ROTATION SUNDAY SCHOOL

A Firm Foundation

A six-year rotational Sunday School curriculum
by Clark Highsmith

Rotation Sunday School: A Firm Foundation
by Clark Highsmith

ISBN 10 - 1451540930
ISBN 13 - 9781451540932

Published by Alacrity Press
www.alacritypress.com

Unless otherwise noted, all Scripture quotations are taken from the Holman Christian Standard Bible®, Copyright © 1999, 2000, 2002, 2003 by Holman Bible Publishers. Used by permission. Holman Christian Standard Bible®, Holman CSB®, and HCSB® are federally registered trademarks of Holman Bible Publishers.

ALACRITY
PRESS

Table of Contents

Preface

In late 2004 our church, Oak Crest Baptist in Midlothian, Texas, decided to replace its traditional Sunday School with a rotational Sunday School. The change caught me off guard and raised many questions in my mind. I wondered why we needed to change. Shortly after the change was approved, the head of the children's department, Carl Roach, approached my wife and me and asked if we would be willing to head up the curriculum aspect of the ministry.

I am curriculum-neutral. I do not believe a rotation Sunday school to be inherently superior nor inferior to any other model, traditional or otherwise. What I have learned over the past couple of years is that teachers are the most important part of the education experience. If a teacher is motivated and excited about teaching, their preparation and presentation will be of a higher quality. The learners will pick up on their excitement, and learning will be more likely to occur. An untrained or unmotivated teacher will find little benefit in a good curriculum, while a good teacher can take a mediocre curriculum and make it great.

The teachers in our church were the ones who pushed for a rotational Sunday School. They were excited and full of creative teaching ideas. What they needed was a foundation on which to build. Thus these lessons were written on an adult level with the aim to prepare teachers to thoroughly understand and know the story they are to teach. Once the material is confidently mastered, it is easier to teach it to children.

Our church wanted to build a six-year curriculum with a comprehensive scope and sequence. At the time, most of the rotational material available was in the form of individual lessons. In addition, I soon realized that there was nothing written from a Southern Baptist perspective. It became obvious that Oak Crest would best be served by a curriculum built from scratch.

Before I began writing, I attempted to plot the scope and sequence for the entire six years. I went through a Bible page-by-page and noted every story that I thought might potentially be appropriate. I then took on the near-impossible task of narrowing the candidates down to seventy-two lessons.

I knew there would be six Christmas lessons and six Easter lessons. I looked for lessons that would have a strong narrative. I tried to make certain large portions of the Bible were not overlooked. Since some children will receive their only Biblical education from Sunday School, I tried to make sure traditional children's stories (ex. *David and Goliath*) were included along with some that are not commonly taught (ex. *Elijah vs. the Priests of Baal*). The sequence was not rigid. Changes were made throughout the writing process, but I found that having a foundational plan made it easier to determine which changes were necessary.

I have found that a curriculum is like a chili recipe. No matter how good a recipe is, cooks cannot resist tinkering. Like preparing a pot of chili, teachers cannot resist tinkering with a curriculum. I think that is a good thing. If I left out your favorite Bible story, replace one of the lessons on the schedule. If you're concerned that your children will become bored because next month's lesson covers the same topic as this month's VBS, rearrange the schedule. Again, having a foundational "map" will help with planning.

While I think any Bible-based church can benefit from this curriculum, my goal (some may say *bias*) was to approach this curriculum from a Southern Baptist perspective. What does that mean?

- **Jesus Christ** — In writing the lessons, I attempted to keep *Jesus*, as the author and perfecter of our faith, at the front of the story.
- **Expository style** — I tried to keep opinion to a minimum and teach only what we can be factually discerned from the Biblical text. Some Bible stories, such as *the Nativity* or *Noah's ark*, have had so much tradition added that it is difficult to discern what is Biblical and what is extra-biblical tradition without a careful study of the text.
- **Use of the Holman Christian Standard Bible** — The HCSB is published by Broadman & Holman, a publishing house familiar to most Southern Baptists. The HCSB is faithful to the original texts while written in contemporary language that is easy for children to understand.
- **Hymns** — The majority of suggested music in the curriculum comes from the *2008 Baptist Hymnal*. Hymns should play an important role in Christian education, as they not only express praise, but teach doctrinal truths. We would do well not only to sing hymns, but to study them.

- **Baptist Doctrine** — The lessons were written from a strong personal belief in traditional Baptist doctrines, including Biblical inerrancy, baptism by immersion, and the security of the believer.

I need to thank God for the strength, perseverance and clarity to see this curriculum to completion. I pray it will in some way serve to advance His kingdom. I would like to thank the members of Oak Crest Baptist Church, who have made us part of their family. I would like to thank the Oak Crest Rotation Sunday School teachers, including Carl Roach, Becky Fontenot, Connie Rowland, Betty Golden, Diane Holt, Jean Volini, Gloria Fields, Linda Horn and Mary Gordon for their encouragement and faithfulness in teaching biblical truth to children.

I thank my parents for taking me to church and teaching me the things of God. I also thank my mother for her assistance in proofreading this book. I thank the pastors and teachers I have had the privilege to learn from over the years, including, but certainly not limited to, Darrell & Betty Molen, Dr. Ron Bracy, Blain Craig, Jerry & Annette Hall, Rich Nuesse, Dr. Bernhard Holmes, Vic Sallis and Dennis & Donna Vogt. I'm thankful for Southern Baptists in remaining faithful to God's Word and providing institutions of learning. I received so much more than just degrees from Southwest Baptist University and Southwestern Baptist Theological Seminary.

I would like to thank my son for his patience. It is my prayer that he and other children will be blessed through this curriculum.

I need to give a special thanks to my wife, Susan. Her influence is found on every page of this book. She proofed every lesson, polished my plethora of grammatical shortcomings and offered many positive, and sometimes challenging, suggestions that I might not have liked, but needed to hear. She encouraged, sacrificed and prayed as this curriculum came together. This curriculum would not be what it is without her support.

Clark Highsmith

Credo ut intelligum
(I belive in order to understand)

ABBREVIATIONS

AMP — The Amplified Bible
HCSB — Holman Christian Standard Bible
KJV — King James Version
NASB — New American Standard Bible
NIV — New International Version

Jesus Teaches Forgiveness

BACKGROUND PASSAGES

Main Passage
Matthew 18:21-35   Unforgiving servant

Related Passages
Luke 17:4   Forgive seven times

Suggested Homiletic Passage
Matthew 18:28-35

MEMORY VERSE

Younger version
Forgive others so that God will forgive you.
            Mark 11:25 (paraphrased)

Older version
And when you stand praying, if you hold anything against anyone, forgive him, so that your Father in heaven may forgive you your sins.
            Mark 11:25

LESSON OBJECTIVE

Jesus taught His followers to forgive others because they had been forgiven much more by God

LESSON

A parable is a simple story illustrating a moral or religious lesson. Jesus used many parables in his earthly teachings. The parable of the unforgiving servant is an illustration of grace and mercy, which illustrates the far-reaching forgiveness of God toward us. It also teaches us to forgive in order to be in right relationship with God.

Matthew 18:21-35

In Matt. 18:15-19 Jesus had just finished telling His disciples how to treat a believer who was sinning. Peter then asked Jesus "Lord, how many times could my brother sin against me and I forgive him? As many as seven times?" (v.21).

Jesus answered, "I tell you, not as many as seven, but 70 times seven." (v.22) The New International Version states, "seventy-seven times." Whether the literal translation is 77 times or 490 times, the point is clear: Christian forgiveness is to be unlimited. But just because believers are commanded to forgive does not mean they are to allow others to take advantage of them. John Calvin states "For when God commands us to wish well to our enemies, he does not therefore demand that we approve in them what He condemns, but only desires that our minds shall be purified from all hatred."[1]

Beginning in verse 23, Jesus told a parable. Jesus used parables as illustrations of what things are like in the kingdom of heaven. The parable begins with a man brought before his king and master. The master demanded that the man repay the debt he owed to him. The man owed his master 10,000 *talents*. We cannot be exact as to the value, but a talent was the highest monetary unit of currency, equivalent to 6,000 *denarii* or *drachmas*. A *denarii* was approximate to the daily wage for a common laborer. A footnote in the New American Standard states the value at "about $10,000,000 in silver content but worth much more in buying power." The point is that the amount owed was immense, and more than any debtor could ever hope to repay.

As the king was ordering the man and his family into slavery to settle the debt, the man pled for leniency. In verse 27 the king "took pity" on the man and canceled the debt. The King James version states that the master was "moved with compassion."

One would expect verse 28 to reflect overwhelming joy and gratefulness exuding from the servant. Unfortunately, the reaction was quite the opposite. The man went out from the master's presence and found (perhaps even actively hunted down) a fellow servant who owed him a hundred *denarii*. As stated earlier, just one *denarii* was comparable to an entire day's wage. Assuming the value of a *talent* at 6,000 denarii, this means the value compared with what was owed to the king was approximately about one part in 600,000. Still, a hundred *denarii* is no small sum of money. Worth approximately four months salary, it reminds us that there will be times that we are wronged or taken advantage of by others. Whatever earthly loss we as believers may suffer, it is virtually nothing compared to what we owe God as a result of our sinful rebellion.

The reaction of the second servant was the same as the first servant's reaction before the master. Falling to his knees, the debtor asks for patience and promises to pay back what he owes. The forgiven servant was unmoved. Showing no mercy, the forgiven servant had the debtor thrown in prison. Other servants, having witnessed or heard about the act of cruelty, reported it to the master.

Enraged, the master called the unforgiving servant to appear before him once more. He berated the servant for not showing mercy after having been shown a great mercy of his own. "You wicked slave! I forgave you all that debt because you begged me. Shouldn't you also have had mercy on your fellow slave, as I had mercy on you?" (vv.32-33). Then the master sent the unforgiving servant to jail to be tortured.

Jesus concluded the parable in verse thirty-five saying "So my heavenly Father will also do to you if each of you does not forgive his brother from his heart." Because of his unforgiving spirit, the servant could not be in a position of forgiveness before God.[2]

A person forgiven by God, through the work of Jesus Christ, will give unmistakable evidence of his gratitude when dealing with others. This holds true even when the debt or trespass is great. No forgiveness can ever surpass that which God did through the work of Jesus to make eternal life possible for a rebellious humanity.

AGE GROUP CONSIDERATIONS

Money may be a vague concept for younger children, so the emphasis should be that the forgiven servant would never, ever have enough money to be able pay back what he owed, nor be able to make things right on his own.

While it is important to forgive others, regaining trust can be difficult and is sometimes unwise. There is a difference between forgiving and trusting. For example, a child who has been abused by an adult needs to forgive that person in order to be right before God, but they do not need to be placed in a position where abuse can reoccur. They do not have to prove their trust in someone who has harmed them. Children need to be taught to discern this crucial difference.

STUDENT APPLICATIONS

1. Students will know that the book of Matthew is found in the New Testament.
2. Students will know that Jesus used parables to teach spiritual truths.
3. Students will learn to forgive those who have wronged them.
4. Students will know that we owe a debt to God for our sin which we cannot humanly repay. Jesus paid our sin debt on the cross.
5. Students will know that their sin "debt" will be forgiven if they trust God as their Lord and Savior.
6. Students will know that in the parable a servant owed his master more than he could ever hope to repay.
7. Students will know that the master mercifully forgave the man's debt.
8. Students will know that the servant mistreated another servant who owed him a relatively minor amount of money.

9. Students will know that the master heard about the forgiven slave's behavior and punished him for his unforgiving spirit.
10. Students will know that Jesus' death on the cross and resurrection is the greatest act of forgiveness ever.

SUGGESTED HYMNS AND SONGS

1. *Praise to the Lord, the Almighty*, 1, 2008 Baptist Hymnal.
2. *Wherever He Leads, I'll Go*, 437, 2008 Baptist Hymnal.
3. *Seek Ye First*, 524, 2008 Baptist Hymnal.
4. *Find Us Faithful*, 598, 2008 Baptist Hymnal.

RESOURCES/CREDIT

1. John Calvin. *Commentary on Matthew, Mark, Luke - Volume 2*, trans. and ed. by William Pringle (Grand Rapids: Christian Classics Ethereal Library, 1999), 226
2. I.H. Marshall, *The New Bible Commentary : Revised, ed.* Donald Guthrie (New York: Wm. B Eerdmans Co.), 840.

Joshua and the Conquest of Canaan

BACKGROUND PASSAGES

Main Passage
Joshua 1-5   Joshua given command
Joshua 6   The battle of Jericho

Related Passages
Joshua 1:1-10   God commissions Joshua
Joshua 2   The Spies and Rahab
Joshua 3-4   Crossing the Jordan

Suggested Homiletic Passage
Joshua 1:1-9

MEMORY VERSE

Younger version
Do not be afraid or discouraged, for the Lord your God is with you wherever you go.

Joshua 1:9b

Older version
Haven't I commanded you: be strong and courageous? Do not be afraid or discouraged, for the Lord your God is with you wherever you go.

Joshua 1:9

LESSON OBJECTIVE

God can do mighty things in the life of a believer when they are obedient. Believers are told to be strong and brave.

LESSON

The book of Joshua begins just after the death of Moses. God gave Joshua charge of the Israelites, who had known nothing but a wandering, tent-inhabiting, nomadic lifestyle. God told them to go into an unknown land to confront and defeat the established people who were living in cities with strong walls. Faith would be of necessity.

Joshua 1-5

In Joshua 1:7, God commanded Joshua to "Above all, be strong and very courageous to carefully observe the whole instruction My servant Moses commanded you." The people agreed to submit to Joshua's leading and promised to obey him just as they had Moses (of course, they had often rebelled against Moses).

Like Moses 40 years earlier, Joshua sent out spies to survey the land and it's inhabitants. It is here that Rahab, an inhabitant of Jericho, is introduced. Rahab is an unlikely hero. Ironically, in an act that placed her life in great danger, she secured safety for herself and her family. Two of the spies stayed at her house. Hiding the spies until after dark, she let them down by a rope through a window and allowed them to escape.

Joshua (chapters 3 and 4) details the crossing of the Jordan river with the Ark of the Covenant which went ahead of the people. The waters started to part, literally, as the priests stepped into the river. The people walked across on dry land, just as the previous generation had crossed through the Red Sea. The children of Israel were finally in the promised land. Something interesting happened at that point of time: "And the day after they ate from the produce of the land, the manna ceased." (5:12).

Joshua 6

The "siege" and subsequent destruction of Jericho took place in chapter 6. The inhabitants of Jericho, confident of their strong fortifications, had barricaded themselves within their city. Jericho was right where the Lord wanted them: "Look, I have handed Jericho, its king, and its fighting men over to you. March around the city with all the men of war, circling the city one time. Do this for six days. Have seven priests carry seven ram's-horn trumpets in front of the ark. But on the seventh day, march around the city seven times, while the priests blow the trumpets. (vv. 3-4). Joshua had been given a battle plan, but it was a plan

Joshua and the Conquest of Canaan

unlike any ever devised by a general. Where were the siege engines and tools?

But Joshua was blessed to know the end result before he began. On the seventh day, when the priests blew the trumpets, the people were to shout; the walls would fall and the people would advance into the city. Following this plan would make it undeniably clear that the battle depended solely upon God. And, due to its unconventional nature, it also challenged the Israelites' faith to follow God completely in what they were required to do. Having the priests blow trumpets used in their religious festivals reinforced that it was God who was in control.[1]

In verse 6, Joshua gave the priests their marching orders. The plan went into action when, in verse 9, an armed guard went out before the ark and the rest of the people followed behind. Everything was done just as God had commanded. The trumpets sounded and the people remained silent. Joshua had told them to not shout until he told them. After marching once around the city, they returned to their camp (v.11).

For the next five days, the Israelites got up early in the morning and proceeded to march once around the city before returning to their camp. What went through the minds of the people as they silently marched around the wall? They must have wondered if the marching would accomplish anything. Hopefully, their faith in trusting God, by following Joshua, did not waver.

On the seventh day, the Israelites, once again, arose early in the morning. On this day Joshua instructed them to march around the city seven times. In verse 16, the trumpets sounded and Joshua commanded "Shout! For the Lord has given you the city!" The trumpets blared, the people shouted, the walls of Jericho collapsed, and the Israelites charged in to take the city.

Through Joshua, God had warned the Israelites not to take any loot from the city for all in Jericho was to be devoted to the Lord. The inhabitants of Jericho, young and old, would be destroyed as a judg-

ment from God for their wickedness. This wholesale destruction also helped deter the Israelites from being tempted by the Canaanite's idolatrous ways. Only the gold, silver, bronze and iron were to be spared. These items were placed in the Lord's treasury as the first fruit to the Lord for the conquest of Canaan.

There was one other exception to the order to destroy everyone and every thing: Rahab and her family. In verse 22, Joshua said to the two spies who had been hidden by Rahab, "Go to the prostitute's house and bring the woman out of there, and all who are with her, just as you promised her." Joshua and the Israelites kept their word. Rahab lived among the Israelites from that time. Rahab married an Israelite man, Salmon, and as the mother of Boaz (married Ruth) and the great-great-grandmother of King David, received a special mention in Matthew 1:5 as part of the lineage of Jesus.

And so began the Israelite's conquest of Canaan. God had honored the obedience of His children. Emboldened, the Israelites, at God's command, went on to conquer many of the people in the land. But despite the dramatic victory at Jericho and other subsequent battles, the Israelites soon started to show disobedience. As a consequence, they never fully conquered the land that God had promised to them, for the surviving Canaanites later caused the Israelites much grief. The Israelites would many times in their subsequent history turn from Yahweh and worship the false gods of the Canaanites.

AGE GROUP CONSIDERATIONS

A discussion of Rahab's profession, prostitution, is probably not appropriate for children. It is best to teach that she was a resident of Jericho and part of the culture. She was spared from the destruction because she feared and obeyed God, in spite of her pagan background.

Joshua 6:21 is a sobering verse for people of any age, especially those with 21st century sensibilities. God commanded the Israelites to destroy every living person and animal in Jericho.

Joshua and the Conquest of Canaan

God alone is the giver of life and in perfect holiness has every right to create and destroy as He sees fit. Sin is a serious thing. It is only by the grace of God's love that He has not destroyed us since all have sinned and fallen short. It is even more amazing that God made a way for us to become holy in His sight. Our sin was placed upon Christ on the cross. In return, to those who repent and follow Him, Christ's righteousness is imputed to them. Thus sinful humans, covered by the blood of Christ, can stand before a Holy God. God's ways may not seem fair, but they are always right.

While the destruction of Jericho is not an easy topic to discuss, it provides a wonderful opportunity to teach older children about God's holiness and His love.

SUGGESTED HYMNS AND SONGS

1. *O the Blood of Jesus*, 226, 2008 Baptist Hymnal.
2. *Awesome God*, 63, 2008 Baptist Hymnal.
3. *The Battle Belongs to the Lord*, 662, 2008 Baptist Hymnal.
4. *Onward Christian Soldiers*, 660, 2008 Baptist Hymnal.
5. *Joshua Fought the Battle of Jericho*, Track 4, Sharing God's Love: 25 Bible Songs for Children. Twin Sister Productions.

STUDENT APPLICATIONS

1. Students will know that the book of Joshua is in the Old Testament.
2. Students will be able to find the book of Joshua in the Bible.
3. Students will know that the conquest of Canaan is chronicled in the book of Joshua.
4. Students will know that God's Law has purpose in our life. Not following God's Law has consequences.
5. Students will know that God tested the faith of the Israelites by asking them to trust Him completely. They then see that God did deliver Jericho and the rest of Canaan.
6. Many things in life seem impossible for to do. If it is God's will, He can make it happen just as easily as He brought down the walls of Jericho.
7. God will judge those who do not follow Him. Followers of Christ will not face His wrath.
8. Students will know that Rahab, a resident of Jericho, hid two Israelite spies, and helped them escape.
9. Students will know that the Israelites marched, in silence, around the city of Jericho one time a day for six days.
10. Students will know that on the seventh day the Israelites walked around Jericho seven times. The priests blew trumpets, the people shouted and the walls fell.
11. Older students will know that God commanded the Israelites to destroy everything in the city as judgment and to deter the Israelites from following the pagan ways.
12. Students will know Rahab and her family were spared because she feared and obeyed God.
13. Students will know that Rahab became the great-great-grandmother of King David.

RESOURCES/CREDIT

1. *Life Application Bible*. (Grand Rapids, Michigan: Zondervan Publishing House, 1991), 341.

Philip and the Ethiopian

BACKGROUND PASSAGES

Main Passage
Acts 8:26-40 — Conversion of the Ethiopian

Related Passages
Acts 8:4-25 — Philip's Samaritan Ministry
Matthew 10:3 — Listed as a disciple
John 1:43-46 — Jesus calls Philip
John 14:8-11 — "Lord, show us the Father..."
Isaiah 53:7-8 — Passage read by the Ethiopian

Suggested Homiletic Passage
Acts 8:30-38

MEMORY VERSE

Younger version
But you will receive power when the Holy Spirit has come upon you, and you will be My witnesses ...
Acts 1:8a

Older version
But you will receive power when the Holy Spirit has come upon you, and you will be My witnesses in Jerusalem, in all Judea and Samaria, and to the ends of the earth.
Acts 1:8

LESSON OBJECTIVE

It is a privilege and an act of obedience for believers to tell others about Jesus and to baptize new followers in His name.

LESSON

All believers, after conversion, soon learn that sharing the Gospel is expected of them. Still, many do not regularly share their faith, whether because of fear or a sense of inadequacy. The gospel is simple enough for a child to share. This month our children will see how God miraculously used Philip to introduce another person, the Ethiopian official, to Christ. This is a story about obedience, evangelism, missions and the importance of baptism. Our children will learn that if they are obedient to just share, God will take care of the rest.

Philip was one of Jesus' twelve disciples and the person who introduced Nathanael (Bartholomew) to Jesus. In the gospels we learn that he was a fisherman by trade, and in John 12:21 it is learned that he is from Bethsaida in Galilee. Later, Philip played a prominent role in the early church as one of the first traveling evangelists. He had a strong ministry in Samaria and is an example of how the gospel can transcend vast cultural barriers since no self-respecting Jew would have desired contact with the Samaritans unless the love of God had led them to have that compassion.

Acts 8:26-40

In verse 26 an angel appeared to Philip and told him, "Get up and go south to the road that goes down from Jerusalem to desert Gaza." This must have seemed an odd command as Philip had a successful preaching ministry in Samaria, and now he was being asked to go, to what was apparently, the middle of nowhere.

It was at this location that he met an Ethiopian official. Today Ethiopia is one of many African nations, but at Philip's time, Ethiopia was a vast kingdom south of Egypt. This man was an important official for Candace, queen of the Ethiopians. Candace was not the name of a specific queen but a royal title which was used much like the title Caesar was used in regard to Roman rulers. The position of queen in Ethiopia held great responsibility, because, deified as the child of a god, the Ethiopian king was considered too holy to serve as a secular leader.[1]

The Ethiopian official had just been to Jerusalem to worship. The journey to and from Jerusalem would have been no short trek, even by chariot. The official was reading from the book of Isaiah. Philip followed the Holy Spirit's leading and approached the chariot. This took faith and courage on Philip's part. In a modern context, this would have been similar

Philip and the Ethiopian

to an ordinary citizen approaching a diplomat or a cabinet official.

Philip asked the man if he understood what he was reading. In verse 31 the Ethiopian said "How can I, unless someone guides me?" He invited Philip to come sit with him. Even in his position of power, the Ethiopian was not insecure nor too prideful to ask for help.

The Ethiopian was reading Isaiah 53:7-8. The passage prophetically described Christ's sacrifice. The Ethiopian had learned enough to recognize that the passage referred to a prophet. But who was this prophet? Philip gladly used the passage as a starting point for telling the Ethiopian about Jesus.

In verse 36 the Ethiopian said to Philip "Look, there's water. What would keep me from being baptized?" Verse 37 is not in the earliest manuscripts and the New International Version places it in the footnotes.[2] Regardless of the authenticity, verse 37 affirms what was already apparent; the Ethiopian, having now heard the good news, had given his life to Christ. Philip would not have been willing to baptize the Ethiopian if he had not felt the conversion was genuine.

In verse 38 the Ethiopian gave orders to stop the chariot. Philip and the Ethiopian walked down into the water where Philip then baptized him. Before they could exit the water "the Spirit of the Lord carried Philip away." (v. 39). The Ethiopian went on his way rejoicing.

Philip reappeared in Azotus and continued to preach the gospel in many towns (v.40). Philip had been obedient to God's command and was prepared to give an account for what he believed. As a result God used Philip to further the spread of His kingdom "...in Jerusalem, in all Judea and Samaria, and to the ends of the earth." (Acts 1:8).

Baptism

Baptism is one of the two *ordinances* observed by the New Testament church. According to Hobbs, "In the Bible the word 'ordinance' is used to refer to either governmental or divine laws."[3] In this context an ordinance is a decree or a command. The *2000 Baptist Faith and Message* states "It is an act of obedience symbolizing the believer's faith in a crucified, buried, and risen Saviour, the believer's death to sin, the burial of the old life, and the resurrection to walk in newness of life in Christ Jesus."[4]

As it is a command, a willingness to submit to baptism should be one of the first steps of faith in a new believer's life of obedience to Christ. Baptism is not a means of salvation and demonstrates to others that one is a follower of Jesus.

New Testament baptism is immersion and emergence from water. The word **baptize** is a Greek transliteration of the Greek word *baptizo*, which means to dip, plunge, and/or immerse. While baptism is symbolic and believers are commanded to be baptized, baptism is a public act. Obedience, therefore, is important not only for the sake of obedience but as a testimony, to the world, of the work of Christ. Immersion, specifically, most accurately reflects New Testament teaching and most graphically pictures the death and resurrection of the believer in Jesus. Baptism, by immersion, must be clearly and thoroughly taught, as children will almost certainly hear about other modes of baptism used in other churches from friends, family and acquaintances.

AGE GROUP CONSIDERATIONS

The Bible passage for this lesson uses the word "eunuch" to describe the Ethiopian. The dictionary definition of a eunuch is "a castrated male." The term was widely used for high male officials who may or may not have been castrated. In order to avoid an awkward explanation, it is probably better to use the term "official" with children, as used in this lesson.

Children may be intimidated by the thought of baptism. Even for adults, it is an act of courage and faith. Participation of the pastor or another minister in any discussion with a child about baptism may prove beneficial.

Suggested Hymns and Songs

1. *Turn Your Eyes Upon Jesus*, 413, 2008 Baptist Hymnal.
2. *Wherever He Leads I'll Go*, 437, 2008 Baptist Hymnal.
3. *Heaven Came Down*, 573, 2008 Baptist Hymnal.
4. *Share His Love*, 358, 2008 Baptist Hymnal.
5. *We've A Story to Tell*, 356, 2008 Baptist Hymnal.

Student Applications

1. Students will know that the story of Philip and the Ethiopian is found in the New Testament book of Acts.
2. Students will know that Philip was one of Jesus' disciples.
3. Students will know that Philip was told by an angel to follow a road into the desert.
4. Students will know that Philip went to the desert where he met an official from the Ethiopian Royal court.
5. Students will know that Philip was able to share the gospel with the Ethiopian.
6. Students will know that the Ethiopian official gave his life to Jesus.
7. Students will know that the Ethiopian was baptized after giving his life to Jesus.
8. Students will know it is a privilege to share the Good News with lost people
9. Students will know that baptism is an important step for people who decide to trust in Jesus.
10. Students will know that God intends for His Good News to be shared with all people groups of the world. (Matt. 24:14)
11. Students will know that when they do not understand the Bible, it is a good idea to ask for help.
12. Students will know that when God tells them to do something, they need to obey, no matter how unusual the request may seem.

Resources/Credit

1. David Alexander & Pat Alexander, eds. *Eerdmans' Handbook to the Bible* (Grand Rapids: William B. Eerdmans Publishing Company, 1973), 556.
2. *Life Application Bible*. (Grand Rapids, Michigan: Zondervan Publishing House, 1991), 1963.
3. Herschel H. Hobbs, *Fundamentals of Our Faith* (Nashville: Broadman & Holman Publishers, 1960), 114.
4. *The Baptist Faith and Message*, 2000. The Southern Baptist Convention.

Easter - Peter's Story

BACKGROUND PASSAGES

Main Passage

Verse	Summary
Luke 22:31-34	Peter's betrayal predicted
Luke 22:54-62	Peter's denial
John 21:1-19	Jesus talks with Peter

Related Passages

Verse	Summary
Luke 22-24	The Passion story
Luke 24:34	Jesus' appearance to Peter
John 18:12-27	John's version of Peter's denial

Suggested Homiletic Passage

John 21:12-19

MEMORY VERSE

Younger version

"He has risen, just as he said."

Matthew 28:6a (NIV)

Older version

"He is not here! For He has been resurrected, just as he said. Come and see the place where He lay. Then go quickly and tell His disciples, He has been raised from the dead"

Matthew 28:6 -7a (HCSB)

LESSON OBJECTIVE

At Easter believers remember the death and resurrection of Jesus. Like Peter, believers have human short comings but can rejoice in the reality that God, through Jesus' death and resurrection, grants forgiveness and salvation to all who call upon His name.

LESSON

At Easter, believers remember the crucifixion, burial, and glorious resurrection of Jesus. While the cross is always central at Easter time, this lesson will have a special focus on Peter and his experience dur-

ing Jesus' final days on earth. Teachers are strongly encouraged to read the entire Passion account in preparation for teaching this lesson. Gospel accounts of the "Easter story" are found in the following places:

> *Matt. 26:47 through Matt. 28:10*
> *Mark 14:43 through Mark 16:13*
> *Luke 22:39 through Luke 24:12*
> *John 18 :1 through John 20:18*

Depending on the age of your group, you may wish to relate your own short version of Jesus' arrest, crucifixion, burial, and resurrection. Teachers may wish to tell the passion story in first-person, as if the events were seen through Peter's eyes.

Luke 22:31-34

Luke's account of the Lord's Supper begins in 22:14. The disciples shared the bread and the cup, the treachery of Judas was announced, and the disciples had a dispute about who would be the greatest. After the dispute, Jesus spoke directly to Peter. Jesus said, "Simon, Simon, look out! Satan has asked to sift you as wheat. But I have prayed for you that your faith may not fail. And you, when you have turned back, strengthen your brothers." (vv. 31-32).

Only ten verses previously (Luke 22:21), Jesus had revealed the betrayal of Judas that would lead to his damnation. One scholar states "...if this is true for Judas, and if even Peter's faithfulness is imperiled, then Luke's readers ought to take seriously how their faith is at risk on account of the stratagems of Satan."[1] Satan had made a request to God to do with Peter much as he had for Job.[2] The important point here is that Jesus prayed for Peter. Peter truly repented after his falling away. That is why he did not suffer the consequences that Judas did.

In verse 33 Peter insisted he would follow Christ regardless of personal safety. Jesus replied in verse 34 "I tell you, Peter, the rooster will not crow until you deny three times that you know me."

Late in the evening after the supper, Jesus and the disciples went to the Mount of Olives. The Mount is a hill just outside of Jerusalem. Jesus went off alone and prayed. Judas, led the chief priests, officers of the temple guard, and the elders to the garden and directly to Jesus. Judas had betrayed Jesus just as Jesus had said he would. Peter briefly scuffled with the captors, until Jesus told him to stop. After Jesus was taken into custody, Peter and John followed at a distance. The other disciples ran away and scattered (Mark 14:50).

Luke 22:54-62

Jesus was taken to the house of the chief priest where a mock court began to assemble to determine Jesus' fate. John was able to gain entrance to see the trial (John 18:16). Peter refused to go inside, and instead milled about in the crowd gathered in the courtyard. Peter was asked by three different people if he was a follower of Christ. Each time Peter emphatically denied any connection to Jesus. In verses 60-61, as Peter finished his third denial, he heard the rooster crow and saw Jesus looking straight at him. Peter realized what he had done and began to weep bitterly.

Death and Resurrection

Luke 23 describes the trial and crucifixion of Christ. The trial and crucifixion is the focus of another Easter rotation lesson. There is no mention of the whereabouts of Peter at this time. The only mention of a disciple present at the crucifixion, is John (John 19:26-27). Jesus was placed on a cross between two thieves. Darkness covered the land in the middle of the day and the curtain of the temple was torn in two. In 23:46, "Jesus called out with a loud voice, 'Father, into your hands I entrust my spirit.' When he had said this, he breathed his last." Joseph of Arimathea requested the body of Jesus. He prepared the body for burial and placed it in his personal tomb.

Several women, including Mary Magdalene and Mary (Mark 16:1), had prepared spices and perfumes for Christ's body. Due to the beginning of the Sabbath, they were unable to immediately prepare the body. Early in the morning on the first day of the week they went to the tomb. An angel appeared to the women; they were the first to learn of the resurrection. They went straight to the eleven disciples to tell them the good news. The disciples at first disbelieved

what the women said. In Luke 24:12, however, Peter ran to the tomb, finding the linens lying by themselves. He then went away, as the Amplified translation states "wondering about and marveling at what had happened."

Luke 24:34 briefly mentions that the risen Lord had appeared to Peter. One scholar calls the lack of information "a yawning gap."[3] He further states "... we must still inquire into why Luke has drawn special attention to Simon. Undoubtedly, this is to indicate Simon's full rehabilitation following his denial of Jesus and repentance."[4] The only other reference to this appearance to Peter is found in I Corinthians 15:5 as written by Paul. Why we don't have more detail remains a mystery, but it is clear that Peter was the first disciple to see the risen Lord.

John 21:1-19

After the initial appearance, Peter had one last (recorded) intimate conversation with Jesus. In John 21, Peter, along with six other disciples, spent a night of fishing on the Sea of Tiberias (Galilee). The fishing had not produced any results. Early in the morning Jesus appeared on the shore; the disciples did not recognize him at first. He told them to cast their nets on the right side of the boat. Miraculously, they hauled in 153 fish. Then, having recognized Jesus, the disciples made their way to shore so they could be with Jesus.

It was then that Jesus had his private talk with Peter. "Simon, son of John, do you love Me more than these?", Jesus asked in verse 15. Peter replied "Yes, Lord, you know that I love you." Jesus told Peter "Feed my lambs." The line of question and response was repeated twice more. Peter had disowned Jesus three times. Now Jesus asked three times if he loved Him. Peter had repented, but Jesus tested and verified his willingness to serve Him. No longer would Peter be a fisherman, but instead an evangelist and an apostle. Peter was forgiven and at last fully understood the significance of Jesus' death and resurrection.[5]

In verse 18 Jesus hinted of Peter's future suffering and death. He then commanded Peter to follow

Him. Though there would be difficult times ahead, Peter was now ready to live a life entirely dedicated to the Lord. Later, in the book of Acts, Peter matured into the prominent leader of the early church. His dedication to Jesus has impacted eternity for believers throughout the centuries and to this day.

AGE GROUP CONSIDERATIONS

Depending on the age of your group, you may want to relate your own short version of Jesus' arrest, crucifixion, burial, and resurrection in keeping with the Easter season.

SUGGESTED HYMNS AND SONGS

1. *Christ Arose*, 273, 2008 Baptist Hymnal.
2. *Were You There*, 254, 2008 Baptist Hymnal.
3. *The Wonderful Cross*, 239, 2008 Baptist Hymnal.
4. *The Power of the Cross (Oh, to See the Dawn)*, 232, 2008 Baptist Hymnal.

STUDENT APPLICATIONS

1. Students will know that Peter was one of Jesus' disciples and became a great church leader.
2. Students will know that the Passion story can be found in all four gospels.
3. Students will know that the true purpose of Easter is to remember the sacrifice Christ made for their salvation and to celebrate His resurrection.
4. Students will know that God can forgive them for anything they have done wrong, but repentance is a must.
5. Students will know that the women were the first people to see the resurrected Jesus
6. Students will know that Peter was the first disciple to see Jesus.
7. Students will know that Jesus really lived, died, and rose again.
8. Students will know the reason Jesus died was to be the sacrifice for their sin and make possible eternal life.

RESOURCES/CREDIT

1. Joel B. Green, *The Gospel of Luke: The New International Commentary on the New Testament*, Gordon D. Fee, ed. (Grand Rapids: William B. Eerdmans Publishing Co., 1997), 772.
2. F.F. Bruce, ed., *The International Bible Commentary, Revised Edition*. (Grand Rapids, Michigan: Zondervan Publishing House, 1979), 1223.
3. Green, 851.
4. *Ibid.*
5. *Life Application Bible*. (Grand Rapids, Michigan: Zondervan Publishing House, 1991), 1929.

Solomon asks for Wisdom

BACKGROUND PASSAGES

Main Passage
I Kings 3:3-15	Solomon asks for wisdom
Proverbs 3:1-8	Benefits of Godly wisdom

Related Passages
I Kings 3:16-28	A wise ruling
I. Cor. 3:18-21	Wisdom of this world is folly

Suggested Homiletic Passage
Proverbs 3:1-8

MEMORY VERSE

Younger version
The fear of the Lord is the beginning of knowledge...

Proverbs 1:7a

Older version
The fear of the Lord is the beginning of knowledge; fools despise wisdom and instruction.

Proverbs 1:7

LESSON OBJECTIVE

Believers learn God's wisdom from knowing God. God's wisdom is superior to earthly wisdom and will guide the obedient in every situation.

LESSON

There is much that the world considers to be wise. As Christians, we know that true wisdom finds its source in God's work. *Wisdom* is seeing and living life the way that God sees it. God gave Solomon a choice; he could ask anything of God . He could have chosen wealth, power, or influence. Instead, Solomon chose God's wisdom. Because of his thoughtful choice, Solomon was blessed in many other ways. Every time we study Solomon's writings in the Bible, we too are blessed by Solomon's God-given wisdom.

I Kings 3:3-15

King David had died, and his son Solomon ruled on the throne of Israel. in verse 3 we learn that Solomon loved the Lord (like his father David had) and sought to please Him. Unfortunately, Solomon was not perfect and offered sacrifices to God outside of the temple at Gibeon. This was explicitly against Old Testament law which forbade sacrifice outside of the tabernacle and later, the Jerusalem temple. Even though Solomon offered a thousand sacrifices, God did not condone his disobedience to a known law.

While at Gibeon, God appeared to Solomon in a dream. In verse 5 God said, "Ask for whatever you want me to give you." Everyone has heard fairy tales about a genie, in the lamp, who grants wishes to the owner of the lamp. Solomon was asked this question, not by a fanciful genie, but by the personal and omnipotent creator God of the cosmos. What would have been your "wish?"

Solomon first gave praise and thanksgiving to God. Solomon thanked God for his faithfulness and kindness to himself and his father David. In verse 7 Solomon showed humility in professing his inadequacy to rule without God's help.

Solomon's answer is not what most people would expect, for in the next verse, instead of seeking something for himself in the way of riches, power, or physical pleasure, Solomon asked for a "obedient heart to judge Your people." More specifically, in verse 9, he asked for the ability "to discern between good and evil."

This request pleased God, who recognized that Solomon could have asked for any number of selfish things. True to His promise, God gave what Solomon asked. God said "I will therefore do what you have asked. I will give you a wise and understanding heart, so that there has never have been anyone like you before and never will be again." (v.12). On top of that, God promised Solomon riches and honor, that would not be matched by any other king during his lifetime.

Solomon asks for Wisdom

After these sure promises, came another, but conditional promise: "If you walk in My ways and keep My statutes and commandments just as your father David did, I will give you a long life." (v. 14). This promise can be made real to children in Ephesians 6:2-3 "Honor your father and mother — which is the first commandment with a promise — 'that it may go well with you and that you may have long life in the land.'" Children who respect their parents are less likely to get into dangerous situations or behaviors that can literally threaten their life.

At this point Solomon awoke and realized he had a dream. He returned to Jerusalem, and he went to offer sacrifices. Since Jerusalem was the proper place to sacrifice, this would have been pleasing to the Lord.

God blessed Solomon to accomplish much in his lifetime. Not only was he, indeed, the wisest man who ever lived, but he was a great diplomat, trader, scientist (I Kings 4:33) and collector of tributes. Under his reign Israel reached its zenith of power, both in riches and size. People from many nations came to listen to the wisdom of Solomon, and it was a time of peace and safety. The pinnacle of Solomon's building program was the temple in Jerusalem. As God had promised (in I Kings 3:14), Solomon had no equal among the kings of his time.

Proverbs 3:1-8

A direct blessing of Solomon's wisdom, that we have today, are his writings in Proverbs, Ecclesiastes and the Song of Songs. Proverbs was written to teach young people about the benefits of wisdom. In the proverbs, Wisdom is often contrasted with the "fool." The fool is the person who despises and/or disobeys God. While Solomon penned most of Proverbs, others contributed, including Agur and King Lemuel in chapters 30 and 31.

A proverb is a short, concise sentence that conveys moral truth. Proverbs are more principles than specific promises. The blessing of following God's wisdom may not be readily apparent and may even appear to be counterproductive from time to time. A look at the life of Job will bear this to be true. However, we can be certain that living by faith ultimately leads to blessing, whether in this world or the world to come.

In the first two verses of Proverbs 3, Solomon charged the reader to not forget his teaching and the first benefits cited are the expectation of long life and prosperity. This blessing may be realized as a result of avoiding dangerous behavior; that is, going the way of the "fool" can result in consequences that cause harm to many.

In verse 3 Solomon encouraged believers to embrace love and faithfulness. The resulting blessing, in verse 4, is "Then you will find favor and high regard (NIV says "'good name') in the sight of God and man." Respect from others is a great blessing.

Verses 5-6 show how to find Godly wisdom. "Trust in the Lord with all your heart, and do not rely on your own understanding; think about Him in all your ways, and He will guide you on the right paths." The key is to know and trust God. One scholar states "To acknowledge him is not mere assent but personal awareness of God that leads to obedience and praise."[1] It does not take long for new Christians to learn that struggles and sufferings are part of this life. When God makes believers' paths straight, He gives peace as He guides them to their final goal.

Verse 7 cautions believers to not be prideful about their own wisdom, but to fear God and avoid evil. Taking undue pride in God's wisdom is as sinful as ignoring His wisdom.

The rest of chapter 3 touts other benefits of wisdom, including health (v.8), happiness (v.13), security (v.23), and confidence (v.24). True wisdom affirms life in the most practical ways.

In conclusion, seeking God and submitting one's life to Him is the key to gaining wisdom. Believers who earnestly seek Godly wisdom will find it and experience God's blessings. "The fear of the Lord — and to turn from evil is understanding." (Job 28:28).

AGE GROUP CONSIDERATIONS

To supplement the lesson, older children may benefit from hearing the story where Solomon showed much wisdom in a ruling between two women fighting over a child (I Kings 3:16-28) . This story probably is not appropriate for smaller children.

Possible video or activity ideas could cover other areas of Solomon's reign, including the construction of the temple.

SUGGESTED HYMNS AND SONGS

1. *When I Look into Your Holiness*, 484, 2008 Baptist Hymnal.
2. *Open Our Eyes, Lord*, 426, 2008 Baptist Hymnal.
3. *I Am Resolved*, 378, 2008 Baptist Hymnal.
4. *O Worship the King*, 24, 2008 Baptist Hymnal.

STUDENT APPLICATIONS

1. Students will know Solomon was king over Israel.
2. Students will know that Solomon asked God for wisdom when he could have asked for riches or a long life instead.
3. Students will know that God was pleased with Solomon's choice to ask for wisdom, therefore He also blessed him with riches, long life, and peace.
4. Students will know that a proverb is a principle for life, not a direct promise.
5. Students will know the difference between those who seek wisdom and the "fool."
6. Students will know that Solomon's wisdom is recorded in Proverbs, Ecclesiastes and the Song of Songs.
7. Students will know that wisdom has many practical benefits, including health, happiness, security, and confidence.
8. Students will know that people came from many nations to hear Solomon's wisdom.

RESOURCES/CREDIT

1. Charles G. Martin, *The International Bible Commentary, Revised Edition*, F.F. Bruce, ed. (Grand Rapids, Michigan: Zondervan Publishing House, 1979), 661.

The Centurion's Faith

Background Passages

Main Passage
Luke 7:1-10   Centurion exhibits faith

Related Passages
Matthew 8:5-13   Matthew's account
Matthew 11:23-24   Capernaum's fall prophesied

Suggested Homiletic Passage
Luke 7:2-10

Memory Verse

Younger version
   Keep asking and it will be given to you; keep searching and you will find.
                                        Matthew 7:7a

Older version
   Keep asking, and it will be given to you. Keep searching, and you will find. Keep knocking, and the door will be opened for you.
                                        Matthew 7:7

Lesson Objective

   God honors believers who place their faith in Him. When a believer trusts God completely, He can work powerfully through his/her life to care for himself/herself and others.

Lesson

   Charles Spurgeon wrote, "The life of your soul lies in faith; its health lies in love."[1] Faith (and repentance) is what God requires of a person for salvation. The merits of faith are commonly taught and discussed in church. Yet believers struggle daily in trusting God to be their *Jehovah-Jireh* (Provider). The story of a faith-filled Roman centurion serves as an example of how God, working through someone who trusts Him completely will bless others.

Background

   The days of Jesus' ministry were a time of much tension in Israel. The Israelites had enjoyed a period of independence under the Hasmoneons (beginning in 167 B.C). That changed when the Romans arrived as conquerors (approximately a century later). The Romans completed the assimilation of Israel into their empire with the crowning of Herod the Great as king of the Jews in 37 B.C. In Jesus' day, Israel was still an occupied country, resentfully paying taxes to Caesar, careful to avoid treacherous acts that would bring Roman retribution, and hoping for a day when they would be free from their control.

   The city of Capernaum was an important setting in the Gospels. Jesus lived there with his family for a time after they left Nazareth. He gave his famous talk about the Bread of Life in Capernaum. He also performed many miracles in the city. The location of the city is uncertain, but was most likely on the northwest coast of the Sea of Galilee.[2] The people of Capernaum did not treat Jesus any better than Nazareth had. In Matthew 11:23-24, Jesus prophesied its ruin. The prophecy came true, and the city was never been rebuilt.

   The scriptures mention the presence of a centurion in Capernaum. When not engaged in a military campaign, Roman soldiers took on a number of duties, including policing subjugated cities. Centurions were Roman officers, who typically had been promoted to their position (based on courage and reliability[3]) and who commanded a unit of 100 soldiers. We know that, since Capernaum warranted the stationing of a centurion, it was a substantial town, with a Roman garrison.

Luke 7:1-10

   A group of Jewish elders walked the streets of Capernaum looking for Jesus. The servant (New American Standard translates as *slave*) of a local centurion was sick and had sent the delegation to seek the Jesus' assistance. Jesus entered Capernaum and was approached by the elders (v.1).

The Centurion's Faith

The elders pleaded earnestly with Jesus to come and heal the servant. For a Jewish elder to show such concern for a Roman (and a servant) would have been unusual. In verse 4 the reason they cared for the centurion is revealed, "He is worthy for you to grant this, because he loves our nation and has built us a synagogue." This centurion did not fit the profile of a conqueror and had embraced, rather than oppressed, the community under his control . In all likelihood, he was a "God-fearer" — a gentile believer of Yahweh. Persuaded, Jesus went with the elders towards the Centurion's house.

In verse 6, friends of the centurion met Jesus a short distance from the house. The friends brought another message from the centurion. Humbly, the centurion communicated through the friends that he was not worthy to have Christ come into his home. In verse 7 he said that he did not even consider himself worthy to come before Christ, but that he had faith to know that if Jesus would merely say the word, the servant would be healed.

The centurion easily related to Jesus' authority. A centurion was also a man under authority, as he was simply one of six *centurions* who comprised a unit called a *"cohort."* Ten cohorts comprised a *"legion,"* and a legion was lead by an officer (called a *tribune*). Centurions knew to obey orders, as well as give them. An officer, such as a centurion, would often delegate his duties to the soldiers under his command, and he expected his orders to be immediately obeyed; in fact, the consequence of disobedience was usually imprisonment or death. The centurion understood authority and the power of a command. This centurion recognized that Jesus had the heavenly authority and all the power required to heal his slave. In faith, he simply requested that Jesus make the command, so that the healing would occur.

Jesus' response in verse 9 was to be "amazed" at the centurion's faith. The King James version states,

"he marvelled at him." The response was unusual in that the only other time in the gospels that Jesus marveled was as a result of Nazareth's unbelief (Mark 6:6). Turning to the crowd he said, "I tell you, I have not found so great a faith even in Israel!" The crowd of Jews would have fully realized that in all of Israel, Jesus was saying the greatest faith He had seen came from a gentile.

The men returned to the house and discovered that the slave had been healed (v.10). The account ends at this point. While the centurion was praised for his faith, he was rewarded by the healing of the slave. The testimony of the centurion was certainly strengthened among the Jews of Capernaum.

Faith tends to be easier for children than adults. Adults tend to try and explain things while children trust. Sunday School (in Southern Baptist and other churches) has historically been the vehicle through which unbelievers first encounter the gospel message. This is a wonderful time for telling children why Christ died and how we can be followers of Him (if we repent and trust Him to be our Lord and Savior). If someone like the centurion can trust Jesus and be accepted, they can too.

SUGGESTED HYMNS/SONGS

1. *Victory in Jesus*, 499, 2008 Baptist Hymnal.
2. *Footsteps of Jesus*, 550, 2008 Baptist Hymnal.
3. *He Has Made Me Glad*, 579, 2008 Baptist Hymnal.
4. *My Life Is in You, Lord*, 518, 2008 Baptist Hymnal.

AGE GROUP CONSIDERATIONS

Older children may need to be reminded that Jesus did not endorse slavery. He recognized that a person's greatest need was (and still is today) salvation from spiritual death.

The Centurion's Faith

STUDENT APPLICATIONS

1. Students will know that the story of the centurion is found in the New Testament books of Luke and Matthew.
2. Students will know that Rome had conquered and occupied the Jews and the land of Israel.
3. Students will know that a *centurion* was a Roman army officer in charge of 100 men.
4. Students will know what the differences are between Jews and gentiles.
5. Students will know that God does great things in the lives of believers who exhibit great faith.
6. Students will know that Jesus praised the centurion for exhibiting great faith.
7. Students will know that God is pleased when His people pray to Him and serve Him in faith.
8. Students will learn that no one has to be perfect to please God, but one must place his/her faith and trust in Him.

RESOURCES/CREDIT

1. Charles H. Spurgeon, *All of Grace* (Chicago: Moody Press), 128.
2. V. Gilbert Veers, *Family Bible Library* (Nashville: The Southwestern Company, 1971) Vol. 6,144-45.
3. David Alexander & Pat Alexander, eds. *Eerdmans' Handbook to the Bible* (Grand Rapids: William B. Eerdmans Publishing Company, 1973), 507.

Queen Esther

BACKGROUND PASSAGES

Main Passage

Esther 2-8   Queen Esther

Related Passages

Esther 1   The king's decree
Esther 9-10   Victory of the Jews

Suggested Homiletic Passage

Esther 4:6-14

MEMORY VERSE

Who knows, perhaps you have come to the kingdom for such a time as this?

Esther 4:14b

LESSON OBJECTIVE

God always takes care of His people. Like Esther, believers may be placed in an uncomfortable or dangerous situation. If they are faithful to trust God, He will use them as an instrument of grace to others.

LESSON

The book of Esther is a marvelous account of how God actively works through history to care for His children. The book of Esther is ten chapters long. It is recommended that you become familiar with the entire book of Esther though the lesson will focus on chapters two through eight.

The events of Esther took place in the city of Susa, in the kingdom of Persia and during the reign of King Xerxes (*Ahasuerus* in some translations, including NASB and NIV). It had been 100 years since the Jews in Persia had been deported from their homeland.[1] They were a minority in a foreign land. The Persian empire stretched from Greece in the west to India in the east and southward to include Egypt and part of the African east coast.

Esther 2-8

At the beginning of chapter 2 Xerxes began a search to replace the wife he had deposed for insubordination (Esther 1). Commissioners were appointed to find beautiful young women in each province and bring them to the king's harem. Mordecai was a Jew who served in Xerxe's palace. Living with him was his cousin Esther (or Hadasah), whom he had raised as if she were his own daughter. Esther was one of the young women taken into the king's harem. After a lengthy preparation time, Esther went before the king, won his favor and was crowned queen (Esther 2:17).

At the end of chapter two something occurred that initially appears irrelevant but was later integral to the story; Mordecai uncovered a plot against the king. Relaying the information through Esther, to the king, Mordecai thwarted the conspirators' plot. Mordecai's deed was recorded in the king's official chronicle.

Haman, the Agagite, entered the scene in chapter 3. Xerxes elevated him to a position subordinate only to his own. All the royal officials, at the gate, would bow as Haman passed. Mordecai refused. Haman was a descendent of King Agag, king of the Amalekites, ancient enemy of Israel. Mordecai refused to bow before one of the people God had commanded Israel to blot out. "Blot out the memory of Amalek from under Heaven" (Deuteronomy 25:17-19). Mordecai's actions angered Haman, and, after learning of Mordecai's heritage, Haman's anger increased until he sought to destroy all of the Jews.

Haman convinced Xerxes that "certain people" did not obey the king's laws and deserved to be destroyed. The king gave Haman his signet ring, symbolic of his personal signature, to do as he had requested. Dispatches were sent to all the provinces that "... on a single day, the thirteenth day of Adar, the twelfth month." (3:13) every Jewish man, woman and child were to be killed and their possessions plundered. Not knowing Esther's nationality, Xerxes had unwittingly approved a law that could be used to kill his queen.

Queen Esther

The new law caused no small commotion among the Jews. Mordecai sent Esther details of Haman's evil plot and urged her to go before the king to plead for mercy for her people. Esther knew that to go before the king without being summoned would mean death unless the king extended his golden scepter as a sign of acceptance. In chapter 4:13-14 Mordecai told her

> *"Don't think that you will escape the fate of all the Jews because you are in the king's palace. If you keep silent at this time, liberation and deliverance will come to the Jewish people from another place, but you and your father's house will be destroyed. Who knows, perhaps you have come to the kingdom for such a time as this."*

Resolved to do what she could, Esther requested Mordecai and the other Jews in Susa to fast and pray for three days.

On the third day Esther took a bold step and went before the king. When the king saw her he extended his scepter. How relieved Esther must have been! The king appeared very pleased to see her, asking "Whatever you want, even to half the kingdom, will be given to you."(5:3) The International Bible Commentary says that "half the kingdom" was likely an ancient exaggeration not to be taken literally.[2] Esther requested the presence of the king and Haman at a banquet she had prepared. Xerxes and Haman joined Esther for the banquet. During the banquet the king asks Esther once more about the nature of her petition. For an unknown reason, Esther hesitated and requested that the king and Haman to come the next day for another banquet.

Haman left the banquet in such high spirits that even the sight of Mordecai, refusing to bow, only distracted him for a moment. Haman called together his friends and family to gloat about being the only person invited to the king and queen's private banquet. Remembering Mordecai tempered his enthusiasm as he confessed that, "Still none of this satisfies me since I see Mordecai the Jew sitting at the King's Gate all the time." (5:13) Zeresh, his wife, suggested building gallows seventy-five feet tall. Haman delighted in the idea and had the gallows built. Not only would he kill Mordecai, but he would utterly humiliate him as well.

At the beginning of chapter 6, the scene shifted to the king's chambers. It was late at night and the king could not sleep. He asked that the chronicles of his reign be brought to him. He found the account of Mordecai exposing the assassination plot. Xerxes asked, "What honor and special recognition have been given to Mordecai?" His attendants replied, "Nothing has been done for him." (6:3) Haman, who was nearby in the court, was brought before the king. Xerxes asked Haman what should be done for the man whom the king delighted to honor. Haman assumed the king was thinking of him and suggested that the man be clothed with royal robes and paraded around the city on one of the king's own horses, all the while being announced as the man whom the king delighted to honor. The king liked his idea and commanded Haman to go at once and do all that he had suggested to Mordecai.

The Bible gives no account of what certainly must have been Haman's shock and reaction to the unexpected turn of events. In verse 6:11 Haman carried out the king's wishes and in verse 12 he rushed home embarrassed, with his head covered. Very shortly thereafter his escort arrived to take him to the second banquet with the king and queen.

The story's climax is reached in chapter 7. At the banquet, the king once again asked Esther about her petition. Esther humbly requested that the king spare her life and the lives of her people because they had "been sold out to destruction, death and extermination" (v.4) . The king demanded of Esther who would do such a thing. Esther replied, "The adversary and enemy is this evil Haman." (v.6) If the sting of humiliation of parading Mordecai around Susa earlier that very day was not enough, now his grand plot against the Jewish people had been revealed in the presence of the king. The king was not happy.

The king got up in a rage and went out into the garden. Haman knew the king would kill him, so he started to beg Queen Esther for his life. Upon his return, the king saw Haman "falling on the couch where Esther was reclining." (v.8) and all chance of forgiveness disappeared with the king's assumption that Haman was molesting Esther. Immediately, attendants covered Haman's face. Persian kings refused to look on the face of a condemned person.[3] Harbona, one of the king's attendants, mentioned the gallows that Haman had built for Mordecai and the king commanded that Haman be hung upon them. Proverbs 26:27 states "The one who digs a pit will fall into it; and whoever rolls a stone — it will come back on him." It was no small irony that Haman was caught by the very trap he had intended for another.

In chapter 8 Mordecai is elevated to Haman's position (8:1, 10:3). Esther pleaded with the king to overturn the evil law Haman had enacted against the Jews. According to the law of the Medes and Persians, even the king could not overturn a law once it was enacted. The king gave Mordecai his signet ring and commanded him to write a new law which would counteract the first one without actually canceling it. The new law allowed the Jews to destroy any enemy who sought to harm them on the day Haman had chosen for them to be slaughtered.

When the appointed day arrived, the Jews turned the tables on their enemies, striking many down with the sword. Even the nobles and governors helped the Jews, as they now feared Mordecai because of his relationship to the king.

While God is not the author of evil, He does allow some evil things to occur for His greater glory. What Haman had plotted for evil, God used as a means to show His providence and grace in protecting His chosen people, the Jews. Being placed in the king's harem was probably not Esther's idea of what to do with her life. Risking her life to go before the king and plead for her people was also probably not what Esther desired. Yet, she was faithful to God, and God used her, and Mordecai, as a tool of deliverance for the oppressed and captive people of Israel.

Children may not fully understand what is happening in their lives and in the world around them, but they need to understand that God is always in control and working for our good. If we believers are faithful to follow Him, we will enjoy His peace and He will bless us in unimaginable ways.

AGE GROUP CONSIDERATIONS

Older students may enjoy hearing about what Esther went through before she became queen. The Persian royal court had many interesting customs, some of which are detailed in Esther chapter 2.

Younger children may not need to hear about Haman's gallows, but can be told that Haman made plans to send Mordecai away forever.

SUGGESTED HYMNS/SONGS

1. *Revive Us Again*, 493, 2008 Baptist Hymnal.
2. *Great and Mighty*, 20, 2008 Baptist Hymnal.
3. *Sweet Hour of Prayer*, 429, 2008 Baptist Hymnal.
4. *I Need Thee Every Hour*, 423, 2008 Baptist Hymnal.

STUDENT APPLICATIONS

1. Students will know that the story of Esther is found in the Old Testament book of Esther.
2. Students will know the story of Esther took place in the Persian Empire, where many Jews were slaves.
3. Students will know that Esther was a Jewish girl who became queen of Persia during the reign of King Xerxes.
4. Students will know that Haman was a descendent of the Amalekites, an ancient enemy of the Jews.
5. Students will know that Haman desired to have every Jew killed.

Queen Esther

6. Students will know that God used Esther and Mordecai to uncover Haman's evil plot and rescue the Jews.
7. Students will know that God providentially cares for His people.
8. Students will learn that doing the right thing is often not easy and can sometimes be uncomfortable or dangerous.

RESOURCES/CREDIT

1. *Life Application Bible.* (Grand Rapids, Michigan: Zondervan Publishing House, 1991), 822.
2. John Bendor-Samuels, *The International Bible Commentary, Revised Edition*, F.F. Bruce, ed. (Grand Rapids, Michigan: Zondervan Publishing House, 1979), 516.
3. *Life Application Bible*, 832.

Jesus Helps on the Sabbath

BACKGROUND PASSAGES

Main Passage
Mark 2:23-3:6   Jesus and the Sabbath

Related Passages
Matthew 12:1-14   Matthew's account
Luke 6:1-11   Luke's account
I Samuel 21:1-6   David eats consecrated bread

Suggested Homiletic Passage
Mark 3:1-6

MEMORY VERSE:

Younger version
"The Sabbath was made for man and not man for the Sabbath"
Mark 2:27b

Older version
Then He told them, "The Sabbath was made for man and not man for the Sabbath. Therefore the Son of Man is Lord even of the Sabbath."
Mark 2:27

LESSON OBJECTIVE

Jesus taught that the Sabbath was created for humans as a day of physical and spiritual rest. While believers should respect the day of rest, Sunday, it is not a day for legalism, but instead, worship and ministering to one another.

LESSON

The gospels teach about Jesus' perspective on the weekly observance of the Sabbath; a day of rest. Christians observe Sunday as the day of rest. Mark recorded two episodes involving Jesus and the Sabbath. In one of these episodes Jesus was accused of breaking Sabbath laws by the Pharisees. Jesus taught them the truth about observing the Lord's Day.

Mark 2:23-3:6

One Sabbath, Jesus and His disciples passed through a grain field. The disciples started to pick some heads of grain to satisfy their hunger. This was not stealing, as the law allowed harvesting by hand from a neighbor's field if one was in need (Deuteronomy 23:25). Cutting it down, however, was not allowed. The Pharisees saw them and confronted Jesus, accusing Him of breaking a Sabbath regulation.

First-century Jews had many regulations about what was acceptable behavior on the Sabbath. These rules were originally passed down orally but, in approximately 220 B.C., rabbis, after much debate, set down the boundaries of the regulations. The result of their work is *The Mishnah.*[1] While the laws were intended to encourage respect for the Sabbath, by Jesus' time, the Pharisees had become more concerned with their regulations than with pleasing God.

As He often did, Jesus made a reference to the Old Testament. The Pharisees would have been familiar with the passage, in this case I Samuel 21:1-6. Jesus asked, "Have you never read what David and those who were with him did when he was in need and hungry — how he entered the house of God in the time of Abiathar the high priest and ate the sacred bread — which was not lawful for anyone to eat except the priests — and also gave some to his companions?" (2:25-26).

In Matthew 12:6 Jesus said "But I tell you that someone greater than the temple is here!" If the Pharisees were to condemn Jesus, they would also condemn David, whom they held in reverence. Jesus always demonstrated the intent of the law. The Sabbath was created for people to rest and worship God. Even the Levites "worked" on the Sabbath, but their actions were a form of worship.

Jesus then quoted from Hosea 6:6 "I desire mercy, not sacrifice." (NIV). God had instituted many worship rituals in the Old Testament, but if they were not carried out with the right attitude, they became empty and hollow. In conclusion, Jesus stated "Therefore the Son of Man is Lord even of the Sabbath." Jesus was greater than and above the law, just as the Creator has always been greater than His creation. He has the authority to overrule man-made traditions and regulations.[2]

It appeared that Jesus had made His point. Yet the Pharisees once more attempted to trap Jesus on an issue regarding the Sabbath. Going from the field into a nearby synagogue (according to Matthew 12:9), a man with a shriveled hand was brought before Jesus. Hoping to trap Jesus, the Pharisees asked, "Is it lawful to heal on the Sabbath?" Their treacherous plan was transparent. Healing the man would break a Sabbath regulation. Not healing the man would reflect poorly on Christ's mercy for the needy.

Jesus commanded the man to stand up before everyone. Jesus asked, "Is it lawful on the Sabbath to do good or to do evil, to save life or to kill?" (3:4). Silence; No answer was given as the Pharisees realized that the "trap" had been turned against them. To agree would mean they admitted that Jesus was correct. To disagree would be to support evil. Jesus looked at them with anger, deeply distressed at their stubbornness and unwillingness to admit fault.

Jesus asked the man to extend his hand. Jesus healed his hand completely. Instead of rejoicing in the miracle or offering any kind of apology, the Pharisees went out to plot with the Herodians how they might kill Jesus. The Herodians were a political group who hoped to restore Herod the Great's line to the throne. The Pharisees and Herodians, normally enemies, joined together against Jesus because He exposed them for what they were.[3]

Jesus taught that the Sabbath is a day created for physical and spiritual rest, and renewal, not a day to deny needed help. It is a day to do good, as we glorify our Creator God. Set an example in word and deed by teaching our children to keep worship as a priority in everything they do on the Lord's Day.

Why don't Christians observe the Sabbath?

God set the pattern of the Sabbath during the creation week. On the seventh day, He rested from the act of creating. The Sabbath was observed on the seventh day of the week. Today, almost 2000 years later, Christians observe Sunday as the day of rest, instead of the Jewish Sabbath.

The change began early in the New Testament church. After Acts the day of rest is always referred to as the Lord's Day, not the Sabbath.

Why the change? It has to do with one special Sunday: Resurrection Sunday. On this first day of the week, believers remember and celebrate the resurrection of our Lord.

Examples of other Sabbath Laws[4]

Sabbath laws often appear outrageously strange and impractical to our modern culture. While well-intentioned and designed to build a "fence" in order to keep people from sinning, some of the regulations were quite absurd. Some of the regulations included:

- Bread could not be put in an oven when darkness was falling on the Sabbath as it would not be done before the Sabbath began.
- One could not drink more than a mouthful of milk on the Sabbath.
- A schoolmaster could watch their students read, but were not allowed to read themselves.

SUGGESTED HYMNS

1. *This is the Day*, 571, 2008 Baptist Hymnal.
2. *We Have Come into His House*, 666, 2008 Baptist Hymnal.
3. *Worthy of Worship*, 3, 2008 Baptist Hymnal.
4. *Come, Now is the Time to Worship*, 30, 2008 Baptist Hymnal.

STUDENT APPLICATIONS

1. Students will know that the Jews call their day of rest "the *Sabbath*."
2. Students will know that the account of Jesus healing on the Sabbath is recorded in the New Testament gospels of Matthew, Mark and Luke.
3. Students will know that Jewish law contained many regulations regarding behavior on the Sabbath.
4. Students will know that the Sabbath/Sunday was created for spiritual and physical rest and as a day of special worship.
5. Students will learn that they need to obey God cheerfully, with the right attitude.
6. Students will know that the Pharisees brought a man with a paralyzed hand to Jesus to see if He would heal the man on the Sabbath.
7. Students will know that Jesus healed the man, even though it was the Sabbath, because it was the right thing to do.
8. Students will learn that Jesus is Lord of the Sabbath/Sunday.
9. Students will know that believers today celebrate Sunday on the first day of the week in celebration of Christ's resurrection.

RESOURCES/CREDIT

1. Garry Hardin "*Sabbath Laws of the First Century*" Biblical Illustrator, Vol. 32, no. 3 (Spring 2006), insert before page 43.
2. *Life Application Bible*. (Grand Rapids, Michigan: Zondervan Publishing House, 1991), 1673.
3. *Ibid.*, 1732.
4. Hardin, 43.

Samuel Listens to God

BACKGROUND PASSAGES

Main Passage
I Samuel 3   Call of Samuel

Related Passages
I Samuel 1:1-2:21   Hannah's prayer answered
Hebrews 11:32-40   Samuel mentioned in Hall of Faith

Suggested Homiletic Passage
I Samuel 3:1-10

MEMORY VERSE

Younger version
Samuel responded, "Speak, for your servant is listening."

I Samuel 3:10b

Older version
The Lord came, stood there, and called as before, "Samuel! Samuel!" Samuel responded, "Speak, for your servant is listening."

I Samuel 3:10

LESSON OBJECTIVE

As a child, Samuel learned to listen to and obey God's voice. Today, God still speaks to His people in several different ways including through prayer and the Bible.

LESSON

While we have very little information about the childhood of most Biblical people, Samuel is a notable exception. Young Samuel serves as a personal example, to all ages, of a person being totally dedicated to God. Later, as an adult, Samuel the judge, prophet and priest exhibited faith that earned him the honor of a mention in the Hall of Faith in Hebrews.

Samuel was the answer to the prayer of a barren, heartbroken woman named Hannah. In I Samuel, verse 1, we see her broken before God and plead-

ing for a child. Eli, who later figured prominently in Samuel's development, saw Hannah in her anguished state and assumed she was drunk. Eli served 40 years as the high priest and judge of Israel. In her prayer to God, Hannah vowed to give her child into God's service if He would answer the prayer. The Lord did answer the prayer and Hannah kept her promise:

We do not know Samuel's age at the time Hannah took him to Eli. The NIV says only "after he was weaned." She reminded Eli of the time she had prayed for the child and of her promise to give Samuel to God. After Hannah left, Samuel lived with Eli and the other priests and assisted them as they performed their duties at the tabernacle. Hannah came to visit Samuel every year and brought a robe for his use. The Lord blessed Hannah again; after Samuel, Hannah had three sons and two daughters (I Sam. 19-21).

While this background information is important to understanding the context of the lesson, this month's story centers on one incident in the life of young Samuel.

The lesson begins with a look back at the first verse of I Samuel. God had spoken audibly to Moses and Joshua, but by the time of the judges, there were no prophets proclaiming God's word. *The Life Application Bible* suggests that the reason for this silence was that the priests were selfish and greedy, as seen in the lives of Eli's sons, Hophni and Phineas.[1] Whatever the reason, things were about to change, starting in the life of Samuel.

I Samuel 3
Samuel had a place to sleep in the Tabernacle, along with the priests, and not far from the Ark of the Covenant (v.3). In verse 4 Samuel audibly heard God speak to him, but mistaking the voice for Eli, Samuel replied "Here I am." ran to Eli. Eli told him he had not called and sent Samuel back to bed.

In verses 6-7 God called Samuel again. Samuel goes to Eli, who again said he had not called Samuel and then sent him back to bed. In verse 8, God spoke a third time to Samuel. Samuel, thinking once more that Eli had called, dutifully went to him. Upon Samuel's third visit, Eli had realized that God had spoken to Samuel. Eli instructed Samuel that if he heard the call again, to answer, "Speak, Lord, for your servant is listening."

What might have gone through Samuel's mind? Was he scared? Excited? Sometimes when God speaks to us, it can make us uncomfortable. Being in the presence of a holy God makes us aware of how sinful we are. God will reveal destructive behaviors and attitudes to us so that He can change our heart for our ultimate sanctification.

Verse 10 states "The Lord came, stood there, and called as before." Samuel might have visually seen the events revealed to him as verse 15 refers to the visit as a vision. Samuel responded, "Speak, for your servant is listening." In verses 11-14 God explained that He was going to judge the house of Eli because of their sins (this judgment was fulfilled in I Samuel 4). In a single day, Eli and his two sons died, and the ark of the covenant was captured by the Philistines. Certainly these events made the ears of all the Israelites "shudder" (The NIV translates the word as "*tingle*"). In the place of Eli's descendants, Samuel became the high priest of Israel.

Verse 15 says Samuel "lay down until the morning." Was he able to get any sleep after what had happened? Samuel was afraid to tell Eli about the vision. Eli cornered Samuel and ordered him to tell every detail of the vision. Samuel obeyed and hid nothing, telling Eli every detail. Eli accepted his judgment, acknowledging that the Lord had authority to do what He thought was best.

That God would speak to a child instead of one of the adult priests of Israel reminds believers that God honors faithfulness, not high position. Believers should not be surprised when God works through unexpected channels. We need to be sensitive to God working in the life of anyone at any place or time.

Verses 19-21 note the progress made by Samuel as he grew up. Verse 19 states, "Samuel grew, and the Lord was with him and let nothing he said prove false." (NIV says, "... he let none of his words fall to the ground.") The mental picture of words falling to the ground is an unusual one. What it teaches is that as a prophet of God, all that Samuel said was true. Anyone who claims to be a prophet but makes even one mistake is a false prophet.

Samuel was then recognized as a prophet by the people of Israel. Israel once again heard directly from God, as He spoke through the prophet Samuel who was faithful to listen and obey. Children and adults today can also learn from his example and listen attentively for God to speak in their lives.

How does God speak to believers today?

God still speaks to His people today. In the Bible He communicated in many different ways. Henry Blackaby, in Experiencing God, teaches that there are four ways which God speaks to believers today.

1. *The Bible* — God reveals Himself and His will to us through the ministry of the Holy Spirit when believers study His word. The Bible is the ultimate authority; if anything contradicts God's word, it is not of God.
2. *Prayer* — Believers have a direct line to God the Creator. He listens and speaks through prayer.
3. *Circumstances* — When believers start to view life from God's perspective, they see God at work through their circumstances.
4. *The Church* — The church is the bride of Christ and center of fellowship. Close Christian friends, Godly teachers, and ministers can help a believer discern God's will.[2]

In seeking God's will, it is important to look for direction in all four ways God speaks. If there are certain circumstance or someone in the church suggests you do something, make sure to verify whether it is of God through prayer and Bible study.

AGE GROUP CONSIDERATIONS

While the focus of the lesson presentation needs to center on Samuel obediently listening to God, feel free to work in the background material (from chapters 1 and 2) about why Samuel was at the tabernacle, how Hannah had prayed for him, and how Samuel would go on to become a great servant of God.

For the younger children, a simpler way to explain to young children how God communicates to believers today, would be to say something like "God talks to us through prayer and learning from the Bible with our parents and our teachers."

Suggested Hymns/Songs

1. *Here I am to Worship*, 130, 2008 Baptist Hymnal.
2. *Be Thou My Vision*, 83, 2008 Baptist Hymnal.
3. *Speak, O Lord*, 432, 2008 Baptist Hymnal.
4. *Speak to My Heart*, 428, 2008 Baptist Hymnal.
5. *Word of God, Speak*, 343, 2008 Baptist Hymnal.

Student Applications

1. Students will know that the story of young Samuel is found in the Old Testament book of First Samuel.
2. Students will know that Samuel was living and serving with the priests because of a vow his mother had made before he was born.
3. Students will know that God blessed Hannah with more children after Samuel.
4. Students will know that Samuel heard God speaking to him in the middle of the night.
5. Students will know that Samuel thought Eli was calling him, when it was really God.
6. Students will know that after the third time, Eli told him that when he heard his name called to say "Here I am" for it was God speaking to him.
7. Students will know that Samuel said "Here I am" when God called the third time.
8. Older Students will know that God told Samuel that he would judge Eli's family because they had done evil things.
9. Students will know while we may not hear Him audibly, God reveals Himself to those who place their faith in Him.
10. Students will know that sometimes when God speaks to us, it is uncomfortable. God works in us to reveal destructive behaviors and attitudes (sin) for our ultimate sanctification.
11. Students will know that God speaks through the Bible, prayer, circumstances and the church.
12. Students will know that Samuel became the high priest and a great judge, serving as the leader of Israel.

Resources/Credit

1. *Life Application Bible*. (Grand Rapids, Michigan: Zondervan Publishing House, 1991), 439.
2. Henry T. Blackaby and Claude V. King. *Experiencing God: Youth Edition* (Nashville: Lifeway Press), 69-103. *Much of this book focuses on how God speaks to us today.*

Ark of the Covenant

Background Passages

Main Passages
I Samuel 5:1-6:15 Ark captured by Philistines
II Chronicles 5:2-14 Ark brought into temple

Related Passages
I Samuel 4   Philistines capture ark
Exodus 25:10-22   God gives instructions concerning
                  the construction of the Ark
Hebrews 9:1-5   Contents of the Ark
II Chronicles 6-7 The Temple dedication

Suggested Homiletics Passage
II Chronicles 5:7-14

Memory Verse

Don't you know that you are God's sanctuary and that the Spirit of God lives in you?

I Corinthians 3:16

Lesson Objective

In the Old Testament, the Ark of the Covenant was God's dwelling place among His people. The capture of the Ark by the Philistines and subsequent return showed that Jehovah was the one true God. Today He dwells in the hearts of believers through the ministry of the Holy Spirit.

Lesson

The Ark of the Covenant played a vital role in the community of Israel in the Old Testament. It was God's dwelling place within the Israelite community and therefore a most precious possession. Originally housed in the tabernacle, it later was housed in Solomon's temple. The story of its capture by the Philistines (in *I Samuel*) and the temple dedication (in *II Chronicles*) further illustrate the importance of the Ark. Today God dwells with His people through the indwelling of the Holy Spirit.

I Samuel 5:1-6:15

In I Samuel 4 the Israelites had displeased God. The Israelites carried the Ark into battle, hoping that God would grant a military victory against the Philistines. The result was a total disaster. The Ark was captured by the Philistines during the battle. Compounding the tragedy, the judge and high priest of Israel, Eli, died the same day upon hearing news of the Ark's capture. The glory of God in the ark had departed Israel as the Philistines basked in the glow of victory. But God was not surprised by these events and He was not about to share his glory with any false god, as the Philistines soon painfully learned.

The narrative picks up just after the capture of the Ark. In 5:2 the Philistines took the Ark to the city of Ashdod and placed the Ark in the temple of Dagon next to a statue of Dagon. The Philistines worshipped many gods, but Dagon was the chief god, to whom was attributed rain and assurance of bountiful harvests.[1] The Philistines may have recognized the importance of the Ark to Israel and hoped that it might help them, too, or they might simply have attributed the victory to Dagon and placed the Ark in the temple as a war trophy.[2]

A curious thing happened that night. When the people entered the temple the next morning, they found the statue of Dagon on its face before the Ark. This is certainly a picture of God asserting His authority over the false god. The Bible does not record the reaction of the Philistines other than to note that they returned Dagon to his original place. The next morning Dagon was once more on his face before the Ark. In addition, his head and arms had been broken off, leaving only the body prostrate before the ark.

The Philistines still did not understand (or refused to accept) what God what trying to tell them. In verse 6 the Lord's hand was heavy upon the people of Ashdod, and he afflicted them with many tumors. The men of Ashdod finally realized they were dealing with a Being who was beyond their control and more powerful than their gods.

Not knowing what to do, they gathered together all the Philistine leaders to discuss the predicament. It was decided to send the Ark away to the city of Gath. Verse 9 states, "After they had moved it, the Lord's hand was against the city of Gath, causing a great panic." Both young and old were afflicted by tumors, just as they had been in Ashdod.

The Gathites sent the Ark to the city of Ekron. News of what had happened to Ashdod and Gath had reached Ekron ahead of the Ark. The Ekronites, wanting nothing to do with the Ark, pleaded with the Philistine leaders to return it to the Israelites. As it was with Ashdod and Gath, the hand of God was heavy upon the Philistines. Many Ekronites were afflicted with tumors while others just died (v.12).

At the beginning of chapter 6 the Philistine leaders met with their priests and "diviners" to decide how to properly return the Ark. The Ark had been in the hands of the Philistines for seven months, and still they were not convinced that all the trouble they had endured was from the hand of the God of the Israelites.

It was suggested that the Ark not be returned without a trespass offering. The Philistines had five rulers, so it was suggested that they make five gold images of the tumors that had afflicted the people, along with five golden mice. Mice were also likely part of the afflictions from God. The mice could have facilitated the rapid spread of disease. In verse 10, the Ark was loaded on a cart and attached to two female milk cows. The symbolic gold tumors and mice were placed in a box on the cart. Since milk cows were used that had never been yoked, it was unlikely they would pull together.[3]

In verse 9 the Philistines had decided that if the cattle went towards Israel on their own accord, then they would know that it was the God of Israel who was judging them. If the cows did not, then "... it was just something that happened to us by chance."

The Philistines followed the cart as the cows worked in tandem and headed toward the Israelite settlement of Beth-shemesh (v.12). They observed the inhabitants of Beth-Shemesh harvesting wheat in the valley. Upon seeing the ark, the Israelites were overjoyed. The Levites were called to come take possession and set the Ark upon a rock. The cart was cut up and used to create a fire. The cows were killed and sacrificed to the Lord. The Philistine rulers returned to the city of Ekron. Despite their attempt at reconciliation, the Lord's hand was against the Philistines all of Samuel's life (I Samuel 7:13). Samuel was Eli's successor.

God had preserved His glory and returned the Ark to the people of Israel. A great revival broke out in Israel, leading to the destruction of the false idols in the land. It would still be several decades before the Ark was properly housed within Solomon's temple. For the time being, the people of Israel rejoiced at God's provision in protecting the Ark.

II Chronicles 5:2-14

In II Chronicles 5 Solomon had completed the first temple. It was time for the dedication of the Temple to God's glory. It would be a grand spectacle and time of worship as all of Israel came to participate. The Levites took up the Ark and, in verse 7, carried it into the inner sanctuary of the temple, which was the most holy place called the Holy of Holies. Not a small space, this was a room 30' by 30' by 30'. Two large winged cherubim were in the room, their wings extending 15' each, covering the entire width of the room. The Ark was placed beneath the wings of the cherubim, so that their wings formed a cover over the Ark. A thick curtain covered the front of the room. This was the curtain that was torn in two at Jesus' crucifixion.

In verse 11 the priests came out of the most holy place as the Levitical singers, accompanied by 120 trumpets and various cymbals and musical instruments, praised God. As they worshiped, the temple was filled with a cloud. The Levites "were not able to continue ministering, for the glory of the Lord filled

God's temple." (II Chronicles 5:14) God had accepted the work of Solomon and the Israelites.

From now on, the Holy of Holies could only be entered once a year on the Day of Atonement, by a consecrated priest. God would dwell among His people, but even then at a distance. Today the presence of God, in the life of the covenant community, is personal. Believers are indwelled with the Holy Spirit. "Don't you know that you are God's sanctuary and that the Spirit of God lives in you?" (I Cor. 3:16) Just as the Israelites were blessed to have God dwelling among them, believers are even more blessed to have Him within our hearts, receiving guidance and teaching from our ever present Lord.

Origin and contents of the Ark

Exodus 25:10-22 is where God gave instructions concerning the construction of the ark. The ark was 45" long, 27" wide, and 27" high. Rings were attached to each corner. Two gold-covered poles were inserted through the rings and were used to carry the ark. The rings may have been attached to the bottom of the Ark, so that it could be lifted "on high."[4] The lid of the Ark was called the mercy seat. On top of the mercy seat were two winged cherubim. Exodus 25:22 states, "I will meet you there above the mercy seat, between the two cherubim that are over the ark of the testimony; I will speak with you from there about all that I command you regarding the Israelites."

What was in the Ark? Hebrews 9:4 speaks of three items. The three items were the tablets of the ten commandments, a gold jar containing manna, and the rod of Aaron's which had budded. It was a common practice in antiquity to place covenant and treaty documents in a sanctuary box.[5] Some believe the staff and jar were removed at some point before Solomon's temple was completed as II Chronicles 5:10 states "Nothing was in the ark except the two tablets ..."

The Ark Today?

Where is the ark today? After the Babylonians conquered Jerusalem and plundered the Temple, the Ark was lost to history. It was possibly destroyed by king Nebuchadnezzar and the Babylonians.

Contrary to the story line of the movie *Raiders of the Lost Ark*, the Nazi's did not find the Ark only to be consumed by the wrath of God and a talented team of special effects artists. Still, there is no lack of theories suggesting that the ark survived to the current day. Several sites around Jerusalem, including under the Temple mount, have been argued as the location of the Ark. Other sites such as caves near where the Dead Sea Scrolls were found and even Ethiopia have been suggested.

If the Ark is ever recovered it would be the greatest archeological discovery of all time. Needless to say, it will only be revealed if God desires so and will be in His perfect timing .

SUGGESTED HYMNS

1. *Abide with Me*, 88, 2008 Baptist Hymnal.
2. *Breathe on Me*, 332, 2008 Baptist Hymnal.
3. *Without Him*, 470, 2008 Baptist Hymnal.
4. *We are Called to be God's People*, 391, 2008 Baptist Hymnal.

AGE GROUP CONSIDERATIONS

The concept of the indwelling of the Holy Spirit may be difficult for some younger children. It may be best to tell them that when we trust in Jesus, God is always with us even though we cannot see Him.

The background information about the Ark may also be taught, though is not essential to the lesson. Older children will find fascinating some of the theories about the possible existence of the Ark today.

STUDENT APPLICATIONS

1. Students will know that the story of the Philistines and the Ark is recorded in the Old Testament book of I Samuel.
2. Students will know that the Ark of the covenant was the symbol of God's presence to the nation of Israel.
3. Students will know that God actually "met" the priests at the Mercy seat on the Ark.

4. Students will know that God indwells believers today through the ministry of the Holy Spirit.
5. Students will know that God caused the idol of Dagon to fall face-first before the Ark.
6. Students will know that God punished the Philistines for stealing the Ark by sending tumors and other punishments.
7. Students will know that the Ark was placed in the Holy of Holies when the Temple, which God had Solomon construct, was finished.
8. Students will know that God's glory descended as a cloud on the temple during the dedication ceremony.

RESOURCES/CREDIT

1. *Life Application Bible.* (Grand Rapids, Michigan: Zondervan Publishing House, 1991), 442.
2. David Alexander & Pat Alexander, eds. *Eerdmans' Handbook to the Bible* (Grand Rapids: William B. Eerdmans Publishing Company, 1973), 233.
3. *Ibid.*, 234.
4. *Manners & Customs of the Bible.* (New Kensington, PA: Whitaker House, 1996), 79.
5. Robert P. Gordon, *The International Bible Commentary, Revised Edition*, F.F. Bruce, ed. (Grand Rapids, Michigan: Zondervan Publishing House, 1979), 175.

The Ten Lepers

BACKGROUND PASSAGES

Main Passage
Luke 17:11-19   Jesus heals ten lepers

Related Passages
Leviticus 14:1-32   Procedure for ritual cleansing
Matthew 25:35-40   Care for the least of these

Suggested Homiletic Passage
Luke 17:11-19

MEMORY VERSE

Younger version
Seeing that he was healed, he returned and ... gave glory to God.

Luke 17:15

Older version
But one of them, seeing that he was healed, returned and with a loud voice, gave glory to God.

Luke 17:15

LESSON OBJECTIVE

Jesus showed compassion toward a Samaritan leper, who had been rejected by society. Like the leper, believers should show gratefulness to God for both physical blessing and spiritual salvation.

LESSON

The story of the ten lepers is a story about the power of God over physical affliction and about thankfulness. Though the account is only nine verses long, there is much that can be learned. Children will learn to acknowledge the power and grace of God, just as the Samaritan leper did.

Luke 17:11-19

Starting with verse 11 Jesus was traveling to Jerusalem. The route he took was literally on the border of Galilee and Samaria. It was common for Jews to take a circuitous route around Samaria because of their disdain for the Samaritans (See *Jews and Samaritans* later in this lesson).

As Jesus neared a village, ten men approached. The men had leprosy (or other similar serious skin maladies) and as such were considered "unclean." They were not allowed to get in close proximity to other people. Per expectations, they kept their distance from Jesus. The lepers cried out, "Jesus, Master, have mercy on us!" Perhaps they were merely begging, but most likely they had heard about Jesus' miraculous works and sought healing.

Instead of healing the lepers where they stood, Jesus commanded them to go present themselves before the priest. Sometimes leprosy would go into remission, and God had made a provision for priests to serve in the role of a "health inspector" to determine whether the leper could rejoin society (See *Leprosy during Bible Times* later in this lesson).

All ten lepers left to present themselves to the priest, "And while they were going, they were healed." (v.14) Jesus had miraculously healed them. Their lives would be dramatically different from now on.

But the story did not end there. One of the lepers, upon seeing that he had been healed, returned to Jesus. The man fell on his face at Jesus' feet and with a loud voice gave glory to God. It is at this point that we learn the man was a Samaritan. To Jews who read Luke's account, this would have been a real shock. Not only was the man an outcast because of his leprosy, but he was also considered a second class citizen because of his heritage. In healing not just anyone, but a Samaritan leper, Jesus had shown great compassion for the lowest of the low.

But how would Jesus react to the man's display of gratefulness? Jesus asked the man, "Were not 10 cleansed? Where are the nine?" (v.17). Only the "foreigner" had returned to show his gratefulness. Jesus told the man, "Get up and go on your way. Your faith has made you well." (v.19). The Samaritan was rewarded spiritually and physically as a result of his faith.

When was the last time you passionately thanked God for some work He has done in your life? When was the last time you passionately thanked God just because of who He is? Jesus cares for all, even those who are social outcasts. He expects believers to show the same compassion (Matt. 25:35-40).

God still works miracles today. In His perfect will, many people are healed of physical maladies. Some however, will not receive healing until they enter Heaven and receive their glorified body. Thankfully, Jesus can be trusted to always "heal" us from our sins when we come to Him, just as we are, and repent and place our faith in Him. We cannot clean ourselves up, our only hope is to trust Jesus to save us from our sins. He will not disappoint or turn away.

Leprosy during Bible Times

While most Americans have likely never encountered or thought of leprosy, it was a dreaded disease in Bible times. The term "leprosy" is used for wide range of skin maladies. Not only did it cause physical distress as it afflicted the body, but because of social stigma, victims were isolated from friends and loved ones. In Biblical times, victims were considered to live under a divine curse and were therefore declared "unclean," pushed to the margins of society, and ostracized.

Sometime the leprosy or skin disease would go into remission. If a victim was healed of leprosy, they still had to go through a long ceremonial ritual before they could rejoin society. Leviticus 14 details this extensive procedure. *The Family Bible Library* gives a summary:

1. The leper must have a priest examine him outside the camp or town to make sure the leprosy was gone.
2. Then the leper must get two clean, living birds. He must kill one bird in an earthen jar with some water in it, letting the blood drip into the water.
3. A piece of cedar wood, some red wool, and part of a plant called hyssop were tied together. Then, holding this with the living bird, whose wings

and tail were held together, all were dipped in the bloody water.
4. The leper was sprinkled with the bloody water seven times.
5. The living bird was turned loose into a field, supposedly taking the leper's uncleanness with it.
6. The cleansed leper was to wash his clothes, shave off all his hair, and take a bath. Then he could come back into camp or town. But he still could not go into his own tent or home for six days.
7. On the seventh day, he was to shave all his hair from his head again, as well as the hair from his eyebrows and beard. He was to wash his clothes again and take another bath. Then he was (proclaimed) clean.
8. On the next day, he was to make an offering of two male lambs, one ewe lamb, and some flour mixed with oil. If the man was poor, he could use one male lamb, two pigeons or turtledoves, and some flour mixed with oil.[1]

Jews and Samaritans

Samaritans were considered foreigners or half-breeds by the Jews. Samaritans were descended from Jews who were left behind after the Assyrians took many (generally the more well-to-do or noble) of their number into captivity. They intermarried with the pagan people brought in by the Assyrians (II Kings 17:24) and developed their own culture. The biggest point of contention, between the Jews and Samaritans, was the temple the Samaritans had built in Samaria. Under the Old Testament covenant, God had commanded worship at the temple in Jerusalem, not Samaria. To 'pure' Jews, the Samaritan temple was an abomination.

The gospels report that Jesus had multiple contacts with Samaritans, including the woman at the well. Jesus was preparing both the Jews and Samaritans for a time when neither temple would be a center of worship, but instead worship would focus on Jesus in the New Testament church. Salvation is now available to anyone who repents and follows Jesus.

STUDENT APPLICATIONS

1. Students will know that the story of the Ten Lepers is found in the New Testament book of Luke.
2. Students will know that Jesus loves all people, even those we consider unlovable.
3. Students will know that Jesus healed 10 lepers of their disease.
4. Students will know that only one of the 10 lepers returned to thank Jesus.
5. Students will know that the man who thanked Jesus was a Samaritan.
6. Students will learn to be thankful for all of God's blessings in their lives.
7. Students will know that leprosy was an especially dreaded disease in Bible times. Besides physical distress, it required separation from loved ones.
8. Students will know that Jews considered Samaritans to be foreigners.
9. Students will know that God still does miracles today but not everyone receives earthly healing.
10. Students will know that saving faith in God is even more important than physical healing.
11. Students will know that it pleases God when they worship Him and give Him the thanks He deserves.

SUGGESTED HYMNS

1. *Count your Blessings*, 585, 2008 Baptist Hymnal.
2. *He is Lord*, 277, 2008 Baptist Hymnal.
3. *What a Friend We Have in Jesus*, 154, 2008 Baptist Hymnal.
4. *God is so Good*, 23, 1991 Baptist Hymnal.
5. *Doxology*, 668, 2008 Baptist Hymnal.
6. *Praise Him, Praise Him*, 149, 1991 Baptist Hymnal.
7. *Thank You Lord*, 582, 2008 Baptist Hymnal.
8. *He is able to Deliver Thee*, 24, 1991 Baptist Hymnal.
9. *He Touched Me*. 628, 2008 Baptist Hymnal.
10. *Praise Him, All Ye Little Children*, 650, 2008 Baptist Hymnal.

RESOURCES/CREDIT

1. V. Gilbert Veers, *Family Bible Library* (Nashville: The Southwestern Company, 1971) Vol. 7,166-67. *List quoted verbatim.*

Christmas - Anna & Simeon

BACKGROUND PASSAGES

Main Passage
Luke 2:21-40   Simeon and Anna see Jesus

Related Passages
Luke 2:1-22   Nativity/Shepherds
Matt. 1:18-2:12   Nativity/Wise Men

Suggested Homiletic Passage
Luke 2:25-32, *may be extended to verse 35.*

MEMORY VERSE

Blessed are the pure in heart, because they will see God.

Matthew 4:8

LESSON OBJECTIVE

Anna and Simeon are representative of obedient Jews who longed for the coming of the Messiah. Almost 2000 years later Christmas is still a special celebration of the remembrance of Jesus' coming to dwell among people.

LESSON

Have you ever waited for something with great anticipation? Did it seem like the anticipated day would never arrive? Did time seem to crawl? The Israelites expectantly awaited the arrival of the Messiah for many centuries. Isaiah had prophesied centuries before that a Messiah would come out of Israel. Christians celebrate the coming of the Messiah, Jesus, every year at Christmas.

Anna and Simeon embraced the promise of the Messiah throughout their long lives. God rewarded their faithful patience by allowing them to see the newborn child, Jesus, who would be "a light for revelation to the Gentiles and glory to Your people Israel." (Luke 2:32). It is important to remember that while sometimes we believers do not see the result of our faith, we must remember God is faithful to keep His promises.

Luke 2:21-40

In keeping with Jewish law, Mary and Joseph waited eight days to name their son; the baby was given the name **JESUS**. Following the birth of a son, a woman was considered impure for seven days, and for the following thirty-three days the woman was not allowed to touch anything holy. At the end of the forty days an offering was given at the temple.

After the time of cleansing was complete, Mary and Joseph took Jesus up to the temple for the dedication and Mary's sacrifice. In verse 24 it says that the offering was a pair of turtledoves or two young pigeons. This was the offering given by people of lesser means (Lev. 12:8).

In verse 25, while in the temple area, the family met a man named Simeon. Simeon is commended by Luke for being righteous and devout. It had been revealed to him by the Holy Spirit that he would not die before seeing the promised Messiah. This meeting was not coincidental, but was preordained as God led Simeon directly to the infant Jesus.

In verse 28 Simeon took Jesus in his arms and began to praise God. His joy at seeing Jesus was so great that he exclaimed in verses 29-32:

> "Now, Master, You can dismiss your slave in peace, according to Your word. For my eyes have seen your salvation. You have prepared it in the presence of all peoples — a light for revelation to the Gentiles and glory to Your people Israel." (Luke 2:29-32).

Now that God had kept his promise, Simeon was more than willing to die. Even as an infant, Jesus was recognized as the cornerstone of God's redemptive plan.

Simeon's powerful and prophetic words amazed Mary and Joseph. In verse 34 Simeon gave a personal prophecy to Mary. He told her that Jesus would cause the rise and fall of many in Israel. While a number of Jews would follow Jesus, most would not. This was would ultimately be fulfilled in the death of Jesus at the hands of the Jews and Romans. Simeon also told her what would transpire in Jesus' life, and that as a result, "a sword will pierce your own soul..." This was an obvious reference to the hurt and grief that Mary would suffer as Jesus was rejected and crucified.

Also in the temple was an elderly widow, Anna. Anna was a prophetess. She, along with Simeon, embodied all that was positive about faithful Jews who looked with longing for the arrival of the Messiah. Most translations say she was eighty-four. Some say she had spent eighty-four years in the temple after the death of her husband, pushing her age well over one-hundred. Regardless of her true age, Luke noted her unfailing devotion and faith in serving God night and day for many years. Anna approached Mary and Joseph while they were talking with Simeon. Anna instantly recognized Jesus as the Messiah and began to thank God and shared the news with others who were looking forward to the redemption of Israel.

After these encounters and completing their duty at the temple according to the law, Jesus was taken by Mary and Joseph to Nazareth. In verse 40 we are told simply that Jesus grew up and was filled with wisdom, and the grace of God was on Him.

Anna and Simeon are wonderful examples of how believers should celebrate Christmas. They rejoiced in the fulfilled promise of the Messiah. Throughout the year, and especially at Christmas, Christians should celebrate the birth of Jesus. Empires have risen and fallen, kings have come and gone, but Jesus established an eternal kingdom and invited anyone who is willing to follow to be co-heirs with Him. All people have deserved spiritual death, but through God's perfect plan, Jesus won victory over death, and secured eternal life for all who repent and place their trust in Him.

The Nativity: Luke 2:1-22

It would not seem to be Christmas without a look at the nativity. This lesson focuses on the wise men, but feel free to precede the narrative of the wise men with what actually happened at Jesus' birth. Two of the other lessons, *Christmas - The Messiah Prophesied* and *Christmas - Shepherds* cover the events surrounding the nativity.

AGE GROUP CONSIDERATIONS

Jewish boys were circumcised on the eighth day after birth. Jesus was no exception as described in Luke 2:21. The topic does not need to come up with children.

SUGGESTED HYMNS

1. *Come, Thou Long-Expected Jesus*, 176, 2008 Baptist Hymnal.
2. *Good Christian Men, Rejoice*, 183, 2008 Baptist Hymnal.
3. *Joy to the World! The Lord is Come*, 181, 2008 Baptist Hymnal.
4. *O Come, All Ye Faithful*, 199, 2008 Baptist Hymnal.
5. *Emmanuel*, 201, 2008 Baptist Hymnal.
6. *I know Whom I Have Believed*, 353, 2008 Baptist Hymnal.
7. *Great is Thy Faithfulness*, 96, 2008 Baptist Hymnal.

STUDENT APPLICATIONS

1. Students will know the story of Simeon and Anna is found in the book of New Testament book of Luke.
2. Students will know that Jesus was presented at the temple, forty days after his birth and according to Old Testament law.
3. Students will know that God had revealed to Simeon that he would not die before seeing the Lord's Christ.
4. Students will know that Anna had spent many years faithfully serving God and was overjoyed to see the Messiah.
5. Students will know that at Christmas Christians celebrate the good news that Jesus was born.
6. Students will know that God always keeps His promises, even if they do not see the ultimate result.

Gideon

BACKGROUND PASSAGES

Main Passage
Judges 7:1-23   Defeat of Midian

Related Passages
Judges 6:11-40   Gideon's call
Judges 7:24-8:21   Pursuit of Midian
Judges 8:22-23   Gideon declines offer to be king

Suggested Homiletic Passage
Judges 7:15-23

MEMORY VERSE

Younger version
> Do not fear, for I am with you;
> do not be afraid, for I am your God.
>   *Isaiah 41:10a*

Older version
> Do not fear, for I am with you;
> do not be afraid, for I am your God.
> I will strengthen you; I will help you
> I will hold on to you with my righteous right hand.
>   *Isaiah 41:10*

LESSON OBJECTIVE

In the time of the book of Judges, God raised up leaders to protect His people. Gideon was one judge that God used in a mighty way to deliver the Israelites from a large Midianite army.

LESSON

Gideon was one of several judges whom God raised to protect the nation of Israel. During the time of the judges, Israel repeatedly went through a cycle of peace and national revival, only to fall away from God, suffer subsequent judgment at the hands of their pagan neighbors, and finally find redemption through God raising a powerful judge. Despite their fickleness, God extended mercy and grace to the Israelites and answered them in their distress. One judge, Gideon, was used mightily by God to deliver the Israelites from a large Midianite army. From the experience of Gideon, we can learn to trust that God will always provide for us, often in the most unexpected of ways.

Gideon was also known by the name of Jerubbaal, meaning, "Let Baal plead his case with him." The name was given after Gideon had destroyed an altar of Baal (Judges 6:25-32). Gideon was called by God during a time of oppression at the hands of the Midianites. Midian is generally believed to have been on the east coast of the Gulf of Aqaba (in modern day Saudi Arabia), though the Bible also describes Midianites in southern and eastern Transjordan.[1] These "fierce camel-riders" would have intimidated any foe.[2]

Judges 7:1-23

At the beginning of chapter 7 Gideon was camped with his army of 32,000 Israelites and facing a horde of Midianite soldiers. It is not until later (Judges 8:10) that we find out the Midianite army was actually 135,000 strong. Outnumbered more than four to one, Gideon could not have anticipated what God was about to do to the Israelite army. "You have too many people for Me to hand the Midianites over to you..." said the Lord in verse 2. God wanted the glory for the victory. He did not want the Israelites to brag about what they had "accomplished."

In verse 3 God told Gideon to announce to the people that any who were "fearful and trembling" would be allowed to return to their homes. 22,000 men left, leaving an army of just 10,000. Once again, God told Gideon that he had too many men. God gave Gideon an unusual way of dividing the army. Gideon was told to take the men to water and observe what method they used to drink. Most of the men got down on their knees and drank up water like a dog. 300 of the men reached over and cupped water with their hands.

God told Gideon "I will deliver you with the 300 men who lapped and hand the Midianites over to you. But everyone else is to go home." (v.7). Gideon was obedient and sent the majority of the men home, keeping just the 300. Thus reduced, Gideon's army was then outnumbered 450 to 1!

The Lord sought to assure Gideon that the battle was already won. God told Gideon to go down near the Midianite camp and listen to what the soldiers were saying (vv.9-11). What Gideon heard comforted him. Approaching the army, Gideon and his servant, Purah, found a huge sprawling mass of humanity and camels. Gideon overheard one of the soldiers talking about a dream, in which "a loaf of barley bread came tumbling into the Midianite camp, struck a tent, and it fell. The loaf turned the tent upside down so that it collapsed." A friend said it "could be nothing less than the sword of Gideon..." In the Midianites' hearts and minds, the battle had already been lost.

Encouraged, Gideon returned to the Israelite camp. In verse 15 Gideon said, "Get up, for the Lord has handed the Midianite camp over to you." The 300 men divided into three equal-sized groups. The men each took a trumpet and a torch which was covered by an empty pitcher. Nothing is mentioned about swords or other weapons. During the middle of the night, the small army neared the Midianite camp. When Gideon blew his trumpet, the men broke their pitchers and blew their trumpets. They lifted high their now blazing torches and cried "The sword of the Lord and of Gideon." (v.20).

Greatly startled, the Midianites drew their swords to defend themselves. In verse 22 it says that the Lord threw the Midianites into great confusion, and they began to attack one another. The vast army began to break and run away.

Gideon and his men pursued the fleeing army. Later in chapter 8 it is revealed that only 15,000 men survived (Judges 8:10). 120,000 had perished as part of God's judgment against Midian. Eventually the two kings of Midian, Zebah and Zalmunna., were captured and killed (Judges 8:12).

For the removal of the Midian menace, Gideon was so admired and revered by the Israelites, that (Judges 8:22-23) the people asked him to be their king and rule over them. Instead of accepting this position of great power and responsibility, he declined, and said, "...the Lord will rule over you." The Lord did indeed rule, and the people of Israel had forty years of peace during the lifetime of Gideon.

God still raises leaders to guide and protect His people. Whether it is a pastor, Sunday School teacher, parent, or other leader, children look up to and need to respect those God has placed in authority. Those in positions of authority need to submit to God's leadership and live and work in a way that is pleasing to Him.

AGE GROUP CONSIDERATIONS

It may be necessary to explain what role judges filled in the life of Israel. Children today have only court judges with which to compare. The judges of the Old Testament took on many roles, including those of judge, administrator, politician and field general in leading the people of Israel.

In addition to the lesson, older children may enjoy learning about the origin of Gideon's other name, Jerubbaal, in Judges 6:25-32.

SUGGESTED HYMNS

1. *Lead On, O King Eternal*, 659, 2008 Baptist Hymnal.
2. *Victory Chant*, 299, 2008 Baptist Hymnal.
3. *Faith is the Victory*, 521, 2008 Baptist Hymnal.
4. *To God be the Glory*, 28, 2008 Baptist Hymnal.

STUDENT APPLICATIONS

1. Students will know that the story of Gideon can be found in the Old Testament book of Judges.

Gideon

2. Students will know that Gideon became a leader (a judge) of the people of Israel.
3. Students will know that Gideon's army faced a Midianite army of 135,000 men.
4. Students will know that God culled Gideon's army down to only 300 men.
5. Students will know that Gideon sneaked up to the Midianite camp and heard that one of the soldiers had a dream about losing the battle to the Israelites.
6. Students will know that Gideon's army sneaked up to the Midianite camp, broke the pitchers covering their torches and shouted.
7. Students will know that God delivered the Israelites in spectacular fashion as the Midianites panicked from the surprise attack and retreated in great disorder.

8. Students will know that Gideon had fears but ultimately trusted and obeyed God. His faith was rewarded with victory over the Midianites.
9. Students will know that judges in the Old Testament served many roles in leading Israel, including judge, administrator, politician and field general.
10. Students will know that Gideon was humble enough to turn down the Israelite's request to become their king.

RESOURCES/CREDIT

1. Bradford S. Hummel, "*Midian: The Land and Its People*," *Biblical Illustrator,* Summer 2006, 18.
2. David Alexander & Pat Alexander, eds. E*erdmans' Handbook to the Bible* (Grand Rapids: William B. Eerdmans Publishing Company, 1973), 556.

The Healing of Naaman

BACKGROUND PASSAGES

Main Passage
II Kings 5:1-19   Naaman is healed

Related Passages
II Kings 5:20-27   Gehazi's greed
Luke 4:24-27   Jesus mentions Naaman's faith

Suggested Homiletic Passage
II Kings 5:8-14

MEMORY VERSE

When pride comes, then comes disgrace, but with humility comes wisdom.

Proverbs 11:2

LESSON OBJECTIVE

Naaman was a man of high position from a foreign land who had a terrible disease. He set aside his pride as God used others as instruments of grace. His humility was rewarded with healing.

LESSON

II Kings chronicles God's relationship with Israel and her kings. Chapter five is unusual in that it is dedicated to an account about a foreign general, Naaman. Through the story of Naaman believers can learn how God used two servants and the prophet Elisha as instruments of grace. The story of Naaman is an example of God using Israel to provide "salvation" to gentiles. Naaman is an example of how to live humbly and heed Godly counsel.

II Kings 5:1-19

Naaman was commander of the army for the king of Aram (modern day Syria). He had an active, successful military career but had developed a skin disease. While Naaman wanted desperately to be healed, the disease was, at the time, not too severe of an impediment to keep him from serving the king.

Aram had paid tribute to Israel during the reign of David, but times had changed, and Aram appeared to hold the upper hand in the days of Naaman (v.2). Aram had raided Israel, bringing back plunder and slaves. One of the Israelites captured during a raid was a young (unnamed) girl. The girl was taken into Naaman's house as a slave to serve his wife. We do not know how she felt about her circumstances, but regarding the skin disease, it is clear that she showed concern for her master. The girl told her mistress about the prophet Elisha, saying that he could certainly heal Naaman. God used her as an instrument of grace.

The information about Elisha was relayed to Naaman. He listened and went before his king (possibly Ben-hadad II[1]) to share what he had been told. Naaman's master granted him permission to seek out Elisha. The king of Aram told Naaman to use the traditional diplomatic channel and go through the king of Israel. Naaman took a fortune of gold and other valuables on the journey, intending to use it as a gift offering to Elisha. The 150 pounds of gold he took would be worth more than a million dollars today.

Naaman went to the court of the king of Israel (the king is not named but was likely Jehoram[2]) and presented a letter from his king. The letter disturbed the king, who said, "Am I God, killing and giving life that this man expects me to cure a man of skin disease?" (v.7) The king feared that Aram was using this incident as an excuse for attacking Israel. Upon hearing about the king's distress, Elisha sent a message to the court, requesting that Naaman be sent to him "... and he will know there is a prophet in Israel." (v.8).

Naaman left the court and traveled until he stood at Elisha's door ... along with his entourage of horses and chariots. Elisha did not even bother to come out to meet Naaman. Instead, he sent a messenger who said, "Go wash seven times in the Jordan and your flesh will be restored and you will be clean." (v.10). Naaman was clearly angered that Elisha had not greeted him in person and provided immediate healing as he had anticipated. In addition to the perceived snub, the proud royal servant was offended that the prophet requested that he dip into what he considered to be an inferior river, the Jordan. If the prophetic healing was only a ritual, he would have much preferred rivers that flowed through his homeland near Damascus, the Abana and Pharpar. Naaman went away angry.

Fortunately for Naaman, he was blessed to have wise and caring servants. First the Israeli servant girl had shown concern. After the incident at Elisha's place another servant bravely approached him and pointed out to Naaman that he would have been willing to try any time-consuming or complex quest that Elisha would have given, but the command given was relatively simple. Why not try it and see what happens?

Naaman's anger subsided and he humbly decided to do as Elisha had commanded. Naaman traveled 25 miles to the Jordan river.[3] At the river Naaman dipped himself in the water. As he came up out of the water, there was no change in his condition. Two, three times he dipped in the river. Still no change was noticed. Did Naaman start to doubt Elisha? Whether or not he doubted, he was obedient. Finally, after dipping himself the seventh time, Naaman's skin was healed. The healing was so thorough that his skin resembled that of a young boy (v.14)

After the healing, Naaman and his entourage traveled back to Elisha's house. Naaman went before Elisha and confessed, "I know there's no God in the whole world except in Israel. Therefore, please accept a gift from your servant." (v.15). Elisha refused to accept the lavish and expensive gifts.

Naaman's newfound faith in God was genuine. He would no longer offer sacrifices to false gods. In an unusual request, he asked to be allowed to take two mule-loads of earth back to Aram to construct an altar to Yahweh. God is omnipresent and can be worshipped anywhere. Yet, it easy for mature Christians to forget that new Christians may still have misunderstandings. Using dirt from Israel for an altar was inconsequential, but in this case would be an encouragement for Naaman. Teachers need to recognize that children especially may have misconceptions that need to be gently corrected.

In verse 18 Naaman made one last request. He requested forgiveness for when he had to enter the temple of Rimmon with his master, the king of Aram. Rimmon was a significant deity of the Syrians. It was likely a part of court etiquette for a king to lean on the arm of a trusted adviser when bowing during public worship.[4] Naaman would be expected to do this as part of his job, but now had no intention in his heart of worshipping anyone except Yahweh. Elisha replied, "Go in peace."

God used two of Naaman's servants and Elisha as instruments of grace to lead Naaman to healing. Naaman, a proud man of high-standing, learned to humbly accept wise counsel and placed his faith in God. Believers can learn from the story of Naaman to humbly follow God and have faith even when he does not seem to make sense. Believers also are reminded that worship of God has no physical boundaries.

AGE GROUP CONSIDERATIONS

Older students may benefit from the additional content found in II Kings 5:20-27. It details the greed of one of Elisha's servants, Gehazi. This account is ironic in that a foreigner, Naaman, gave glory to God, while an Israelite who had ministered with Elisha on a daily basis gave in to greed and deceit.

SUGGESTED HYMNS

1. *Have Faith in God*, 508, 2008 Baptist Hymnal.
2. *Surely Goodness and Mercy*, 91, 2008 Baptist Hymnal.
3. *Shall We Gather at the River*, 604, 2008 Baptist Hymnal.
4. *Open Our Eyes, Lord*, 426, 2008 Baptist Hymnal.

The Healing of Naaman

STUDENT APPLICATIONS

1. Students will know that the story of Naaman is found in the book of II Kings
2. Students will know that II Kings is in the Old Testament.
3. Students will know that Naaman was the military commander of the army of Aram (Syria).
4. Students will know that Naaman had a form of leprosy and sought to be healed.
5. Students will know that Naaman was told by an Israeli servant girl that there was a prophet in Israel who could heal him.
6. Students will know that the prophet Naaman sought was Elisha.
7. Students will know that Naaman initially resisted Elisha's instructions, but humbly submitted to them after the wise counsel of a servant.
8. Students will know that Naaman was healed by God after washing himself seven times in the Jordan river.
9. Students will know that Naaman became a follower of God.
10. Students will know that Naaman took back two mule-loads of dirt to use in constructing an altar to God.
11. Students will know that worship of God is not restricted to a specific location, for God is, eternally, omnipresent.
12. Students will know that the conversion of Naaman is a picture of how God worked through Israel to bring salvation to the gentiles.

RESOURCES/CREDIT

1. R.C. Sproul, ed. *The Reformation Study Bible.* (Orlando, Florida: Ligonier Ministries, 2005), 521.
2. *Ibid.*
3. Charles G. Martin, *The International Bible Commentary, Revised Edition*, F.F. Bruce, ed. (Grand Rapids, Michigan: Zondervan Publishing House, 1979), 423.
4. *James M. Freeman, Manners & Customs of the Bible* (New Kensington: Whitaker House, 1996), 173-4.

Jesus is Tempted

BACKGROUND PASSAGES

Main Passage
Matthew 4:1-11   Temptation of Jesus

Related Passages
Mark 1:12-13   Mark's account of temptation
Luke 4:1-13   Luke's account of temptation
Hebrews 2:14-18   Why Jesus was tempted
Deut. 8:1-5   Parallel - Israel's 40 years

Suggested Homiletic Passage
Matthew 4:1-11

MEMORY VERSE

Younger version
He Himself was tested and ... is able to help those who are tested.

Hebrews 2:18

Older version
For since He Himself was tested and has suffered, He is able to help those who are tested.

Hebrews 2:18

LESSON OBJECTIVE

Temptation is a part of every believer's life. Jesus used prayer and scripture to overcome temptation and so can believers.

LESSON

This lesson will focus on the temptation of Jesus Christ. Jesus faced strong temptation in order to show His power over sin and to give an example for all believers, who will face temptations, of how to deal with it.

Matthew 4:1-11

The time of Jesus' tempting was carefully planned as "Jesus was led up by the Spirit into the wilderness to be tempted by the Devil." (v.1). Facing and defeating temptation was necessary. Adam had failed when tempted. Jesus, as the second "Adam," had to conquer temptation before He could be the perfect sacrifice for our sins.

While in the wilderness, Jesus endured extreme circumstances. Jesus had been alone and without food for 40 days. We are tempted greatly when we are hungry. In fact, food often distracts us from God. The first tool Jesus used in combatting temptation was fasting. Abstaining from food served as an act of self-discipline that focused His attention on the Father and His mission.

Perhaps Satan had tempted Jesus many times during the 40 day period. However, three instances are recorded. These three temptations appeal to motivations and desires which are common to all human beings.

Satan seemingly wasted no time and attacked directly. His first attack, in verse 3, appealed to the a common physical need. Specifically, great hunger after a lack of food for 40 days. Satan tempted Jesus to turn stones into bread. Jesus answered, quoting from Deuteronomy 8:3; "Man must not live on bread alone but on every word that comes from the mouth of God." A reading of Deuteronomy 8:1-5 reveals that the 40 days Jesus spent in the wilderness closely parallels the 40 year wilderness wandering of the nation of Israel. Also note that Jesus was not carrying any scripture; having scripture memorized beforehand is a tool Christians can draw upon when tempted.

Having been rebuffed in his first attack, Satan took Jesus to Jerusalem, specifically to the highest point on the temple. One scholar writes that this point would have been the summit of the royal gallery built by Herod on the edge of the Kedron valley, the height of which is supposed to have been close to 700 feet.[1] Satan was tempting Jesus to throw himself off the point knowing that angels would catch Him. Here Satan was tempting Jesus' human pride. Jesus answered with a quote from Deuteronomy 6:16, "It is written: Do not test the Lord your God." Jesus did not have to do anything on a dare to prove Himself. Having been twice thwarted, Satan tried a third time to tempt the Lord.

This time Satan targeted the Lord's human desire for earthly power and wealth (possessions). Satan took Jesus to a very high mountain (the specific mountain is unknown) where the kingdoms of the world lay before them. Satan as the prince of this world (for a time, as limited by the Providence of God) claims ownership of Earth (Luke 4:6). Satan offered the kingdoms of the world to Jesus if only He would bow down and worship him. Jesus knew, even then, that one day He would reclaim rightful ownership of Earth, but at that moment He was very hungry (Luke 4:2), and physically tired. The temptation was real. Nevertheless, He responded from Deuteronomy 6:13, "Go away, Satan! For it is written: Worship the Lord your God, and serve only Him." This verse was from the same passage which Jesus used to refute Satan at the Temple.

After this final rebuff, Satan fled from Jesus' presence while angels came to minister to Jesus (v.11). Refreshed and energized, Jesus went out in the power of the Spirit and began to minister in Galilee (Luke 4:14-15).

Christians and Temptation

Hebrews 2:18 states, "For since He Himself was tested and has suffered, He is able to help those who are tested." Jesus understands what people experience when tempted. In His human body He experienced all the desires and drives that cause struggles. Since He successfully overcame those temptations, believers can lean on, and learn from, Him in dealing with their temptations.

So how are Christians to deal with temptation? This study will review four ways. The first way is through prayer and fasting. Prayer is not specifically mentioned in the temptation passage, but it goes hand-in-hand with fasting. Jesus spent much time communing with the Father while being tempted, so should Christians.

The second way is through Bible study and memorization. Puritan William Whitaker had this to say, "If Christ defended Himself against Satan with the scriptures, how much more needful are the scriptures to us against the same enemy!"[2] Satan used scripture to tempt Jesus, but Jesus had a better understanding of scripture, and it proved powerful in defense. Simply stated, the more time one spends studying scripture and committing it to memory, the more one has to draw upon during times of temptation.

The pull of temptation can be strong even for a Spirit-indwelled child of God. "No temptation has overtaken you except what is common to humanity. God is faithful and He will not allow you to be tempted beyond what you are able, but with the temptation He will provide a way of escape, so that you are able to bear it." (I Corinthians 10:13). Thus, the third way to avoid temptation is to leave (or better yet, avoid) tempting situations. Sometimes this may require physically fleeing from a situation. An example of this can be seen in the life of Joseph. In Genesis 39 Joseph was pressured by his master's wife to sin. When she attempted to physically have her way with him, Joseph literally ran from the scene, leaving his garment in her grasp.

Temptation is inevitable, but Christians can limit temptation by carefully choosing their friends and guarding the situations in which they place themselves. This is especially relevant for children as they approach the teen years. Many, otherwise responsible, teens make poor choices and end up in trouble because of being with the wrong people or in the wrong place at the wrong time.

The fourth and final way is to be encouraged and to encourage others to remember God's amazing grace. Believers need to understand that they will not be perfect in this life. When temptation overtakes a believer, confession and repentance are required. God then restores and forgives.

Jesus is Tempted

AGE GROUP CONSIDERATIONS

What are temptations for children? Children typically do not face adult temptations. While we may think of a child's misbehavior as innocent immaturity, it can really be disobedience.

Children are to obey their loving (though imperfect) parents. Obedience even comes with a scriptural promise "Children, obey your parents in the Lord, because this is right. Honor your father and mother — that it may go well with you and that you may have a long life in the land." (Ephesians 6:1-3). If children focus on being obedient to their parents, they will be doing the will of God for their lives and will avoid many pitfalls and temptations. Encourage children to put this lesson into practice by showing honor and obedience to their parents.

Also note that fasting is not appropriate for the developing bodies of young children. It is for adults who can observe proper limits so as not to harm themselves.

SUGGESTED HYMNS/SONGS

1. *I am Resolved*, 378, 2008 Baptist Hymnal.
2. *Turn Your Eyes Upon Jesus*, 413, 2008 Baptist Hymnal.
3. *Victory in Jesus*, 499, 2008 Baptist Hymnal.
4. *Leaning on the Everlasting Arms*, 453, 2008 Baptist Hymnal.

STUDENT APPLICATIONS

1. Students will know that the account of Jesus being tempted is found in the New Testament.
2. Students will know that Jesus spent 40 days in the wilderness.
3. Students will know that Jesus was tempted by Satan, at least three times.
4. Students will know the temptations of Christ are temptations which are common to all humans; physical drives, pride and desire for possessions.
5. Students will know that Jesus rebuffed Satan's temptations by quoting scripture.
6. Students will learn that temptations come, but can be resisted, avoided, or conquered through Christ.
7. Students will know that prayer, scripture memory, avoidance, and Biblical encouragement can all help to overcome life's temptations and lead many to Christ.

RESOURCES/CREDIT

1. James M. Freeman, *Manners & Customs of the Bible* (New Kensington: Whitaker House, 1996), 173-4.
2. William Whitaker, *Disputations on Holy Scriptures*, trans. and ed. by William Fitzgerald (Orlando: Soli Deo Gloria Publications) 237.

Easter - The Emmaus Road

BACKGROUND PASSAGES

Main Passage
Luke 24:13-49   Emmaus Road

Related Passages
Mark 16:12-13   Mark's account of Emmaus road
Luke 21-24:12   Luke's account of the Passion

Suggested Homiletic Passage
Luke 24:44-49

MEMORY VERSE

Younger version
He also said to them, "This is what is written: the Messiah would suffer and rise from the dead the third day."

Luke 24:46

Older version
He also said to them, "This is what is written: the Messiah would suffer and rise from the dead the third day, and repentance for forgiveness of sins would be proclaimed in His name to all the nations, beginning at Jerusalem."

Luke 24:46-47

LESSON OBJECTIVE

On Easter, as on every Sunday, believers celebrate the resurrection of Jesus. Jesus appeared to His disciples and taught them that all these things had happened so that He could triumph over sin and offer forgiveness of sins. He told them that they would be His witnesses of all these things.

LESSON

With our benefit of hindsight, it is easy to overlook the uncertainty that Jesus' followers surely experienced in the dark days between His crucifixion and resurrection. Their hope and sense of purpose were extinguished.

This year, the Easter lesson will focus on two of Jesus' followers who left Jerusalem after the Passover and the crucifixion. These followers could not make sense out of what they had witnessed but, after a "surprise" encounter with the risen Savior, everything changed. In fact, their lives would be forever changed.

Luke 24:13-49

It was the day of the resurrection, and since the tomb was empty, Jesus' followers knew something had happened. Still, what exactly had happened was not readily agreed upon, even after the women had made the fantastic claim that He was alive.

Two of Jesus' followers, Cleopas and an unnamed man, were traveling from Jerusalem to the village of Emmaus (the location of which is now unknown). The two men discussed what had taken place during the unforgettable Passover week. As they were "discussing and arguing," Jesus came along side and started to walk with them. Verse 16 explicitly states that the men were prevented from recognizing Jesus as he asked them about their dispute. Perhaps they discussed whether Jesus had truly been resurrected, as the women had claimed. We cannot know, though Cleopas' response lets us know that they did, indeed, discuss the events surrounding Jesus' death and that the men were discouraged at how they believed things had ended.

Jesus asked the men, "What is this dispute that you're having with each other as you are walking?" (v.17). Cleopas was incredulous that anyone this close to Jerusalem could possibly not know what had transpired. Jesus responded by asking, "What things?" The men told Him about how they had placed their hope in Jesus. In verse 19 they said they believed Jesus was a "Prophet, powerful in action and speech." They blamed the Jewish leaders, not the Romans, for His death (v.20).

We understand that Jesus went willingly to the cross out of love for sinners. It was our sin that He died for on the cross. God had a plan of redemption in place before the creation of the world (I Peter 1:20). The Jews and Romans were merely instruments used by God to achieve His own purposes through the cross.

In verse 21 it is apparent that the men did not understand why Jesus had died. They were looking for a political leader, a Messiah that would end Roman rule and introduce a time of prosperity for Israel. Jesus was (and will be) the one to "redeem Israel" but not in the way and time frame they had hoped.

The men recounted how some women had come from the tomb, claiming to have seen angels who said that Jesus was alive. Some men from their group had gone to the tomb but found nothing. Doubt was likely prevalent among the believers despite the testimony of Mary Magdalene and the other Mary.

Jesus had heard enough. He chastised them for not comprehending, nor believing, what had happened. Jesus began to teach them the prophecies of the Old Testament that foretold and explained, what had just happened in Jerusalem (v.27).

Upon their arrival in Emmaus, it was close to evening. So, the men invited Jesus to stay with them. Verse 30 states that they were reclined at the table to eat (as was the custom of their day). Jesus took on the role of a host, broke and blessed the bread, and then served it to them. It was at this very moment that they recognized Jesus and, instantly He disappeared from their sight.

What went through their minds in those first few seconds? Was it a rush of excitement? Was it embarrassment? We do not know, but we do know what they were feeling while they were walking with Jesus. After Jesus departed, they said to one another, "Weren't our hearts ablaze within us while He was talking with us on the road and explaining the Scriptures to us?" (v.32). Even though it was likely dark by this time, and travelers usually did not travel at night, they immediately returned to Jerusalem.

When they arrived back in Jerusalem, the men went directly to the gathered believers and the disciples (Judas was now dead). Cleopas and his companion were describing their encounter on the Emmaus road, when Jesus suddenly appeared in their midst and said, "Peace to you!" (v.36). Even after this, the believers reactions were troubled, not joyous.

Jesus immediately sought to calm and end any lingering doubt. "Why are you troubled?" He asked them (v.37). He invited the believers to touch his body so that they could feel He was real. The truth was finally beginning to sink in. He asked if they had anything to eat. Jesus was given a piece of fish that He ate in their presence to prove He was not just spirit. There was no longer any doubt. Their Lord and Savior had conquered sin and death and was alive.

Jesus then shared with them the same reminder he had given the two men on the Emmaus road. Everything that had happened had been foretold by the prophets in the Old Testament. "These are my words that I spoke to you while I was still with you — that everything written about Me in the Law of Moses, the Prophets, and the Psalms must be fulfilled." said Jesus (v.44). Then, in verse 45, Jesus "opened their minds to understand the Scriptures." It is important to note that the believers did not yet have the benefit of the indwelling of the Holy Spirit, who reveals and teaches God's truths.

Jesus continued to teach His followers, "...the Messiah would suffer and rise from the dead the third day..." (v.46). How exciting it must have been to be in the midst of fulfilled prophecy. Jesus had appeared to them because they were to be the witnesses of all that had transpired and, were to be the instruments through which God would spread His message of repentance for the forgiveness of sin. It was vital that they comprehend what was expected of them.

Finally Jesus told them to remain where they were, for a time, until they were "empowered from on high" (v.49). Jesus knew He would soon ascend to heaven, but that He would leave a gift (the Holy Spirit).

For Jesus' followers, Easter Sunday had begun without hope but ended with great joy. Their Lord and Savior, Jesus Christ, was alive! The followers experienced a renewed sense of purpose as Jesus prepared them for the birth and expansion of the church.

The followers would, indeed, testify about what had happened and lead many more to believe what they believed — Jesus is alive!

Age Group Considerations

It is suggested that teachers not assume that students know what events led up to Resurrection Sunday. At some point during this lesson it would be a good idea to summarize what happened during the passion week as is found in the gospels. Luke's account of the Passion may be found in Luke 21-24:12.

Remember that each Easter rotation focuses on a different aspect of Passion week, but remember to always include the crucifixion, resurrection, and triumph of Jesus Christ over sin and death.

Suggested Hymns/Songs

1. *Christ Arose*, 273, 2008 Baptist Hymnal.
2. *Christ the Lord Is Risen Today*, 270, 2008 Baptist Hymnal.
3. *He Is Risen! He Is Risen!*, 166, 1991 Baptist Hymnal.
4. *Because He Lives*, 449, 2008 Baptist Hymnal.

Student Applications

1. Students will know that believers celebrate the resurrection of Jesus every Sunday, and especially on Easter.
2. Students will know that Jesus appeared bodily to His believers after His resurrection.
3. Students will know that the story of the Emmaus road is found in the New Testament gospel of Luke.
4. Students will know that Jesus appeared to two men leaving Jerusalem and walking toward the town of Emmaus.
5. Students will know that the men could not make sense of events during the Passion week.
6. Students will know that Jesus shared with the men many things from the Old Testament concerning Himself.
7. Students will know that the men did not recognize Jesus until He disappeared while they were eating dinner.
8. Students will know that the men returned to Jerusalem to tell the others that they had seen Jesus.
9. Students will know that Jesus appeared to the believers and ate food and allowed them to touch Him to prove He was truly alive.
10. Students will know that the reason Jesus died and came back from the dead was so that (through belief and repentance) they can be forgiven of their sins and spend eternity in God's presence.
11. Students will know that Jesus commanded His followers to tell others about what they had witnessed.
12. Students will know that Jesus promised to send the Holy Spirit to indwell and to guide His followers.
13. Students will know that Jesus is still alive today.

Conversion of Saul

BACKGROUND PASSAGES

Main Passage
Acts 8:1-3   Saul persecutes the church
Acts 9:1-25   Damascus Road

Related Passages
Acts 22:61-6   Paul's testimony of Damascus
Acts 7:54-60   Saul at the stoning of Stephen

Suggested Homiletic Passage
Acts 9:3-9 or 3-18

MEMORY VERSE

Younger version
... for there is no other name under heaven given to people by which we must be saved.

Acts 4:12b

Older version
There is salvation in no one else, for there is no other name under heaven given to people by which we must be saved.

Acts 4:12

LESSON OBJECTIVE

Saul was a persecutor of the church until a life-changing encounter with Jesus on the road to Damascus. God changed Saul's heart and still changes hearts today.

LESSON

Christians venerate Paul as a champion of the Faith since he bravely went on mission trips and wrote letters of instruction to churches which comprise a large part of the New Testament. Paul, however, was not always this way. Before his conversion, Paul (or Saul as he was known at that time) was an enemy of the church. God worked miraculously in Saul's life and can change our lives as well.

Acts 8:1-3

The first encounter with Saul in Acts is not a positive one as he stood by at the stoning of a Christian, Stephen, by the Jewish leaders. Saul might have not thrown any stones, but he gave his approval to Stephen's stoning (v.1). The Christian men who buried Stephen were described as "devout." They were also very brave to have associated themselves with Stephen since they could easily have met the same fate.

The stoning signaled the start of a great persecution against the church in Jerusalem. As a result, the believers scattered throughout the land. While this was certainly an injustice, it had a positive side effect. Instead of suppressing the church, as intended, believers spread the gospel as they were forced into new areas.

In verse three, Saul moved into action, entering house after house looking for believers. When believers were found, man or woman, Saul would drag them to prison. His persecution of the church was thorough and reflected a passion that would one day be put to use in spreading the gospel.

If anyone would have appeared unreachable for God, it was Saul. God, though, had another plan which unfolded as Saul embarked on a journey to Damascus to further persecute Christians. On the way to Damascus, Saul had a personal encounter with Jesus Christ.

Acts 9:1-22

What type of person would breathe "threats and murder" against God's people? This is what the future writer of much of the New Testament was doing in Acts 9:1. The persecution of the church had caused many believers to scatter to other parts of the country (Acts 8:1). Saul went before the high priest and requested permission to arrest any followers of "The Way" that he could find in Damascus. Any man or woman who was part of "The Way" (an early name for Christianity) would be taken back to Jerusalem as a prisoner. The Romans allowed Judea to exercise extradition rights (even extending to the priesthood) from surrounding provinces.[1]

Saul's choice of Damascus is curious since the 175 mile journey was no small endeavor. Damascus was a commercial city located on several trade routes in the Roman province of Syria. Perhaps Saul thought stomping out Christianity in Damascus might prevent its spread to other places.[2]

Saul's plans were radically changed during his journey to Damascus. Saul and his traveling companions were nearing Damascus when a bright light from Heaven shined about him. Saul fell to the ground as he heard the voice of Jesus speak to him, "Saul, Saul, why are you persecuting me?" (v.4). Saul answered with, "Who are you, Lord?" (v.5). Jesus then commanded Saul to go into Damascus and await further instructions. The men traveling with Paul heard the voice and realized it was supernatural. The experience left Saul blinded. His companions led him into the city. While waiting to see what God would reveal, he did not eat or drink.

In the city of Damascus, there was a certain believer named Ananias. The Lord spoke to Ananias in a vision. Ananias obediently responded "Here I am Lord!" (v.10). God commanded him to go to Saul, who was praying in a house on Straight street. Ananias was further told that Saul had already had a vision of Ananias coming to him. Ananias was to place his hands upon Saul so that he would regain his sight.

Saul's reputation and mission had preceded him. In verses 13 and 14 Ananias understandably did not want to go, protesting that Saul had done much harm to the believers and had come to Damascus to continue what he had started in Jerusalem. The Lord reassured Ananias that His ways were greater than Ananias' concerns. "Go, for this man is My chosen instrument to carry My name before Gentiles, kings and the sons of Israel. I will certainly show him how much he must suffer for my name!" (v.15-16).

Ananias obeyed and went to Saul. Saul was staying somewhere on Straight street. Straight street is still a main artery in Damascus today.[3] There he laid his hands on Saul, and "something like scales fell from his eyes, and he regained his sight." Even before eating, Saul was immediately baptized (at the urging of Ananias (Acts 22:16)). After this, he broke his three day fast.

Saul's conversion was apparent to all he met in Damascus. All who observed were astounded by the change in Saul's life. Instead of seeking out Christians to imprison, Saul entered the synagogues and preached that Jesus, "He is the Son of God." (v.20). Ever the scholar and now empowered with the leading of the Holy Spirit, Saul grew more proficient in proving that Jesus was the promised Messiah.

After some time, the Jews in Damascus started plotting to assassinate Saul. Word of the plot got to Saul. One night, after dark, Saul's friends lowered him down the city wall in a large basket . The believers whom Saul had originally sought to persecute had now saved his life.

Saul would later become known as Paul, an apostle of Jesus. As God had informed Ananias, Paul would experience much suffering as he gladly spread the Gospel. He would embark on three major missionary expeditions (detailed in another rotation lesson) and start churches throughout the Roman empire. If God could forgive and use a man who was so opposed to God's ways, He can also forgive us and change the hearts of people today.

SUGGESTED HYMNS/SONGS

1. *We Have Heard the Joyful Sound*, 361, 2008 Baptist Hymnal.
2. *Shine, Jesus, Shine*, 491, 2008 Baptist Hymnal.
3. *Amazing Grace*, 104, 2008 Baptist Hymnal.
4. *Open Our Eyes, Lord*, 426, 2008 Baptist Hymnal.
5. *Turn Your Eyes upon Jesus*, 413, 2008 Baptist Hymnal.

Conversion of Saul

STUDENT APPLICATIONS

1. Students will know that the story of Saul's conversion is found in the book of Acts in the New Testament.
2. Students will know that Saul was a Jewish Pharisee and that he persecuted the early church.
3. Students will know that Saul had a personal encounter with Jesus on the road to Damascus.
4. Students will know that Saul was blinded by a light from Heaven.
5. Students will know that Ananias was faithful to follow God and go to Saul, even though it must have been scary.
6. Students will know that God used Ananias to cure Saul's blindness by laying hands on him
7. Students will know that Jesus can forgive any sin if we genuinely repent and follow Him.
8. Students will know that Saul's conversion was so dramatic that he began to teach about Jesus at every opportunity.
9. Students will know that God later changed Saul's name to Paul.
10. Students will know that God used Paul to write many of the books of the New Testament.
11. Students will know that Paul later went on missionary trips and started churches throughout the Roman empire.

RESOURCES/CREDIT

1. Frederick Fyvie Bruce, *Paul: Apostle of the Heart Set Free* (Grand Rapids: William B. Eerdmans Publishing Co., 1995), 72.
2. *Life Application Bible.* (Grand Rapids, Michigan: Zondervan Publishing House, 1991), 1963.
3. David Alexander & Pat Alexander, eds. *Eerdmans' Handbook to the Bible* (Grand Rapids: William B. Eerdmans Publishing Company, 1973), 556.

Jeremiah - Fall of Judah

BACKGROUND PASSAGES

Main Passage
Jeremiah 1:4-19   Call of Jeremiah
Jeremiah 36:1-26   Jehoiakim burns the scroll
Jeremiah 39   Jerusalem, temple destroyed
Jeremiah 23:5-8   A Righteous Branch

Related Passages
Lamentations   Jeremiah laments fall of Judah
2 Kings 23:34-24:6 Jehoiakim's reign
2 Kings 2410-25:21 Fall of Jerusalem, deportation

Suggested Homiletic Passage
Jeremiah 1:4-10

MEMORY VERSE

Call to Me and I will answer you and tell you great and wondrous things you do not know.
Jeremiah 33:3

LESSON OBJECTIVE

Jeremiah was commissioned by God to tell the nation of Judah to repent and return to Him, Judah rejected the message and eventually suffered the consequences of their disobedience. Jeremiah was faithful through many trials, and God delivered him.

LESSON

This study of Jeremiah begins a three-month arc covering the fall of Judah to the Babylonians, their seventy-year exile in Babylon, and the eventual rebuilding of the temple and the walls of Jerusalem. The book of Jeremiah repeatedly demonstrates God's love for His people and His desire to see them turn from their unfaithfulness.

Through Jeremiah, God spoke, imploring His people to turn back to Him and away from their evil practices. Ultimately, Judah did not listen and they suffered the consequences of their sin. However, even before judgment was exercised, Jeremiah spoke of the grace of God. God already had a plan to redeem His people: first by restoring them to their land after the exile and, ultimately, through Jesus, "...a righteous Branch of David." (Jer. 23:5).

Jeremiah was called to minister during a difficult time and to preach a message that few would heed. As modern day culture becomes increasingly hostile towards Christianity, children need to know that God is still in control and still seeks their faithfulness. Believers can always trust that it is only God's will which will be accomplished. If we are faithful to Him, we can live with hope.

The book of Jeremiah is composed of various materials that make it difficult to read as an unfolding narrative. While it is recommended that teachers take time to read the entire book to understand the broader context, the lesson will focus on four key passages.

The call of Jeremiah
Jeremiah 1:4-19

Josiah was king of Judah when God called Jeremiah. In verse 5 God said to Jeremiah "I chose you before I formed you in the womb; I set you apart before you were born. I appointed you a prophet to the nations."

Children at times may feel insignificant or useless. From the example of Jeremiah, it is clear that God has a purpose and plan for each life, even before conception. While Jeremiah had a call to a specific duty, God may not call each believer to a specific role but all Christians need to be faithful to love, serve and obey the Lord. We need to trust Him with our lives and how we live them.

Jeremiah protested, saying that he was too young. God allayed his fears, telling Jeremiah, "Do not be afraid of anyone, for I will be with you. This is the Lord's declaration." (v.7). God always provides what is needed to accomplish His purposes. Notice in verse 8 the phrase "*to deliver you.*" The New American Standard uses the term "*rescue.*" God did not promise Jeremiah that he would avoid trouble, as He knew that Jeremiah would suffer many things, including imprisonment. God did however, promise to be with him and to rescue him from distress. Obedient believers can trust that God will also be with them as they face various trials.

Verse 9 begins to detail Jeremiah's responsibilities. Jeremiah was to speak to the nations about God's judgment and to call them to receive His mercy. In Jeremiah's lifetime this message would be to the people of Judah. Ultimately, however, God's plan is to communicate this message to every nation and person. God knew that Jeremiah's life would be an example to all believers as they read and study his inspired writings even today.

In verse 11 Jeremiah had a vision in which he saw the branch of an almond tree. Blooming early in the spring, the branch symbolized that God's judgment was at hand. In verse 13 Jeremiah saw a boiling pot, tipping from the north to the south. A kingdom from the north (Babylon) would soon overrun Judah. In verse 16 it was revealed that idolatry was the reason for the judgment: Judah had "abandoned Me to burn incense to other gods and to worship the works of their own hands."

After this, specific instructions were given to Jeremiah, "Now, get ready. Stand up and tell them everything that I command you." (v.17). In verse 19 God told Jeremiah that the message would not be well-received, but that He would certainly rescue him. Jehoiakim Rejects God

Jeremiah 36:1-26

The book of Jeremiah contains a number of accounts in which Jeremiah spoke to the people of Judah about God's impending judgment. Chapter 36 gives an account of what happened when Jehoiakim, king of Judah, heard Jeremiah's message from the Lord.

In verse 2 Jeremiah was commanded by God to write down all the words spoken to him concerning Israel, Judah and all the nations during and since the reign of Josiah. God would give the people of Judah another chance to repent. Jeremiah summoned his friend Baruch, a scribe, to write down the dictation.

At the time, Jeremiah was imprisoned by the king (Jeremiah 32:2) and could not go to the temple to read the scroll. Jeremiah requested that Baruch go and read the scroll before the inhabitants of Jerusalem and the Jews who were visiting from other cities. Baruch agreed, took the scroll, and read it in the hearing of all the people (v.10).

One of the king's officials, Micaiah, heard Baruch and reported back to the other officials. They summoned Baruch and asked him to read the scroll in their presence. The officials agreed that the king must hear what had been written. Anticipating a negative reaction from their king, the officials told Baruch to go back to Jeremiah and warn him to hide. After Baruch left, they took the scroll to King Jehoiakim.

In the presence of the king and all his officials, a man named Jehudi read the scroll. This took place in the king's winter quarters . A fire was burning in front of him for warmth. After Jehudi would read three or four columns, Jehoiakim would cut off a portion of the scroll and toss it on the fire. Several officials asked the king to not burn the scroll, but their pleas along with the scroll's message were ignored. Jehoiakim ordered Baruch and Jeremiah to be seized. Jeremiah and Baruch could not be found. Scripture tells us that God had hidden them (v.26).

Given a chance to repent, Jehoiakim had refused. Instead Jehoiakim "did what was evil in the Lord's sight just as his ancestors had done." (2 Kings 23:37). Nebuchadnezzar invaded Judah for the first time in 604, forcing Jehoiakim to become his vassal (2 Kings 24:1). Jehoiakim's "reign" also was continually harassed by raiders from surrounding territories (2 Kings 24:2). Jehoiakim and Judah experienced the consequences for their disobedience.

Fall of Jerusalem
Jeremiah 39

Jeremiah 39 details the fall of Jerusalem. After Jehoiakim died, Jehoahaz became king for a short time. Nebuchadnezzar had him deported and replaced with Zedekiah. King Zedekiah lived peacefully under Babylonian oversight until 588 B.C. In that year, he rebelled, and the Babylonian army responded with their final invasion of Judah. Jerusalem was placed under siege for eighteen months.

In verse 2 the Babylonians finally assaulted and entered the starving and demoralized city. Desperate, many of Jerusalem's defenders, along with Zedekiah fled, escaping during the night. They were caught, and Zedekiah was bound with chains and sent into exile (verse 7).

The Babylonians began to systematically destroy Jerusalem. The temple and all houses were burned down. The city walls were dismantled. Most of the people were taken into custody and exiled to Babylon, just as Jeremiah had prophesied. The Babylonians plundered the temple, taking all that was valuable and destroying everything else (Jeremiah 52:17-19).

Where was Jeremiah during the destruction of Jerusalem? Jeremiah came to the attention of Nebuchadnezzar, who commanded "...do him no harm, but deal with him as he tells you." (v.12). Jeremiah was left under the care of Gedaliah, the governor appointed by Nebuchadnezzar (v.14). In verse 16-18 Jeremiah prophesied to his friend Ebed-melech the Ethiopian that he too would be delivered because he had placed his trust in the Lord. Jeremiah had suffered much derision from his own countrymen. He had endured an eighteen-month siege, and he witnessed the destruction of his beloved city. Though danger was seemingly ever near, God was faithful and delivered Jeremiah.

"The Righteous Branch of David"
Jeremiah 23:5-8

God would also keep His promise to restore the nation of Judah after seventy years of exile. Even then peace would be fragile and temporary. The Jews would eventually come under the rule of the Roman empire. They would effectively cease to exist as a nation after rebelling against their Roman masters in the first and second century A.D.

Jeremiah prophesied about one who would be the perfect Savior, the "Righteous Branch of Da-

---

Jeremiah Timeline
All dates B.C.

627 Jeremiah called to be a prophet.

609 Pharaoh Necco deposes the new king, Jehoahaz, placing Jehoiakim on the throne.

604 Nebuchadnezzar subdues much of Judah in first Babylonian invasion. Jehoiakim became his vassal.

597 Jehoiakim dies. Nebuchadnezzar invades Judah again. Jerusalem falls to Babylon after a two-month seige.

588 King Zedekiah rebels against Babylon. Babylon places Jerusalem under seige for eighteen months.

587 Babylonians sack Jerusalem, destroying the walls, city and Temple. Many people are deported to Babylon.

---

vid" under which Jerusalem will dwell securely. This was a prophecy about the Messiah. While Christians have varying views concerning the end-times, it is likely that the reign prophesied will be literal, and that during the millennial reign Jesus will physically reign in Jerusalem. Believers can look beyond our world in turmoil to the promised, perfect reign of Christ.

More importantly, all people can experience the reign of Jesus in their lives if they repent of their sins and follow Him. Like Jeremiah, all believers will likely experience times of sorrow in their lives, but God is faithful to deliver those who trust in Him.

Next month's lesson will focus on how God cared for His people while they were captives in Babylon. Our children will learn how four young Jews were determined to be obedient to God no matter what. Their faithfulness was rewarded and God's name was exalted among their Babylonian conquerors.

The book of Jeremiah ended solemnly as Jerusalem burned. Yet, for the people of God, Jew and gentile, their hope for the future is certain.

Jeremiah - Fall of Judah

AGE GROUP CONSIDERATIONS

Some of the detail in Jeremiah is too graphic for younger children. While even young children must learn that sin always has consequences, the focus of this lesson should demonstrate that believers who trust in God and are obedient will always have hope even when bad things happen.

SUGGESTED SONGS

1. *He Lives*, 269, 2008 Baptist Hymnal.
2. *I'd Rather Have Jesus*, 530, 2008 Baptist Hymnal.
3. *Tell the Good News*, 360, 2008 Baptist Hymnal.
4. *Tis so Sweet to Trust in Jesus*, 502, 2008 Baptist Hymnal.
5. *Tell it to Jesus*, 425, 2008 Baptist Hymnal.

STUDENT APPLICATIONS

1. Students will know that the book of Jeremiah is found in the Old Testament.
2. Students will know that Jeremiah was one of several prophets whom God spoke through to His people.
3. Students will know that Jeremiah wrote the books of Jeremiah and Lamentations.
4. Students will know that Jeremiah prophesied that Judah, because of their sinfulness, would fall at the hands of the Babylonians.
5. Students will know that Jeremiah suffered abuse and ridicule, but remained faithful to God.
6. Students will know that God had in place a plan to restore Judah even before their captivity.
7. Students will know that Jerusalem and the temple were destroyed by the Babylonians and that many of the Israelites were taken into captivity for the next seventy years.
8. Students will know that, even before they were born, God had a plan and a purpose for their lives.
9. Students will know that Jesus is the "Righteous Branch of David" and the Messiah of Israel as prophesied by Jeremiah and promised by God.
10. Students will know that if they are faithful to God as Jeremiah was, God will deliver them through any trials they face.

Daniel Stays Pure

BACKGROUND PASSAGES

Main Passage
Daniel 1:1-21   Daniel rejects choice foods

Related Passages
Daniel 2   Daniel interprets a dream

Suggested Homiletic Passage
Daniel 1:11-20

MEMORY VERSE

Younger version
Be diligent to present yourself approved to God, a worker who doesn't need to be ashamed...

2 Timothy 2:15a

Older version
Be diligent to present yourself approved to God, a worker who doesn't need to be ashamed, correctly teaching the word of truth.

2 Timothy 2:15

LESSON OBJECTIVE

While exiled in a foreign land, God continued to protect and care for His people. Daniel and his friends are a perfect example of how God rewards faithfulness under difficult circumstances.

LESSON

The year is 605 B.C. Imagine that you have been taken captive by an invading army which has just conquered your homeland. You and others, like you, are taken from your home and transported hundreds of miles away to a foreign city. Everything is unfamiliar and strange. It would be easy to despair and believe that God has let you down. This was the situation Daniel and his friends found themselves in when they arrived at the king's court in Babylon. Instead of despair or compromise, the young men decided to trust that God would take care of them.

This is the second lesson of a three-part series. In last month's lesson Jeremiah implored Judah to turn from their sin and return to God. Judah did not repent and was subsequently conquered by the Babylonians. Next month, the third lesson will focus on the exiles return to their homeland and the rebuilding of Jerusalem and the temple under the leadership of Nehemiah and Ezra.

The inhabitants of Judah spent seventy years in captivity. The book of Daniel records several events in which God protected His people and glorified His name among their Babylonian masters. This lesson will focus on an event that happened shortly after the first captives arrived in Babylon. Despite the refusal of Judah to return to God, a remnant had, and would, remain faithful even during this difficult time.

Daniel 1:1-21

The book of Daniel opens with the fall of Jerusalem during the reign of Jehoiakim. This was eleven years before the final destruction of Jerusalem. The temple was not destroyed at this time, but unspecified "vessels" were removed and taken as tribute by Nebuchadnezzar to Babylon and placed in "the house of his god." (v.2). According to Freeman, the name of Nebuchadnezzar's god was *Belus*.[1]

Temple items were not the only things removed from Jerusalem. In verse 3 the king ordered the removal of some of the young Israelite men "...from the royal family and from the nobility — young men without any physical defect, good-looking, suitable for instruction in all wisdom, knowledgeable, perceptive, and capable of serving in the king's palace..." These young men were instructed and trained for three years in Babylonian culture and knowledge. They lived in the king's palace and served in his court, a life of privilege, but wholly dependent upon the royal whim.[2]

As part of their total assimilation into Nebuchadnezzar's inner circle, Daniel and his friends received new names. Daniel was renamed Belteshazzar which means: "*he who Bel favors*," a Babylonian god. The others were renamed "to Hananiah, Shadrach; to Mishael, Meshach; and to Azariah, Abednego." (v.7). The Babylonians sought to change their thinking through a Chaldean education, their loyalty through name changes, and their life-style through changing their diet.[3]

While eating from the king's table was a privilege that extended to all who served in the court, Babylonian kings and nobles were not known for their nutritious diet. They dined on wheaten bread, meats in great variety, luscious fruits, fish, and game. The usual beverage was wine of the best varieties, and they were fond of drinking to excess.[4]

Daniel determined not to defile himself with the king's food or wine (v.8). This was no small decision, and one that might have had grave consequences as it might have been viewed as rebellion. In verse 9 God gave Daniel favor with the king's chief official. The official hesitated after Daniel shared his desire to avoid the choice foods. "I'm afraid of what would happen if he [the king] saw your faces looking thinner than those of the other young men your age. You would endanger my life with the king." (v.10).

Undaunted, Daniel talked until he had convinced the guard to test them for 10 days. The guard brought them vegetables to eat and water to drink instead of food from the king's table. At the end of the ten days Daniel and his friends looked healthier and better than the other young men. God had honored their faithfulness. After this, the guard continued to bring them vegetables.

The four young men were blessed by God with "knowledge and understanding in every kind of literature and wisdom. Daniel also understood visions and dreams of every kind." (v.17). At the end of their three years of training, the men were brought before Nebuchadnezzar. As the king tested them, he realized that there was something special about Daniel and his friends. "In every matter of wisdom and understanding that the king consulted them about, he found them ten times better than all the diviner-priests and

mediums in his entire kingdom." (v.20). God's wisdom is infinitely greater than any thing humans can think up.

Verse 21 hints at the longevity of Daniel's career. Daniel's career would outlast Nebuchadnezzar and even the Babylonian empire. Cyrus was not a Babylonian king, but a Persian king who conquered Babylon. Yet Daniel found favor with Persians much as he had with Nebuchadnezzar.[5] Daniel 9:1 notes that Daniel was still serving during the first year of Darius the Mede. His time in the king's court lasted throughout the reign of at least nine kings and the entire 70-year exile.

During their time in Babylon, Daniel and his friends had other adventures as chronicled in the book of Daniel (and covered in other lessons in this curriculum), in which they continued to trust in God in difficult situations. God continued to intercede in their lives as Daniel was delivered from within a den of lions and Shadrach, Meshach and Abednego were kept safe in the fiery furnace. They were proof that, even in captivity, God was still working in the lives of His chosen people. In our darkest times we can live secure in the knowledge that God is with us, He knows us, and He knows our future.

The longevity of Daniel's service in Babylon serves as a bridge between the fall of Judah and the return of the exiles recorded in Ezra and Nehemiah. In the first lesson of this series the consequences that accompanied unrepentance were seen in the fall of Judah. In next month's third and final lesson of the series we will see restoration of the people of Judah as they returned to their homeland. While their restoration was political in nature, remember that the ultimate restoration, guaranteeing eternal, abundant life, is to be found only when sinners repent and give their lives to Jesus.

AGE GROUP CONSIDERATIONS

The purpose of this lesson is not to convert children into vegetarians. God has given a great variety of foods to enjoy in moderation. This is a story about unwavering faith. As we live in a time and place of abundance it also reminds believers to practice self-control (in eating and other areas of their lives). Remind the children that they can enjoy things in life but, led by the Holy Spirit, do not have to allow their impulses and urges to control them.

The ages of Daniel and his friends are never mentioned. Given the length of Daniel's career, they were possibly as young as twelve or thirteen when they arrived in Babylon. Even very young people can be bold and stand up for what is right and pleasing to God.

SUGGESTED HYMNS/SONGS

1. *Have Faith in God*, 508, 2008 Baptist Hymnal.
2. *Surely Goodness and Mercy*, 91, 2008 Baptist Hymnal.
3. *Great Is Thy Faithfulness*, 96, 2008 Baptist Hymnal.
4. *Trust and Obey*, 500, 2008 Baptist Hymnal.

STUDENT APPLICATIONS

1. Students will know that the book of Daniel is found in the Old Testament.
2. Students will know that events in the book of Daniel took place during Judah's Babylonian captivity.
3. Students will know that Daniel and his friends had been taken from their homes in Judah and to the city of Babylon.
4. Students will know that Daniel was renamed Belteshazzar which means : "*he who Bel favors,*" a Babylonian god.
5. Students will know that Hananiah, Mishael and Azariah were renamed Shadrach, Meshach and Abednego.
6. Students will know that Daniel and his friends showed great faith and will power in choosing not to eat the king's food.
7. Students will know that God rewarded Daniel and his friends for their faithfulness.
8. Students will know that while the exile was a consequence of Judah's sin, God still loved His people and cared for them.
9. Students will know that the exile did not last, but God restored them to their homeland after 70 years.
10. Students will learn that it is important for them to show self-restraint and moderation as they go through life in activities such as eating or video games.

RESOURCES/CREDIT

1. James M. Freeman, *Manners & Customs of the Bible* (New Kensington: Whitaker House, 1996), 311.
2. A.R. Millard, *The International Bible Commentary, Revised Edition*, F.F. Bruce, ed. (Grand Rapids, Michigan: Zondervan Publishing House, 1979), 853.
3. *Life Application Bible*. (Grand Rapids, Michigan: Zondervan Publishing House, 1991), 1476.
4. Freeman, 310.
5. *The International Bible Commentary, Revised Edition*, 851.

Nehemiah/Ezra

BACKGROUND PASSAGES

Main Passage

Ezra 1:1-7	Proclamation of Cyrus
Ezra 3:8-4:5	Rebuilding of temple began
Ezra 6:13-18	Temple completion
Ezra 8:21-34	Ezra leads second group
Nehemiah 1-6	Nehemiah rebuilds wall
Nehemiah 8-10	Ezra reads law/Israel repents

Related Passages

II Chronicles 36:22-23	Proclamation of Cyrus
Deuteronomy 30:1-5	Repent and be restored

Suggested Homiletic Passage

Nehemiah 8:1-6   Public reading of the Law
You may wish to read all the way to verse 10.

MEMORY VERSE

Younger version

... if my people ... pray and seek my face and turn from their wicked ways, then I ... will forgive their sin...

II Chronicles 7:14 (NIV)

Older version

... if my people who are called by my name, will humble themselves and pray and seek my face and turn from their wicked ways, then I will hear from heaven and will forgive their sin and will heal their land.

II Chronicles 7:14 (NIV)

LESSON OBJECTIVE

Israel spent seventy years in exile as a consequence of their disobedience. God, in grace and mercy, raised up leaders for the rebuilding of the nation and to lead the people in repentance. These godly leaders included Ezra and Nehemiah.

LESSON

"Did you hear the news? We're going home!" The word must have spread quickly that King Cyrus had issued a decree allowing many of the exiled Jews to return to Judah. Older people would have remembered what it was like before the Babylonians came. Younger people would have known only what they had experienced while living first under the Babylonian and then Persian empires. God kept His promise to restore the Israelites. The returning exiles faced tough times during the coming decades as they sought to reestablish their nation. But God had a plan to care for His people. He sent Ezra and Nehemiah to help rebuild Jerusalem and to lead the people to true repentance, leading to full restoration in their relationship with God.

This is the final installment of a three-lesson study. In the first lesson, the people of Judah had turned from God. As a consequence, they were conquered by the Babylonians and sent into exile. The second lesson taught how even in a foreign land and pagan society, God raised up righteous men (such as Daniel) who remained true to God. This third and final lesson focuses on the return of the people to their homeland, the rebuilding of the temple and the walls of Jerusalem, and their spiritual repentance.

Ezra 1:1-7

Overnight the mighty Babylonian empire had come to an end. The Persians, led by their king Cyrus, swept in and took control of the empire and the fate of the Jews. Verse 1 clearly states that it was God who led Cyrus to make a proclamation regarding the exiled Jews. "The Lord, the God of heaven, has given me all the kingdoms of the earth and has appointed me to build Him a house at Jerusalem in Judah. Whoever is among His people, may his God be with him, and may he go to Jerusalem in Judah and build the house of the Lord..."

Not only would a great number of the Jewish people be allowed to return to their homeland, (Ezra 2:64 states that 42,360 returned) but they would be allowed to rebuild the temple. The political leader of this group would be a man named Zerubbabel, son of Shealtil. Zerubbabel was the grandson of King Jehoiachin who had been conquered and taken into exile by the Babylonians in 597 B.C.

The people made preparations to leave. The Israelites who remained in Babylon collected a freewill offering for the others (v.6). Cyrus showed generosity by returning the temple articles that had been seized by Nebuchadnezzar.

Ezra 3:8-4:5

The rebuilding of the temple did not begin immediately upon their return, but began during the second month of the second year (536 B.C.). Zerubbabel, the high priest Jeshua, and the Levites all participated in the rebuilding. As in any building project, the first order of construction is to prepare the foundation. So the foundation was prepared.

After the foundation was prepared, the priests held a service to thank and glorify God. The people sang "For He is good; His faithful love to Israel endures forever." (v.11). Then all the people gave a great shout, but not all the people were happy. While many shouted for joy, others wept. The older people who had seen the first temple wept loudly because they remembered the splendor of the temple built by Solomon (v.12). They could tell that this rebuilt temple would not be as beautiful, therefore they wept.

The Israelites would soon run into resistance. Decades before, after the Assyrian King Sargon II conquered the northern kingdom, people were relocated from other parts of the empire to repopulate the land left by the exiles. This practice of uprooting and moving people made rebellion more difficult.

Some of the Jews who were left behind by the Babylonians intermarried with these immigrants and became known as Samaritans.[1] The foreigners and the Samaritans asked to help in the rebuilding of the temple, and in Ezra 4:3, Zerubbabel answered "You may have no part with us in building a house for our God, since we alone must build it ..." Displeased with this answer, the foreigners intimidated the people of

Judah to the point that they gave up building. They also bribed Persian officials, stopping construction for almost 20 years.

Why did Zerubbabel reject their offer? There are two reasons. The first was many of the inhabitants of the land, while still worshipping the God of Israel, also embraced idolatrous practices by worshipping other gods. The second reason was that Cyrus had given the exiles exclusive permission to rebuild.

Ezra 6:13-18

It was not until the second year of King Darius (approximately date 522 B.C.) that construction resumed. The Israelites were emboldened by the prophesying of Haggai and Zechariah. Tattenai, governor of the region, inquired of the Jews as to what authority they had to build. While we cannot discern his true feelings about the situation, he sent a letter to Darius inquiring whether construction should be allowed to continue. Darius allowed the building to proceed. Tattenai and other officials were diligent in following Darius' orders and allowed the temple to be finished (v.13). In 517 B.C., twenty-one years after the exiles first returned to Judah, the temple was finished.

The temple dedication included the sacrifice of 100 bulls, 200 rams, 400 lambs and 12 male goats as a sin offering for the twelve tribes of Israel. Lavish as it may have appeared, it paled in comparison to the dedication of Solomon's temple when 22,000 cattle and 120,000 sheep were sacrificed. The Israelites observed the Passover and the Festival of Unleavened Bread, joyful that the temple had been completed. With the resumption of temple worship, the seventy year exile officially ended.

Ezra 8:21-34

But all was not well in Jerusalem. Over the years the exiles struggled, for while temple worship had been restored, the walls and much of the city of Jerusalem was still in ruins. The people found it easier to build new homes outside the city than to clean up and rebuild. Fifty-eight years after the resumption of temple worship, God raised up two leaders who would bring new hope to Israel: Ezra and Nehemiah.

Ezra was a scribe and Levite, a direct descendant of Aaron (Ezra 7:5). Ezra received permission from the Persian king, Artaxerxes, to lead a delegation back to Judah. The generosity of the king may have been motivated by the recent loss of Egypt due to rebellion. To foster loyalty in Judea would be strategic.[2]

Ezra asked the returning exiles to fast and pray before the journey and to ask God for safe passage (v.21). Their prayers were answered and the exiles arrived in Judea unharmed as they were "strengthened by our God" (v.31).

After their arrival Ezra was asked by the leaders to help bring the people back to God. Like the Samaritans before them, the first exiles were guilty of intermarrying and had therefore exposed themselves to idolatrous practices. The book of Nehemiah records how Ezra led the Israelites to return to God's Word, which convicted them to the point of repentance.

Nehemiah 1-6

Nehemiah served in successive roles as cup bearer, builder and governor. In the first chapter of Nehemiah, we find him serving in the court of King Artaxerxes as cup bearer. Nehemiah inquired about the Jewish remnant in Jerusalem and received word that they were struggling. Brokenhearted, Nehemiah prayed to God, seeking help, for the exiles. God impressed upon his heart the desire to personally go and help the Israelites.

The cup bearer would have been a servant in whom the king had great trust. As cupbearer, Nehemiah tested what the king ate and drank; so the king's life was in the cupbearer's hands. In chapter 2 Nehemiah was serving Artaxerxes when the king noticed that he was uncharacteristically sad. Nehemiah became fearful, thinking the king might suspect something was wrong and punish him. Nehemiah shared his heartache over the state of Jerusalem, and boldly asked to be allowed to go to Jerusalem and rebuild the city and its walls (2:5).

The king was willing to meet all of his requests "... for I (Nehemiah) was graciously strengthened by my God" (2:8).

Upon arriving in Jerusalem, Nehemiah initially kept quiet about his intent to rebuild the walls. He went so far as to use the cover of darkness to make a survey of the damaged walls. Once he had a grasp of what would be required, he revealed his plan to the leaders and the work soon commenced. Nehemiah was now a builder.

Not everyone was happy about the project. In Nehemiah 2:19 local leaders Sanballat, Tobiah, and Geshem expressed their displeasure, claiming the Jews were rebelling against the king. At the beginning of chapter 4 they mocked and tried to intimidate the builders. As the building progressed, they plotted an attack (4:7-8), but God worked it so that Nehemiah learned about their plans (4:15).

Led by Nehemiah, the Jews responded with prayer and a plan of defense: there would be guards day and night (Neh. 4:9, 16-18), the workers would be divided such that half worked and half stood guard. Those working would still be armed. Everyone was ready to meet any attack that Sanballat and the others might bring. In addition, all the workers were to sleep inside the city, and not take off their clothes. Nehemiah instructed that they carry their weapon even when washing (4:23).

The expected attack never came, but as the wall neared completion, Sanballat, Tobiah, and Geshem still sought to stop Nehemiah. They sent unsealed letters four different times to Nehemiah asking him to come meet them. God gave Nehemiah the discernment to see that "they were planning to harm me" (6:2). Each time he declined their invitation, saying that he was too busy. A fifth letter was sent accusing Nehemiah of rebuilding the wall so that he could become king and lead a rebellion. Being a man of integrity, Nehemiah simply dismissed the rumor. Finally, in their most devious plan, Tobiah and Sanballat hired a false prophet to warn Nehemiah to flee or face imminent death. Nehemiah easily discerned that the prophet was false and that this was yet another effort to intimidate and discredit him.

Finally, the wall was completed. In just 52 days a new wall had been erected in place of the rubble that had sat untouched for over 140 years. "When all our enemies heard all of this, all the surrounding nations were intimidated and lost their confidence, for they realized that this task had been accomplished by our God." (6:16). Jerusalem was secure and God's name had been glorified.

Nehemiah 8-10

Several days after the completion of the wall, on the first day of the seventh month, the Israelites gathered together at one of the gates of Jerusalem (the Water Gate). Ezra brought out the "... book of the law of Moses ..." (8:1). We recognize the law of Moses as the first five books of the Bible. Ezra stood up on a platform (the first recorded pulpit?) and read from the law while all the people stood and listened.

Ezra read from daybreak until noon. Levites helped interpret the law to the people (8:7). The people wept as they were convicted by God's word. Nehemiah was there also, and along with Ezra and the Levites, encouraged the people saying, "This day is holy to the Lord your God. Do not mourn or weep." (8:9). The people stopped weeping and began to eat and drink, breaking into celebration, because they now understood what had been told to them.

In chapter 9, on the twenty-fourth day of the month, the people gathered for a more somber occasion: the confession of sin. God's Word had convicted their hearts, and now they would seek full restoration of fellowship with God. The people wore sackcloth and put dust on their heads as a sign of humility. The Israelites separated themselves from the foreigners and confessed their sins and the wickedness of their ancestors before the assembly. A fourth of the day was spent reading from God's Word and another fourth in confession and worship. The leaders and Levites drew up a binding agreement in which all the people agreed "...to follow the law of God given through God's servant Moses and to carefully obey all the commands, ordinances, and statutes of the Lord our Lord." (10:29). God's chosen people had finally, truly, returned to the Lord Almighty.

Approximately two-hundred years had passed since Jeremiah first implored Judah to return to God. They refused and, as a result of their disobedience, they suffered many consequences, but God had a plan to redeem and restore his people. God sent leaders, such as Ezra and Nehemiah, to meet the nation's spiritual and physical needs. These leaders were also imperfect, so God sent Jesus, the promised Messiah, as the perfect sacrifice for our sin. If we trust and follow Him, we will also experience redemption and restoration in our lives.

Age Group Considerations

A good application of this lesson is to examine one's life for sin, to confess, and to repent. Even Christians lose their focus. Children may come with feelings of guilt or wrongdoing, and want to confess. Allow them time to share their feelings and assure them that they are loved by God and that they can be sure of His forgiveness. Be prepared to share the sinner's prayer. If the situation allows, say a prayer with the child, thanking God for the child and for his willingness to repent and follow Him. Thank God that Jesus died on the cross to cover our sins and for His promise of forgiveness, when we repent and turn to Him.

Suggested Hymns/Songs

1. *Turn Your Eyes upon Jesus*, 413, 2008 Baptist Hymnal.
2. *Seek Ye First*, 524, 2008 Baptist Hymnal.
3. *Be Strong in the Lord*, 504, 2008 Baptist Hymnal.
4. *I Know Whom I Have Believed*, 353, 2008 Baptist Hymnal.

Nehemiah/Ezra

STUDENT APPLICATIONS

1. Students will know that the books of Ezra and Nehemiah are found in the Old Testament.
2. Students will know that the people of Judah spent seventy years in Babylon, just as God had prophesied.
3. Students will know that the resumption of sacrifices in the rebuilt temple marked the end of the exile.
4. Students will know that Zerubbabel led the first of three groups of exiles back to Jerusalem.
5. Students will know that the returnees struggled for survival for almost sixty years until Ezra and Nehemiah arrived.
6. Students will know that Ezra led the second group of exiles back to Jerusalem
7. Students will know that Ezra was a scribe and priest sent by God to teach the people.
8. Students will know that Nehemiah was the cupbearer and a servant of king Artaxerxes.
9. Students will know that Nehemiah led the third group of exiles back to Jerusalem.
10. Students will know that Nehemiah led the Jews to rebuild the wall around Jerusalem and served as their governor.
11. Students will know that Ezra and Nehemiah led the people to study God's Word, to confess, and to repent of the sins.
12. Students will know that confession and repentance of sin is required of anyone desiring to have a right relationship with God.

RESOURCES/CREDIT

1. Bob Dunston, "*Ezra, Nehemiah, Esther,*" *Explore the Bible Adult Commentary*, Lifeway (Winter 2006-07 Volume 11, Number 2), 21-22.
2. A.E. Cundall, *The New Bible Commentary: Revised*, ed. Donald Guthrie (New York: Wm. B Eerdmans Co.), 397.

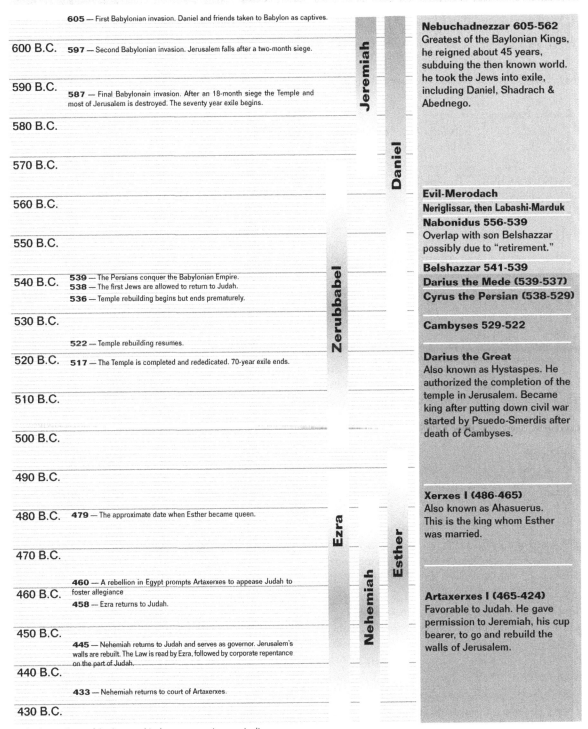

605 — First Babylonian invasion. Daniel and friends taken to Babylon as captives.

600 B.C. 597 — Second Babylonian invasion. Jerusalem falls after a two-month siege.

590 B.C. 587 — Final Babylonain invasion. After an 18-month siege the Temple and most of Jerusalem is destroyed. The seventy year exile begins.

580 B.C.

570 B.C.

560 B.C.

550 B.C.

540 B.C. 539 — The Persians conquer the Babylonian Empire.
538 — The first Jews are allowed to return to Judah.
536 — Temple rebuilding begins but ends prematurely.

530 B.C.

522 — Temple rebuilding resumes.

520 B.C. 517 — The Temple is completed and rededicated. 70-year exile ends.

510 B.C.

500 B.C.

490 B.C.

480 B.C. 479 — The approximate date when Esther became queen.

470 B.C.

460 — A rebellion in Egypt prompts Artaxerxes to appease Judah to foster allegiance
460 B.C. 458 — Ezra returns to Judah.

450 B.C. 445 — Nehemiah returns to Judah and serves as governor. Jerusalem's walls are rebuilt. The Law is read by Ezra, followed by corporate repentance on the part of Judah.

440 B.C.

433 — Nehemiah returns to court of Artaxerxes.

430 B.C.

Jeremiah

Daniel

Zerubbabel

Ezra

Esther

Nehemiah

Nebuchadnezzar 605-562
Greatest of the Baylonian Kings, he reigned about 45 years, subduing the then known world. he took the Jews into exile, including Daniel, Shadrach & Abednego.

Evil-Merodach
Neriglissar, then Labashi-Marduk
Nabonidus 556-539
Overlap with son Belshazzar possibly due to "retirement."

Belshazzar 541-539
Darius the Mede (539-537)
Cyrus the Persian (538-529)

Cambyses 529-522

Darius the Great
Also known as Hystaspes. He authorized the completion of the temple in Jerusalem. Became king after putting down civil war started by Psuedo-Smerdis after death of Cambyses.

Xerxes I (486-465)
Also known as Ahasuerus. This is the king whom Esther was married.

Artaxerxes I (465-424)
Favorable to Judah. He gave permission to Jeremiah, his cup bearer, to go and rebuild the walls of Jerusalem.

Author's note: Some of the dates on this chart are approximate or in dispute.

Jesus Teaches about Prayer

BACKGROUND PASSAGES

Main Passage
Matthew 6:5-15   The model prayer
Matthew 7:7-12   Keep knocking (asking)

Related Passages
Matthew 5-7   Sermon on the Mount
Luke 11:1-13   Luke's account of model prayer

Suggested Homiletic Passage
Matthew 6:9-15

MEMORY VERSE

Don't worry about anything, but in everything, through prayer and petition with thanksgiving, let your requests be made known to God.

Philippians 4:6

LESSON OBJECTIVE

One of the great privileges of being a Christian is direct access to God through prayer. In His longest sermon, the Sermon on the Mount, Jesus taught His followers important principles about prayer.

LESSON

What if you had a need to talk to an important person, say a celebrity or the President of the United States? How easily could one gain access to such a person? Unless you had a special clearance or connection, it would most likely be impossible. Even with good connections, it might take weeks or months to arrange a meeting of even a few minutes. As Christians, we have direct access to God the Father through prayer. Jesus taught about prayer and even gave a model prayer to follow when He preached the Sermon on the Mount.

Early in His ministry, large crowds began following Jesus. *The Sermon on the Mount* took place on a hillside near Capernaum. The hill is believed to have been a natural amphitheater which allowed Jesus to address a large crowd. Three chapters in Matthew are devoted to this sermon. This lesson will focus only on the portions dealing with the topic of prayer.

Matthew 6:5-15

Where should we believers pray? Prayers can be lifted up anywhere, but is there a time and place where it is inappropriate? In verses five and six, Jesus taught that prayers are not to be publicly spoken to impress other people. Public prayer is an important part of corporate worship, but Jesus wanted those who would follow Him to know that most prayers are to be offered privately. When believers get away from distractions and get alone with God, they can focus on and listen to Him alone. They do not have to worry what others think or be tempted to impress them.

In verse seven Jesus said to not babble in prayer. Babbling may manifest itself in several different ways as there are several different interpretations. One author believed that some rabbis, during Jesus' time, taught that oft-repeated prayers were more effective. This author also states that this is a common practice in false religions.[1] In our contemporary culture, it may manifest itself in flowery prayers, using big words or repeating parts of others' prayers. Prayer is to always be sincere and from the heart. Jesus gave the comforting reminder that God knows what we need even before we pray.

Verse nine begins the model prayer. While prayer should never be condensed to a formula, much insight is to be gleaned from the example Jesus offered. Let's examine the prayer verse-by-verse.

"Our father in heaven, Your name be honored as holy." God the Father is the one to whom Christians pray, so it is only natural that they first acknowledge Him for who He is, holy and worthy of honor. Believers are also reminded that they can approach God reverently as a loving father.

"Your kingdom come. Your will be done on earth as it is in heaven." While believers can take any concern to God, they should always seek to pray for His will to be done.

"Give us today our daily bread." God knows what is need even before one asks. By asking Him to provide, believers acknowledge their trust in Him for their very existence. As a further example of trust, God desires His followers to trust daily. He holds the future, and believers need not concern themselves with what is to come. It is prudent and wise to plan for the future but not to worry about it.

"And forgive us our debts, as we also have forgiven our debtors." When an individual is saved, their sins are "paid in full." This does not mean they cease to sin. Sin will be a struggle for all believers until they physically die. Christians are commanded to regularly examine their lives for sin, to confess and repent.

Failure to forgive others will create a barrier which will hinder prayers being heard. Luke 11:26 states, "But if you don't forgive, neither will your Father in heaven forgive your wrongdoing." Christians must first forgive others who have wronged or hurt them. This is often difficult, but holding a grudge or holding onto anger only allows the hurt to continue. Jesus reminded His listeners that they could forgive because they too had been gracefully forgiven.

"And do not bring us into temptation, but deliver us from the evil one." One scholar states, "The forgiven pray this petition because they trust God and they distrust themselves."[2] God may test His people but does not tempt them. Rather "each person is tempted when he is drawn away and enticed by his own evil desires." (James 1:13-14).

The great promise from God is that "... He will not allow you to be tempted beyond what you are able, but with temptation He will also provide a way of escape ..." (I Cor. 10:13). People rarely choose their temptations, but for a child of God, indulging the temptation is not a foregone conclusion. The Christian will have an escape, but one must exercise the will in order to resist the temptation.

"For Yours is the kingdom and the power and the glory forever. Amen" The closing of the prayer is a reminder that believers are to pray for the will of God to be accomplished. God has the power and every right to do His will for His own glory.

Matthew 7:7-12

There is another teaching about prayer in the Sermon on the Mount. It comes later, after the model prayer. Jesus taught that persistence is an important aspect of prayer. Like Bible study and scripture memory, prayer is to be a discipline which is practiced consistently and regularly.

Jesus said, "Keep asking, and it will be given to you. Keep searching, and you will find. Keep knocking, and the door will be opened to you." (v.7). Jesus commanded His followers to be bold in prayer. Hebrews 4:16 also encourages believers to "... draw near with confidence to the throne of grace, that we may receive mercy and find grace to help in time of need." (NASB).

What things are appropriate for a believer pray for? A large house and a new car are nice, but hardly a necessity. Jesus had already taught His followers to pray that God's will be done. So when Christians earnestly pray, they are learning to seek the heart of God. Then their prayers are less self-focused and more God-focused. Believers can then see what God is already doing in the world and in their lives. For children, a practical application is to pray for family, friends and church ministries.

God answers prayer. His answers are usually yes, no, or wait. His answer may not be immediately clear, nor what the believer envisioned. In fact, a prayer may not be answered in a believer's lifetime. God's answer is sometimes 'no' because the believer is not seeking God's will, and God knows that saying 'yes' may actually be harmful.

Parents do the best they can to provide for their children and, in verse 9-11, Jesus used the example of a parent to illustrate how God responds to prayer. "What man among you, if his son asks him for bread, will give him a stone?" (v.9). While some parents may mistakenly withhold something that a child needs, the greater temptation is to give too much, therefore spoiling the child. God, in His perfect wisdom,

Jesus Teaches about Prayer

knows exactly what His children need, and as a loving parent, desires to give it. Like children, believers may not understand what the Father is doing when He says 'no' or 'wait' but they may rest in the assurance that God always does what is best.

Access to the very throne of grace is a Christian's privilege. Prayer is not a formula, but rather, an act of worship where there is fellowship with God, intercession for others, and growing intimacy with the Father.

AGE GROUP CONSIDERATIONS

The Sermon on the Mount takes up three chapters in Matthew 5, 6, and 7. These chapters are also rich with additional teachings which may be used to deepen the lesson for older children.

SUGGESTED HYMNS/SONGS

1. *The Lord's Prayer*, 431, 2008 Baptist Hymnal.
2. *Tell It to Jesus*, 425, 2008 Baptist Hymnal.
3. *Sweet Hour of Prayer*, 429, 2008 Baptist Hymnal.
4. *Only Trust Him*, 465, 2008 Baptist Hymnal.

STUDENT APPLICATIONS

1. Students will know that the Lord's prayer can be found in the Bible books of Matthew and Luke.
2. Students will know that Jesus taught about the Lord's Prayer during the Sermon on the Mount.

3. Students will learn that prayer is direct communication with God.
4. Students will learn that prayer is not a formula, and does not require fancy words nor many words.
5. Students will learn that God desires to fellowship with them through prayer.
6. Students will learn that prayer is a form of worship in which they come before God, acknowledge who He is, and fellowship with Him.
7. Students will learn that prayer is not something done to impress other people.
8. Students will learn that God will willingly forgive them of wrongdoing, but they must first forgive those who have wronged them and must seek forgiveness.
9. Students will learn that God is not a tempter, nor will He ever tempt anyone.
10. Students will know that when they are tempted God will provide a way out. A believer must choose to take the escape from the temptation.
11. Students will know that God usually answers prayer with one of three answers: yes, no, or wait.

RESOURCES/CREDIT

1. James M. Freeman, *Manners & Customs of the Bible* (New Kensington: Whitaker House, 1996), 340-1.
2. R.C. Sproul, ed. *The Reformation Study Bible*. (Orlando, Florida: Ligonier Ministries, 2005), 1370.

Zacchaeus

Background Passages

Main Passage

Luke 19:1-10   Zacchaeus

Related Passages

Luke 18:18-23   Rich young ruler (contrast)

Suggested Homiletic Passage

Luke 19:1-10

Memory Verse

Younger Version

"For the Son of Man has come to seek and save the lost."

Luke 19:10

Older version

"Today salvation has come to this house," Jesus told him, "because he too is a son of Abraham. For the Son of Man has come to seek and save the lost."

Luke 19:9-10

Lesson Objective

Jesus demonstrated that He came to seek and save the lost by changing the heart of Zacchaeus, a man who extorted his fellow Jews while working as a tax collector for the Romans.

Lesson

The story of Zacchaeus is typically one of the first Bible stories learned by children. Children can identify with Zacchaeus' most memorable characteristic: he was a small man. The King James version states, "He was little of stature." But there is much more to the account of Zacchaeus than what is apparent on the surface. In this lesson Jesus surprised many by changing the heart of a man who was thought of as unworthy and unreachable.

Luke 19:1-9

Zacchaeus lived in the town of Jericho, the same Jericho which had been devoted to destruction in the Old Testament. In fact, God had pronounced a curse on it, which would be inflicted upon anyone who attempted to rebuild it (Joshua 6:26). The curse was fulfilled when Hiel rebuilt the city, but at the cost of his oldest and youngest sons (I Kings 16:34) . During the time of Jesus, Jericho apparently had never regained its former status, but was inhabited by many, including Zacchaeus.

Two things are immediately apparent about Zacchaeus; He was a chief tax collector and he was rich. While Americans have little love for the IRS, taxes were a completely different ballgame in Zacchaeus' day. A Jew who was a tax collector in Jesus' day was considered a traitor to his people. Many collectors also enforced high taxes in order to gain wealth, breaking the Jewish law against usury in the process. The fact that Zacchaeus was also rich probably implied that he too gained his wealth from his occupation. Several verses before, Luke gave the account of a rich young ruler (Luke 18:18-23) whose wealth had become an insurmountable barrier to following Jesus. Would Jesus now reach out to a traitor? Would Zacchaeus' riches also keep him from following Jesus?

Scriptures do not say why Zacchaeus wanted to see Jesus. Perhaps he had heard that Jesus was "a friend of tax collectors" (Luke 7:34)? Regardless, he was among the crowd surrounding Jesus. His efforts to see Jesus were hindered because of his height. Grown men rarely climb trees, but Zacchaeus did; this most likely meant he a had great desire to see Jesus. Sycamore trees were commonly planted by the roadside and were easy to climb.[1]

Zacchaeus was successful! As he watched from the tree, Jesus passed his way. In verse 5 Jesus looked up and said to Zacchaeus, "Zacchaeus, hurry and come down, because today I must stay at your house." What surprised Zacchaeus most? Was it that

Zacchaeus

Jesus picked him out of the crowd? Was it that Jesus knew his name? Was it that He asked to go to Zacchaeus' home?

Zacchaeus' heart had been changed, and without hesitation, he scrambled out of the tree and joyfully welcomed Jesus. Zacchaeus surely knew what everyone was thinking (even if he didn't hear them actually say, "He's gone to lodge with a sinful man" (v.5)). Yet he willingly showed his public commitment to his new Lord. "Look, I'll give half of my possessions to the poor, Lord! And if I have extorted anything from anyone, I'll pay back four times as much," (v.8). Zacchaeus showed true confession and repentance. Good works follow true faith (James 2:18). How did Jesus respond?

"Today salvation has come to this house, because he too is a son of Abraham. For the Son of Man has come to seek and save the lost," Jesus said (v.9). Three important things are said here. First, Zacchaeus had received salvation. Second, he was a "son of Abraham," (meaning that salvation through Jesus was as valid as the old covenant). Third, Jesus stated His purpose, "For the Son of Man has come to seek and save the lost." Is there anything that gives more hope and joy than that? While we were yet sinners, God became man in the form of Jesus and died to save us from that sin (Romans 5:8).

The account of Zacchaeus ends at this point, but his new life was just beginning. While many may never cheat people like Zacchaeus probably had, all have sinned and are in need of a Savior. Rejoice in the fact that Jesus came to seek and save the lost, and that He has the power to change hearts and save from sin, and make life anew.

Why tax collectors were despised

Why were Roman tax collectors so utterly despised by Israelites in Jesus' time? Some background information provides insight. After a long subjugation to the Babylonians and Persians, the Jews finally realized a period of independence under the Hasmo-

neon kings (beginning in 142 B.C.) Their freedom was short-lived. In 63 B.C., Jerusalem was occupied by the Roman general Pompey. The Romans exacted tribute on occupied nations in the form of taxes. This taxation without representation embittered the Israelites (much like it did Americans while under British colonial rule), and the burden was compounded since Rome was an "unclean" empire.

The Romans did not personally collect the taxes, but used locals in each area who submitted bids as to how much they would collect. The winner was not paid a salary, but collected as much as possible and kept what was left after paying the Romans the promised sum. While a businessman is entitled to make a profit, it is easy to see how the tax collectors often abused the people as Zacchaeus had confessed.[2]

Since Zacchaeus was a "chief tax collector" he was likely an overseer of a large area. In addition, Jericho was near a major trade route (and famous balsam groves) so there was much to tax.[3] Working for the despised Roman occupiers and greatly benefitting financially from the partnership would have made Zacchaeus and all the other tax collectors very unpopular indeed.

Suggested Hymns/Songs

1. *I Love You Lord*, 555, 2008 Baptist Hymnal.
2. *Wonderful Words of Life*, 338, 2008 Baptist Hymnal.
3. *Jesus, Keep Me Near the Cross*, 233, 2008 Baptist Hymnal.
4. *Jesus, What a Friend for Sinners*, 156, 2008 Baptist Hymnal.

Student Applications

1. Students will know the story of Zacchaeus is recorded only in the gospel of Luke.
2. Students will know that the book of Luke is found in the New Testament.

3. Students will know that Zacchaeus was an Israelite who cooperated with the Romans by collecting taxes.
4. Students will know that Zacchaeus was considered a traitor by his fellow Israelites, because of his occupation.
5. Students will know that Zacchaeus lived in Jericho.
6. Students will know that Zacchaeus repented and became a follower of Jesus.
7. Students will know that Zacchaeus sought to pay back fourfold what he had extorted from others and gave away half of his belongings.

8. Students will know that Jesus will accept and forgive anyone who repents and follows Him (regardless of his/her past actions).

RESOURCES/CREDIT

1. R.C. Sproul, ed. *The Reformation Study Bible*. (Orlando, Florida: Ligonier Ministries, 2005), 1492.
2. I.H. Marshall, *The New Bible Commentary : Revised, ed.* Donald Guthrie (New York: Wm. B Eerdmans Co.), 916.
3. Sproul, 1492.

David Becomes King/Psalms

BACKGROUND PASSAGES

Main Passage
I Samuel 16   David Anointed King
Psalm 8
Psalm 23

Related Passages
I Chronicles 16   David leads in worship
Psalm 150   Instruments of praise

Suggested Homiletic Passage
Psalm 23

MEMORY VERSE

Younger version
Man does not see what the Lord sees, for man sees what is visible, but the Lord sees the heart.

I Samuel 16:7b

Older version
Do not look at his appearance or his stature, because I have rejected him. Man does not see what the Lord sees, for man sees what is visible, but the Lord sees the heart.

I Samuel 16:7

LESSON OBJECTIVE

God chose David for a special job, to be king of Israel. While others looked at the outside, God looked at David's heart. Later, David expressed his faith in God through the composing of psalms of praise. Studying these Psalms can help us learn more about how to worship God by praising him from our heart.

LESSON

The ascension of David to the throne of Israel, as its greatest king, was most unexpected by those who were around him. Even the prophet Samuel mistakenly formed preconceived notions about the future king. Samuel and Jesse's family quickly learned that God does not look upon outward appearances, but upon the heart. Believers must worship Him purely for the sake of worshipping Him, and not for any benefit they may hope to receive. Worship must come from the heart.

"Why do we worship? Because we cannot help worshipping. Worship is not a human invention; rather it is a divine offering. God offers Himself in a personal relationship and we respond," says Franklin M. Segler.[1] God used David in many ways, but perhaps the way that is most meaningful to believers is the legacy of the many psalms he composed. David personally experienced a heartfelt walk with God and knew that He desired worship from the heart. There is much to learn about worship from the psalms which God inspired David to write.

I Samuel 16

King Saul's reign began with much promise, but Saul eventually forsook the Lord This was manifested by God pulling His anointing and rejecting his kingship. Though he was still legally king, God's Spirit was no longer present. In verse 1 Samuel was still mourning the tragedy of Saul's fall when God told him it was time to move ahead, for He had already chosen a new king. Samuel filled his horn with anointing oil and traveled to visit the family of Jesse of Bethlehem. God told Samuel that one of Jesse's sons would be the new king.

In verse 2 Samuel stated an obvious fact: Israel already had a king. God reassured him by simply telling him to take a young cow along for the sacrifice and to anoint the one He had chosen. God would handle the rest. It was part of God's perfect plan for David not to take the throne until years later.

Despite any lingering fears he might have had, Samuel was obedient and "... did what the Lord directed and went to Bethlehem." (v.4). In a small village like Bethlehem the arrival of a High Priest was a major event. Samuel, also a prophet and judge, caused a stir just by his presence. The elders came before him, trembling, fearing that he would deliver bad news as prophets sometimes did. Samuel assured them he came in peace and he invited them and Jesse's family to gather for the sacrifice.

Sacrifice first required that participants be consecrated. Consecration required a time of reflection and washing of clothes (Ex. 19:10) . After consecration, Jesse and his seven oldest sons arrived for the sacrifice. Samuel surveyed the young men and wondered which one was to be chosen. Perhaps he thought the new king would be tall and handsome like Saul. Samuel's attention gravitated to the oldest child, Eliab. "Certainly the Lord's anointed one is here before Him," he said. In verse 7 the Lord said to Samuel, "Do not look at his appearance or his stature, because I have rejected him. Man does not see what the Lord sees, for man sees what is visible, but the Lord sees the heart."

Jesse began to call his sons forward one at a time (v.8). First came Abinadab, then Shammah. Soon, all seven sons had come before Samuel. Directed by God, Samuel rejected each one. It is easy to envision an awkward and uneasy moment of silence before Samuel asked Jesse, "Are these all the sons you have?"

There was another son whom Jesse had left at home to watch the sheep. Jesse probably did not know what Samuel was planning to do (other than that it involved a sacrifice). Still, leaving David behind may give a clue as to David's lower status even within his own family. Samuel said to Jesse, "Send for him. We won't sit down to eat until he gets here." In verse 12 David arrived. "Anoint him, he is the one," the Lord said. Samuel poured the anointing oil on David in the presence of his family. The Spirit of the Lord then came upon David and led him from that day forward. Imagine the shock and wonder that might have come over those present for this crucial event in Israel's history. Verse 14 illustrates the stark contrast between David and Saul. David was led by the Spirit, but "the Spirit of the Lord had left Saul."

David patiently waited until the Lord decided to elevate him in Saul's place. In the meantime their paths crossed a number of times. After God removed his protective hand from Saul, an evil spirit tormented him. One of Saul's advisors suggested that having a court harpist might soothe Saul (v.16). Saul commanded that a search be carried out for such a musician.

The search led to David. One of Saul's advisors knew of David and vouched for his character and musical skill. Jesse sent David to Saul's court where David was admired by Saul so much that he even made him his armor-bearer. As an armor-bearer, David would care for and account for Saul's military weapons and armor. But David's main duty was to play his harp for Saul. When he played the harp, "Saul would then be relieved, feel better, and the evil spirit would leave him." (v.23).

David's harp was a stringed instrument which was held in by an arm and hand and played with the fingers. The body was made of wood or metal and may have had eight or ten strings.[2]

Throughout his life, David would continue to express himself through music. He would also plan the music in the house of the Lord and put men in charge of it (I Chronicles 6:31). David endured many lows and highs during his life. Several of these experiences are immortalized in God's Word as psalms. These psalms provide insight into how to worship God. Two of David's psalms will now be studied.

Psalm 8

This psalm declares the Glory of God and attributes the dignity of man to God the Creator. In verse 1 David affirmed that God's glory is evident throughout all creation. In verse 2 David proclaimed that God capably defends Himself against those who would attack Him. He is in control of all aspects of creation. True worship acknowledges that God is the only One worthy of worship.

In verse 3 David started to ponder his place in the cosmos. Looking at the broad scope and grandeur of God's creation, David realized how miniscule he was. He then asked an honest question that all of us ask at one time or another, "What is man that You remember him, the son of man that You look after him?" (v.4). This is an example of a poetic device common in psalms. Two successive lines carrying the same thought (they are "parallel" in the idea they convey).

The rest of the psalm explains what is special about humans. We are made a little lower than God and have been given glory and honor (v.5). We have been made lords (or stewards) over God's creation here on earth(v.6). Verses 7-8 beautifully describe the earthly creations that have been given to humans to manage. None of this is deserved or earned, but is freely given by God. When we worship we acknowledge that every heartbeat, each possession, our very being is a gift from God.

It is important to see that we are made in the image of God because this is what separates humans from other living creatures. A secular view inevitably concludes that humans are just one type among all living things; therefore there is no rational basis for human dignity. In addition, once we realize we are made in God's image, we realize that we are accountable to Him and need to seek His will, not our own.

Psalm 23

Psalm 23 is probably the most well-known of the Psalms. In this psalm, David drew upon imagery from his time as a shepherd. As a shepherd David would have understood the importance of sheep having someone to watch over them. Unlike cattle or other livestock, sheep require constant surveillance and protection. It is little wonder that God compares humans in need of a Savior to sheep in need of a shepherd.

In verse 1 David confessed that God is the perfect shepherd who meets every need. What are the needs of sheep? Sheep need food, water, and protection. God alone meets these needs in human lives. Also in

verse 2 God provides green pastures and fresh water. In verse 3 the perfect shepherd leads the sheep down the right paths, protecting them from getting lost or injuring themselves in a dangerous place. Why does God do this? At the end of verse 3 we see another worship principle as God leads believers "for His name's sake." When believers worship, they acknowledge that God's will is perfect and submit to that will. It also serves to remind that God alone deserves the glory. Worship is not about the worshiper.

In verses 4-5 David took comfort in knowing that God would guide and protect him even in the darkest valleys of life. An earthly example is a little child falling asleep in the back of a car without a concern for his/her safety, knowing his/her parent is in control. When, in faith, we give our concerns to God, we can live a life of peace in a world of constant strife.

In verse 6 David affirmed that God had his best interests at heart and would meet his needs. Life is rarely easy, but God's goodness overcomes any obstacle.

AGE GROUP CONSIDERATIONS

Psalm 150 also discusses worship and even describes the instruments used in worship during the time of David. This psalm would be good for further study with older children.

SUGGESTED HYMNS/SONGS

1. *This is My Father's World*, 46, 2008 Baptist Hymnal.
2. *All the Way My Savior Leads Me*, 474, 2008 Baptist Hymnal.
3. *Doxology*, 668, 2008 Baptist Hymnal.
4. *He's Got the Whole World in His Hands*, 346, 1991 Baptist Hymnal.
5. *The Lord is my Shepherd*, Track 17, Praise Him: 25 Praise Songs for Children. Twin Sister Productions.

STUDENT APPLICATIONS

1. Students will know the story of David's anointing as king is found in the book of I Samuel.
2. Students will know that I Samuel is found in the Old Testament.
3. Students will know that David was the youngest son of his family.
4. Students will learn that God does not look upon the outward appearance of a person. He looks upon their heart.
5. Students will know that the book of Psalms is found in the Old Testament.
5. Students will know that David wrote many of the passages in the book of Psalms as praise songs to God.
6. Students will know that David was a musician who played the harp (lyre).
7. Students will know that before he was king, David was a shepherd.
8. Students will know that human life is valuable because humans are created in God's image and are valued by God.
9. Students will know that true worship will exalt God solely for who He is.
10. Students will know that true worship acknowledges that all that the worshiper has and ever will have is because of God.

RESOURCES/CREDIT

1. Franklin M. Segler (Revised by Randall Bradley), *Understanding, Preparing for, and Practicing Christian Worship* (Nashville, TN: Broadman & Holman), 5-6.
2. V. Gilbert Veers, *Family Bible Library* (Nashville: The Southwestern Company, 1971), Vol. 4, 55.

Christmas - Wise Men

BACKGROUND PASSAGES

Main Passage
Matthew 2 :1-12   Wise Men visit

Related Passages
Luke 2:1-22   Nativity/Shepherds
Luke 2:21-40   Simeon and Anna see Jesus
Micah 5:2   Prophecy about Bethlehem

Suggested Homiletic Passage
Matthew 2:3-12

MEMORY VERSE

Younger version
"...they saw the child with Mary ... and they worshipped him."

Matthew 2:11b

Older version
"Entering the house, they saw the child with Mary His mother, and falling to their knees, they worshipped him."

Matthew 2:11

LESSON OBJECTIVE

At Christmas time Christians celebrate the birth of Jesus, Savior of the world. Wise men from the east saw His star and went to find Him. Today those who seek Him will find Him.

LESSON

During Christmas the events surrounding Jesus' birth are told again and again. One of the story's more intriguing elements has to do with wise men. Who were these wise men? Why did they travel so far to find Jesus? What can we learn from them today? This lesson will examine these questions, and more, as the Church once again prepares to celebrate Christmas.

Matthew 2 :1-12

Only one gospel, Matthew, talks about the wise men. The narrative begins with the first verse of chapter 2. King Herod was ruling Palestine under the watchful eyes of the Romans. Herod was the name of the family that ruled from 37 B.C. to 95 A.D. The particular king visited by the wise men was Herod I (also known as Herod the Great), who ruled from 37 B.C. to 4 A.D. He rebuilt the temple and engaged in other major construction projects. His son Herod Antipas killed John the Baptist and mocked Jesus.

One day the wise men arrived unexpectedly in Jerusalem. Who were they? What is known about them? How many wise men were there?

The identity of the wise men has prompted much speculation. The King James version uses the term "wise men" but many modern translations use the term "magi" to describe these mysterious travelers. According to one scholar, the magi were priestly or influential order of men with origins among the Chaldeans or Assyrians.[1] The wise men may have been descendants of the diviner-priests, mediums, sorcerers and Chaldeans in the court of king Nebuchadnezzar in the Old Testament (Daniel 2:2). After a time, the meaning of "magi" became more extended, when learned men, devoted to astronomy and the sciences, were called magi whether they were of the priestly sort or not.[2] The idea that they were kings is not supported by the Biblical text.

Where they came from is also up to much conjecture. Various writers have suggested their origin as Babylonian, Arabian, Persian, or even Indian. All we know for certain is that they came from the east.

How many wise men were there? Three is the traditional number. While rarely questioned, the Bible does not tell us how many there were. Three has been generally assumed since the wise men brought three gifts. A close look at verse 3 hints that their entourage may have been rather large ... "When King Herod heard this, he was deeply disturbed, and all Jerusalem with him." It is unlikely that the arrival of just three men would have created a stir in a city like Jerusalem. Also, for safety reasons, it is unlikely that prominent men of learning would travel a great distance without servants or armed guard. Most likely, the wise men traveled as part of a large caravan.

Herod gathered the chief priests and scribes and asked where the Messiah was to be born. Bethlehem (Ephrathah) was the answer. Bethlehem was a village five miles southwest of Jerusalem. Ruth and David were famous inhabitants of Bethlehem. The prophecy concerning the birthplace came from Micah 5:2, "Bethlehem Ephrathah, you are small among the clans of Judah; One will come from you to be ruler over Israel for Me. His origin is from antiquity, from eternity."

Herod summoned the wise men to a secret meeting. He asked when the star appeared. In verse 8 Herod told them to go to Bethlehem and search for the child. Once they found Him, Herod would join them ... to worship. This was a lie, as Herod had no intention to worship anyone who might be a threat to his kingship. Herod decided to use the wise men to find the potential rival for the throne so that he could then kill him.

In verse nine the star reappeared. There has been speculation that the Christ star was a supernova or similar natural phenomenon. The timeliness of its reappearance would support the argument that this was a supernatural light. The star served as a "global positioning system" leading the wise men directly to Jesus' location. That would be an impossible task for any natural heavenly feature.

Did the wise men actually go to Bethlehem? Possibly. Mary and Joseph's stated purpose for being in Bethlehem was to register in the Roman census. While Joseph had family ties in Bethlehem, both he (Luke 2:4) and Mary (Luke 1:26-27) were almost certainly citizens of Nazareth. We know that they returned to Nazareth after Jesus' temple dedication (Luke 2:39). Based on Herod's decree to kill chil-dren two and under, it could be argued that it took the wise men as much as two years to make the journey to find Jesus in a "house" (Matthew 2:11) as opposed to a stable or cave.

But Matthew's account seems to suggest the wise men believed Herod and would have headed to Bethlehem. Also, Nazareth was in Galilee, and nowhere near Bethlehem. Why would God direct Joseph to take his family to Egypt if the threat to young boys was only in Bethlehem and the surrounding area? When the family returned from Egypt, they apparently looked first to settle in Judea, not Galilee (Matthew 2:22). Perhaps Jesus' family stayed in Bethlehem until going to Jerusalem for the temple purification. This would have allowed six weeks or so for the wise men to see the star and make their journey. Regardless, the fact is that we do not know whether Jesus was visited by the wise men in Bethlehem or Nazareth.

Verse 11 states that the wise men found Jesus with His mother Mary in a house. Their first response was to drop to their knees and worship Jesus. How humbling to think about these "important" men traveling from afar in order to bow before a young child.

They then presented their gifts: gold, frankincense, and myrrh. Frankincense was a type of incense made from the aromatic gum resin of specific trees grown in the middle east. Myrrh was similar in that it also came from tree gum resin, but was used primarily to make perfumes. The gifts were expensive and lavish, and may have helped finance the later flight to Egypt. While several efforts have speculated as to the symbolism of the gifts, perhaps the only sure symbolism is related to the prophecy of Gentiles bringing gifts to The King during the millennial reign (Isaiah 60:6). Gifts fit for a king were brought at Christ's birth and will be brought during His future earthly reign.

Having been alerted by God in a dream to Herod's deception, the wise men did not go back to Jerusalem but took another route home. The wise men found Jesus when they sought Him. Jesus is no longer on

Christmas - Wise Men

Earth in human form but He still seeks us. He stands at the door of our hearts and knocks. If we "seek" Him, we will find Him. At Christmas, while many seek presents, happiness, and world peace, Christians know that the greatest gift ever is that God sent His Son to save a fallen world.

The Nativity: Luke 2:1-22

It would not seem to be Christmas without a look at the nativity. This lesson focuses on the wise men, but feel free to precede the narrative of the wise men with what actually happened at Jesus' birth. Two of the other lessons, *Christmas - The Messiah Prophesied* and *Christmas - the Shepherds* cover the events surrounding the nativity.

AGE GROUP CONSIDERATIONS

While *magi*, instead of *wise men*, has been the more common term used in this lesson, younger children can better relate to the term *wise men*. Older children may benefit from the use and explanation of the term *magi*.

To supplement the lesson for older children, material about the flight into Egypt and return to Nazareth may be taught in addition (Matthew 2:23).

SUGGESTED HYMNS/SONGS

1. *Joy to the World*, 181, 2008 Baptist Hymnal.
2. *We Three Kings of Orient Are*, 215, 2008 Baptist Hymnal.
3. *As with Gladness Men of Old*, 193, 2008 Baptist Hymnal.
4. *What Child Is This*, 198, 2008 Baptist Hymnal.

5. *Good Christian Men, Rejoice*, 183, 2008 Baptist Hymnal.

STUDENT APPLICATIONS

1. Students will know that the story of the wise men is found only in the book of Matthew in the New Testament.
2. Students will know that the wise men were not present at the nativity but likely visited not long after Jesus' birth.
3. Students will know the wise men came from the East and gave three gifts to the infant Jesus.
4. Students will learn that the number of wise men who came is unknown; but that, for safety and practical reasons they likely traveled with a large entourage.
5. Students will know that the wise men decided to seek out Jesus because they had seen His star.
6. Students will know that the wise men asked King Herod where Jesus was born. Herod tried to trick them into finding Jesus for him.
7. Students will know that the wise men found Jesus at a house.
8. Students will know that the wise men were warned by an angel to not report the location of Jesus to Herod. They returned to their country another way.

RESOURCES/CREDIT

1. James M. Freeman, *Manners & Customs of the Bible* (New Kensington: Whitaker House, 1996), 330-331.
2. *Ibid.*, 332.

BACKGROUND PASSAGES

Main Passage
Ephesians 6:10-20   Armor of God

Related Passages
Acts 19:11-20   Revival in Ephesus
Hebrews 4:12   God's Word a two-edged sword

Suggested Homiletic Passage
Ephesians 6:10-18

MEMORY VERSE

Younger version

This is why you must take up the full armor of God, so that you may be able to resist in the evil day.

Ephesians 6:13a

Older version

This is why you must take up the full armor of God, so that you may be able to resist in the evil day, and having prepared everything, to take your stand.

Ephesians 6:13

LESSON OBJECTIVE

Paul used the imagery of Roman soldiers to teach believers about spiritual warfare. There are three ways to prepare spiritually: prayer, Bible study, and scripture memorization.

LESSON

Over the years, much has been made of spiritual warfare. Some Christians believe that demons are everywhere while others dismiss the spirit world all together. Scripture teaches us that it does indeed exist and that spiritual warfare is real. While much of what goes on in the supernatural realm is shrouded in mystery, how to train for spiritual warfare can be known. Inspired by God, Paul used vivid imagery of the Roman soldier to instruct believers in how to prepare for action in spiritual warfare.

Ephesus was a major city of the first century Roman Empire. As a port city on the western portion of what is now modern-day Turkey, Ephesus was a bustling port and center of trade. Ephesus' most famous landmark was the temple of Artemis. Ephesus had a reputation as a great center of magic.[1] Nevertheless, Paul started a local church and many came to know Christ. As God's Spirit began to move in the city, fewer people purchased idols, so the local merchants dependent on the sale of these items stirred up a riot against Paul (Acts 19:21-41). Many of Ephesus' new believers had come from a background of magic. They rejected their old ways and burned their books (Acts 19:19). The church in Ephesus understood that spiritual warfare was real and would have easily been able to relate to Paul's teaching on the Armor of God.

Ephesians 6:10-20

Paul gave instructions for spiritual warfare in the book of Ephesians. Believers are to first and foremost depend on the strength of the Lord. All too often believers look at things through the eyes of the world and lose heart. It is easy to forget that God has "vast strength."

In verse eleven believers are told to put on the full armor of God. Do not wield just one or two parts, but the full armor, then we can stand against the Devil's tactics.

Verse twelve reminds believers that evil has a strong presence in this world. Satan is allowed to work for a time. Humans are both the battleground and the prize. Christians must keep in mind that non-believers have been deceived and need to know the Lord. Non-believers are not the enemy, Satan is the enemy.

Christians struggle with their fleshly nature but do not have to be held by the bonds of sin. Believers need to actively prepare themselves both to live a holy life and to minister to others. When Christians "put on the armor" they can stand and be faithful.

Starting in verse fourteen Paul described what the Christian's armor should look like by comparing it to elements of a first-century Roman soldier's armor. Classes of soldiers ranged from the lightly armed *velites* to the heavily armed *hastati*. Paul probably had the latter in mind when he wrote about the Armor of

Armor of God

God as it closely resembles Roman historian Polybius' description of the *hastati*.[2]

First mentioned is the *Belt of Truth* (v.14). Roman soldiers wore two belts: the first was under the armor and held the tunic and undergarments in place, while the second belt was outside the armor and used to hold the sword. Bolt belts were crucial to holding the rest of the armor in place. The spiritual inference is obvious. Knowledge of Truth is essential to the Christian, giving confidence and a firm foundation from which to witness. In one commentary William Barclay stated, "Others may guess and grope; the Christian moves freely and quickly because he knows the truth."[3]

Next is the *breastplate of righteousness* (v.14). Breastplates were made of one (or sometimes many) pieces and were usually made of brass. As the name implies, they covered the chest area, protecting the heart and other vital organs. Christians are to guard their hearts. They do this best by keeping their attention on Jesus and avoiding or fleeing situations that involve temptation.

Paul then compared sandals with "readiness for the gospel of peace" (v.15). Roman military sandals were made of a strong leather, and the bottoms were studded with hobnails, much like modern day cleats. These sandals provided sure footing.[4] Just as it is important to know what is true, a Christian needs to be prepared to share and defend the Truth, to be ready to stand firm.

The Christian is to wield the *shield of faith* (v.16). On the arm of Roman soldiers there was a shield. The Roman shield was made of wood and leather. Some soldiers soaked their shields in water before a battle. Burning arrows shot by the enemy would bury themselves in the shield and be snuffed out. Shields could also be used offensively to hit and stun the enemy without exposing the Roman to harm. Roman shields could also be interlocked with one another, providing more and better protection for a group of soldiers. This also gives a beautiful illustration of how the Body of Christ can be stronger when Christians exercise faith together.

Personal trust was a necessity on the battlefield. Ancient battles rarely lasted long. The side that lost commonly was the one that first lost its nerve, panicked and attempted to flee the field of battle. Great leaders were vital as they had the dual effect of building up the courage of their men while their reputation unnerved the enemy. A veteran army led by a feared commander could almost win a battle just by showing up. Christians place their faith not in an earthly general, but in the omnipotent Creator. No matter how intimidating the enemy may appear, God is in control and believers can stand strong.

The Roman helmet protected not only the skull, but the cheek and neck as well.[5] The *helmet of salvation* evokes imagery of the battleground of the mind. The mind is where sin is conceived and then either indulged in or overcome. The enemy seeks to deceive the lost and to discourage the saved. While the helmet is a defensive weapon, it was used in conjunction with an offensive weapon. Wielding the sword of the Spirit will proactively assist the helmet of Salvation to do its job.

Roman soldiers used a two-edged sword. Paul compared God's Word, the *sword of the Spirit* (v.17), to such a sword. Hebrews 4:12 states "For the word of God is living and effective and sharper than any two-edged sword, penetrating as far as to divide soul, spirit, joints and marrow; it is a judge of the ideas and thoughts of the heart." The sword of the Spirit confronts and reveals God's truth without favor. It is a giver of life to those who trust in it and a terror to those who reject it.

While the sword of the Spirit is powerful, prayer just might be the Christian's best weapon. Verse 18 teaches much about prayer. Believers put on the armor each time they pray. The Christian is to "pray at all times in the Spirit." It is a continual awareness of the presence of God in the believer's life.

Unfortunately, we are often only aware of the television constantly blaring in the background. Prayer should be lifted up throughout the day as people and concerns come to mind to the point where it is continuous as to almost be unconscious. We are reminded to stay alert in doing this and to persevere in it. Paul then requested that intercessory prayer be made for other Christians, and specifically for himself. It is important not only to pray for Christian leaders, but for all other believers.

Note that Paul's request for personal prayer was not for a personal need. It was for the spread of the gospel (v.19). While Paul never seemed to be afraid, he understood that his boldness came from God, and that in a moment of fleshly weakness he might miss an opportunity to minister. We do know that Paul made it to Rome as a prisoner. We do not know if he had the opportunity to stand before the emperor, but his ministry did impact the Imperial guard (Phil. 1:13). Paul wanted to be prepared to share the gospel with whomever he might have opportunity, whether it was a soldier guarding him, a slave serving him or the emperor himself.

The Armor of God is about preparation that leads to ministry. When believers "wear" the armor, they grow closer to God and better comprehend His will as the enemy's attacks are proved useless. Believers gain confidence, experience the joy of ministry, and become better ministers to a world that needs to know Jesus.

Age Group Considerations

Younger children may struggle with the abstract nature of this lesson. Reinforce the lesson with examples to which they can relate (*e.g.* putting on a coat and boots before going out in the rain).

The focus of this lesson is not on what is "out there" demonically. While Satan and demons do exist, the danger is to think we can use the armor to manipulate them. The armor is about setting our hearts and minds on God and devoting ourselves to Christian disciplines that lead to service, not trying to root out demons that may or may not be present. Take extreme care not to frighten little ones with truths they cannot yet understand fully.

Suggested Hymns/Songs

1. *Lead On, O King Eternal,* 659, 2008 Baptist Hymnal.
2. *I'm in the Lord's Army,* 7, *Praise Him: 25 Praise Songs for Children.* Twin Sister Productions.

3. *Onward Christian Soldiers,* 660, 2008 Baptist Hymnal.
4. *Soldiers of Christ, in Truth Arrayed,* 661, 2008 Baptist Hymnal.

Student Applications

1. Students will know that the Armor of God is found in the book of Ephesians.
2. Students will know that Ephesians is found in the New Testament and was a book written by Paul to believers in the city of Ephesus.
3. Students will know that Christians will continue to struggle with sin but can make conscious decisions to avoid sinning.
4. Students will know that it is upon the truth of the Gospel that they should build their life upon.
5. Students will know that righteousness means "living right."
6. Students will know that Christians need to be prepared to share the Gospel at any time.
7. Students will know that faith in God allows the Christian to resist evil.
8. Students will know that the Bible is true and certain and is a powerful weapon for spiritual warfare.
9. Students will know that Christian soldiers must pray continually and be always alert.
10. Students will know that Christians should pray for one another.

Resources/Credit

1. James M. Freeman, *Manners & Customs of the Bible* (New Kensington: Whitaker House, 1996), 448.
2. Gregory T, Pouncey, *"First-Century Armor,"* *Biblical Illustrator,* Lifeway (Summer 2005 Volume 31, Number 4): 16-19.
3. William Barclay, *The Daily Bible Series: The Letters to the Galatians and Ephesians* (Philadelphia: The Westminster Press, 1976), 183.
4. Freeman, 462.
5. Pouncey, 19.

Nicodemus

BACKGROUND PASSAGES

Main Passage
John 3:1-21   Nicodemus' visit

Related Passages
Numbers 21:4-9   Bronze snake
John 7:50-51   Nicodemus defends Jesus
John 19:38-42   Nicodemus buries Jesus

Suggested Homiletic Passage
John 3:13-21

MEMORY VERSE

For God loved the world in this way: He gave His One and Only Son, so that everyone who believes in Him will have eternal life.

John 3:16
(This is the HCSB version - other, more familiar, versions may be used as long as teachers agree to be consistent)

LESSON OBJECTIVE

Nicodemus visited Jesus at night and learned how to be "born again." We can come to Jesus at anytime for forgiveness and salvation.

LESSON

The book of John records the nighttime encounter of a man with Jesus. This man, Nicodemus, a Pharisee and a "ruler of the Jews," sought out Jesus and learned what it meant to be "born again." Today, anyone can have an encounter with Jesus at anytime. If one repents and confesses Him as Lord, he/she too can be "born again."

According to the Bible Family Dictionary, Pharisees were "A jewish sect, strictly orthodox in religion, and politically opposed to foreign supremacy."[1] Other sects in Jesus' day included the Sadducees and the Essenes. The name Pharisee is usually derived from the Hebrew word *"parush"*,

meaning "separated."[2] Pharisees were those who separated themselves from something. "What" is debated. The twin pillars of Pharisaic belief were the "Torah and Tradition." The Torah being the first five books of the Old Testament. Tradition developed out of the Torah as the Pharisees sought to keep the Law from becoming dead ritual by giving it new meaning and life.[3] One legacy of the Pharisees was the Mishnah, a vast collection of specific rules and regulations that affected everyday areas of life. The Mishnah was developed fully between 50 B.C. and 220 A.D.[4]

John 3:1-21

The story of Nicodemus' meeting with Jesus begins in John chapter three. Nicodemus is introduced as a Pharisee and as "a ruler of the Jews." This meant that as a member of the Pharisees, Nicodemus helped lead the Jews in matters pertaining to the law.

Nicodemus came to visit Jesus at night. Why at night? The obvious assumption is that Nicodemus did not want to be seen visiting Jesus. This is plausible since Nicodemus was in a prominent position and a visit to a controversial teacher might have invited criticism. Another possibility is that both Jesus and Nicodemus were very busy, and nighttime was the only time they could meet. Scripture does not reveal Nicodemus' motivation for visiting at night.

Nicodemus was first to speak, "Rabbi, we know that You have come from God as a teacher, for no one could perform these signs You do unless God were with him."(v.2) Nicodemus had already observed Jesus and apparently was convinced that he was a prophet, but would he believe Jesus was the Son of God?

Jesus replied, "Unless someone is born again, he cannot see the kingdom of God." Nicodemus' reaction was to think in worldly terms, wondering how a grown man could accomplish such a feat.

There is a debate about the meaning of how Jesus replied. In verse five Jesus answered, "I assure you:

Unless someone is born of water and the Spirit, he cannot enter the kingdom of God." Did He mean regeneration by the Spirit followed by baptism? Probably not, as it is most likely a contrast between physical birth (water) and spiritual birth (Spirit). Jesus followed up the statement by saying, "Whatever is born of the flesh is flesh, and whatever is born of the Spirit is spirit."

Jesus then compared being "born again" with the wind; while wind cannot be seen, its reality is undeniable. Giving one's life to Jesus is truly a spiritual rebirth. The theologian F.F. Bruce wrote, "The operation of the wind is a parable of the work of the Spirit."[5]

Nicodemus still did not understand and asked, "How can these things be?" (v.9). He, who had been a teacher of Israel, telling others how to keep God's commandments and striving to do the same was still spiritually blind. This teaching about spiritual birth must have sounded foreign, showing that knowledge does not equal salvation. It is a work of the Holy Spirit.

In verses eleven through thirteen Jesus contrasted earthly and heavenly things. Like birth, accepting Jesus is just the first step. Persons can reach the point where they know they need to follow Jesus, but until they actually do yield to Him, they cannot begin to fathom the depths of heavenly things. Only Jesus (in the form of the Holy Spirit) can teach these things.

Jesus then gave Nicodemus a preview of what was to soon come at the cross. In verse fourteen Jesus recalled how Moses lifted up the bronze serpent to heal the Israelites bitten by poisonous snakes (Numbers 21:4-9). The bronze snake met an earthly need: physical healing. Jesus also would be lifted up (literally on the cross) and exalted to meet our spiritual need.

But why would Jesus do this? Jesus gave a concise and direct statement about the purpose of his ministry (v.16). It was out of God's love that He gave His Son to save all who would (and will) believe in Him.

God's purpose was not condemnation, though for salvation one must acknowledge his/her sinful nature and admit he/she is powerless to overcome it. In verse eighteen Jesus warned that anyone who would not trust in Him had no other option for salvation. This parallels Moses' snake in which not all looked, but those who did were spared.

As Christians, we recognize this as the most exciting message of hope ever spoken. Salvation does exist and is available not only to a select few but to everyone. Unfortunately, many people refuse this wonderful gift. In verse nineteen Jesus talked about how people love the darkness more than the light. They actively seek to avoid the light. God has chosen to reveal Himself to all people, so they are without excuse (Romans 1:19-22). As believers tell others about Jesus, some will readily accept Him while others will outright reject Him. Obedient Christians will tell others and let God take it from there. The "power" is in the message, not the messenger. Do not take rejection personally.

The narrative of Nicodemus' conversation ends after verse 21. How did Nicodemus respond to what Jesus told him? The Scriptures do not say, but there are two other passages concerning Nicodemus that give us hope that he did indeed become a follower of Jesus. In John 7:51 Nicodemus defended Jesus before his fellow Pharisees, asking them to listen to Jesus before passing judgment on Him. In John 19:39 Nicodemus assisted Joseph of Arimathea in preparing Jesus' body for burial. If Nicodemus had agreed with the Sanhedrin that Jesus was a blasphemer and false prophet, it is unlikely that he would have assisted with Jesus' burial. The strategic placement (beginning, middle and end) in John's gospel of these episodes clearly indicates that God wants the reader to notice Nicodemus.[6]

AGE GROUP CONSIDERATIONS

Many of the concepts in this lesson are abstract. Still, sin and salvation are concrete concepts that can

Nicodemus

be understood even by young children. Choose your words carefully as you teach this lesson.

Encourage those who are already Christians to seek ways to tell others about Jesus. To those who have yet to make a decision, do not push, but check to make certain they understand what is required for one to receive Christ.

SUGGESTED HYMNS/SONGS

1. *People Need the Lord*, 359, 2008 Baptist Hymnal.
2. *I'd Rather Have Jesus*, 530, 2008 Baptist Hymnal.
3. *Shine, Jesus, Shine*, 491, 2008 Baptist Hymnal.
4. *We've a Story to Tell*, 356, 2008 Baptist Hymnal.

STUDENT APPLICATIONS

1. Students will know that Nicodemus is only mentioned in the book of John.
2. Students will know that John's gospel is found in the New Testament.
3. Students will know that Nicodemus was a Pharisee.
4. Students will know that Pharisees were a Jewish sect who followed strict religious rituals and resented foreign (Roman) supremacy.
5. Students will know that Nicodemus visited Jesus at night.
6. Students will know that Jesus told Nicodemus that he must be "born again."
7. Students will know that Jesus taught that all who follow Him will have eternal life.
8. Students will know that Nicodemus assisted in the burial of Jesus.
9. Students will know that God loves them so much that He sent His Son Jesus to die for their sins (and that He rose again).
10. Students will learn that Jesus is the only way to salvation.
11. Students will know that while many people will follow Jesus, many others will choose not to follow Him and perish for their sins.

RESOURCES/CREDIT

1. *The Family Bible Dictionary*, 1958 ed. Avenir Books, s.v. "*Pharisee.*"
2. Everett Ferguson, *Backgrounds of Early Christianity* (Grand Rapids: William B. Eerdmans Publishing Co., 1993), 480-1.
3. Ibid., 482-3.
4. Gary Hardin, "*Jewish Sabbath Laws,*" *Biblical Illustrator*, Lifeway (Spring 2006 Volume 32, Number 3): 43-45.
5. Frederick Fyvie Bruce, *The Gospel & Epistles of John* (Grand Rapids: William B. Eerdmans Publishing Co., 1983), 85.
6. Randall L. Adkisson, "*A Man named Nicodemus,*" *Biblical Illustrator*, Lifeway (Winter 2006-07 Volume 33, Number 2): 12-15.

BACKGROUND PASSAGES

Main Passages

Luke 23:32-56	Crucifixion and burial
Luke 24:1-12	Resurrection

Related Passages

Matthew 27:27-28:5	Passion account
Mark 15-16	Passion account
John 19-20	Passion account
Leviticus 16	Day of Atonement

Suggested Homiletic Passage

Luke 23:35-43

MEMORY VERSE

Younger version

The Son of Man must ... be killed ... and be raised the third day.

Luke 9:22

Older version

The Son of Man must suffer many things and be rejected by the elders, chief priests, and scribes, be killed, and be raised the third day.

Luke 9:22

LESSON OBJECTIVE

On the cross, Jesus won victory over death, and any person, like the repentant thief by Jesus' side, can receive the free gift of salvation until the Lord returns.

LESSON OBJECTIVE

At Easter time Christians celebrate the resurrection of Jesus. Victory over sin was bought at a terrible price on the cross by Jesus' death. His subsequent resurrection gives the certain hope of salvation to all who believe and follow Him. Each year the Easter rotation lesson focuses on a different aspect of the Passion week. While the cross is always central, this lesson will focus on the events of the crucifixion and the subsequent resurrection.

Luke 23:32-56

Events passed in rapid succession the night before the crucifixion. Jesus shared His final supper with His disciples, He spent intimate time in prayer before Judas betrayed Him, an illegal court found Him guilty of blasphemy, and Herod's decree forced Him to carry a cross to a hill called "*The Skull*" where he was to be crucified. These and other events, as chronicled in the Gospels, led up to the crucifixion.

Jesus was not the only person to be crucified that day: two criminals were also condemned to the same sentence (v.32). The crosses were arranged side by side, and Roman soldiers hung Jesus on the cross in the middle. A crowd had gathered and were waiting for the men to die.

Death by crucifixion was a regular means of execution by the Romans. Death on a cross was an agonizing and drawn-out process. Jesus would have been weak from the brutal beating administered shortly before the crucifixion. The pain from the nails, which were in his wrists and feet, and served as his sole support would have only intensified as time progressed. Jesus would become weaker and weaker until finally, completely exhausted, he died.

The cross was not an accident. It was not God's "*plan B*" after the fall in the Garden of Eden. The cross was part of God's providential plan for the redemption of mankind from before the beginning of time. Jesus' blood would redeem us because "He was destined before the foundation of the world..." (I Peter 1:20). In verse 34 Jesus said, "Father forgive them, because they do not know what they are doing." In the midst of His suffering, Jesus still showed love and compassion on those who were murdering Him.

The soldiers gambling for His clothing fulfilled one of many prophecies concerning the crucifixion (Psalm 22:18). Clothing was valuable and not to go to waste.

Easter - Crucifixion

Members of the Sanhedrin were among the crowd watching the proceedings (v.35). Mocking him, they acknowledged that Jesus helped others but asserted that if He were the true Messiah, he would also save Himself. The soldiers joined in the mocking. Fueling the mockery was a sign above the cross reading, "This is the king of the Jews."

One of the criminals echoed the mocking of the leaders and soldiers, "Aren't You the Messiah? Save Yourself and us!" he cried (v.39). The other criminal rebuked him saying, "Don't you even fear God, since you are undergoing the same punishment? We are punished justly, because we are getting back what we deserve for the things we did, but this man has done nothing wrong." (v.40).

But even at this time of apparent hopelessness, there was grace. The second criminal said "Jesus, remember me when You come into Your kingdom!" Jesus' reply in verse 43 was, "I assure you: Today you will be with Me in paradise."

A criminal receiving what was due to him for any number of heinous crimes, who never joined a church, and who was never baptized, was allowed, that day, to enter into the presence of God. He rightly recognized that there was nothing he could do to save himself and placed his total faith in Jesus, the one who could and did save him. Children need to learn that salvation cannot be earned through good living. Children also need to know that once they place their faith in Jesus, they cannot do anything bad enough to be rejected. Just as the criminal received the free gift of salvation, they too can receive Jesus' free gift today.

The crucifixion began at 9 a.m. Around noon time the skies began to darken, and for the next three hours the skies were as dark as night. The end came suddenly as Jesus cried out, "Father, into Your hands I entrust My spirit." and then died (v.46).

At the moment of death several things happened simultaneously. First, Luke (23:45) and Matthew (27:51) record that the curtain in the Temple was torn in two from top to bottom. The curtain had separated the Holy Place from the Most Holy Place. The Most Holy Place was God's dwelling place and was hidden from view by a large curtain. This curtain served to keep sinful people away from God's presence. Once a year, on the Day of Atonement, bearing the blood of sacrifice, the High priest would enter the Holy of Holies (Lev. 16). To do so at any other time or way would have brought instant death to the trespasser (Lev. 16:2). The tearing of the curtain signified that an earthly priest was no longer required, and all people were free to approach God because of Jesus' perfect once-for-all sacrifice upon the cross.

Second, Matthew recorded that a number of "saints", people, rose from the dead, and went into the city (Matt. 27:52-3). These two verses raise many questions that remain unanswered. It did foreshadow Jesus' ultimate victory over death.

Third, one of the Roman centurions overseeing the crucifixion felt convicted that Jesus "...really was righteous!" (Luke 22:47). Mark 15:39 quotes the centurion as exclaiming, "This man really was God's Son." The crowd that witnessed the crucifixion also realized that this was not a normal crucifixion and that a great wrong had been done. They went home "striking their chests" (v.48) in a show of mourning or regret.

Perhaps only members of the Sanhedrin were pleased with the events of the day. But even among their ranks, there was dissent. One member, Joseph of Arimathea asked Pilate for the body of Jesus. Along with another member, Nicodemus, Joseph prepared Jesus' body for burial and placed it in his own new, unused tomb. They hurried to finish before the Sabbath began at sunset. The women from Galilee that had become followers of Jesus observed the preparations from a distance. Once they knew where the body was, they went to prepare spices and perfumes to put on Jesus after they observed the Sabbath.

Christians know that tragic day was the beginning of the story, rather than the end. To the early believers, who did not yet comprehend why Jesus had to die, the future was without hope. That bleak outlook changed dramatically.

In Luke 24:1 the women returned to the tomb on the first day of the week. They found the stone rolled away and entered the tomb. There was no body there. The women were perplexed but had little time to worry, as two angels appeared. The women were terrified, but one of the angels gave them the most wonderful news they would ever hear, "Why are you looking for the living among the dead? He is not here, but He has been resurrected!" (Luke 24:5-6). Jesus had foretold His resurrection, but only now did the women seemingly remember.

The women rushed to tell the other believers about the good news. At first the disciples refused to believe the women, but soon Peter and John were running to the tomb to see if there was any truth to the claim. Peter looked into the tomb (v.12). Jesus was not there, only His linen burial clothes. Peter was amazed at what had happened.

It would be some time before all the followers were convinced that Jesus was alive. Jesus made several post-resurrection appearances and gave final instructions to his disciples before He ascended to Heaven. Of these first followers, many would suffer greatly and die for their beliefs, but just as the repentant thief on the cross, those early Christians received an eternal inheritance for their belief. Their work laid the foundation of our Church today.

AGE GROUP CONSIDERATIONS

Crucifixion was a brutal, offensive way to die. It is offensive to our sensibilities, yet it is necessary to understand how much Jesus suffered for our sins. Young children do not need to know every detail of the crucifixion. It is enough for them to know that Jesus was willing to die, and rise again, in order to save them. We should not avoid the cross because of its unpleasantness, but adult Christians should recognize that they can also reach a point of familiarity where they become irreverently casual in discussing the cross. We should strive to remain sensitive to the Lord's sacrifice and His gospel.

SUGGESTED HYMNS/SONGS

1. *When I Survey the Wondrous Cross*, 234, 2008 Baptist Hymnal.
2. *The Old Rugged Cross*, 230, 2008 Baptist Hymnal.
3. *At the Cross*, 255, 2008 Baptist Hymnal.
4. *The First Lord's Day*, 162, 1991 Baptist Hymnal.
5. *Christ the Lord is Risen Today*, 270, 2008 Baptist Hymnal.
6. *Wherever He Leads, I'll Go*, 437, 2008 Baptist Hymnal.

STUDENT APPLICATIONS

1. Students will know that all four gospels in the New Testament talk about Jesus' death and resurrection.
2. Students will know that Jesus was executed on a cross.
3. Students will know that Jesus' death on a cross was part of God's master plan of salvation.
4. Students will know that two criminals were crucified alongside Jesus.
5. Students will know that one of the criminals asked for and received forgiveness from Jesus.
6. Students will know that Jesus was innocent and died to be a sacrifice for their sins.
7. Students will know that Jesus arose from the dead three days after the crucifixion.
8. Students will know that it is because of the resurrection of Jesus that Christians celebrate Easter Sunday and every day.
9. Students will know that the tearing of the temple curtain meant that all people could approach God because of Jesus' once-for-all sacrifice on the cross.
10. Students will know that Jesus is still alive today.

Early Church - Peter Rescued

BACKGROUND PASSAGES

Main Passage

Acts 4:32-37   Believers share
Acts 6:1-7   Deacons appointed
Acts 12:1-19   Peter freed from prison

Suggested Homiletic Passage

Acts 4:32-37

Memory Verse

And they devoted themselves to the apostles' teaching, to fellowship, to the breaking of bread, and to prayers.

Acts 2:42

LESSON OBJECTIVE

After Jesus ascended to Heaven, He sent the Holy Spirit to lead the believers in establishing the church. First century believers demonstrated what it means to be the body of Christ through selfless giving, prayer and evangelism.

LESSON

The first chapter of the book of Acts (also known as The Acts of the Apostles) begins with an ending. Jesus' time on earth ended when he ascended into the sky, and left his disciples staring at the clouds. They must have wondered what would happen next. Jesus had commanded them to continue His work by telling others about Him. He also promised to send a "Helper." On the day of Pentecost, the Holy Spirit descended upon them and the New Testament church was born. The early church serves as an example to all modern churches through their selfless giving, prayer and evangelism.

Acts 4:32-37

One of the defining marks of the early church was their unity, as manifested through their sacrificial giving. The followers were of "one heart and soul." (v.32). No one held back. This unified giving was not a communist system because their giving was solely voluntary and on an "as needed" basis.

In verse 33 the apostles were obedient in proclaiming the good news. With the help of the Holy Spirit, sent at Pentecost, the message went out with power and grace. Many people responded to the message.

As people believed, the church grew and began to expand its ministry. Believers freely and extravagantly gave. They clearly put the needs of others ahead of their own desires. Believers willingly sold homes and land to provide for those in need. There was a man named Joseph. The disciples called him Barnabas, meaning "Son of Encouragement." Barnabas, like others, sold land and brought the money to the disciples feet (v.36-37).

The early church took joy in giving. They made it an act of worship and thanksgiving. While children are limited in how they can give monetarily to support ministry, they can still learn to give. They can give of whatever resources they may have in a way that is a joyful act of worship.

Acts 6:1-7

It is easy to look at the early church and wish that today's church could be so "perfect"; however, churches have always faced issues and the early church was no exception. While the early church was unified and focused on eternal matters, practical needs and concerns also needed to be addressed.

Growth, while a positive thing, usually brings challenges . In verse 1, Grecian Jews complained to the Hebraic Jews that, as the number of believers had grown, their widows were being overlooked in the daily distribution of food. Hebraic Jews were native Jewish Christians who spoke Aramaic. Grecian Jews were most likely Jews from other countries who had been become believers on the day of Pentecost. Most likely the oversight of the widows was not intentional, but caused by a language barrier.

In verse 2 the Apostles gathered to discuss the situation. In their God-given wisdom, the Apostles realized that they needed to keep their main focus on proclaiming the gospel. Service is important but was not their primary call. They decided to delegate the food distribution to seven men. Maturity and character counted as the men were to be of , "... good reputation, full of the Spirit, and wisdom."

In verse 5, the seven men were chosen for the task. Most notable, among the men, was Stephen (who would later be stoned for his faith). The Apostles laid hands on and prayed for the seven men. The church had ordained its first deacons.

After this, the early church continued to minister and grow, and even a number of Jewish priests became Christians (verse 7).

While various definitions of the office of deacon have been given by many, their Biblical purpose is clear: a deacon is one who willingly and graciously serves. Ordination for ministerial positions mainly occurs for two reasons: service and evangelism. Thus the two ordained offices in Southern Baptist churches, and many other evangelical churches, are for *deacons* and *pastors*. The roles of pastoral and deacon ministry have always been closely tied together. According to Hobbs, "When both function properly, the work of the church prospers."[1]

Acts 12:1-19

The success of the early church attracted the attention of powerful authorities. Unfortunately, as has happened throughout history, Satan used the authorities to persecute the early church. The believers responded then, as they do now, with prayer.

King Herod (*Herod Agrippa I*, grandson of Herod the Great) persecuted Christians in order to please the Jewish leaders. Herod also had James, the brother of John killed (verse 2). He then arrested Peter, and, put him in prison under heavy guard (v.4). Peter's arrest came during the feast of Unleavened Bread. The timing of the arrest probably allowed Herod to impress out-of-town Jews which had come for the festival.[2]

In verse 5 the church was praying earnestly for Peter. They knew, with the death of James fresh on their minds, that Peter's safe release would require a miracle. His execution scheduled for the next day, their prayers continued well into the night.

In verse 6 Peter, bound with chains, was asleep between two guards . Sentries stood watch at the prison doors. Suddenly an angel of the Lord appeared in Peter's cell. He awakened Peter. As Peter stood up, the chains fell from his wrists. The angel then told Peter to get dressed and to follow him. Peter followed and found himself escorted beyond the prison and into Jerusalem, where the angel suddenly disappeared. But what about the guards? They had simply walked past them. Perhaps God lulled them into a deep sleep. Despite Herod's extravagant precautions, Peter was providentially enabled to leave without the slightest resistance. The prayers of the church were effective in helping Peter!

In verse 11 Peter realized that he had not been dreaming. He acknowledged that God had rescued him. He headed to the home of Mary, mother of John Mark. John Mark is best known as the author of the Gospel of Mark.

Many believers had gathered at the house to pray for Peter. Peter knocked at the door and a servant girl, named Rhoda, approached the door. She recognized Peter's voice and became so excited that she forgot to open the door. She announced to everyone that Peter was at the door. Their initial reaction was disbelief. In fact they said, "You're crazy!" (v.15). They truly believed in the power of prayer, but the circumstances were so dire that when Peter was actually released, it still caught them by surprise. Peter kept knocking. Eventually someone opened the door and discovered that Rhoda had been telling the truth. The believers were astounded and filled with joy.

Unable to speak over the excitement, Peter motioned for the group to be quiet. He then testified about how God had rescued him. He told them to tell James (brother of Jesus) and the others. Then Peter left to a different, unknown, place.

Verse 18 states, "At daylight, there was a great commotion among the soldiers as to what could have become of Peter." The sixteen soldiers who had been guarding Peter did not have a clue as to how he escaped. Understandably, Herod was very upset and, believing the guards must have collaborated with Peter, cross-examined them and ordered them to be executed.

A short time later, Herod died, but the gospel continued to flourish. Throughout the rest of the book of Acts the Apostles and other believers boldly evangelized, prayed, and served one another sacrificially. God affirmed their faith and through them, began the ministry of His church, which continues today.

Age Group Considerations

Due to the behind-the-scenes nature of the deacon ministry, most children will have little, if any, concept of how deacons minister. It would be a good idea to have a deacon visit the class and explain the different ways that deacons benefit the church.

Why did God allow John's brother James to be executed by Herod, yet spared Peter? Life is full of tough questions as to why bad things are allowed to happen. All we can do is trust God since He has a plan and purpose in all things. Children need to know that bad things sometimes come as a consequence of our sins, but not because God loves one person more than another.

Suggested Hymns/Songs

1. *The Church's One Foundation*, 346, 2008 Baptist Hymnal.
2. *The Family of God*, 393, 2008 Baptist Hymnal.
3. *Our God Reigns*, 58, 2008 Baptist Hymnal.
4. *Serve the Lord with Gladness*, 382, 2008 Baptist Hymnal.

Student Applications

1. Students will know that Jesus is the founder and head of the Church.
2. Students will know that Jesus sent the Holy Spirit to lead the Church.
3. Students will know that the history of the early church is found in the book of Acts.
4. Students will know that the book of Acts is found in the New Testament.
5. Students will know that the early believers gave sacrificially to one another because they so loved Jesus.
6. Students will know that the early church appointed deacons to assist the apostles by ministering to others, while the Apostles preached and prayed.
7. Students will know that Peter was arrested for preaching the gospel.
8. Students will know that members of the early church prayed fervently for Peter's release.
9. Students will know that God freed Peter from prison by sending an angel to assist his escape.
10. Students will know that deacons still minister as servants in today's church, as do pastors.
11. Students in Southern Baptist churches will know that there are two ordained offices: deacons and pastors.

Resources/Credit

1. Herschel H. Hobbs, *Fundamentals of Our Faith* (Nashville: Broadman & Holman Publishers, 1960), 131.
2. *Life Application Bible*. (Grand Rapids, Michigan: Zondervan Publishing House, 1991), 1974.

Josiah the Boy King

BACKGROUND PASSAGES

Main Passage
II Kings 22:1-23:25   Josiah's reign

Related Passages
II Chronicles 33:25-35:27 Josiah's reign
I Kings 13   Josiah prophesied

Suggested Homiletic Passage
II Kings 22:8-13

MEMORY VERSE

Younger version
    He did what was right in the Lord's sight ... he did not turn to the right or the left.
                    II Kings 22:2

Older version
    He did what was right in the Lord's sight and walked in all the ways of his ancestor David; he did not turn to the right or the left.
                    II Kings 22:2

LESSON OBJECTIVE

After learning how Judah had forsaken God and turned to idols, Josiah turned to the Lord with all his heart and mind. Boldly, he led his people to remove temptation by destroying all idols in the land and also led them to return to worshiping the Lord Almighty.

LESSON

Who was the greatest of the kings of Judah and Israel? David? Solomon? David was a man after God's heart. His son Solomon ruled over a vast area and was the wisest man who ever lived. Either one would seem to be a sound choice as the greatest king, but there was another king who freed his people from the grip of idolatry and led them to worship the Lord Almighty: Josiah.

Josiah was the king of Judah between 641 and 609 B.C. While often referred to as "the boy king", Josiah is more noteworthy for his faith than his age. He led Judah from pagan worship back to the worship of God. He showed that one person with resolve, conviction, and a strong faith in God, could make a deep and lasting impact on his country.

II Kings 22

Josiah's rise to power came as a result of traumatic circumstances. His father, King Amon, was killed in his own house by his own servants after reigning for only two years. At the age of eight, Josiah was fatherless and the leader of a nation.

Why the servants spared Josiah, we do not know. In fact, little is known of Josiah's early years, but the writer of II Kings is quick to tell us that Josiah, "...did what was right in the Lord's sight..." (v.2). This was in stark contrast to the idolatrous lifestyle his father had lived (II Kings 21:20-21). Did Josiah's mother, Jedidah, or an unnamed advisor, plant the seed that would lead to Josiah's passion for God? Regardless, Josiah earnestly began to seek God as a teenager in the eighth year of his reign (II Chron. 34:3).

In verse 3 Josiah showed concern for the Temple. In a land where idols were everywhere, the temple had fallen into disrepair and misuse. He directed the high priest Hilkiah to use temple funds and spare no effort to repair the temple.

During the temple renovation, Hilkiah alerted the court secretary, Shaphan, that a book of the law had been found (v.8). This might have been a single book like Deuteronomy, but might also have been the entire Pentateuch (first five books of the Bible). Regardless, the fact that it had been "lost" was another indicator of how far Judah had wandered from God.

Shaphan took the law and read it to Josiah. Josiah was now in the eighteenth year of his reign. The king's first reaction was to tear his clothes as a sign of great remorse and anguish. Josiah rightly discerned that the nation was far from God and had likely incurred His wrath. He instructed Hilkiah, Shaphan and several

Josiah the Boy King

others to inquire of the Lord about what could still be done.

In verse 14, Huldah, a prophetess was consulted. What she reported was what Josiah feared: God was displeased that His people had continued in sin by worshipping false idols. He would soon punish Judah. But in verses 19-20, God granted grace to Josiah because his heart was tender and he humbled himself before the Lord. Judgment would come on Judah, but not until after Josiah's death. Because of the humility and faith of Josiah, an entire generation was spared.

II Kings 23:1-25

The revival that began in Josiah's personal life would extend through his rule to the entire nation. In verse 1, Josiah sent messengers to all the elders throughout the kingdom. The elders, along with all the men of Judah and the inhabitants of Jerusalem, met Josiah at the temple. He read to them the same words found in the temple that had convicted his own heart. Then, before all the people, Josiah made a personal covenant to follow the Lord. The people also agreed to the covenant. Josiah set an example for all the people follow.

Words ring hollow if they are not backed with action. After the time of covenant renewal, Josiah embarked on the greatest spiritual cleansing Judah would ever see. It began with the temple.

In verse 4, the king commanded Hilkiah, the high priest, to remove from the temple any articles which had been brought in for the use of idol worship. These items, including an Asherah pole erected by King Manasseh (II Kings 21:7), had been brought in by past kings. The items were carried outside the city and burned. Next, Josiah did away with all the pagan priests in Jerusalem and surrounding areas. In verse 7 he commanded the tearing down of houses of male prostitutes and the female weavers that were part of the worship of *Asherah* (sea goddess and mistress of *Baal*).[1]

Josiah then gathered all the Levitical priests together in Jerusalem. Many had participated in the idolatrous practices and were not allowed back in the

temple (v.9). Josiah destroyed the high places. He also destroyed Topheth, the place where children had been heinously sacrificed to the false god Molech.

Josiah destroyed altars built by previous kings by smashing them into dust. This included altars erected by King Solomon on the Mount of Destruction (v.13), a slur for what is known in the New Testament as the Mount of Olives.[2] Where the Asherah poles had stood, he filled with human bones. This was a defilement of the false god's place of worship and discouraged anyone from ever trying to resume worship at the site.

A prophecy was also fulfilled during Josiah's reforms. Approximately three-hundred years before Josiah, an unnamed prophet had confronted king Jeroboam as he worshipped Baal at an altar he had built at Bethel. The man of God prophesied that a king (named Josiah) would one day arise and destroy Jeroboam's altar (I Kings 13). Here in verse 15 Josiah fulfilled the prophecy.

Josiah traveled far from Jerusalem to the city of Samaria, the northern kingdom's former capital. There he removed the shrines and high places and killed the pagan priests. After this he returned home to Jerusalem.

Bad habits are easy to slip back into and need to be replaced with good ones. After thoroughly removing the false religions, Josiah commanded the people to carefully observe the Passover as God had given it to them. A casual reading might lead to the conclusion that the observance of the Passover had been abandoned since the time of the Judges; however, a Passover celebration (by Josiah's grandfather, King Hezekiah), is recorded in II Chronicles 30. Hezekiah's effort was somewhat haphazard, while Josiah sought to meticulously follow the Passover as prescribed by God. II Chron. 35 describes Josiah's attention to detail in preparation and observance, although this is not this lesson's focus. Truly, "No such Passover had ever been kept from the time of the judges ..." (v.20).

In addition to all he had already done, Josiah removed "all the detestable things that were seen in the land of Judah."(v.24). His persistence in personally following and leading the nation to worship God resulted in the following being written about him in verse 25:

> *"Before him there was no king like him who turned to the Lord with all his mind and with all his heart and with all his strength according to all the law of Moses, and no one like him arose after him."*

The nation of Judah would ultimately face God's judgment, but the faithfulness of one man saved his generation. Josiah ruthlessly removed all forms of idolatrous temptation and set the example of how to worship and serve the living God. Today, we too can learn from his examples of how to deal with temptation and seek God with all our heart and mind.

Age Group Considerations

The details of idol worship in ancient Israel is full of sordid details including sexual rites and torture. Obviously, these are not appropriate for children. In reference to the male prostitution that Josiah ended in II Kings 23:7, it is suggested that children be told that Josiah tore down houses of people, who assisted in the worship of idols, so that they would no longer tempt the people to follow false gods.

Children may not be able to identify with the ancient practice of worshipping idols nor understand why it was so important to destroy them. There are everyday situations to which they can relate. For example, if they have trouble concentrating on schoolwork while the television is on, they might need to go to a room where no television is present. Josiah did an excellent job in removing temptation from the people. He replaced bad habits with Godly ones, as should we.

Suggested Hymns/Songs

1. *Seek Ye First*, 524, 2008 Baptist Hymnal.
2. *I Have Decided to Follow Jesus*, 434, 2008 Baptist Hymnal.
3. *I'd Rather Have Jesus*, 530, 2008 Baptist Hymnal.

Student Applications

1. Students will know that the story of Josiah is found in the Old Testament book of II Kings.
2. Students will know that Josiah became king of Judah when he was only eight-years-old.
3. Students will know that, as an adult, Josiah worked to repair the temple.
4. Students will know that the book of the law was found and brought to Josiah while the temple was being restored.
5. Students will know that Josiah was convicted by what he heard from the book of the law.
6. Students will know that Josiah thoroughly and systematically destroyed idols and idolatrous practices throughout Judah.
7. Students will know that Josiah led all of Judah to renew their covenant with God.
8. Students will know that Josiah reinstated proper observance of the Passover.
9. Students will know that no other king turned his heart and mind to God like Josiah did, according to God's Word.
10. Students will know that Judah ultimately paid the consequence of their rebellion by being taken into captivity by the Babylonians.
11. Students will know Jesus is the perfect king and wants them to live holy and righteous lives.
12. Students will know that the best way to avoid giving in to temptation is to walk with God and obey Him.

Resources/Credit

1. *Life Application Bible*. (Grand Rapids, Michigan: Zondervan Publishing House, 1991), 650.
2. William Sanford LaSor, *The New Bible Commentary : Revised*, ed. Donald Guthrie (New York: Wm. B Eerdmans Co.), 366.

Moses Part 1 - Birth to Midian

BACKGROUND PASSAGES

Main Passage
Exodus 1-4   Moses

Suggested Homiletic Passage
Exodus 4:11-20

MEMORY VERSE

Younger version
"Now go! I will help you speak and I will teach you what to say."

Exodus 4:12b

Older version
The Lord said to him, "Who made the human mouth? ... Is it not I, the Lord? Now go! I will help you speak and I will teach you what to say."

Exodus 4:11-12

LESSON OBJECTIVE

When the children of Israel cried for deliverance from their oppression, God called and then sent Moses to deliver them. We, like Moses, are imperfect, but God will give us everything we need to accomplish what He wills.

LESSON

This is the first of three lessons covering the life of Moses and the deliverance of the Israelites from the Egyptians. This lesson will focus on the early life of Moses and his call. The second lesson will focus on the ten plagues and exodus of the Israelites. The third lesson will cover the events which occurred at Mt. Sinai (including the giving of the Ten Commandments).

At the conclusion of Genesis, all twelve sons of Israel were living safely in Egypt, having been providentially delivered by God, through Joseph, from the famine that had engulfed the region. Late in his life, Joseph made his Israelite brethren make an oath to return his bones to the Promised Land when God saw fit to return them there (Gen. 50:24-25).

Exodus 1-2

Exodus begins with the descendants of Israel still in Egypt almost 430 years later (Ex. 12:40). The Israelites' numbers had grown innumerably until the land was filled with them (v.7). Joseph had held a position of privilege and prestige in the eye of Pharaoh (Possibly the Pharaoh named Amenehet I)[1]. But many generations later, another Pharaoh was in power (Possibly Amenhotep II)[2]. He felt threatened by the multitude of Israelites and feared they could rebel and overcome his people.

His solution was to enslave the Israelites and force them to hard labor. "They (the Egyptians) worked the Israelites ruthlessly and made their lives bitter with difficult labor in brick and mortar..." (Ex. 1:13-14a). Enslavement was not Pharaoh's worst act in attempting to control the Israelites: Pharaoh met with the Hebrew midwives and commanded them to kill the newborn boys. The girls were to be allowed to live.

Exodus gives the names of two Hebrew midwives: Shiphrah and Puah. Perhaps they were representatives of a larger group of midwives, as the number of Israelites almost certainly would have required the services of more than two. The midwives took a bold stand and disobeyed Pharaoh's order. Pharaoh summoned them to answer for their disobedience. The midwives told Pharaoh that the Israelite women gave birth quickly before a midwife could arrive. For doing the right thing that might have cost them their own lives, God blessed them with families of their own. Pharaoh, however, then turned to his own people and they began to hunt down the Israelite boy infants.

At this time a son was born to Amram and Jochebed (Ex. 6:20) and they successfully hid him for three months. Jochebed realized it was inevitable that her son would be found and put to death. In an act of desperation, she placed the baby in a papyrus basket coated with pitch (so it would float) and then set it afloat on the Nile River. The baby's sister watched from a distance. Perhaps Jochebed knew that Egyptian royalty was nearby and hoped that they would find the basket and have mercy on the child. By any rational reasoning the plan was desperate, but God's Providence is clearly evident in what happened next.

Pharaoh's daughter, along with her attendants, came to the river to bathe. They discovered the basket in the reeds. Pharaoh's daughter had mercy on the child. The baby's sister, Miriam, approached and offered to find a nurse for the child. Pharaoh's daughter accepted the offer. Naturally, the nurse that was "found" was the baby's natural mother. After he was weaned, Pharaoh's daughter adopted the baby and named him Moses. Despite the evil intentions of Pharaoh, God's own perfect plan was never in danger.

Exodus 2:11 moves the story ahead many years. Moses was grown and clearly aware of his heritage. He saw how poorly the Egyptians were treating his people. One day Moses observed the beating of an Israelite, and believing that no one was watching, he killed the Egyptian responsible. The next day he learned that another knew of the murder and, in fear, Moses fled the country. He ended up in Midian, a region east of the Sinai peninsula.

While in Midian, Moses came to the aid of the seven daughters of Reuel, the priest of Midian. In Midianite culture, clan and tribal leaders also served as priests.[3] Reuel is also referred to as Jethro. Reuel may have been a title or clan name and Jethro a personal name.[4] Jethro's daughters were watering their father's flock when some shepherds arrived and tried to drive them away. Moses defended their rights, drove away the shepherds, and then assisted the women in watering their flock. Jethro invited Moses into his home. Later, Moses married one of the daughters, Zipporah (2:21). They had a son named Gershom.

Moses stayed in Midian for quite some time, and eventually the oppressive pharaoh of Moses' childhood died and another took his place. The Israelites cried out to God. God, in His great mercy, "... re-membered His covenant with Abraham, Isaac, and Jacob. God saw the Israelites, and He took notice." (2:24-25).

How encouraging it is to know that God understands human trials and shows mercy. Little did the Israelites know that God was about to reveal His plan for deliverance through the call of a man, deep in the Midian wilderness.

The Burning Bush (Exodus 3-4)

Moses was watching the flocks of his father-in-law, Jethro, near Horeb. Here, "the Angel of the Lord" appeared to him as a fire within a bush (3:2). This is an example of a theophany; *i.e.*, a physical manifestation of God.

Moses was intrigued that the bush was not consumed by the fire. He approached to investigate the unusual phenomenon. God spoke to him from the bush. He commanded Moses to remove his sandals because he was standing on holy ground. He told him that He was the God of Moses' forefathers. Like others in the Bible who were in God's presence, Moses hid his face (out of fear) .

God told Moses that he had seen the Israelites struggling for survival in Egypt. He had heard their cry and was going to rescue them and lead them to the Promised Land. Moses was not prepared for what came next, "Therefore, go. I am sending you to Pharaoh so that you may lead My people, the Israelites, out of Egypt." (3:10).

What would be your reaction if you were commanded to take up such an important role? Moses was considered the greatest prophet by the Jews in Jesus' day. Moses' faith is presented to us as a Godly example in the book of Hebrews (Heb. 11:23-29). But Moses was fallible. He began to make excuses and argue with God.

In Exodus 3:11 Moses basically asked, "Why me?" To which God replied that as a sign, all the Israelites would worship at the very mountain where they were standing. Next Moses asked, "Who do I say sent me?" God replied, "**I AM WHO I AM.**" Moses was to meet with the elders of Israel and relate to them the things God had told him at the burning bush. After which, Moses was to go before the Pharaoh and request the Israelites be allowed a three-day trip into the wilderness to worship their God.

God already knew Pharaoh would be resistant and had given Moses warning. God performed many glorious miracles before Pharaoh allowed the people to leave. It was clear to Israelite and Egyptian alike that there was only one true God. By the end of it all, the Egyptians would no longer be reluctant to let the Israelites leave but would actually plead for them to leave, giving them their gold, jewelry and clothing in an effort to hasten their departure.

Still hesitant, Moses asked, "What if they won't believe me and will not obey but say 'The Lord did not appear to you'?" (4:1). God then commanded Moses to throw his staff to the ground. Moses complied and it became a snake. Grabbing the snake by the tail, it once again became a staff in Moses' hand. God told him that he should repeat this in Egypt as confirmation that he had been sent by God.

As further proof, God told him to put his hand in his cloak and then remove it. When Moses withdrew his hand it was diseased, probably with a form of leprosy. Moses placed it back in his cloak and pulled it out once more and found that it had returned to normal.

Again Moses hesitated, asking, "Please, Lord, I have never been eloquent — either in the past or recently ..." (4:10). God replied, "... Now go! I will help you speak and I will teach you what to say." (4:11). God always equips those whom He calls. Moses was no exception.

Finally Moses argued, "Please, Lord, send someone else." (4:13). God's anger burned against Moses because of his lack of faith. God is not pleased when doubted, and while it is true that believers should not put God to the test, He is a God of mercy. God told Moses that He was sending Moses' brother Aaron to meet him and that Aaron would serve as spokesman for Moses.

Moses asked no other questions nor made any further excuses. He returned home and told his father-in-law, Jethro, of his plan to return to Egypt. He then packed up his wife, sons, and his staff for the journey. God reminded Moses once more to perform all the signs he had been shown with the expectation that Pharaoh would harden his heart. Moses was to be faithful in delivering the full message. God was to handle the consequences of Pharaoh's resistance.

In Ex. 4:27 Aaron was led by God to the wilderness where he met Moses. It was a joyous meeting. Moses shared with Aaron all that the Lord had revealed to him. Together, they went before the Israelite elders. Moses performed the signs according to God's command. The people believed and knew that God had heard them in their distress. They bowed to worship God and thank Him.

God had shown the Israelites that He is faithful to remember His people at all times and in every situation. Moses, while initially reluctant stepped out in faith to do what God commanded. His first audience with Pharaoh was to come.

AGE GROUP CONSIDERATIONS

Exodus 4:24-26 was purposely skipped in this lesson. The content of the three verses was deemed appropriate only for adults and is not necessary for this lesson.

SUGGESTED HYMNS/SONGS

1. *Awesome God*, 63, 2008 Baptist Hymnal.
2. *Holy Ground*, 72, 2008 Baptist Hymnal.
3. *Praise Him, All Ye Little Children*, 650, 2008 Baptist Hymnal.
4. *We Praise You, O God, Our Redeemer*, 9, 2008 Baptist Hymnal.

STUDENT APPLICATIONS

1. Students will know that Exodus is found in the Old Testament.
2. Students will know that the birth and call of Moses is found in Exodus.

3. Students will know that the children of Israel were enslaved by the Egyptians.
4. Students will know that Pharaoh ordered all Israelite male infants be put to death.
5. Students will know that, as a baby, Moses was placed in wicker basket and floated down the Nile river.
6. Students will know that Moses' basket was found by the daughter of Pharaoh, who both named and raised him.
7. Students will know that Moses killed an Egyptian who was physically harming an Israelite.
8. Students will know that Moses fled to Midian and was eventually called by God to return to Egypt during the encounter at the burning bush.
9. Students will know that God called Moses from within a burning bush.
10. Students will know that God will equip them with everything they need for ministry.
11. Students will know that Moses met his brother, Aaron, on his way back to Egypt, because God sent him as promised.
12. Students will know that the Israelites acknowledged that God had heard them in their distress by worshiping Him.
13. Students will know that they too should seek to recognize when God is at work and regularly thank, praise, and worship Him.

RESOURCES/CREDIT

1. Steven R. Miller, "*The Egypt Joseph Knew*," *Biblical Illustrator*, Lifeway (Spring 2008 Volume 34, Number 3): 74.
2. *Ibid*, 75.
3. Hywel R. Jones, *The New Bible Commentary : Revised*, ed. Donald Guthrie (New York: Wm. B Eerdmans Co.), 122.
4. Robert P. Gordon, *The International Bible Commentary, Revised Edition*, F.F. Bruce, ed. (Grand Rapids, Michigan: Zondervan Publishing House, 1979), 157.

Moses Part 2 - Plagues & Exodus

BACKGROUND PASSAGES

Main Passage
Exodus 5-14   Ten Plagues & Exodus

Suggested Homiletic Passage
Exodus 6:1-8

MEMORY VERSE

Younger version
   I will take you as My people, and I will be your God.

Exodus 6:7a

Older version
   I will take you as My people, and I will be your God. You will know that I am Yahweh your God, who delivered you from the forced labor of the Egyptians.

Exodus 6:7

LESSON OBJECTIVE

   God's omnipotence and providence was displayed when He used plagues and the parting of the waters to deliver the nation of Israel from their Egyptian oppressors. Believers can trust Him to meet every need in their lives in a way that brings Him the glory.

LESSON

   This is the second of three lessons covering the life of Moses and the deliverance of the Israelites from the Egyptians. The first lesson focused on the early life of Moses' call. This lesson covers the ten plagues and the exodus of the Israelites. The third, and final, installment will cover the events at Mount Sinai, including the giving of the Ten Commandments.

Exodus 5-6:9

   Moses and Aaron arrived in Egypt with the good news that God had observed the Israelites' distress and was going to deliver them. Only one person stood in the way ... the Pharaoh. To the Egyptians, the Pharaoh was not only their national leader, but he was a god. What could possibly motivate him to relinquish such a valuable resource as the Israelites' free labor?

   In 5:1 Moses and Aaron made their first of several appearances before the Pharaoh. They made it clear that they were speaking on behalf of the Lord, the God of Israel. They asked for three days to go and worship God in the wilderness. Pharaoh refused to even acknowledge the Lord, and summarily dismissed any notion of letting the Israelites go forth. He told Moses and Aaron to stop bothering him, for they were distracting the people from their labors.

   Pharaoh stated that the Israelites must be lazy and not have enough work to do if they had time to listen to such lies. He promptly commanded the overseers of the Israelites to withhold straw from the laborers. Straw was integral to the creation of bricks, and so the Israelites then had to gather it themselves. As could be expected, the Israelites were unable succeed and their foremen were beaten.

   The foremen went to Pharaoh to appeal their case. Pharaoh refused to give them straw or to reduce their quotas. The Israelites then went to Moses and Aaron, whom they chastised as the cause of their misery. Moses went before the Lord and asked God why He had brought harm to His people. God answered Moses, "Now you are going to see what I will do to Pharaoh; he will let them go because of My strong hand ..." (6:1). God also told Moses to tell the Israelites that He remembered the covenant which He had made with Abraham and that He was the Lord their God and would deliver and lead them to the land promised to Abraham, Isaac and Jacob.

   The Israelites did not listen because of their hard labor and broken spirits (6:9). But God had a plan that would work for their deliverance. Even when things are not going the way we hope, believers can know that God is working all events for His Glory. God will work for His best in our lives.

Moses Part 2 - Plagues & Exodus

The Ten Plagues
Exodus 6:26 - 13

God commanded Moses to speak to Pharaoh, but, because of Pharaoh's actions after the first meeting, Moses was hesitant. God reminded him that Aaron would be allowed to speak for him. God also reminded him that everything that had happened so far was within His purposes. Pharaoh would continue to resist, but God would ultimately deliver the Israelites.

Once in the presence of Pharaoh, Moses performed the first of the signs as commanded by God. He threw down his staff and it turned into a snake. Pharaoh's magicians apparently did the same, although their transformation may have been an illusion. God showed His superiority by having Moses' snake swallow theirs.

Then Moses announced the first of what would eventually be ten plagues to afflict the Egyptians. Notice that each plague came after Pharaoh refused to let the Israelites go free.

Plague of Blood: Moses and Aaron met Pharaoh as he came to the Nile. Aaron struck the river with his staff and all the water in the Nile turned to blood. The magicians used their magic arts to duplicate the feat, and Pharaoh was unmoved.

Plague of Frogs: Seven days later Moses and Aaron were back before Pharaoh. Aaron stretched out his staff over the Nile and hordes of frogs came up out of the water and covered the land. Once again the magicians duplicated the miracle and Pharaoh was unmoved, but the magicians could not make the frogs go away. Pharaoh verbally promised to let the people go and asked Moses to ask his Lord to remove the frogs.

Plague of Gnats: God allowed all the frogs to die; their rotting bodies caused a great stench in the land. Once the frogs were gone Pharaoh "hardened his heart" and refused to let the people go. Aaron stretched out his staff and struck the dust. The dust turned into great clouds of gnats that inflicted distress on all the people and animals of Egypt. Pharaoh's magicians were unable to duplicate this feat

and confessed to Pharaoh that it was their belief that this was "the finger of God" (8:19). Pharaoh still would not listen.

Plague of Flies: God commanded Moses to again meet Pharaoh in the morning, as he came to the water (most likely the Nile). Moses announced that flies would swarm over the land. God said that He would make a distinction between the Israelites and the Egyptians. The Israelites would not be afflicted with the flies. As no distinction was given, it is likely that the first three plagues afflicted Israelite and Egyptian alike. The flies came the next day and even infiltrated Pharaoh's palace. Pharaoh agreed to let the Israelites go a short ways into the wilderness. Moses said this would not do; a three day's journey was required. As soon as the flies were removed, Pharaoh once more hardened his heart and refused to let the people go.

Plague of Livestock: Next God sent a plague on all the livestock of Egypt. Horses, donkeys, camels, herds and flocks were all decimated. Messengers reported back to Pharaoh that the plague had not affected the Israelite animals. Pharaoh refused to let the Israelites go.

Plague of Boils: God told Moses to go before Pharaoh and throw handfuls of furnace soot into the air. Moses obeyed and the people, the magicians themselves, and remaining animals of Egypt broke out with festering boils. The magicians, in fact, were so personally afflicted with boils that they could not stand before Moses. Nonetheless, Pharaoh remained defiant.

Plague of Hail: Life and land in Egypt was already in tatters, but more was to come. God told Moses to tell Pharaoh that he and his people could have already been obliterated, "However, I have let you live for this purpose: to show you My power and to make My name known in all the earth." (9:16). The next plague was a terrible hailstorm. God gave prior warning to Pharaoh to see that all his people and animals were in shelters, for anyone or anything that remained outside would die. Those in Egypt who feared the Lord listened, the rest did not. Some of

Moses Part 2 - Plagues & Exodus

Pharaoh's officials did heed the warning while others did not. It is amazing to think that even after the first six plagues, Pharaoh and some of his officials still refused to believe.

Moses stretched out his staff towards the sky and hail fell and lightning struck the earth. "The hail struck down everything in the field, both man and beast. The hail beat down every plant of the field and shattered every tree in the field." (9:25). Only the land of Goshen, home of the Israelites, was spared.

This time Pharaoh admitted his sin to Moses and confessed that "The Lord is the Righteous One..." (9:27). Moses went out of the city, raised his arms, and the plague ended. But Pharaoh's confession did not lead to submission. Pharaoh's heart hardened once more and he did not let the Israelites go.

Plague of Locusts: At the beginning of chapter ten, one reason for Pharaoh's stubbornness is revealed: God was using the severity of the plagues to impress upon the hearts of the doubting Israelites, His power and love for them. Thus, the Israelites would remember and recount the events to future generations.

Moses and Aaron went before Pharaoh and announced that a plague of locusts would swarm over the land. They would fill every house and destroy any plants that were not already destroyed. Pharaoh's officials begged him to let the people go. Still resistant, Pharaoh insisted on negotiating, wanting only the men to leave and was not willing to compromise. Moses and Aaron were driven from Pharaoh's presence.

Moses lifted his staff, and in the morning, wind from the east brought in the cloud of locusts. The locusts were everywhere, and nothing green was left on any tree or plant in Egypt. Pharaoh asked Moses for forgiveness; however, once the locusts were gone, his heart only hardened again. The Israelites were not to be freed.

Plague of Darkness: This plague of darkness may not have seemed destructive, but was possibly the most terrifying of the plagues. God told Moses that "there will be darkness over the land of Egypt, a darkness that can be felt." (10:21). Three days the Egyptians were paralyzed by a blinding darkness. No one left their home. In Goshen, the Israelites still had light where they lived.

Pharaoh summoned Moses and Aaron. He said he would allow all them to go, but that they must leave their livestock behind. Moses was unyielding: everyone and everything must be allowed to leave. Pharaoh angrily sent them away, threatening them with immediate death if he ever saw them again.

Plague of Death of Firstborn: The deliverance and exodus of the Israelites was imminent. God would send a final plague before Pharaoh, and the people of Egypt would indeed, not only allow, but plead, for the Israelites to leave their land. So Moses was to have all the Israelites ask for silver and gold from the demoralized Egyptians. Egypt would be plundered just as God had promised (Ex. 3:20-22). This event would be so profound that the Israelites would start a new calendar based on the timing of the exodus (12:2).

God told Moses to make preparations for what would become known as the Passover. On the designated night, the people were to prepare to leave on a moment's notice. Preparations were to include unleavened bread for the journey, as there would not be time for yeast bread to rise. Most importantly, each family was to slaughter an unblemished lamb and brush its blood on the home's door posts and lintel. The lamb's meat was to be consumed in the subsequent Passover meal.

All the Israelites were to stay indoors as the Lord passed over Egypt and struck down every firstborn male, person and livestock, that was not in a house marked with a lamb's blood. The blood of a lamb on the door posts satisfying God's wrath as He "passed over" foreshadowed the work of Jesus, the true Lamb of God, on the cross at Calvary.

There was great wailing and grief in Egypt as death struck everywhere at once. Pharaoh was not spared as his firstborn son was among those who died. In the middle of the night, despite his vow to never see them again, Pharaoh summoned Moses and Aaron. His will broken, he begged them to leave, all the people along with their flocks and herds and to bless him also.

The Egyptians also pleaded with the people to leave, showering them with gifts of gold and jewelry as had been prophesied (Ex. 3:22). The Israelites took up their belongings along with the unleavened bread and gifts from the Egyptians and set out to Succoth, a days journey from where Pharaoh lived in Rameses.[1] They also took the bones of Joseph (Ex. 13:19), keeping the oath to return them to the promised land (Gen. 50:25). The Israelites had lived in Egypt for 430 years.

God went before them in a pillar of cloud by day and a pillar of fire by night. He did not lead the Israelites on the well-traveled road beside the sea, but took them into the wilderness of the Sinai peninsula. Eventually they camped by the sea at a place called Baal-zephon (14:2). God warned Moses that Pharaoh would once more change his mind and come after the Israelites with the intention of enslaving them once more.

Some time (possibly several days or weeks) after the departure of the Israelites, Pharaoh felt remorse over releasing the Israelites. He prepared his chariot along with more than 600 chariots from his army. He then took his troops in pursuit of the Israelites.

As the Israelites saw Pharaoh's army approaching, panic spread throughout the camp. After having witnessed miracle after miracle in Egypt, the people showed little faith and blamed Moses for bringing them into the wilderness to die. God told Moses to stretch out his staff over the sea. The waters separated and a dry pathway was created. The pillar of cloud and the Angel of the Lord moved behind the Israelites, blocking the Egyptians from making an attack. Throughout the night the wind blew, creating dry land by separating the waters. The Israelites crossed over the dry land to the opposite side. It probably took hours for the group of at least 600,000 men and a likely greater number of women and children to cross.

After all the Israelites were across, the pillar of dust moved, allowing the Egyptians to enter the dry sea bed to continue their pursuit. During the morning watch God threw the Egyptians into confusion. Their chariots swerved and operated with great difficulty. Recognizing that God was once more thwarting their plans, they began to retreat. On the far shore, Moses stretched out his hand, and the waters came crashing back to normal at daybreak. The water swallowed the Egyptians. There were no survivors.

God clearly demonstrated, to the pagan nation of Egypt, that He alone was (and is) sovereign, that He alone is omnipotent. He showed grace, and was merciful toward Israel in accordance with His covenant with Abraham. We, too, can experience His grace and mercy through a relationship with Jesus. We can know that He will always meet our needs, even in the midst of desperate times.

AGE GROUP CONSIDERATIONS

The plagues may be strong material for some younger children. Please be sensitive to this as you teach.

How were the magicians able to replicate several of the plagues? The fact that there is power in evil cannot be denied and is not to be trifled with. However, notice that the magicians' power was limited; God's power is never limited.

SUGGESTED HYMNS

1. *Rejoice in the Lord Always*, 586, 2008 Baptist Hymnal.
2. *Let My People Go*, African-American spiritual hymn. http://my.homewithgod.com//moses.html
3. *How Deep the Father's Love for Us*, 101, 2008 Baptist Hymnal.

4. *Lead On, O King Eternal*, 659, 2008 Baptist Hymnal.

STUDENT APPLICATIONS

1. Students will know that Pharaoh, the plagues, and the deliverance of Israel are all found in the Old Testament book of Exodus.
2. Students will know that the children of Israel were enslaved by the Egyptians years after Joseph died.
3. Students will know that God raised up leaders in Moses and Aaron to free and guide the Israelites from Egypt to the Promised Land.
4. Students will know that God forewarned Moses that the Pharaoh would not listen to him.
5. Students will know that God spared the Israelites from experiencing seven of the plagues.
6. Students will know that after the plagues, the Egyptians pleaded with the Israelites to leave their land and gave them many valuables.
7. Students will know that God's creation of the Passover foreshadowed Christ's work on the cross.
8. Students will know that God made a way of escape for the Israelites from the Egyptian army by creating a dry path across the sea.
9. Students will know that they can experience God's grace and mercy through a relationship with Jesus Christ.

RESOURCES/CREDIT

1. *The Family Bible Dictionary*, 1958 ed. Avenir Books, s.v. *"Succoth."*

Moses Part 3 - Ten Commandments

BACKGROUND PASSAGES

Main Passage
Exodus 16-17   God meets physical needs
Exodus 19-20   Giving of Ten Commandments

Related Passages
Verse	Summary
Exodus 32-34	Golden Calf

Suggested Homiletic Passage
Exodus 20:2-17

MEMORY VERSE

Younger version
All Scripture is inspired by God and is profitable for teaching, for correcting, [and] for training in righteousness.

II Timothy 3:16

Older version
All Scripture is inspired by God and is profitable for teaching, for correcting, [and] for training in righteousness, so that the man of God may be complete, equipped for every good work.

II Timothy 3:16-17

LESSON OBJECTIVE

After their deliverance from the Egyptians, God led the Israelites into the wilderness . While in the wilderness, God gave the Israelites His Law, including the Ten Commandments, which would show them the way of life.

LESSON

This is the third and final lesson covering the life of Moses and the deliverance of the Israelites from the Egyptians. This lesson will focus on events in the wilderness and at Mount Sinai (including the giving of the Ten Commandments).

Exodus 16-17

The Israelites had just witnessed one of the greatest miracles ever known. Not only had God parted the sea and allowed them to escape the pursuing Egyptian army, but God had annihilated the pursuers themselves. The way for the Israelite exodus appeared to be clear, but challenges still awaited them as their faith was to be tested time and again in the wilderness. God led the Israelites to Mount Sinai where He gave them His Law. Unlike false gods who are seen but not heard, the Lord God clearly outlined His expectations for His people. Would they be faithful and obey?

At the beginning of Exodus 16, the Israelites were wandering in the wilderness of Sin on the Sinai peninsula. The entire community began to grumble against Moses and Aaron. They wished to be back in Egypt where they remembered food being plentiful. After the devastation of the plagues, Egypt was probably the last place to find food, but their lack of faith in God quickly became apparent.

The Lord said to Moses that He would "... rain bread from heaven ..." (16:4). The people were go out and gather enough bread for each day. It was a test of their faith; any bread left over would spoil the next day. On the seventh day (this was the establishment of the Sabbath) there would be no bread. So, on the sixth day, they were to gather double a day's amount, which would not spoil for two days.

The Israelites would not only have bread. God told Moses that they would eat meat before the day ended. Moses announced this to the people. As promised, God provided. A large bevy of quail descended upon the camp at twilight and in the morning "dew" appeared. As the morning dew evaporated, a flaky bread was left behind. Some gathered a little and some a lot, but there was no shortage or surplus, each had exactly what they needed. The people named the bread *manna*, meaning, "What is this?"[1] Some people did not obey; they saved their leftover manna and in the morning it was infested with maggots.

Water was another physical need. The Israelites camped at a place called Rephidim. The people had no water and once again began to grumble against Moses, and said to him, "Give us water." Moses was commanded to take some elders and go ahead of the people to a rock at Horeb. Moses struck the rock with his staff and water gushed out of the rock, providing all that the people needed.

While still at Rephidim, the Amalekites came out to battle the Israelites. Moses told Joshua to lead the men to fight with the Amalekites. Moses, Aaron and Hur went to the top of a hill overlooking the battlefield. Moses held up his hands and the battle went in favor of the Israelites. When he grew tired and lowered his hands, the Amalekites began to prevail. Aaron and Hur seated Moses and then each took one his hands and held it up until the sun went down and the battle was decided. God allowed Joshua and the Israelites to win the battle.

The Israelites would eat manna for the next 40 years, until they entered Canaan (Ex. 16:35). Their clothing would not wear out despite the rugged environment. They would be protected militarily from the people in whose lands they wandered. Despite suffering severely for their disobedience, the fullness of God's wrath never fell upon the people.[2] God continued to be faithful and provided for the Israelites.

Exodus 19-20

God led the Israelites to the foot of Mount Sinai. The traditional site of Mount Sinai is in the southern part of the Sinai peninsula. Ancient Midian (the western area of modern day Saudi Arabia) has also been suggested as the location of Mount Sinai (Horeb).

The Israelites set up camp while Moses ascended the mountain. In Exodus 19:9 God told Moses that He would appear to Moses in a dense cloud and audibly speak so that the Israelites would hear and believe Moses forever.

Preparations needed to be made before God would come down on Mt. Sinai. The Israelites observed two days of purification which included the washing of their clothes and abstaining from sexual intimacy. Barriers were erected around the mountain base to protect the people. No one nor anything was to go up on the mountain nor touch its borders or they would die.

On the third day there was thunder and lightning from a thick cloud that enveloped the mountain. Smoke went up as if from a furnace, and the mountain shook. A loud trumpet sound made all the people shudder. Then, Moses led the people to the base of the mountain. The trumpet sound grew as God spoke with Moses and summoned him to go up on the mountain.

In chapter 20, God spoke to the people. In verse 2 He introduced himself: "I am the Lord your God, who brought you out of the place of slavery." He then went on the give what we call the *Ten Commandments*. These commandments and other laws would be invaluable to the Israelites as they did not have a Bible or a heritage of theological thought to guide their living. Pagan peoples around them groped blindly to ascertain what pleased "god" while the Israelites would now know with certainty because God had revealed His expectations to them. *Note: In the Age Group Considerations at the end of this lesson is an excellent adaptation of the Ten Commandments that children can understand.*

The first commandment, to worship no other gods before God, laid the foundation for all the other commandments. Whenever a person sins, they are placing something or someone above or before God.

How did the Israelites react in the presence of God? They trembled. Keeping their distance, they pleaded with Moses to speak to them instead of God, because they feared for their lives (20:19). Moses reassured them that God was only testing them so that they would have a healthy respect for Him and not sin. Today, believers still need to show God utmost respect for He desires us to follow Him and not sin.

The Ten Commandments would not be the only laws God gave the Israelites. Part of the purpose of the Law was to show people that their own efforts to reach God are futile; people need a savior. Despite good intentions, the Israelites always fell short in keeping God's laws. God's mercy showed in that despite the apparently negative "do not ..." tone of the commandments, they were life-protecting and not the instrument of death.[3] Ultimately, Jesus would "fulfill all righteousness" (Matthew 3:15) and obey the law perfectly. He would suffer the wrath of sin on the cross and make a sure way for us to be pure in God's sight.

AGE GROUP CONSIDERATIONS

Concepts about worshipping idols and adultery are likely beyond younger children and would not be appropriate. In his book, *First Bible Stories*, Stuart Branch gives a wonderful adaptation of the Ten Commandments for young children:

1. We must worship only God.
2. Nothing is to take God's place.
3. We must not misuse God's name.
4. The seventh day of the week is for rest and prayer.
5. We must respect our mothers and fathers.
6. We must not kill.
7. Husbands and wives must keep their love for one another.
8. No stealing.
9. No lying.
10. We must not be jealous of what belongs to other people.[4]

You may supplement this lesson with the account of the golden calf found in Exodus 32-34.

SUGGESTED HYMNS/SONGS

1. *Trust and Obey*, 500, 2008 Baptist Hymnal.
2. *Thy Word*, 342, 2008 Baptist Hymnal.
3. *Holy Ground*, 71, 2008 Baptist Hymnal.
4. *Holy is the Lord*, 67, 2008 Baptist Hymnal.
5. *Holy, Holy, Holy*, 68, 2008 Baptist Hymnal.

STUDENT APPLICATIONS

1. Students will know that the wilderness wanderings of Israel and the giving of the Ten Commandments are found in the Old Testament book of Exodus.

2. Students will know that God raised up Moses and Aaron to help lead the Israelites out of Egypt and into the Promised Land.
3. Students will know that God loved and cared for the Israelites despite their grumbling and lack of faith.
4. Students will know that God provided meat for the Israelites by sending quail into their camp.
5. Students will know that God provided *manna* for the Israelites for the entire 40 years they spent in the wilderness. He also took care of their clothing.
6. Students will know that God provided water for the Israelites by causing it to come up out of a rock.
7. Students will know that God protected the Israelites by helping them defeat an Amalekite army and to see Joshua as a leader.
8. Students will know that God led the Israelites to Mount Sinai in order to worship Him.
9. Students will know that Moses was given the Ten Commandments at Mount Sinai.
10. Students will know that God spoke the Ten Commandments audibly to the Israelites.
11. Students will know that God gave the Law to show the Israelites how to live.
12. Students will know that only Jesus could fulfill the law perfectly and would suffer the wrath of sin on the cross to make a sure way for them to be pure in God's sight.

RESOURCES/CREDIT

1. *The Family Bible Dictionary*, 1958 ed. Avenir Books, s.v. "*manna*."
2. Burk Parsons, ed., "*One with His People*," Tabletalk, Ligonier Ministries (January 2008 Volume 32, Number 1): 52.
3. Hywell R. Jones, *The New Bible Commentary : Revised, ed.* Donald Guthrie (New York: Wm. B Eerdmans Co.), 131.
4. Stuart Branch, *First Bible Stories* (Bath, United Kingdom: Parragon Publishing, 2003), 29.

Martha & Mary

BACKGROUND PASSAGES

Main Passage
Luke 10:38-42	Jesus visits Mary & Martha
John 12:1-11	Mary anoints Jesus' feet

Related Passages
Matt. 26:6-13	Matthew: Mary anoints Jesus' feet
Mark 14:3-11	Mark: Mary anoints Jesus' feet
Luke 7:36-50	Luke: Mary anoints Jesus' feet
John 11:1-44	Raising of Lazarus

Suggested Homiletic Passage
John 12:1-8

MEMORY VERSE

I have called you friends, because I have made known to you everything I have heard from My Father.

John 15:15b

LESSON OBJECTIVE

Mary and Martha showed friendship toward Jesus and discovered that He is a true friend to sinners.

LESSON

Who are your friends? The word *"friend"* is typically used in a casual manner in everyday conversation. Often, we refer to coworkers, neighbors and even acquaintances (whom we actually don't know very well) as friends. True friendships are rare in life. Despite His full-time ministry, Jesus developed meaningful friendships not only with the disciples, but with three siblings: Mary, Martha and Lazarus. We can learn much about how God views friendship through Jesus' relationships with His friends.

Luke 10:38-42

Only a few people, in the gospels, are recorded as having more than one interaction with Jesus. Mary and Martha (and their brother Lazarus) are mentioned several times in the gospels.

The first recorded episode concerning Martha and Mary is found in the gospel of Luke. Jesus and the disciples were traveling. They met Martha, who invited Jesus into her home (v.38). Also present was Mary, her sister, who like, Martha wanted to be in the presence of Jesus.

The two sisters had different ways to show their concern and care for Jesus: Mary sat at Jesus' feet, listening to every word He said, while Martha set about serving by doing "many tasks" (v.40). Martha's tasks were likely well-intended, but they proved to be a distraction and a source of worry for Martha. Perhaps feeling frustrated or overwhelmed, she asked Jesus, "Lord, don't you care that my sister has left me to serve alone? So tell her to give me a hand." (v.40).

In verse 41 Jesus responded by saying, "Martha, Martha, you are worried about many things, but one thing is necessary. Mary has made the right choice, and it will not be taken away from her." What was the "right choice" that Mary had made? It was spending time with her new friend. Chores need to be done, but are not as important as our relationships with others. Mary was aware that her time with Jesus was limited (as it is in all relationships) and sought to learn and share as much as she could. The chores could wait for a time.

The passage ends abruptly after Jesus' response. We do not know how Martha then responded. What do you think? Perhaps Martha set aside her chores and joined Mary in fellowship with Jesus. Perhaps she again asked Mary to help her with the dishes ... later. Ask the children how they would have responded.

Children may not consciously realize it, but they are acutely aware of the principle of time in friendships. The actual activity they do is often immaterial if they are doing it with someone they like or from whom they desire attention. Jesus wants believers to spend time with Him through prayer and studying His Word.

Lazarus is not mentioned in this passage; perhaps he was present in Martha's house, or perhaps he lived somewhere else or was traveling. We do not know.

John 12:1-11

The time of Jesus' crucifixion was drawing near. It was the evening before Jesus would make His triumphal entry into Jerusalem. He was sharing a dinner with His disciples, Mary, Martha and Lazarus at the home of Simon the Leper in Bethany. Lazarus had recently been raised from the dead. The friends were undoubtedly sharing an intimate and meaningful time together.

Martha was serving them as they reclined at the table. People of Jesus' time would typically lie down and eat off a short raised area or table. Unlike today, where feet are hidden under a table, a guest's feet would be more accessible. During the gathering, Mary did something that was most unexpected; something that showed how much she truly cared for her friend, Jesus. Mary took a pound of fragrant *nard* (an expensive oil or perfume) and anointed Jesus' feet with it. Mary then showed even greater love by using her own hair to wipe the oil off of His feet as the fragrance filled the house.

Mary's actions may have seemed strange, but the oil itself is what initially got the attention of one of the disciples, Judas Iscariot. He was well aware that the oil was very rare and of great value. He suggested that a more appropriate action would have been to sell the oil and estimated that it would have sold for 300 *denarii*. A *denarius* was generally equivalent to a day's wages.

His suggestion might appear sensible, but he had an ulterior motive. Judas was in charge of the money bag and essentially served as treasurer for Jesus and the disciples. Judas was dishonest and often stole from the money bag. He was not expressing concern for the poor, just remorse for the loss of ill-gotten gain he might have realized from the sale of the oil.

Jesus responded, "Leave her alone; she has kept it for the day of My burial. For you always have the poor with you, but you do not always have Me." (v.7). Mary was showing her love for Jesus through her great sacrifice and humility. The sacrifice came from giving up the valuable oil and the humility from using her hair to clean Jesus' feet.

Jesus had referred to His impending death when He said, "...she has kept it for the day of My burial." Did Mary know Jesus was about to die? Despite Jesus' many references to the cross, even the disciples did not comprehend what was about to happen. Perhaps Mary was more attuned to the events that were unfolding? We do not know, but the oil used by Mary was typically used for burial. Perhaps this was another affirmation of God's plan.

Developing friendships takes effort. Our lives often intersect with the lives of many others. Building a friendship takes time and sacrifice. Building a Godly friendship should be slightly easier for Christians, since they have the common foundation of Christ. We can never really know what it is to be a true friend until we understand and accept what Jesus did for us. His perfect model of sacrifice and love are examples for us. While Mary was referred to as having lived a "sinful life" (Luke 7:37), she sacrificed greatly to bless her friend, Jesus. Even as sinners, we can learn to be a true friend.

AGE GROUP CONSIDERATIONS

The raising of Lazarus is covered in detail in another lesson but may be used as supplemental material.

Also, the account of Mary anointing Jesus' feet appears in all four gospels. It would be worth the effort to study all four passages. See "Related Passages."

SUGGESTED HYMNS/SONGS

1. *What a Friend We Have in Jesus*, 154, 2008 Baptist Hymnal.
2. *Jesus! What a Friend for Sinners*, 156, 2008 Baptist Hymnal.
3. *No, Not One*, 152, 2008 Baptist Hymnal.
4. *Jesus Loves Me*, 652, 2008 Baptist Hymnal.

Martha & Mary

STUDENT APPLICATIONS

1. Students will know that Mary, Martha and their brother Lazarus are mentioned in all four of the Gospels.
2. Students will know that Jesus valued and built friendships.
3. Students will know that sacrificial giving is an act of worship to God.
4. Students will know that Mary, Martha and Lazarus lived in the small town of Bethany.
5. Students will know that Mary did well by choosing to spend time with Jesus.
6. Students will know that God desires for them to spend time with Him through prayer and the study of His Word.
7. Students will know that Jesus' disciple, Judas Iscariot, stole from the money bag.
8. Students will know that true friendships are rare and require effort to maintain.
9. Students will know that it is important to carefully choose Godly Christian friends and to seek to build Godly relationships.

The Lost Son

BACKGROUND PASSAGES

Main Passage
Luke 15:11-32   The Lost Son

Related Passages
Luke 15:1-7   Parable of lost sheep
Luke 15:8-10   Parable of lost coin

Suggested Homiletic Passage
Luke 11:17-24

MEMORY VERSE

Look at how great a love the Father has given us, that we should be called God's children. And we are!
I John 3:1a

LESSON OBJECTIVE

Just as the father, in the parable, extended grace to his lost son, God will extend His grace to any person who repents of his/her sins and follow Jesus.

LESSON

Have you ever wondered why Jesus did what He did? What was His purpose in taking human form and dwelling among us? While many have missed the point, the reason is straightforward: Jesus came to seek and to save the lost. One day the Pharisees and scribes complained about Jesus spending time with "sinners." Jesus took the opportunity and told three parables which explained His purpose. We will study the final of the three parables, the Parable of the Lost Son.

Have you ever done something that you really regretted? Have you ever had a broken relationship that you thought could not possibly be restored? The young man in the Parable of the Lost Son found himself in just such a situation. He also found the depth of his father's love for him.

Luke 15:11-32

The parable begins in Luke 15:11. A man had two sons. The younger son approached his father and asked for his share of the inheritance. He was unwilling to wait until after his father's death. Such a bold request would be audacious at any time or in most any culture in history. No explanation is given, but the father granted the son's request and gave him his share of the inheritance. The older son also received his portion (a larger one) at the same time.

The son then severed his family ties (v.13) as he packed, and left for a foreign land. There, he squandered his money by living an extravagant lifestyle. After the money ran out, things were bad and then got worse as a famine fell upon the land, "... he had nothing." (v.14).

The dire circumstances forced the young son to go work in the fields tending pigs for a local farmer. His poverty increased until he longed to eat what he was feeding to the pigs.

At this point in the parable, the Pharisees likely thought the son was getting exactly what he deserved for his brash and rebellious behavior. While we may not envy the son, most modern people still think of farm work as honest, good work. To the scribes and Pharisees listening to Jesus, they would have seen the son as having to seek out the lifestyle of a Gentile. Compounding their disdain was the fact that pigs were considered to be spiritually unclean animals. To reach a point where one would be compelled to care for pigs would have been a great humiliation to an Israelite.

In verse 17 the son reasons that even his father's slaves (*servants* in most translations) were treated better than what he was experiencing. He resolved to return and beg for a "job" as a slave to his father.

He returned home, but as he neared his father's place, his father saw him first. Filled with compassion, the father ran to his son, whom he embraced and kissed. This was not the reception the son expected. The father's joy is so complete that the son never gets around to his plan to beg a position as a slave. What a burden is lifted when one knows that they have been forgiven.

While this is just a parable, it is easy to imagine that a person in the son's situation would be dressed in little more than tatters. The father called for a fine robe, sandals, and a ring to be put on his son. Next he announced that they would celebrate his return with a lavish party, including the slaughter of a prized calf for a great feast.

It is at this point where Jesus' purpose is made clear in the parable. Why the grand celebration? "...because this son of mine was dead and is alive again; he was lost and is found!" (v.24). Like the father in the parable, Jesus takes great pleasure when a sinner returns to Him.

As the celebration started, the older son was out working in the fields. When he returned to the house, he noticed the commotion caused by the celebration and, summoning a servant, learned that the party was celebrating the return of the lost son. Was the man happy to know his brother was back home safe and sound? No, he became so angry that he refused to go in to the party.

The father left the party to talk to the older brother. He pleaded for his son to join the celebration. The older son complained to his father that he had "...been slaving many years for [him]..." He asks why he was never given a young goat to celebrate with friends. He then accused his brother of having wasted all his money on prostitutes. While that may have been true, he was missing the point his father was celebrating: a lost son restored and wiser.

Instead of getting angry or chastising his son, the father responded graciously, "Son, you are always with me, and everything I have is yours. But we had to celebrate and rejoice, because this brother of yours was dead and is alive again; he was lost and is found." (v.31-32). Compared to the view of fathers in Roman times as being authoritarian and controlling, the father in the parable is remarkably caring and compassionate.[1]

The parable ends at this point, but even short parables can contain many nuances of truth. By taking a closer look at this parable, it is easy to wonder who is really the lost son. Was it the son who ran away or the one with the ungrateful attitude? Even though the second had continued to live under his father's roof, in spirit he had been just as far away as the younger son.[2] Jesus was comparing the older brother with the Pharisees. They said and did the right things, but their hearts were not in tune with the father's. While most people may identify with the younger son, there is just as much to learn from the older son.

There is nothing on earth as precious as a human soul. Humans were created for fellowship with God the Father. Sin breaks that fellowship, but Jesus came to seek and save the lost. Just as the father in the parable celebrated the return of his son, Jesus takes great joy and welcomes anyone "home" who repents and returns to him.

AGE GROUP CONSIDERATIONS

The Parable of the Lost Son was the third of three parables told by Jesus to the same audience. The other two, the Parables of the Lost Sheep and the Lost Coin, are found at the beginning of Luke 15. These may be studied and used to supplement the lesson.

SUGGESTED HYMNS/SONGS

1. *Softly and Tenderly*, 414, 2008 Baptist Hymnal.
2. *Lord, I'm Coming Home*, 634, 2008 Baptist Hymnal.
3. *I Have Decided to Follow Jesus*, 434, 2008 Baptist Hymnal.
4. *What a Friend We Have in Jesus*, 154, 2008 Baptist Hymnal.

STUDENT APPLICATIONS

1. Students will know that the parable of the *Lost Son* is found in the New Testament book of Luke.
2. Students will know that the younger son took his inheritance and foolishly spent all the money on lavish living.
3. Students will know that God, like the father in the parable, loves them despite any wrongdoing.
4. Students will know that God, like the father in the parable, will accept them when they ask for forgiveness.
5. Students will know that the older brother displayed a poor attitude over the treatment shown towards the younger brother by their father.
6. Students will know that both sons were in need of their father's forgiveness.
7. Students will know that the reason Jesus came to earth was to seek and save lost people.

RESOURCES/CREDIT

1. Joel B. Green, *The Gospel of Luke: The New International Commentary on the New Testament*, ed. Gordon D. Fee (Grand Rapids: William B. Eerdmans Publishing Co., 1997), 579.
2. Laurance E. Porter, *The International Bible Commentary, Revised Edition*, F. F. Bruce, ed. (Grand Rapids, Michigan: Zondervan Publishing House, 1979), 1214.

Elijah and the Widow

BACKGROUND PASSAGES

Main Passage
I Kings 17   Elijah and the Widow

Related Passages
James 1:27   Help widows and orphans
I Kings 16:29-34   Ahab's background

Suggested Homiletic Passage
I Kings 17:8-16

MEMORY VERSE

A father of the fatherless and a champion of widows is God in His holy dwelling.

Psalm 68:5

LESSON OBJECTIVE

God showed His concern for the poor by sending Elijah to a widow and her son. Through Elijah, God would meet their basic needs in a time of distress. God cares for and loves children who have experienced tragedies such as poverty, the loss of a parent, or a grave illness.

LESSON

God showed mercy by meeting the needs of the prophet Elijah, a widow, and her son. Children who have lost a close loved one and endured subsequent hardship can know that God always loves them and will meet their needs.

The northern kingdom of Israel was under the rule of a tyrant. For 22 years King Ahab not only forsook worshipping the Lord, but led the nation to worship the false gods Baal and Asherah. Among his evil acts were the construction of a temple for Baal and his marriage to a pagan Sidonian princess, Jezebel.

I Kings 17

At the beginning of I Kings 17, God sent a messenger, the prophet Elijah, to speak to Ahab. Elijah delivered bad news for the nation: because of Ahab's evil acts, Israel would suffer a prolonged drought. Rain would not fall until Elijah said so (he would be told by God). It was to be over two years before it would rain again in Samaria.

God led Elijah into the wilderness to a wadi (a seasonal stream) near the Jordan river (v.5). He stayed there for an unknown period of time. God took care of Elijah by having ravens bring him meat and bread. Because of the lack of rain, the brook (Clarith) eventually dried up.

God then directed Elijah to go to Zarephath which, at that time, was under the control of the Sidonians (Jezebel's people). There Elijah was to meet a widow. Elijah obeyed God and made his way to Zarephath.

The dire effect of the drought was evident when Elijah met the widow near the city gate. She was gathering wood when Elijah asked her for a cup of water. As she went to get it, he also asked her for a piece of bread. She responded to his request, "As the Lord your God lives, I don't have anything baked — only a handful of flour in the jar and a bit of oil in the jug. Just now, I am gathering a couple of sticks in order to go prepare it for myself and my son so we can eat it and die."

Elijah asked the woman to step out in faith. He asked her to prepare some bread for him first and then make some for herself and her son. Elijah told her God had promised that the flour jar would not become empty nor the oil jug run dry until the famine had ended. The widow obeyed and found that what Elijah said came true. God kept His word, and the household had food for many days. Imagine the joy and hope that came into her life that day on account of God's provision.

Elijah stayed with the widow and her son for a time. One day the son became ill. The illness became "very severe until no breath remained in him." (v.17). The widow blamed Elijah for bringing such a tragedy on her. Most likely this harsh response came out of anguish, but perhaps the woman thought it was the result of past sin, "Man of God, what do we have in common? Have you come to remind me of my guilt and to kill my son?" (v. 18) Elijah apparently did not rebuke her but merely asked her to give him her son.

Elijah carried the boy's body to the upper room where he was staying and placed him on his own bed. Just as people today often ask "why?" when faced with tragedy, Elijah asked a similar question. He cried out to God asking, "My Lord God, have You also brought tragedy on the widow I am staying with by killing her son?" (v.20). He then stretched himself out over the boy's body three times and called to God that He might allow the child's life to return.

God honored the prayer and allowed the boy to come back to life. Elijah took the boy downstairs and gave him back to his mother. Even with the daily reminder of provision, the widow's faith was greatly strengthened as she exclaimed, "Now I know you are a man of God and the Lord's word in your mouth is the truth." (v.24).

Later Elijah left to confront Ahab and his pagan priests. Shortly thereafter, God once again showed His omnipotence and the drought ended. In the middle of a catastrophe brought about by the actions of evil King Ahab, God still met the needs of the destitute. Believers can worship God with acts of ministry to children, widows, and others who have experienced tragedy. Believers can also be certain that God loves them and will care for them no matter what tragedy or distress they may experience. God desires that they obey, seek, and trust Him just as Elijah did.

AGE GROUP CONSIDERATIONS

Children (and adults) who have faced tragedy are often uncertain how to "approach" God. A typical response is with an anger that accuses God of being the cause of an injustice. While it is important to always trust that God is doing what is best, human feelings are genuine and God-given. God knows every detail of what we are thinking and feeling and will allow us to share them with Him (just like Elijah did). When we are transparent with God, it becomes much easier for us to accept His guidance and provisions.

God still works miracles today. Often the news is not as good as it was for the widow and her son. At these times it is okay to ask "Why did You allow this to happen, God?" God can handle our questions and He understands them. Just as was the case with the widow and Elijah, suffering and loss can create a great desire to know and understand the purpose beyond the tragedy. The truth is we will rarely be given true insight into why a tragedy occurred. We must learn to trust even when we cannot understand.

What is dangerous is when a sufferer becomes resentful and blames God for inflicting them with an injustice. God is the only One Who can truly identify with us in times of grief as He gave up His Son to die cruelly upon the cross. We can have the faith and hope that God's will was (and will be) accomplished regardless of what we face in life. We live in a sin-infested world wrecked with peril. The real miracle is that we can have eternal life through a personal relationship with Jesus. All the troubles of this life pale in comparison to knowing Him (Jesus).

SUGGESTED HYMNS/SONGS

1. *Have Faith in God*, 508, 2008 Baptist Hymnal.
2. *It is Well with My Soul*, 447, 2008 Baptist Hymnal.
3. *Victory in Jesus*, 499, 2008 Baptist Hymnal.
4. *I'll Fly Away*, 601, 2008 Baptist Hymnal.
5. *On Jordan's Stormy Banks*, 611, 2008 Baptist Hymnal.

Elijah and the Widow

STUDENT APPLICATIONS

1. Students will know that the story of Elijah and the widow is found in the Old Testament book of I Kings.
2. Students will know that Elijah was a prophet.
3. Students will know that prophets are messengers chosen by God to proclaim His word.
4. Students will know that Israel suffered a drought as a result of King Ahab's unfaithfulness to God.
5. Students will know that God used birds to bring food to Elijah.
6. Students will know that God takes special care of widows, orphans and those who are in need.
7. Students will know that God took care of the widow of Zarephath, and her son, by not allowing their flour jar and oil jug to run out during the long drought.
8. Students will know that God raised the widow of Zarephath's son back to life after he died.
9. Students will know that it pleases God when we minister to widows, orphans and others who have unmet needs.

Christmas - Joseph

BACKGROUND PASSAGES

Main Passage

Verse	Summary
Matthew 1:18-25	Joseph's dream
Matthew 2:13-23	Joseph cares for his family

Related Passages

Verse	Summary
Luke 2:1-22	The Nativity
Luke 2:39-50	Jesus as a boy
Isaiah 7:14	Jesus' birth foretold

Suggested Homiletic Passage

Matthew 1:18-23

MEMORY VERSE

Younger version

She will give birth to a son, and you are to name Him Jesus...

Matthew 1:21a

Older version

She will give birth to a son, and you are to name Him Jesus, because He will save His people from their sins.

Matthew 1:21

LESSON OBJECTIVE

Joseph's life changed when an angel announced to him that his betrothed was to be the mother of the Messiah. Joseph obeyed God and was faithful to care for Mary and Jesus.

LESSON

As Christmas approaches, Christians once again turn their focus toward the birth of Jesus. This unit will focus on Jesus' birth from Joseph's perspective. Under difficult circumstances, Joseph was faithful to do what God requested of him. As a result, he was blessed to have an important role in God's redemptive plan through Jesus.

Matthew 1:18-25

Weddings are a time for celebration of life and hope as a couple looks toward their future together. Joseph probably had feelings of joy and anticipation as he looked forward to his marriage with Mary. A Jewish marriage was different from a modern wedding in that there was a betrothal period, similar to an engagement, in which the couple still lived apart. The difference was that it was binding and could not be legally broken without a divorce. It was during Mary and Joseph's betrothal and before the wedding Joseph's joy turned to concern and disappointment: He learned that Mary was pregnant.

Joseph knew the child was not his. Since the marriage was not final and there had been no physical intimacy, Joseph naturally assumed that Mary had been unfaithful. No conversations between Mary and Joseph during this period are recorded. Mary knew the child was from God, but even if she spoke the truth to Joseph he would have, understandably, had difficulty believing it.

In verse 19 Joseph decided to divorce Mary. Pregnancy outside of marriage was punishable by death in Joseph's day, death by stoning. Joseph is referred to as "righteous" for the way he dealt with Mary. He chose not to have Mary stoned or even put up for public criticism and humiliation. He would divorce her secretly.

While considering these things, Joseph had a dream. An angel appeared and assured Joseph that Mary had not been unfaithful and that the child she was carrying had been conceived by the Holy Spirit (v.20). Moreover, the Angel commanded Joseph to name the child Jesus and revealed that He would save His people from their sins. Jesus means "the Lord saves." Joseph's wife-to-be Mary was carrying the long-awaited Messiah!

Hundreds of years before, the prophet Isaiah had spoken about Jesus' birth, and prophesied that He would be born of a virgin and that He would be named *Immanuel*. Had not the angel

Christmas - Joseph

told Joseph to name the child Jesus? *Immanuel* means "God with us." It is one of many titles for Jesus. It tells us that God became fully man (while still fully God) through the person of Jesus and dwelt among humans.

After Joseph awoke, he obeyed. He took Mary as his wife and cared for her. When Mary gave birth to her son, Joseph named him Jesus.

Matthew 2:13-23

Joseph received a second dream from an angel. This dream occurred shortly after the visit from the wise men. While the first dream had been reassuring and joyful, this dream was a warning of imminent danger. Joseph was commanded to get up immediately and take Mary and Jesus to Egypt. They were to stay there until they were told to return. The reason? King Herod was seeking Jesus to destroy Him. He feared that Jesus might try to become king in his place.

Interestingly, in several ways Joseph's life paralleled that of Joseph, the Old Testament patriarch. Both Josephs were presented as examples of righteousness. Both received dreams from God. Both of their families were providentially saved by spending time in Egypt.

Joseph did not hesitate. During the night he immediately took Jesus and fled for Egypt (v.14). Herod's threat became reality as he slaughtered all the male children (age 2 and under) in Bethlehem and its surrounding areas (v.16-18). During this time Jesus was safe in (or on his way to) Egypt.

After a period of time in Egypt, Joseph had a third dream. An angel told him to take his family back to Israel. They would be safe because Herod had died.

Joseph once again was faithful to obey. He took Mary and Jesus and returned to Israel. It is likely that he intended to move back to Bethlehem. He changed his plans upon learning that Archelaus, Herod's son, was now ruling over the region of Judea. Bethlehem was only several miles from Jerusalem.

Even with the angel's assurance, living so close to the son of Herod would have been uncomfortable. Especially as Archelaus was a violent ruler, as evi-denced early in his reign when he slaughtered 3000 influential people.[1]

It is at this point that more prophecies were fulfilled. One was the "exodus" out of Egypt: "Out of Egypt I called my son." (v.15). Joseph moved his family to Nazareth in the region of Galilee. Galilee was north of Judea. Upon Herod's death, Israel was divided into three parts; Archelaus did not rule Galilee. Sandwiched between the two regions was Samaria. Jews did not like to pass through Samaria, so it served as a buffer zone of safety. Another prophecy was fulfilled in that Jesus would be known as a "Nazarene."

Joseph is mentioned only one more time in the Bible (Luke 2:41-50) . Jesus was twelve and Joseph took his family to Jerusalem to observe the Passover.

When Jesus began his ministry two decades later Joseph is never again mentioned. It is almost certain that he had passed away during that time. We are left to speculate what it must have been like for Joseph to see the Messiah grow up.

Joseph could have never imagined how he would have a role in God's great plan for redemption. We may have no idea what God will do in our lives or in the lives of our children. We have God's Word and the command to raise our children in the fear and respect of God. This Christmas our children can learn from the example of Joseph — to be a faithful, responsible Christian and, someday, a caring and responsible parent.

The Nativity: Luke 2:1-22

It would not seem to be Christmas without a look at the nativity. This lesson focuses on Joseph, but feel free to precede the narrative of the wise men with what actually happened at Jesus' birth. Two of the other lessons, *Christmas - The Messiah Prophesied* and *Christmas - Shepherds* cover the events surrounding the nativity.

Age Group Considerations

The slaughter of the Bethlehem infants is probably too graphic for the youngest children. It is enough to say that a king was jealous of Jesus and wanted to hurt Him.

SUGGESTED HYMNS/SONGS

1. *O Little Town of Bethlehem*, 196, 2008 Baptist Hymnal.
2. *Angels, from the Realms of Glory*, 179, 2008 Baptist Hymnal.
3. *O Come, O Come, Emmanuel*, 175, 2008 Baptist Hymnal.

STUDENT APPLICATIONS

1. Students will know that Joseph's story is found in the New Testament book of Matthew.
2. Students will know Joseph was betrothed to Mary.
3. Students will know that betrothal was more binding than an engagement.
4. Students will know that Joseph wanted to divorce Mary after he found out she was expecting a child.
5. Students will know that an angel or angels appeared to Joseph three different times via dreams.
6. Students will know that an angel told Joseph that the child had been conceived by the Holy Spirit and that it was okay to marry her.
7. Students will know that an angel told Joseph that Jesus would save His people from their sins.
8. Students will know that the birth of Jesus fulfilled many prophecies (many more than were mentioned in this lesson).
9. Students will know that Joseph obeyed and took his family to Egypt.
10. Students will know that King Herod sought to harm (kill) Jesus.
11. Students will know that, while in Egypt, Joseph received the third message from an angel.
12. Students will know that Joseph obeyed and left Egypt with his family.
13. Students will know that Joseph settled his family in the town of Nazareth in the region of Galilee.

RESOURCES/CREDIT

1. *Life Application Bible.* (Grand Rapids, Michigan: Zondervan Publishing House, 1991), 1644.

David & Goliath

BACKGROUND PASSAGES

Main Passage
I Samuel 17   David and Goliath

Suggested Homiletic Passage
I Samuel 17:45-52

MEMORY VERSE

Younger version
And this whole assembly will know that it is not by sword or by spear that the Lord saves, for the battle is the Lord's.

I Samuel 17:47a

Older version
And this whole assembly will know that it is not by sword or by spear that the Lord saves, for the battle is the Lord's. He will hand you over to us.

I Samuel 17:47a

LESSON OBJECTIVE

Despite being only a youth, David had enough faith that he was willing to face the giant who taunted God's chosen people, the Israelites. Just as God equipped David to defeat the giant, He gives believers everything they need to face giant-sized challenges.

LESSON

Life is full of challenges. Some are small, but some are daunting and appear to be impossible. The nation of Israel faced such a challenge. Led by a hesitant king, it appeared that Israel would soon be overrun by their enemy, the Philistines. Little did they know that God would use a mere youth, David, to turn the war in their favor.

I Samuel 17

The Israelite army, under King Saul, had gathered for battle against a troublesome foe, the Philistines. The place was the Valley of Elah (I Sam 17).

Each day, for forty days, the armies had lined up on opposite hills facing one another. A stream wandered through the valley between them. Instead of battle, the Philistines sent out their champion to challenge the Israelites. They were to send a champion of their own to fight him one-on-one. The battle would be decided by this contest of individuals.

The Philistine champion, Goliath, was truly a giant of a man. Standing nine feet, nine inches tall and wearing 125 pounds of armor (v.4-5), no Israelite was willing to step forward and face him (v.11).

Goliath wore bronze scale armor and bronze shin guards. He carried a bronze sword and a spear with a head that weighed fifteen pounds. Imagine trying to throw a spear with a head that weighed more than most bowling balls! In addition a shield bearer propped a shield in front of Goliath. According to one scholar, a shield bearer of that era carried a shield (approximately five feet tall) that he set on the ground before his warrior, protecting his entire body and providing a mobile defensive wall.[1] The citizen soldiers of the Israelites likely had little if anything in the way of armor.

As the Israelites cowered before the Philistines, a young man named David arrived in their camp. David was the youngest of the eight sons of Jesse and the great-grandson of Ruth and Boaz. David's three oldest brothers were serving in Saul's army. Jesse had sent David with roasted grain, bread and cheese to give to his brothers and the army (v.17). The cheese might have been a Middle Eastern cheese made into salty small cakes that were soft when first made but then became hard and dry.[2]

Jesse, as a concerned parent, also hoped to hear camp news as to how the war was going. He specifically asked David to bring back "a confirmation" of the brothers (v.18). The confirmation (or "*pledge*" as found in some translations) might have involved the brothers returning a token such as a ring or a lock of hair.[3]

In verse 20 David arrived just as the two armies formed up lines. Undeterred by the possibility of hostilities, David ran to the line and asked his brothers how they were. As they talked, Goliath strode out and issued his challenge. Greatly intimidated, the Israelite line retreated (v.24).

David & Goliath

David overheard a conversation between several of the Israelites discussing the situation. He asked what the King would do for the man who would kill Goliath. He learned that the king was offering a generous monetary reward and the hand of his daughter in marriage to such a warrior. David defiantly stated, "Just who is this uncircumcised Philistine that he should defy the armies of the living God?" (v.26).

David's oldest brother, Eliab, listened as David talked. He became angry with David and accused him of coming only to see the battle. He insulted David by asking, "Who did you leave those few sheep with in the wilderness?" (v.28) as if David's responsibility as a shepherd was unimportant. David was not discouraged.

Word of David's defiance reached king Saul, and he asked that David be brought before him. David told Saul that he was willing to battle Goliath. Saul refused David, saying that he was only a youth and that Goliath (besides being large and well-armed) was a seasoned warrior. David told Saul that he was not totally inexperienced in battle and that he had a weapon greater than anything man could wield. By the strength of the Lord God, David had battled lions and bears who attempted to attack the sheep under his care and had been victorious. David was convinced that God would save him from the Philistine just as He had from the wild animals (v.34-7). Saul then agreed to let David fight.

Saul, as God's anointed king and warrior, should have accepted Goliath's challenge himself and faced Goliath the first day he offered to fight. Saul was something of a giant himself, as he was a head taller than all the other Israelites (I Samuel 9:2). Instead, Saul had neglected his rightful place along with his army and was now going to send a youth to do what he should have done long before. He offered his personal armor to David, but David was not used to armor and it restricted his movement. Since Saul was a tall man, the armor was most likely too large for anyone else. David declined the use of the armor.

David took only his staff and sling. He stopped in a small wadi (a seasonally dry stream) and collected five smooth stones. He then moved out from the Israelite line to meet the giant. Goliath approached with his shield bearer before him. He was not impressed with David, especially as he noticed that David was not carrying a sword but a staff. "Am I a dog that you come against me with sticks?" the giant bellowed (v.43). Goliath probably no longer expected a battle in the normal sense. He would make a point by quickly striking David down like a defenseless animal.

David also did not expect a battle in the normal sense. "You come against me with a dagger, spear and sword, but I come against you in the name of the Lord of Hosts, the God of Israel's army." (v.45). David expected the Lord to fight the battle for him. Goliath would be handed over to David.

The Philistine moved toward David. David ran toward the Philistine. David reached in his bag and pulled out one of the stones. His sling was not like the slingshots of today. It was a small pouch of leather just big enough to hold a stone. Two strings were attached to the pouch. The bearer would hold the ends of the two strings and swing the pouch over his head. He would then release one of the strings, allowing the stone to fly out of the pouch. David loaded the first stone, slinging, he let the stone fly. It found its mark, as it "sank" into Goliath's forehead.

The giant fell face forward to the ground. David ran to the giant, drew his sword, and cut off his head. At this most unexpected turn of events, the horrified Philistines began to run away. The battle had indeed been decided by the Lord.

The men of Judah and Israel gave a mighty shout and charged the enemy. They routed the Philistines throughout the valley and all the way to Ekron, one of the five major Philistine cities. The men then returned and plundered the Philistine camp. David kept Goliath's weapons as his personal souvenirs.

According to I Samuel 16 David had already been in the presence of Saul as a harpist and armor-bearer. So it seems odd that Saul inquired of his commander

David & Goliath

of the army, Abner, "Find out whose son this young man is." One scholar points out that Saul wasn't so much asking about David as he was about his family.[4] This would only make sense as the young man would be marrying his daughter. It is also possible that Saul's mental state had already deteriorated to a point where he had not recognized David.[5] David, still clutching the giant's head, came before Saul. He told Saul that he was the son of Jesse of Bethlehem.

David remained in Saul's house. He married Saul's daughter Michal and became the best friend of Saul's son, Jonathan. David would experience dark times before he became king, but on that day he had already taught the nation that the battle was the Lord's. When we trust in Him and walk in His ways, God will go ahead of us and fight our battles. Our children should know that God is trustworthy and powerful enough to lead and protect them.

AGE GROUP CONSIDERATIONS

In I Samuel 17:26 David refers to Goliath as an "uncircumcised Philistine." Circumcision was a practice unique to Israelites at the time. It distinguished them from their pagan neighbors. For children, it is probably best to use a word such as "unclean" or "foreign" in referencing this verse.

SUGGESTED HYMNS/SONGS

1. *Onward, Christian Soldiers*, 660, 2008 Baptist Hymnal.
2. *Stand Up, Stand Up for Jesus*, 665, 2008 Baptist Hymnal.
3. *He Leadeth Me! O Blessed Thought*, 81, 2008 Baptist Hymnal.

STUDENT APPLICATIONS

1. Students will know that the story of David and Goliath is found in the Old Testament book of I Samuel.
2. Students will know that the Israelite and Philistine armies had gathered for battle.
3. Students will know that the Israelites were intimidated by the Philistines because of their giant, Goliath.
4. Students will know that Goliath daily challenged the Israelites over the course if 40 days to send out a man to battle him one-on-one. .
5. Students will know that no soldier of the Israelite army accepted the challenge until David.
6. Students will know that David was a youth and a shepherd.
7. Students will know that Jesse, David's father, sent him to the Israelite camp with goods requesting he report back about his brothers.
8. Students will know that David offered to face Goliath.
9. Students will know that King Saul, as leader of Israel, should have faced the giant but refused.
10. Students will know that David went before Goliath in the power of the Lord.
11. Students will know that David collected five smooth stones before fighting Goliath.
12. Students will know that David slew Goliath by slinging a single stone that embedded itself in Goliath's forehead.
13. Students will know that the Israelite army pursued and routed the Philistines after Goliath's death.
14. Students will know that David married King Saul's daughter, Michal.

RESOURCES/CREDIT

1. James M. Freeman, *Manners & Customs of the Bible* (New Kensington: Whitaker House, 1996), 135-6.
2. *Ibid.*, 136.
3. *Ibid.*
4. Laurance E. Porter, *The International Bible Commentary, Revised Edition*, F.F. Bruce, ed. (Grand Rapids, Michigan: Zondervan Publishing House, 1979), 367.
5. R.C. Sproul, ed. *The Reformation Study Bible*. (Orlando, Florida: Ligonier Ministries, 2005), 405.

Jesus is Baptized

BACKGROUND PASSAGES

Main Passage
Matthew 3:1-17   John's preaching and Jesus' baptism

Related Passages
Mark 1:1-11   John the Baptist and Jesus' baptism

Luke 3:1-22   John the Baptist and Jesus' baptism

John 1:19-42   John's account of John the Baptist

Suggested Homiletic Passage
Matthew 1:11-17

MEMORY VERSE

Younger version
Having been buried with Him in baptism, you were also raised with Him through faith...

Colossians 2:12a

Older version
Having been buried with Him in baptism, you were also raised with Him through faith in the working of God, who raised Him from the dead.

Colossians 2:12

LESSON OBJECTIVE

John was faithful to help Jesus carry out the Father's will by preparing the people for Jesus' message. Jesus set an example for us through His willingness to be baptized.

LESSON

Before Jesus began His public ministry, God was preparing hearts to receive His message. John the Baptist played an important role in preparing Israel for the unveiling of the Messiah by preaching a message of repentance and consecration.

John the Baptist is one of the most unforgettable persons in the Bible. He was the last Old Testament prophet, even though we read of him in the New Testament. Even the first encounter with John in Luke 1:44 is quite memorable. While still in his mother Elizabeth's womb, he "leaped for joy" when an expecting Mary came for a visit. John is talked about in all four gospels.

Matthew 3:1-17

John the Baptist had a ministry that resembles nothing today. He did not have a modern sanctuary with a sound system in which to deliver his message. He preached in a highly unusual place. The Wilderness of Judea was his sanctuary.

His God-given message of repentance bespoke the arrival of the kingdom of heaven and the appearance of the Messiah. Jesus was to reign in the hearts of His believers. John then, was the fulfillment of the prophecy from Isaiah 40:3; he was the "voice of one crying out in the wilderness."

What probably makes John most memorable is the description of his appearance. John wore a camel-hair garment and a leather belt. Even more curious was his diet, "locusts and wild honey." Freeman says that grasshoppers were a food used only by the poor, dried and often eaten with butter or honey, as they were considered an inferior form of food.[1]

In addition to his unusual appearance, John was memorable because he was the first prophet sent by God in 400 years. During the intertestamental period, there were no prophets. He was also the last Old Testament prophet as he ministered before the new covenant was initiated with Christ's death and resurrection. His message was a stark contrast to the scripted lifestyle taught by the Jewish leaders. It is no wonder that the crowds flocked to hear him preach and to be baptized (v.5).

John attracted the attention of the religious leaders. He did not mince his words and even called them a "brood of vipers!" (v.7). The leaders rejected John and proclaimed that they placed their faith in being children of Abraham (v.9). Salvation is not to be found through genealogy, but only through repentance and faith in Jesus. Verse 10 reminds believers that true repentance will be followed by righteous works. Right belief and right living will align. God's transformation of new believers is always shown through their actions and ministry to others.

In verse 11 John made it clear that he was a messenger only and not the Messiah himself. "I baptize you with water for repentance, but the One coming after me is more powerful than I." John preached salvation through repentance, but only Jesus had the power to save. Carrying the sandals of the master was one of the most menial tasks that a servant or slave could do.[2] John clearly realized he was unworthy to do for Jesus even the most trivial of tasks when he said, "I am not worthy to take off His sandals." (v.11).

In verse 12 John preached not only that Jesus had the authority to save or condemn, but that He would also sit as judge over all. A threshing floor would have been a common site in Jesus' day; thus John used one as a relevant illustration. Grain was harvested along with the stalks and other inedible parts and taken to the threshing floor. To gather the needed grain, a winnowing fork was used to toss the harvested materials into the air. The denser, heavier grain would fall straight down on the floor, while the "chaff" would simply blow away. Just as a thresher easily separated the wheat and the chaff, Jesus would (will) judge the world.

Baptism of Jesus

John not only preached that the Messiah was coming, but had a direct part in the initiation of Jesus' ministry. In verse 13 John was at the Jordan river, baptizing people. Jesus came to John and asked to be baptized by him. John recognized the irony, that the Messiah was asking a sinful mortal to baptize Him.

Jesus answered John's concern, saying "Allow it for now, because this is the way for us to fulfill all righteousness." (v.15). Clearly, it was God's will for Jesus to be baptized by John. The baptism foreshadowed

Jesus death and resurrection. More importantly for us, it set the example for all believers to follow Jesus in the ordinance of baptism.

After Jesus was baptized, He saw the heavens open and the Spirit of God descending like a dove. A voice came from heaven, saying, "This is My beloved Son. I take delight in Him!" (v.17). The presence of all three members of the Trinity: Holy Spirit, God the Father and Jesus, demonstrated that Jesus' will and the Father's will were in complete agreement.

John, preaching repentance, prepared the way for Jesus. John, willing to submit to God's will, helped Jesus start His ministry to redeem those who would repent. Jesus, in setting the example, taught believers to submit to God the Father in all things, including baptism.

BAPTISM

Baptism was a central focus in the story of Philip and the Ethiopian, which is covered in another lesson. More information about baptism may be found in that lesson.

Since baptism is an *ordinance* (command), it should be a new believer's first act of obedience to Christ. There are occasionally rare cases in which extenuating circumstances, such as a medical condition, or a parent who will not give permission for a child, in which a person cannot be baptized. They should be reminded that baptism is not a means of salvation and is simply an action which testifies to others that one is a follower of Jesus.

AGE GROUP CONSIDERATIONS

Younger children may be afraid of baptism. Be sensitive to their emotional concerns and seek to reassure them so that it will be a positive experience. This month may be a good time to take a tour of the baptistry and explain how your church observes baptism. Perhaps the pastor or another staff member could be recruited to assist in this tour.

Jesus is Baptized

SUGGESTED HYMNS

1. *Let Jesus Come into Your Heart*, 416, 2008 Baptist Hymnal.
2. *Now I Belong to Jesus*, 503, 2008 Baptist Hymnal.
3. *He Lives*, 269, 2008 Baptist Hymnal.
4. *Trust and Obey*, 500, 2008 Baptist Hymnal.

STUDENT APPLICATIONS

1. Students will know that John the Baptist was the last prophet of the Old Testament and the fulfillment of prophecy given by God through Isaiah (Isaiah 40).
2. Students will know that Jesus was baptized in the Jordan river by John the Baptist.
3. Students will know that all three members of the Trinity were present at Jesus' baptism.
4. Students will know that baptism is symbolic and is a testimony of Christ's death, burial and resurrection. It is not a means of salvation.
5. Students will know that after an individual becomes a Christian, Jesus expects them to obediently follow His example of public baptism.
6. Students will know that baptism is a command of God for every believer.

RESOURCES/CREDIT

1. James M. Freeman, *Manners & Customs of the Bible* (New Kensington: Whitaker House, 1996), 333.
2. *Ibid.*

Ruth

BACKGROUND PASSAGES

Main Passage
Ruth 1-4   Story of Ruth

Suggested Homiletic Passage
Ruth 2:3-12

MEMORY VERSE

Younger version
... your people will be my people, and your God will be my God.

Ruth 1:16c

Older version
For wherever you go, I will go, and wherever you live, I will live, your people will be my people, and your God will be my God.

Ruth 1:16

LESSON OBJECTIVE

Ruth showed faithfulness, kindness, and integrity in caring for her mother-in-law Naomi. She is an example of God's protection and blessing on those who are true to Him.

LESSON

The story of Ruth is one of the warmest and most uplifting to be found in the Bible. Written hundreds of years before Jesus' birth, it clearly shows how God works to redeem His people. It also demonstrates that even though God had made Israel His people, a faithful foreigner, such as Ruth, could become part of that covenant.

Ruth 1-4

At the beginning of the book of Ruth, a famine gripped the land of Israel. A Bethlehemite, named Elimelech, took his wife, Naomi, and two sons, Mahlon and Chilion, to the land of Moab. Moab was a nation descended from Lot's incestuous relationship.

Located on the eastern side of the Dead Sea, Moab was involved in a number of conflicts with its neighbor Israel. In the Old Testament Moab had a negative influence on Israel because of their pagan rituals and worship of Chemosh, their national god. That an Old Testament book is named after a Moabite woman may be because Ruth was so "un-Moabite" in her ways, faithfully worshipping the True God.[1]

While the family escaped the famine, they still experienced tragedy. While in Moab, Elimelech died. The family stayed in Moab and the two sons took Moabite wives, Orpah and Ruth. Ten years after moving to Moab, both of Naomi's sons also died.

Having heard that conditions had improved in Israel, the three widows decided to leave Moab. Along the way, Orpah turned to her daughters-in-law and implored them to return to their Moabite families. Hopefully, they could find men among their own countrymen and be remarried. Both daughter-in-laws resisted. Finally after more persuasion, Orpah relented, kissed Naomi goodbye, and headed home to Moab.

Ruth, however, would not be so easily convinced. "Do not persuade me to leave you or go back and not follow you. For wherever you go, I will go, and wherever you live, I will live; your people will be my people, and your God will be my God. Where you die, I will die, and there I will be buried. May the Lord do this to me, if anything but death separates you and me."(1:16-17). Naomi realized that she could not persuade Ruth. The two women traveled on to Bethlehem.

The two women arrived at the beginning of the barley harvest. The whole town was excited to see Naomi return after her long absence. The return was not joyful for Naomi. She requested her friends call her "Mara", for she was bitter and felt that the Lord had judged her.

The two women set about meeting their everyday needs. Ruth went out into the fields to gather grain. The Law provided for the poor by forbidding farmers to reap all of their field. Leviticus 19:9-10 commanded farmers to leave the edges of the field alone and to not go back over already-harvested areas. While the law allowed the poor to work in a field, several comments in the book of Ruth infer that these gatherers were commonly subject to mistreatment.

The field that Ruth began to work belonged to Boaz, who was a relative of Elimelech (2:1). When Boaz arrived at the field he greeted his workers, "The Lord be with you." (2:4). Boaz noticed Ruth, and inquired as to her identity, and then went to Ruth and encouraged her to stay work only in his field. He told her to stay by his maidens and told his workers to leave her alone and to share their water with her.

Ruth was understandably curious as to why Boaz was showing such generosity to a Moabitess and a stranger. Boaz told her that he had heard of her faithfulness and kindness towards Naomi. At mealtime, Boaz extended further kindness to Ruth by encouraging her to eat bread with his harvesters. He himself gave her roasted grain until she was satisfied and even had some left over to take home to share with Naomi.

Boaz commanded his men to leave extra grain for Ruth to collect. By the end of the day she had collected 26 quarts of barley, similar in volume to 4 gallons of milk.[2] Naomi was amazed at the amount of grain and food brought home by Ruth. "Where did you gather barley today, and where did you work?," Naomi asked (2:19). When Naomi discovered that Ruth had met Boaz, she informed Ruth that he was a close relative, a family (kinsmen) redeemer. She encouraged Ruth to remain in his fields. Naomi's stated reason was "... so nothing will happen to you in another field ..." (2:22).

Naomi probably had Ruth's safety first in mind; however, she might also have begun contemplating the providence behind Ruth "finding" the field of a family redeemer. A family redeemer was a 'next of kin'. God retained ownership of the land so it was not possible for one to own the land outright. The responsibility of a family redeemer was to restore dispossessed family property and to protect family rights.[3] The rights of the family of Elimelech, Naomi and their sons had been stripped with the untimely deaths of their men. If not yet at that moment, in time Naomi would hope that Boaz would take on the family redeemer role for her and Ruth.

Ruth continued to work with Boaz's gleaners during the barley, and then the wheat, harvests. We can only speculate about the relationship between Ruth and Boaz, and how it had developed during this time. Regardless, after this time, Naomi had a talk with Ruth regarding the future. She encouraged Ruth to make a bold move to see if Boaz would be willing to take on the responsibility of kinsman redeemer.

"Now isn't Boaz our relative? Haven't you been working with his young women?" (3:2) Naomi asked Ruth. Naomi probably knew that Boaz was a good man, and that He was quite possibly attracted to Ruth.

Naomi told Ruth to clean herself, put on perfume, and get dressed. She then told her to go to the threshing floor where Boaz would be that evening. During harvest, workers slept on the threshing floor in order to protect the grain from robbers.[4] They also threshed at night so they could harvest during the daylight hours.[5] After he went to sleep, she was to go uncover his feet and lie down next to him. This was a position of submission as servants often slept at the feet of their masters.

Ruth obeyed everything that Naomi asked. After Boaz fell asleep, Ruth went secretly and, after she uncovered Boaz's feet, she lay down. About midnight, Boaz awoke, startled to find a woman lying at his feet! In the dark of the night, his first question was "Who are you?" Ruth replied "I am Ruth, your slave (most translations use "servant"). Spread your cloak (or *wings* in ESV or *skirt* in KJV) over me, for you are a family redeemer." (3:8)

Ruth

It was the moment of truth. Would Boaz reject her and send her away? Would he grudgingly agree? Boaz responded by praising Ruth for her kindness. He also praised her for coming to him instead of a younger man. Boaz's age is never mentioned, but he was likely middle-aged or older. Finally he praised Ruth for being a woman of good character and expressed his desire to fulfill the duties of the family redeemer. But there was a catch: one other man was a redeemer closer than Boaz. Boaz would talk to the man. If he declined to redeem Ruth, Boaz would do so gladly. He told Ruth to go back to sleep. In the morning he gave Ruth some grain and sent her on her way, before anyone knew (3:14).

When Ruth arrived home, Naomi naturally wanted to know all that had happened. After telling her story, Naomi told Ruth to be patient for a time, since she knew Boaz would not rest until the matter was settled.

Boaz went to the town gate, where the town elders conducted business and waited for the other redeemer to arrive. When the man passed by, Boaz asked him to sit down to discuss business. Boaz gathered ten other men to witness their business dealing. Boaz told the man that he had the right to buy the land of Elimelech. The unnamed man initially agreed to buy the land, but after being told that he would also have to take Ruth into his home, he declined to take on the responsibility of the family redeemer.

In what we would consider a real legal oddity, the man took off his shoe and handed it to Boaz and said, "Buy back the property yourself " (4:8). The exchange of a sandal was the legally binding method in matters concerning the right of redemption or the exchange of property (4:7).

Boaz turned to the witnesses and announced that he would indeed take the role of family redeemer and buy everything that belonged to Naomi's family.

He would also take Ruth as his wife. The witnesses blessed Boaz and Ruth and their forthcoming union.

Boaz married Ruth. She gave birth to a son, Obed, who would later become the grandfather of David the king. The women of the town praised Naomi as being blessed by God. They said that Ruth's faithfulness was better than seven sons.

Of course, no one was more proud of the child than Grandma. Naomi took the child and placed him on her lap and cared for him. Her bitterness had turned to a joy that she would have never experienced if Ruth had not shown such faithfulness. Ruth and Naomi found redemption through a mortal man, Boaz. Believers know that we ultimately find our redemption in the work of Jesus through His sacrifice on the cross. Like Naomi, believers will experience heartache and loss in this world. In the world to come, believers will find only exceeding joy. Ruth is an example of how God cares for, and blesses, those who love Him.

AGE GROUP CONSIDERATIONS

Be sensitive to children who may have lost a parent or who live in a blended home. God does not always send another adult to take the place of a lost spouse or parent. Children can take comfort in knowing that "A father of the fatherless and a champion of widows is God in His holy dwelling" (Psalm 68:5).

The term "family redeemer," used in the HCSB, may be easier for children to understand than "kinsman redeemer," as found in other translations.

SUGGESTED HYMNS/SONGS

1. *Great is thy Faithfulness*, 96, 2008 Baptist Hymnal.
2. *Amazing Grace*, 104, 2008 Baptist Hymnal.
3. *What a Mighty God We Serve*, 64, 2008 Baptist Hymnal.

STUDENT APPLICATIONS

1. Students will know that the book of Ruth is found in the Old Testament.
2. Students will know that Naomi was the mother-in-law of Ruth and Orpah.
3. Students will know that Naomi, Ruth and Orpah were all widowed.
4. Students will know that Ruth and Orpah were from the land of Moab.
5. Students will know that Naomi decided to return to her home, Bethlehem, in Israel.
6. Students will know that Orpah stayed in Moab while Ruth insisted on going with Naomi.
7. Students will know that Ruth worked hard to care for herself and Naomi by going to the fields to glean grain.
8. Students will know that Ruth found favor in the eyes of a farmer named Boaz.
9. Students will know that Boaz was a family (or kinsman) redeemer.
10. Students will know that Boaz and Ruth were married and had a son, named Obed.
11. Students will know that Jesus is our Redeemer.

RESOURCES/CREDIT

1. Robert Bergen, "*Moab,*" *Biblical Illustrator,* Lifeway (Spring 2006 Volume 32, Number 3): 54-57.
2. Charles A. Oxley, *The International Bible Commentary, Revised Edition*, F.F. Bruce, ed. (Grand Rapids, Michigan: Zondervan Publishing House, 1979), 345.
3. *Ibid.*
4. J. Mark Terry, "*Threshing Floors,*" *Biblical Illustrator*, Lifeway (Spring 2008 Volume 34, Number 3): 26-29.
5. *Life Application Bible.* (Grand Rapids, Michigan: Zondervan Publishing House, 1991), 426.

Easter - Trial/Judas

BACKGROUND PASSAGES

Main Passages
Matthew 26:14-16   Judas takes a bribe
Matthew 26:36-26:68 Jesus on trial
Matthew 27:1-26   Judas' fate, Pilate
Matthew 28:1-10   Resurrection

Related Passages
Acts 1:16-20   Peter on Judas' fate
Jeremiah 32:6-9   Prophecy of Judas' treachery

Suggested Homiletic Passage
Matthew 26:36-46

MEMORY VERSE

For to those who are perishing the message of the cross is foolishness, but to us who are being saved it is God's power.

I Corinthians 1:18

LESSON OBJECTIVE

Jesus knew that His death was imminent. First would come betrayal by His friend Judas. He also knew that this betrayal leading to His death and subsequent resurrection was the only way He could gain salvation for all who would (and will) believe and trust in Him.

LESSON

On Easter Sunday, believers celebrate Jesus' resurrection and victory over sin and death. The days leading up to Jesus death were filled with much drama and intrigue. There was the resurrection of Lazarus and the triumphal entry. There was the plotting against Jesus and the last supper. Perhaps the saddest thing, was the betrayal of Jesus by His close friend. Judas had been with Jesus and watched Him minister for quite some time. All this took place to fulfill prophesy and pay the price for sin, but knowing who Jesus is, and trusting Him, are two different things (as shall be learned from the story of Judas).

Matthew 26:14-16

It was two days before the Passover. On the evening of the Passover Jesus would be turned over to the authorities and crucified the next day. Jews from all over Palestine and surrounding areas were gathering in Jerusalem for the observance.

Jesus and the disciples were at the home of Simon the Leper. After this event, one of Jesus' followers, Judas Iscariot, went to the chief priests. He asked them, "What are you willing to give me if I hand Him over to you?" (v.15). Judas showed a desire to betray his friend for personal gain. After the resurrection of Lazarus, the chief priests had resolved to put Jesus to death (John 11:45-53). Jesus' popularity kept them from following through with their plan. The people at that time believed that Jesus might be the leader who would lead a successful rebellion against Roman rule, thus, the chief priests would have to take Jesus into custody outside of the public eye. Judas, as one who was close to Jesus, could easily assist them.

For his betrayal, Judas was given thirty pieces of silver. From that point forward, Judas looked for an opportunity to discretely hand Jesus over to the religious authorities.

Matthew 26:36-26:68

Judas found his opportunity while Jesus and the disciples were observing the Passover meal. Late in the evening, Judas slipped out and went to get the religious authorities in order to lead them to Jesus.

After the Passover meal, Jesus and His disciples went to the garden of Gethsemane on the Mount of Olives just outside of Jerusalem. Knowing His death was less than 24-hours away, Jesus was sorrowful and desired to spend the time in prayer with the Father. Twice Jesus checked with His disciples and both times found them asleep.

When Jesus returned the third time, He said, "Are you still sleeping and resting? Look, the time is near. The Son of Man is being betrayed into the hands of sinners. Get up; let's go! See — My betrayer is near." (26:45). At this moment Judas arrived with an armed group sent by the chief priests and elders.

This late-night drama played out in an age before electricity and photography. Everyone had heard of Jesus, but unless they had personally seen Him, they would not likely recognize Him. Also, in the dark of the night without any electrical illumination, the task of identifying Jesus would be near impossible. There needed to be a sign. Judas walked up to Jesus and kissed him on the cheek (26:49). This was the prearranged sign identifying Jesus. While men in our culture do not greet one another with a kiss, it was (and still is) a common custom of the region. Once identified, Jesus was promptly arrested.

Before He was taken away for His trial, one of His followers jumped to His defense. Peter took a sword and cut off the ear of one of the servants, named Malchus (John 18:10). Jesus rebuked Peter, saying that He could call more than 12 legions of angels to defend Himself. A legion is comprised of approximately five thousand or more. One angel would likely have sufficed. Jesus knew that the coming events needed to happen in order to fulfill Scriptural prophecies. In a true act of compassion, while surrounded by enemies who wanted Him dead, Jesus healed Malchus' ear. While this took place, all of the disciples deserted Jesus.

Jesus was led to the home of Caiaphas, the high priest. The religious authorities had convened to put Jesus on trial. A trial at night before only a portion of the Sanhedrin was a mockery of justice.

We know that Peter and John followed at a distance. John was able to gain access to Caiaphas' courtyard for both of them (John 18:15-16). The religious authorities hardly brought forth a compelling case against Jesus. In verse 59 they were looking for false testimony but despite a number of "witnesses" they could not find two that agreed as was prescribed by the law to validate truthfulness.

Finally two witnesses came forward who were willing to agree that Jesus said, "I can demolish God's sanctuary and rebuild it in three days." (26:61). Jesus had made a similar statement after cleansing the temple (John 2:19). However, He was talking about His death and resurrection. The religious authorities misunderstood and thought He was referring to the temple in Jerusalem. They put much faith and pride into the temple and considered it blasphemy to make a "threat" against it.

As much as they revered the temple, the Jewish leaders considered one thing to be even more treacherous: claiming to be God. The high priest asked Jesus, "By the living God I place you under oath: tell us if You are the Messiah, the Son of God!" (26:63). Jesus replied, "You have said it, But I tell you, in the future you will see the Son of Man seated at the right hand of the Power and coming on the clouds of heaven." (26:64).

Jesus rightfully claimed to be the Messiah and while in this position of submission, He let it be known that one day He would return as rightful ruler and Lord of all. The religious authorities cried out, "He deserves death!" and began to slap and spit on Jesus. Despite their desire to kill Jesus, they still needed the permission of the Roman authorities. For this they had to take him to the Galilean governor: Pilate. Having no interest in Jewish religious affairs, Pilate would only allow the execution if He were guilty of a political crime. Therefore, they needed to persuade Pilate that Jesus was a political threat.

Matthew 27:1-26

Judas must have been at the trial or nearby . When he heard that Jesus had been condemned, Judas was filled with remorse and attempted to return the 30 pieces of silver to the religious authorities. They refused to accept it, so Judas threw the money into the sanctuary in the temple.

Judas was so despondent that he went and hung himself. The priests did not want to keep the money since they considered it blood money; so they used the money to buy the field where Judas had killed himself. It was then used as a burial ground for foreigners. Peter, in Acts 1:19, also states that this field was thereafter known as "The field of blood." This fulfilled a prophecy found in Jeremiah 32:6-9 that 30 pieces of silver would be used to buy a field.

Easter - Trial/Judas

At dawn the Jewish leaders bound Jesus and took Him before Pilate. Pilate was governor and embodied the law as an occupying ruler; but, even he had to answer to Rome. Keeping relative peace and a steady flow of taxes back to Rome was his only way to guarantee favor and his position with his superiors.

Now there was a tradition during the Passover in which the Roman governor pardoned one criminal chosen by the people. Pilate had discerned that Jesus was almost certainly innocent and that He had been accused by the leaders out of envy. Pilate had also received an unusual message, from his wife, asking him not to have anything to do with Jesus because of a troubling dream she had experienced (27:19). He decided to take the issue to the people. They could either have Jesus released, or Barabbas, a known murderer.

The chief priests thwarted his efforts by stirring up the crowd. When Pilate asked whom he should release, the crowd demanded Barabbas. Pilate asked, "What should I do then with Jesus, who is called the Messiah?" (27:22). The now angry crowd responded, "Crucify Him!" Pilate tried to persuade them that Jesus had done nothing wrong. He saw that he was getting nowhere and feared that a riot might begin. He took some water and washed his hands in a symbolic gesture, claiming innocence in Jesus' death. He released Barabbas and sentenced Jesus to be crucified. Jesus was flogged and led away to His death.

The crucifixion is covered in another Easter rotation lesson. The good news is that Jesus' death was more of a beginning than an ending. In three days, tragedy would turn to triumph.

Matthew 28:1-10

Just having seen their Lord and Master killed horribly on a cross, Mary Magdalene and Mary set out early in the morning of the first day of the week for Jesus' tomb. Their purpose in going was to anoint His body with spices (Mark 16:1). The quiet of the morning was broken by the rumbling of a violent earthquake.

The cause of the earthquake was an angel who had come to earth. The angel had moved the stone from the front of Jesus' tomb. His appearance was striking, "... like lightning, and his robe was as white as snow." (v.3). Guards, who were on duty in order to prevent Jesus' disciples from stealing the body, at the sight of the angel, "... they became like dead men" (v.4).

The angel spoke to the women and gave them good news, "Don't be afraid, because I know you are looking for Jesus who was crucified. He is not here! For He has been resurrected, just as He said." (v.5). The angel invited them to view the empty tomb and then told them to go and tell the disciples. The women left quickly, excited to share the wonderful news, yet fearful. On their way, Jesus met them and calmed their fears. They fell at His feet and worshipped Him. He then told them to go to the disciples and inform them that they too would soon also see Him.

It's interesting to note that Jesus did not appear first to His disciples or someone in a position of importance, but to two ordinary women. What a privilege for those two faithful followers! Their faithfulness stood in contrast to that of Judas. It is one thing to know Jesus and another to trust Him. Today, anyone who repents and places his/her faith in Jesus will be saved. This is the wonderful news that we can share, not only on Easter Sunday, but every day of the year!

AGE GROUP CONSIDERATIONS

The issue of Judas' death is too strong for younger children. It would be appropriate to explain that Judas felt very badly and tried to return the money. He never was a true follower of Jesus and missed out on the joy of His resurrection.

Some children may wonder if they can do something so bad, like Judas, that God would stop loving them. As long as we live, we will do things that are not pleasing to God. Children need to be assured that God will forgive them and restore them to fellowship when they ask Him. The awareness of sin and shortcoming in our lives and the desire to repent and restore our relationship with God is actually evidence that we are saved. There is nothing we can do to earn God's favor: salvation is a free gift that cannot be lost.

SUGGESTED HYMNS/SONGS

1. *Softly and Tenderly*, 414, 2008 Baptist Hymnal.
2. Jesus is Lord of All, 294, 2008 Baptist Hymnal.
3. *Jesus, Keep Me Near the Cross*, 233, 2008 Baptist Hymnal.
4. *Low in the Grave He Lay*, 273, 2008 Baptist Hymnal.
5. *Crown Him with Many Crowns*, 3041, 2008 Baptist Hymnal.

STUDENT APPLICATIONS

1. Students will know that the story of Jesus' death and resurrection is found in the gospels of Matthew, Mark, Luke and John in the New Testament.
2. Students will know that Judas was one of Jesus' original twelve disciples.
3. Students will know that the religious authorities wanted to take Jesus into custody and sentence Him to death but were afraid to do it publicly.
4. Students will know that Judas made a deal with the religious authorities to turn Jesus over to them at a discrete opportunity
5. Students will know that Judas was paid 30 pieces of silver to betray Jesus.
6. Students will know that Judas led the religious authorities to the Garden of Gethsemane late one night, to capture Jesus.
7. Students will know that Jesus was put on trial and sentenced for blasphemy, even though He was not guilty.
8. Students will know that Jesus was crucified on a cross.
9. Students will know that Jesus was resurrected from the dead after three days and appeared to Mary, Mary Magdalene and the disciples.
10. Students will know that Judas was so remorseful for his actions that He returned the thirty pieces of silver and committed suicide (older children).
11. Students will know that all the events concerning the crucifixion and resurrection were part of God's plan, which has been in place since before the beginning of time, so that all who repent and believe in Jesus will be saved.

Jesus' Miracles

Background Passages
Main Passage
Matthew 14:13-36   Jesus' Miracles

Related Passages
Mark 6:30-56   Mark's version Jesus' Miracles
Luke 9:10-17   Luke's version Jesus' Miracles
John 6:1-21   John's version Jesus' Miracles

Suggested Homiletic Passage
Matthew 14:13-21

MEMORY VERSE

Younger version
...He saw a huge crowd and had compassion on them, because they were like sheep without a shepherd.

Mark 6:34b

Older version
So as He stepped ashore, He saw a huge crowd and had compassion on them, because they were like sheep without a shepherd. Then He began to teach them many things.

Mark 6:34

LESSON OBJECTIVE

Jesus performed many miracles, proving not only His Divinity, but that He had great compassion for people as should all believers.

LESSON

Who was Jesus? Some people have reached the erroneous conclusion that He was simply a man who was a good teacher. While Jesus taught many things, He came as the Savior of the world and was God in flesh. While on the earth, He showed His great love and compassion when He used miracles to meet everyday concerns (food and health) and when He died on the cross as the atonement for the sins of humankind. These simple acts of kindness, miracles which could only be accomplished by God, proved His deity in a way that still gives testimony today.

Matthew 14:13-36

In verse 13 Jesus received news that John the Baptist had been beheaded at the order of Herod the Tetrarch. Jesus withdrew to a remote place, by boat, in order to pray and spend time with the disciples. By this point of His ministry, people were constantly seeking to be with Him. He could only rest while on retreat. As Jesus stepped out of the boat, he was immediately greeted by a large crowd that had run ahead of Him.

Rather than feeling harassed or resenting their presence, Jesus felt great compassion for the crowd (v.14). Jesus saw them as "sheep without a shepherd." (Mark 6:34). He began to teach them and to heal those with physical needs.

The place, where the crowd had caught up to Jesus, was a wilderness. As evening drew near, the disciples became concerned and asked Jesus to send the crowd away to surrounding towns that they might find food. Jesus replied "They don't need to go away. You give them something to eat." (v.16).

There was no way possible that the disciples could have had the money or the means to provide food for such a large crowd. Instead, the only food available was five loaves of bread and two fish, brought by a young boy. This paucity of food probably reinforced their belief that feeding the crowd was impossible (John 6:9). Jesus, however, can take what is considered insufficient and make it sufficient. He asked for the bread and the fish, and commanded the crowd to sit down.

The loaves (flat barley cakes that were typically cooked on hot stones) and the fish (likely small and salted, and may have served as a relish on the bread.) were taken and blessed.[1]

Jesus blessed the food, broke it, and had the disciples distribute it to the crowd. Everyone ate until they were full. Cleaning up afterwards, they gathered twelve full baskets of leftovers. Scripture records that there were 5,000 men plus an unknown number of women and children. Jesus, as God, had miraculously met their physical need.

Having fed them, Jesus dismissed the crowd to return to their homes. He also had the disciples get back into the boat and go on ahead of Him, allowing Him a brief retreat. The land rises quickly from the eastern shore of the Sea of Galilee. This area is known today as the Golan heights. Jesus went up onto a mountain in order to pray. Jesus found it important to make time for prayer. We would do well to follow His example.

The disciples found the trip home to be rather difficult as a contrary wind worked against their efforts. At approximately three in the morning, as the waves continued to buffet their craft, the disciples saw Jesus walking toward them on the water. The disciples, not immediately recognizing Jesus and thinking Him to be a ghost, were terrified. Jesus called to them, "Have courage! It is I. Do not be afraid." (v.27).

Not completely convinced, Peter asked, "Lord, if it is You, command me to come to You on the water." (v.28). Jesus said, "Come!" Peter stepped out of the boat and found that the water supported him! It was another miracle. As he began to walk toward Jesus, he noticed how strong the wind was and began to be afraid. He then began to sink and yelled out, "Lord, save me!" (v.30). Jesus reached out, pulled him up, and asked, "You of little faith, why did you doubt?" As they climbed into the boat, the wind ceased. This small group of men, whom God would soon use mightily to spread the gospel, began to worship Jesus. They knew He was the Son of God.

They landed at Gennesaret (likely not long after daybreak). Some people recognized Jesus and news of His arrival swept throughout the whole vicinity. Many sick were brought to Jesus. Now, even after the previously long day and night, Jesus refused to turn away them away. Once again, He showed compassion and healed many. His power as God was evident as "They were begging Him that they might only touch the tassel on His robe. And as many as touched it were made perfectly well." (v.36.).

The Bible clearly shows that a person's greatest need is salvation from their sinful condition. Jesus met that need by atoning for those sins on the cross. Like the ancient crowds, we can also find that Jesus understands and meets our daily needs. We too have food, shelter, and clothing only by God's grace and providential care. We can confidently take our "small" concerns to God in prayer, and remember to thank Him for all the blessings we receive- big or small.

AGE GROUP CONSIDERATIONS

This lesson is a good one for children of all ages. They can readily identify with the needs of the hungry and sick. They can see that Jesus cared for them. Be sensitive to children who may personally suffer from, or have close relatives suffering, from a physical illness. God can still heal people today, but oftentimes it is in the ultimate healing through death. Encourage children that one day, all who trust in Jesus, will have perfect bodies and be free from physical suffering.

All four of the gospels record the events found in this lesson. Please take the time to read all four accounts, as each reveals details that will enrich your teaching.

SUGGESTED HYMNS/SONGS

1. *O How He Loves You and Me*, 170, 2008 Baptist Hymnal.
2. *Love Lifted Me*, 107, 2008 Baptist Hymnal.
3. *I'd Rather Have Jesus*, 530, 2008 Baptist Hymnal.
4. *Sweet Hour of Prayer*, 85, 2008 Baptist Hymnal.

Jesus' Miracles

STUDENT APPLICATIONS

1. Students will know that Jesus' works while on Earth are recorded in the four gospels: Matthew, Mark, Luke and John.
2. Students will know that Jesus cares deeply about the needs of people
3. Students will know that Jesus is fully God and in His earthly body was fully human.
4. Students will know that Jesus used five loaves and two fish to miraculously feed over 5000.
5. Students will know that Jesus spent time alone in prayer.
6. Students will know that Jesus walked on water.
7. Students will know that Jesus rescued Simon Peter from sinking into the sea.
8. Students will know that the disciples recognized Jesus as the Son of God.
9. Students will know that Jesus healed many of the sick.
10. Students will know that ultimate healing comes when a believer is with Jesus in Heaven.
11. Students will know that Jesus cares about our everyday needs.
12. Students will know that they need to thank God for everything (for meeting their everyday needs such as clothing, food and shelter).

RESOURCES/CREDIT

1. Frederick Fyvie Bruce, *The Gospel & Epistles of John* (Grand Rapids: William B. Eerdmans Publishing Co., 1983), 144.

Paul & Silas

BACKGROUND PASSAGES

Main Passage
Acts 16:4-15   Macedonian Call
Acts 16:16-30   Jailer is Saved

Related Passages
Acts 15:36-41   Paul and Barnabas part company

Suggested Homiletic Passage
Acts 16:25-34

MEMORY VERSE

Younger version
How welcome are the feet of those who announce the gospel of good things!

Romans 9:15b

Older version
And how can they preach unless they are sent? As it is written: How welcome are the feet of those who announce the gospel of good things!

Romans 9:15

LESSON OBJECTIVE

The apostle Paul was obedient to go wherever God sent him. During his missionary journeys many people heard and received the Good News about Jesus, including a jailer and his family.

LESSON

Whenever someone travels far from home, something unexpected often happens during the journey: getting lost, forgetting to pack something important, or even foul weather. These things can drastically alter travel plans. Paul and Silas experienced many unexpected things during their missionary travels . They ended up traveling to a country they had not initially planned to visit. In fact, they ended up in jail, even though they had committed no crime. But despite these circumstances, God used them to lead others to the saving knowledge of Jesus.

Acts 16:4-15

Paul and Barnabas had just completed a missionary journey when they had a disagreement and eventually decided to go their separate ways. Paul then teamed up with Silas and traveled throughout Asia Minor (now known as modern day Turkey). They stopped to minister to and encourage established churches (including Derbe, Lystra and Iconium). The churches were strengthened and their numbers increased daily (v.5).

The plan was to go into the Roman province of Asia (not the continent) in northeastern Turkey, but, the Holy Spirit prevented them from entering. How this was manifested is unknown, but Paul and Silas readily discerned that it was not God's will for them to enter the province.

They soon found themselves in the city of Troas where one night Paul received a vision. In the vision, a Macedonian man pleaded with Paul to come over and help his people. Paul and Silas immediately prepared to head to Macedonia, confident that God was calling them there to proclaim the Gospel (v.10).

Macedonia was across the Aegean sea from Asia. The modern day Republic of Macedonia is much smaller than the Roman province of the same name. Much of the ancient province is now part of modern day Greece.

Paul and Silas set sail from Troas, and passed through Samothrace and Neapolis on their way to the city of Philippi (a Roman colony and a major city of Macedonia). They stayed in the city for a number of days.

On the Sabbath, they went outside the city to a nearby river where they hoped to find a place of prayer. Some scholars believe that it was common for Jews to have places of worship distinct from their synagogues. These places were typically located outside of town, and near water so that ritual cleansing could be performed.[1] The likelihood of such a place was probably greater in cities that were home to Jewish nationals, outside of Israel, and where there was no synagogue.

They found a number of women gathered at a place of prayer. One of the women who listened to their gospel presentation was Lydia, a businesswoman

Paul & Silas

who sold purple cloth. She worshiped God but had never heard the gospel message. God spoke to her heart and she believed. She was soon baptized, along with her family, as the first step of obedience in following Jesus (v14-15). She opened up her home to Paul and Silas. Thus they had a place to stay while ministering in Philippi.

Acts 16:16-30

The ministry in Philippi was off to a strong start, but an unexpected event would soon test Paul and Silas. While traveling through the city, they passed a slave girl. She brought in much money for her masters by telling fortunes. Scripture shows this was a case of demon possession.

What is particularly intriguing is that the demon not only recognized the Holy Spirit's presence in Paul and Silas, but drew attention to them by saying, "These men are the slaves of the Most High God, who are proclaiming to you the way of salvation." (v.17). This was not a one-time event as it happened again and for many days.

This annoyed Paul, who finally spoke directly to the spirit and commanded it, in the name of Jesus Christ, to leave the girl. Immediately the spirit left her. While the girl must certainly have been relieved, her owners were not. They were furious because they could no longer profit from her fortune telling!

Her owners "dragged" Paul and Silas before the authorities in the marketplace. A crowd began to gather as the girl's owners accused the two men of disturbing the city with their Jewish ways. The crowd joined in on the attack. The city officials had Paul and Silas stripped and beaten. They were then placed in the prison's inner cell, with their feet in stocks.

How could things have gone wrong so quickly? While our reaction to such an injustice and humiliation against us would likely include shock, dismay, resentment and anger, Paul and Silas were able to see things in a positive light. Late that night (about midnight, verse 25), Paul and Silas were praying and singing hymns. After the horrible events of the day, they found solace in worshiping God. While they probably

had little choice, the other prisoners listened to them. Again, Paul and Silas were giving a powerful witness.

Suddenly the foundations of the jail were shaken by a great earthquake. The jail itself was not damaged but all the doors came open and the everyone's chains came loose.

When the jailer realized what had happened, he feared that under the cover of darkness all the prisoners had escaped. Under Roman law, if a prisoner escaped, the jailer would be compelled to suffer the prisoner's penalty.[2] Faced with that dreadful prospect, the jailer decided to draw his sword and kill himself. Just then Paul called out with a loud voice, "Don't harm yourself, because all of us are here!" (v.28).

The jailer called for lights and went to Paul. He fell before them, trembling. He released them from their restraints. God had done a mighty work on His heart as he asked, "Sirs, what must I do to be saved?" (v.30). "Believe on the Lord Jesus, and you will be saved — you and your household." answered Paul and Silas (v.31). This is the Gospel message. It is quite another thing to believe in someone, rather than simply believing something about them. When one believes in Jesus, he/she realizes his/her sinfulness and the need to repent and give Him the proper authority over his/her life. Perhaps Paul and Silas had witnessed to the jailer early in the evening. Perhaps he had been impressed with their attitude and their joyful singing. Whatever led up to that moment, he knew then that he needed the Savior and willingly gave his life to Jesus.

After this point, the jailer's behavior towards Paul and Silas was that of a host. He took the men to his home, where they shared the gospel with his family. The jailer washed their wounds. Then, in their first act of obedience to God, the jailer and his family were baptized (v.33). The jailer had a meal prepared, and everyone sat down and rejoiced that salvation had come to the household (v.34).

In the morning, orders came to the jailer to release the men. Paul then let it be known that he and Silas were Roman citizens and that the beating they had received was illegal. If the city magistrates wanted them to leave, they would have to come escort them out themselves. Alarmed, the leaders came and escorted Paul and Silas out of the jail and begged them to leave town. Now officially freed, the two men returned to Lydia's house where they ministered to and encouraged their Christian brothers and sisters. After some time they left to minister elsewhere.

Paul and Silas had many other adventures while sharing the gospel. Next month's lesson will cover their adventure in the Greek city of Athens. Despite many unexpected turns and hardships, they had the joy and privilege of seeing lives changed as people came to know and grow in the Lord. Believers can live each day in confidence, knowing that whatever may come, God has a purpose and a plan for all.

AGE GROUP CONSIDERATIONS

Speaking too much about demons, like the spirit in the young girl, may scare younger children. Simply state that God says that no one but He alone knows the future. Any person or being who claims to know the future is not pleasing to God.

Older children may be quite curious about demons and the supernatural realm. Demons are real and, while limited, have powers that we do not. Remind older students that God forbids believers to experiment with the occult. While it may seem harmless on the surface, like any other sin, it can lead to much trouble. Do reassure the children that God alone is sovereign and omnipresent, while Satan and demons are created beings. When believers trust and follow God, demons cannot have power over them.

SUGGESTED HYMNS/SONGS

1. *Shine, Jesus, Shine*, 491, 2008 Baptist Hymnal.
2. *Make Me a Blessing*, 380, 2008 Baptist Hymnal.
3. *Let Others See Jesus in You*, 363, 2008 Baptist Hymnal.
4. *Come Thou Fount of Every Blessing*, 98, 2008 Baptist Hymnal.

STUDENT APPLICATIONS

1. Students will know that the story of the jailer's salvation is found in the New Testament book of Acts.
2. Students will know that Paul and Silas were on a missionary journey spreading the good news about Jesus.
3. Students will know that Paul and Silas were put in prison after removing a demon from a young girl.
4. Students will know that demons, as well as angels, are real.
5. Students will know that the power of demons is real, but limited, and subject to God's authority.
6. Students will know that believers are commanded by God not to experiment with the supernatural (occult).
7. Students will know that Paul and Silas prayed and sang while in prison.
8. Students will know that an earthquake occurred which opened every door and loosened every chain in the jail.
9. Students will know that the jailer was prepared to kill himself because he thought the prisoners had escaped.
10. Students will know that Paul and Silas calmed the jailer by reassuring him that no one had escaped.
11. Students will know that jailer asked Paul and Silas what he needed to do to be saved.
12. Students will know that the jailer trusted in Jesus, he and everyone in his home, and that they were immediately baptized.
13. Students will know that the city officials released Paul and Silas; the two men continued to encourage the believers and spread the good news.

RESOURCES/CREDIT

1. James M. Freeman, *Manners & Customs of the Bible* (New Kensington: Whitaker House, 1996), 445.
2. *Ibid.*, 446.

Paul's Missionary Journeys

BACKGROUND PASSAGES

Main Passage
Acts 17:10-34   Paul in Athens

Related Passages
Acts 17:1-10   Paul and Silas in Thessalonica

Suggested Homiletic Passage
Acts 17:23-31

MEMORY VERSE

Younger version
The God who made the world and everything in it — He is Lord of heaven and earth...

Acts 17:24a

Older version
The God who made the world and everything in it — He is Lord of heaven and earth and does not live in shrines made by man.

Acts 17:24

LESSON OBJECTIVE

Paul was always ready to defend his faith as he preached the gospel. Just as Paul reasoned with the Greeks who lived in Athens, believers can know their faith is valid and learn to share it with people who do not follow Jesus.

LESSON

Paul had many opportunities to speak to people from many different cultures and backgrounds during his missionary trips. One of Paul's great messages was delivered in Athens, Greece. There he met the intellectual elite of his day and soundly communicated and defended the Gospel in their presence.

Acts 17:10-34

Paul was in the city of Berea before he made his way to Athens. He had already faced many difficult situations and would face more in the days to come. He had been arrested, imprisoned in Philippi, and chased out of Thessalonica. Later, his ministry would spark a riot in Ephesus. But in Berea, his work was accompanied by much joy.

Upon arriving in Berea, Paul and Silas went to the synagogue and spoke to the Jews. In many synagogues they were met with distrust or even outright rejection. Those in Berea "were more open-minded than those in Thessalonica, since they welcomed the message with eagerness and examined the Scriptures daily to see if these things were so."(v.11). As a result, many believed and became followers of Jesus.

Today believers are blessed to have easy access to the Bible, multiple translations, and many outside study aids which allow us to learn from centuries of study. The Bible has all the answers we need for life and eternity. Our children should be encouraged to study the Bible — on their own, at church, and with their family.

As the work at Berea continued to grow, some old antagonists arrived in town. Some of the people responsible for Paul leaving Thessalonica found out he was preaching in Berea and came to town to stir up the people against him. What they planned for harm, however, God would use for His good. Timothy and Silas strengthened the Berean ministry while Paul moved on to Athens.

In Athens, Paul waited for Silas and Timothy to catch up. Even though he would have already seen many idols during his travels in the ancient world, Paul was troubled that the Athenian idol worship was diverse and prolific. The Athenians apparently took much pride in "collecting" many idols and religions.

Paul employed a favorite strategy of his by going to the local synagogue and engaging the Jews of the city. He also went into the marketplace and found other God-worshippers, people who worshipped God but had yet to hear about Jesus.

Paul's Missionary Journeys

While in the marketplace, or as it was known to the Greeks, the *agora*, Paul engaged some of the Epicurean and Stoic philosophers. Athens was famous for being a center for schools of philosophical thought. Stoics taught that self-sufficiency was the highest good, while Epicureans taught that the pursuit of pleasure was what mattered most. When people first heard Paul speaking about Jesus, several of the philosophers used a slang word meaning "*babbler*," or *peddler of false ideas and religion*, to insult Paul.[1]

Others, curious about this new teaching, took Paul before the *Areopagus*, an ancient institution meaning "*Mars Hill*." Mars Hill was said to be over 1,000 years-old. Members of the Areopagus had, in times past, actually met on Mars Hill near the Acropolis. During Paul's time they met in the Royal Portico in the agora below the Acropolis.[2] Mars Hill had a reputation for being a center of debate. Learned men would gather there to share new ideas and debate the philosophical and religious questions of the day. The Areopagus, therefore, was the sanctioned place for oral debate. To Paul, this openness was a door through which he would enlighten the Athenians as to the nature and message of the one true God.

Paul began his address with a curious statement, "Men of Athens! I see that you are extremely religious in every way." (v.22). The Athenians were sincere and zealous in their religious pursuits of philosophy. Their zeal, however, was misplaced. Paul had seen, within the myriad of idols adorning the city one inscribed, "To an unknown god." (v.23). The Athenians probably reasoned that they might overlook and offend a god or his followers and thus had erected an altar to the "unknown." Paul seized on this opportunity to introduce the Athenians to the One True God.

Paul made it clear that no idol nor any false god compared with God Almighty. "He is the Lord of heaven and earth and does not live in shrines made by hands.", he preached to the Athenians (v.24). He told them God did not need anything from human hands because He is the giver and sustainer of all things. All the nations had come from one man, Adam, and God desired for them to reach out and seek Him, because He is ever near (v.26-7).

Next, Paul did a curious thing, he quoted two ancient writers who were likely familiar to his audience. "For in Him we live and move and have our being" and "For we are also His offspring" were quotes from Greek poets. While the second quote originally had been written about Zeus, Paul expertly argued that only God was worthy of such praise.

Paul moved to the point of his message. What did God want of the Athenians? He wanted them to repent. There is a day coming in which God will judge the world righteously. The proof of all this is that Jesus was raised from the dead.

Those who listened had one of three reactions as Paul talked about the resurrection of the dead: some began to ridicule him, others were uncertain but wanted to hear more, and some believed and gave their life to Jesus. Among the Athenians who believed were Dionysius, a member of the Areopagus, and a woman named Damaris.

We don't know how long Paul stayed in Athens. As soon as his speech to the Areopagus is concluded, the author of Acts quickly switches the scene to the founding of the Corinthian church. Yet, some Athenians had believed because of Paul's readiness to proclaim the gospel.

The culture today faces temptations similar to what the Athenians faced. While most modern people do not have actual statues or idols, many things compete for attention. Children are not immune to this as video games, sports, possessions and school activities often take priority over the things of God. Children need to know that it is their life purpose to seek the kingdom of God and to be ready to explain why they believe. They can do this by attending Sunday school, Bible studies, and studying at home personally with their family and by themselves.

Also, as other cultural religions grow — real idols and the believer's need to witness against them, are becoming a reality in the modern world.

Paul's Missionary Journeys

AGE GROUP CONSIDERATIONS

In-depth apologetics are best left for older students. However, it is never too early to start building a child's foundation of faith. Memory verses, thoughtful questions, and repetition can prepare a child for more in- depth study at an older age. Take the time to explain things clearly and ask children to reflect back what they have been taught. Do not be surprised when children understand more than one ever thought they could!

SUGGESTED HYMNS/SONGS

1. *Take the Name of Jesus with You*, 313, 2008 Baptist Hymnal.
2. *We Have Heard the Joyful Sound*, 361, 2008 Baptist Hymnal.
3. *Come, Now is the Time to Worship*, 30, 2008 Baptist Hymnal.
2. *Because He Lives*, 449, 2008 Baptist Hymnal.

STUDENT APPLICATIONS

1. Students will know that the book of Acts is found in the New Testament.
2. Students will know that Paul and Silas went on a missionary trip to tell others about Jesus.

3. Students will know that the Bereans readily accepted the Gospel and loved to search the scriptures.
4. Students will know that Paul went to the city of Athens to tell others about Jesus.
5. Students will know that the Athenians worshipped many idols, and an "unknown god."
6. Students will know that Athens was a place where people liked to discuss and debate ideas.
7. Students will know that Paul debated and defended the gospel to the philosophers in the Areopagus.
8. Students will know that God is superior to all false gods.
9. Students will know that one day all people will be judged by God; some for their heavenly reward, and others to eternal separation from God, through judgment.
10. Students will know that it is important to study The Bible and learn all they can about God.

RESOURCES/CREDIT

1. F.F. Bruce, *The New Bible Commentary : Revised*, ed. Donald Guthrie (New York: Wm. B Eerdmans Co.), 996.
2. *Ibid.*

Paul's Letters

BACKGROUND PASSAGES

Main Passage

Acts 27-28   Paul travels to Rome

Philippians 1-4   Paul writes from captivity

Related Passages

Acts 22-26   Paul arrested

Suggested Homiletic Passage

Philippians 4:4-13

MEMORY VERSE

I am sure of this, that He who started a good work in you will carry it on to completion until the day of Christ Jesus.

Philippians 1:6

LESSON OBJECTIVE

Paul was not only a church planter, but a prolific writer. Inspired by God, he wrote letters to instruct, challenge and encourage the early churches. These letters continue to benefit the church today.

LESSON

This is the final of a three lesson series on the life and ministry of Paul. In the first two lessons Paul ministered to his own Jewish brothers and to Gentiles in Philippi and Athens. Paul invested much effort and endured great hardship in starting and nurturing churches.

When Paul returned to Jerusalem from his third missionary journey, he was arrested and spent two years in a Palestinian jail. Paul appealed to Caesar and was sent to Rome to stand trial. This was his right as a Roman citizen. During this time, Paul likely wrote several of the letters we now know as books in the New Testament. Despite the loss of his freedom, God allowed Paul to continue to minister to the churches of his day and throughout all the centuries since.

Acts 27-28

In Jerusalem, a riot broke out as Jews from Asia (the Roman province) accused Paul of teaching against Judaism and profaning the temple. The charges were false, but Paul appealed his case to Caesar. The Roman officials in Jerusalem could take no further action. Paul would have to go to Rome to stand trial.

Paul spent the next two years in captivity in the port city of Caesarea. He was moved there shortly after the Jerusalem riot. When the time finally came for Paul to sail to Rome, Paul was placed under the charge of a centurion named Julius (27:1). Luke gave a detailed account of the ports-of-call and route of the journey.

The sailing was difficult as the ship arrived at Fair Havens on the island of Crete. Paul warned the centurion and the captain that they would risk disaster if they attempted any further travel at that time (27:10). The captain and owner decided that since the harbor at Fair Havens was unsuitable for wintering, they would nonetheless attempt to reach Phoenix. It was a more suitable port in which to spend the winter months.

Ships during Paul's time rarely ventured out on the open sea. For safety, they preferred to hug the shoreline. Paul's ship tried to stay near the coast of Crete, but a fierce wind drove the ship out to sea. The sailors did everything they could to save the ship: They used ropes and tackle to gird the ship. They lowered their drift anchor, and began to jettison cargo to lighten the ship. As the storm entered a third day, they began to throw the ship's gear overboard. They stopped eating (probably because of sea sickness).

Hope waned on the ship as "For many days neither sun nor stars appeared, and the severe storm kept raging..." (27:20). In verse 22, Paul gave all on board encouragement. An angel had appeared to him saying that he must stand before Caesar, and that God would not only spare his life but all those traveling with him. He told the men to eat and take courage; God had revealed to him that the ship would be lost but everyone's life would be spared.

On the fourteenth night of the storm, the sailors sensed they were approaching land. Several soundings (a measure of the depth of the water) confirmed the water was getting more shallow. The sailors, afraid of smashing against a rocky shore in the darkness, dropped anchor and prayed for daylight.

Some sailors attempted to secretly lower their skiff (similar to a lifeboat) and flee the ship. When Paul was made aware of this, he told the centurion that it was imperative for all to remain aboard in order to be saved. If any men left the ship, they would not be saved. The soldiers cut loose the empty skiff and let it free. Despite being a prisoner (and not a sailor), Paul's shipmates clearly had learned to trust him. As daylight approached, Paul encouraged them to eat some food. He gave thanks to God and began to eat. His shipmates followed his example and were further encouraged. Despite his position as a prisoner, God continued to use Paul to minister to others.

When daylight came, the ship made for a beach. The ship ran aground on a sand bar and began to break up. The soldiers wanted to kill all the prisoners to prevent their escape. The centurion, wanting to protect Paul, prevented the soldiers from carrying out the deed. Each person swam or floated on debris to the shore as they could. 276 people had been aboard the ship (27:37). All made it safely to shore. Just as it had been revealed by God to Paul, not a single life was lost.

The island was *Malta*, a small island southwest of Italy. The local people showed kindness to the castaways, lighting a fire and providing shelter. While Paul helped gather firewood, a viper came out of the brushwood and bit him. Paul shook the viper off into the fire. The locals assumed that Paul was a murderer and that *Justice* (a goddess) was punishing Paul in spite of his surviving the shipwreck. They waited for

the poison to take its effect. When Paul suffered no ill effect from the viper, they changed their minds and said that he was a god.

Paul certainly was not a god, but was a faithful servant of the True God. While on Malta, he stayed in the house of an official named Publius. Publius' father was ill, and after Paul prayed for and laid hands on him, God healed him. News of this spread quickly on the small island, and anyone with a disease came to Paul and all were cured. Again, the inconvenience of Paul being a prisoner did not get in the way of God accomplishing His will.

After three months on Malta, Paul set sail for Syracuse on the island of Sicily. They then sailed along the Italian coast to Rhegium, and finally Puteoli, a port not far from Rome. After spending seven days with some believers in Puteoli, Paul went to Rome. Some of the believers in Rome met Paul outside the city to greet and escort him.

While Paul was in Rome, he was permitted to stay by himself with a soldier guard. His impending trial did not keep him from ministering. He called in the leaders of the Jews and "expounded and witnessed about the kingdom of God." Some were persuaded while others were not. Paul had spent two years in Caesarea, and he next spent another two in Rome, welcoming all who came to visit him and teaching them about Jesus.

The book of Acts ends at this point and there is no definite record of the outcome of his trial. Tradition claims that Paul was released after the charges were revealed as unfounded. He then went on other missionary journeys before eventually being arrested once again, that time to be executed during the reign of emperor Nero.

Paul's Letters

Paul worked tirelessly to keep in touch with the churches sprawled across the Roman empire. The New Testament contains no less than thirteen letters of his sent to various churches. The author of Hebrews is unknown, but also may have been written by Paul.

In four of his letters, *Ephesians, Colossians, Philippians* and *Philemon*, Paul mentioned that he was in captivity. Tradition favors Rome as the location from which these letters were written; though other sites, such as Caesarea, have been suggested.[1]

The book of Philippians is uplifting and encouraging. Paul related to the believers in Philippi that his imprisonment had opened doors of ministry (Phil. 1:12). He was so focused on doing God's will that he not only did not fear death, but actually longed to be in God's presence (Phil. 1:22).

Paul told the Philippians that God would finish the good work that He had started in their lives. As they sought His will, they would see, "I am able to do all things through Him who strengthens me." (Phil 4:13).

In his other letters Paul spoke to many issues concerning the church and personal spiritual growth. Whether defining and clarifying important doctrinal issues or giving warm personal greetings, Paul was faithful to continue to minister under every circumstance. Inspired by God, his letters continue to instruct and minister to believers in the twenty-first century.

Suggested Hymns/Songs

1. *We've a Story to Tell*, 356, 2008 Baptist Hymnal.
2. *Take the Name of Jesus with You*, 313, 2008 Baptist Hymnal.
3. *All the Way My Savior Leads Me*, 474, 2008 Baptist Hymnal.

Student Applications

1. Students will know that the book of Acts is found in the New Testament.
2. Students will know that Paul was an apostle sent by God to travel and minister to many people.
3. Students will know that Roman authorities sent Paul to Rome in order to stand trial.
4. Students will know that Paul, under the inspiration of the Holy Spirit, wrote letters to encourage, challenge and instruct believers.
5. Students will know that Paul was falsely accused and imprisoned.
6. Students will know that Paul was shipwrecked on the island of Malta during his journey to Rome.
7. Students will know that Paul, while on Malta, was bitten by a viper but was unharmed.
8. Students will know that Paul continued to minister even while under house arrest in Rome.
9. Students will know that some people will choose to follow God and some will choose to reject Him.
10. Students will know that, regardless of people's response or life's circumstances, believers are to remain faithful in proclaiming the gospel.

Resources/Credit

1. Donald Guthrie. *Eerdmans' Handbook to the Bible* (Grand Rapids: William B. Eerdmans Publishing Company, 1973), 574-5.

Faith of Job

BACKGROUND PASSAGES

Main Passage

Job 1:1-2:10   Testing of Job

Job 42:1-17   Job Restored

Related Passages

Job 38:1-41:34   God addresses Job

Suggested Homiletic Passage

Job 2:3-10

MEMORY VERSE

Throughout all this Job did not sin or blame God for anything.

Job 1:2

LESSON OBJECTIVE

Despite never learning why he endured great calamity and suffering, Job trusted God unconditionally.

LESSON

Everyone eventually asks the question, "Why do some suffer more than others?" Tragedy and suffering are everyday realities, yet many struggle to make sense of events which do not appear to have a purpose. Often the wicked prosper at the expense of the weak. The Bible teaches that nothing can happen outside of God's control and that seemingly pointless sufferings will lead to good. This lesson will study the story of Job where it will be seen that even in the midst of tragedy, God is still in control.

Job 1:1-2:10

Job is introduced as a man of perfect integrity who fears God and despises evil. He had seven sons, seven daughters, and thousands of livestock. He was the greatest man among his people in the land of Uz. The location of Uz is uncertain, but was likely an area synonymous with ancient Edom, northeast of Israel.[1]

Job regularly offered sacrifices and prayed for his children — just in case they had done something that displeased God (v.5). The days in which Job lived are unknown. Job might have lived in the days before Abraham when there was no covenant nor any priests. In those days, it was the father who took the role of priest as the spiritual leader of the family.

If we could name anyone as undeserving of suffering, Job would certainly merit nomination.

In verse 6 the "sons of God" (most translations use the term "angels") appeared before God. God rules all things — even Satan — and works in the world to accomplish His will.

Satan is a created being and can therefore only be in one place at a time and at any moment. Now, standing before God, he told Him that he had been roaming the earth. God commended the faith of His servant Job to Satan (v.8). Satan responded that Job only followed God because he had been materially blessed and had never faced real adversity. "But stretch out your hand and strike everything he owns, and he will curse You to Your face," Satan argued (v.11).

It was at this point that God allowed Satan to take away all that Job owned. It was a time of testing. A time which was still under God's authority. Satan could do only what was allowed by God. Today, death and suffering are still part of this world. As with Job, some suffering in the life of a believer, may be a test of faith.

Job experienced more loss in a span of a couple minutes than most people experience in a lifetime. On that tragic day a servant came to Job and told him that a group of Sabeans (nomads from southwest Arabia)[2], had attacked the servants tending the oxen and donkeys. The Sabeans had taken the livestock, and killed everyone except the messenger himself.

Before this servant finished his tale, another servant arrived and reported that he too was the sole survivor of a great lightning storm which had killed all of Job's sheep and their tending servants.

While the second servant was still speaking, a third servant arrived. He told that a Chaldean (nomads from south Mesopatamia)[3] raiding party had stolen all of Job's camels and their tending servants (with the exception of the messenger).

The three servants had not finished speaking, when a fourth arrived with the worst news of all: Job's sons and daughters had been feasting at the house of his oldest child, when a powerful wind swept over, causing the house to collapse, and thus, killing them all.

How would you react if everything you owned was suddenly taken away? Job's first reaction was to go into a state of mourning: he shaved his head and tore his robe. His next reaction was both unusual and unexpected: he worshiped God. Job admitted that he had come into the world with nothing and would leave with nothing. He knew that anything he had or ever would have had come from God. Thus, in verse 21, he shouted, "Praise the name of the Lord." He did not blame God.

Job chapter two records that Satan was again in God's presence. God once again commended the faith of His servant Job, to which Satan replied, "Skin for skin! A man will give up everything he owns in exchange for his own life." (2:4). Satan believed Job would curse God if he were allowed to harm Job's personal being. God agreed to let Satan physically afflict Job, but to not kill him.

Satan infected Job with incurable boils. The boils extended from the top of his head down to his toes. Job must certainly have been in constant pain, agitated every time he moved. His wife offered little encouragement when she said, "Curse God and die!" (2:9). Job refused to curse God and told his wife that they should be willing to accept not only good from God, but adversity.

Three friends (Eliphaz the Temanite, Bildad the Shuhite, and Zophar the Naamathite) came to offer comfort and sympathy. The next thirty-five chapters record parts of their conversations with Job. Finally, in chapter 38, God, within in a whirlwind, spoke. God reminded them all that He alone is the one in control of everything and that they had no power or authority to question Him.

Job 42:1-17

When God finished speaking, Job humbly confessed that, "Surely I spoke about things I did not understand, things too wonderful for me to know." (v.3). He had not cursed nor turned from God, but had given up hope during his deep suffering. He repented.

It's worth noting that God never explained to Job, the reason for his suffering. Readers of the book of Job are afforded inside knowledge and are privy to the meetings between God and Satan. Job, however, had no knowledge of them. Believers, too, need to realize that they may or may not learn why they or others go through specific times of suffering, but they can be assured that God works all things according to His purpose.

God chastised Job's three friends for not speaking the truth about Him (as Job had). While well-intentioned, they had assumed Job's suffering was the result of sin. God commanded them to bring seven bulls and seven rams and offer them as a sacrifice. They then had to have Job pray for them or God would not accept their prayers (v.8). The men went and did as God commanded, and the Lord did accept Job's prayer. Intercessory prayer is an important responsibility of believers as God truly listens to the prayers of His righteous people.

God then doubly restored Job's prosperity (v.10). His relatives (brothers, sisters, etc.) and friends gathered at his house and offered sympathy and comfort.

In this way, God blessed Job's life: 14,000 sheep, 6,000 camels, 1,000 yoke of oxen and 1,000 female donkeys (v.12) as well as seven more sons and three daughters (who were considered to be the most beautiful in the land). Notice that Job went against ancient customs and gave each daughter a portion of his inheritance. Job lived until the age of 140. He saw his children, grand children, and great-grand children. His faith, tried and true, honored the Lord for generations untold.

Faith of Job

AGE GROUP CONSIDERATIONS

The story of Job provides an opportunity to teach about suffering. Like adults, children naturally wonder why bad things happen. One only needs to watch the news to see multiple examples of what appears to be pointless suffering. When faced with adversity, such as divorce or family illness, children may reach the erroneous conclusion that they are, in some way, responsible. The story of Job reminds believers that God is in control. God will work out all things for His purposes and glory.

Like Job, we may never understand why certain things happen to us, but we can trust our Lord. We can know that God is not malicious, but is loving towards us. The trials of this world are a result of sin, though not always our personal sin. Life circumstances for all reflect man's choice, God's will, and Satan's rebellion. God, however, rules eternal and, in light of eternity, any suffering on earth will be fleeting by comparison.

SUGGESTED HYMNS/SONGS

1. *Great is the Lord*, 61, 2008 Baptist Hymnal.
2. *It Is Well with My Soul*, 447, 2008 Baptist Hymnal.
3. *Love Lifted Me*, 107, 2008 Baptist Hymnal.
4. *Only Trust Him*, 465, 2008 Baptist Hymnal.
5. *His Eye is on the Sparrow*, 93, 2008 Baptist Hymnal.
6. *Sweet Hour of Prayer*, 429, 2008 Baptist Hymnal.

STUDENT APPLICATIONS

1. Students will know that the book of Job is found in the Old Testament.
2. Students will know that Job loved God more than his earthly possessions.
3. Students will know that God allowed Satan to test Job.
4. Students will know that Job never learned the reasons behind his testing.
5. Students will know that despite immense hardship, Job never sinned by cursing or blaming God for his circumstances.
6. Students will know that three friends came to visit and console Job.
7. Students will know that God spoke directly to Job and his friends.
8. Students will know that Job honored God throughout his trials and that God blessed him with family and possessions greater than he previously had owned.

RESOURCES/CREDIT

1. David J.A. Clines, *The International Bible Commentary, Revised Edition*, F.F. Bruce, ed. (Grand Rapids, Michigan: Zondervan Publishing House, 1979), 522.
2. Derrick Kiddner. *Eerdmans' Handbook to the Bible* (Grand Rapids: William B. Eerdmans Publishing Company, 1973), 320.
3. *Ibid.*

Peter & Cornelius

BACKGROUND PASSAGES

Main Passage

Acts 10   Peter and Cornelius

Related Passages

Leviticus 11   Unclean Animals

Suggested Homiletic Passage

Acts 10:34-40

MEMORY VERSE

...but in every nation the person who fears Him and does righteousness is acceptable to Him.

Acts 10:35

LESSON OBJECTIVE

God first sent His message of salvation to the Israelites, but as Peter learned, God commands believers to share the Good News with all people.

LESSON

First century Judea was an exciting and troubling time for the Jewish people. Soldiers occupied the land, maintained order, and ensured allegiance to the Roman Empire. The Jews yearned for the day when they would throw off the yoke of their oppressors. The Israelites worshiped the True God while the Romans and other nations engaged in pagan practices.

In the early days of the church, the Jewish followers focused almost exclusively on preaching the Good News to other Jews. That Jewish law that forbid association with foreigners was still a powerful stigma. The idea that Jesus would overthrow the Roman empire, free the Jews, and rule as Messiah over the Jews alone was seen in a new light. Peter was quick to see that many Jewish teachings were to forever change. He had a vision from God, and led by the Holy Spirit, he saw that God does not show favoritism, but desires that all people know Him.

Acts 10:1-48

Caesarea, famous for its excellent harbor on the Mediterranean Sea, was the Roman capitol of the province of Judea. It was also home away from home, for a man named Cornelius. He was a centurion in the Italian Regiment. Although a part of the occupying Roman army, Cornelius was not a cold-blooded, pagan-worshiping soldier. Rather, he was devout and God-fearing. He prayed regularly to God. He showed compassion on the inhabitants of Caesarea by giving to those in need. However, he was not a Christian. He had not heard and accepted the Gospel message of Christ. Cornelius' experience would prove that those who earnestly seek God will find Him.

One day while praying, Cornelius had a vision. An angel appeared before him. The angel commended him for his prayers and gifts to the poor. The angel then commanded Cornelius to send men to Joppa to bring back a man named Simon Peter. The angel gave some details as to the exact location of Peter and then was gone. Cornelius immediately called two servants and a devoted soldier. He told them about the vision and dispatched them to Joppa to find Peter.

Joppa, located approximately 20 miles south of Caesarea, was also on the Mediterranean coast. About noon the next day, Peter, while waiting for dinner, went up on the roof to pray. It was common in Bible times for a home to have a flat roof that could be accessed by stairs. It was during his prayer time that Peter fell into a trance.

While in the trance, Peter had a vision that resembled a large sheet being lowered to the earth. Inside the sheet were four-footed animals, reptiles and various kinds of birds. A voice told Peter, "kill and eat!" (v.13). All of the animals were considered unclean under the Mosaic law. Peter refused, claiming he would never eat anything unclean. Old Testament law prohibited eating certain "unclean" animals (Leviticus 11). These laws reminded the Israelites that God had set them apart from the pagan nations. When followed, the laws prevented

Peter & Cornelius

them from adopting pagan worship practices and had other practical benefits regarding sanitation and nutrition.

The voice responded, "What God has made clean, you must not call common (unclean)." (v.15). The importance of the vision was emphasized as it repeated two more times.

Peter was perplexed and did not immediately understand the vision. As he pondered the meaning, Cornelius' men arrived at the house. The Holy Spirit informed Peter that three men were waiting for him downstairs. He was go with the men, without fear, because God had sent them.

The three men spent the night with Peter; the next day the men, Peter, and several of the Joppa Christians made the journey to Caesarea. Expecting their arrival, Cornelius had called together his friends and relatives.

When Peter first entered the house, Cornelius fell at his feet. Peter helped him up saying, "Stand up! I myself am also a man." (v.26). Peter refused to take any of the glory that belonged to God alone.

Peter then addressed the awkward question that was surely on the mind of all present. Why did Peter come to visit Cornelius when it was forbidden for Jews to associate with foreigners? While it is true that the Levitical law commanded the Israelites to live holy lives (unlike the pagan nations), God intended Israel to be the light of the world. They failed in that mission. It was Jesus who truly was (and is) the light of the world. Over time, the Israelites added more and more rules to God's law to the point that they effectively walled themselves off from ministering to foreigners. It was these extra-biblical laws that Peter addressed.

Peter now fully understood the meaning of his vision. God wanted Peter (and all believers) to know that no person is common nor unclean. Not only could they socialize, their time together had been ordained by God.

Cornelius talked with Peter and shared the vision that he had experienced several days prior. He was glad that Peter had come, and was eager "to hear everything you have been commanded by the Lord." (v.33).

Peter began to speak to the crowd, sharing the good news of Jesus with the Gentiles. He had learned that God does not show favoritism. Anyone who desires to follow God may do so through Jesus Christ. As Peter began to share about the good news of peace through Jesus, he talked about Jesus' miraculous acts, His death, and resurrection on the third day. Peter said that he and others were witnesses to these events. The resurrected Jesus was not a ghost nor a spirit, as He had proven when He dined with His followers before he ascended to heaven (v.41). Jesus had commanded Peter and all of His followers to preach the Gospel message to all people. Jesus is the God-ordained judge of the living and the dead. The good news is that "... through His name everyone who believes in Him will receive forgiveness of their sins." (v.43).

God's message, through Peter, had a powerful effect on those gathered in Cornelius' home. It was not because of Peter's speaking skills, but because of the working of the Holy Spirit. The Holy Spirit came upon those present and they began to speak in other languages and praise God for His greatness.

The Jewish believers who had traveled with Peter were astounded to see the Spirit poured out on Gentiles. It was then clear to them that God desires that all people would come to know Him.

The new Gentile believers were baptized, in the name of Lord Jesus, as their first act of obedience. They asked Peter to stay with them for a few days. Their journey with Jesus had just begun and as long as Peter would be willing, they desired to learn all they could from him about their new Lord.

The early church had learned an important lesson through Peter's experience. God desires that all people hear the Gospel message and be saved. Today there are believers in almost every nation who worship and follow the True and Living God. As followers of Jesus, believers should also be prepared to share the Good News of Jesus with unbelievers.

AGE GROUP CONSIDERATIONS

The focus of this lesson could easily turn toward the evil of racism. It would be better to emphasize the preaching of the Gospel to all peoples. Realizing that Jesus died for all people helps believers to see them the way He does. This in itself should make great strides in helping believers accept others who are different from themselves.

SUGGESTED HYMNS/SONGS

1. *Revive Us Again*, 493, 2008 Baptist Hymnal.
2. *He Lives*, 269, 2008 Baptist Hymnal.
3. *Because He Lives*, 449, 2008 Baptist Hymnal.

STUDENT APPLICATIONS

1. Students will know that the story of Peter and Cornelius is found in the New Testament book of Acts.
2. Students will know Cornelius was a centurion in the Roman army that occupied Israel.
3. Students will know that Peter was one of Jesus' disciples, and an apostle.
4. Students will know that one day, while Cornelius was praying, an angel spoke to him and told him to send for Peter (whom he did not know).
5. Students will know that Peter saw a vision in which unclean animals were lowered to earth in a sheet.
6. Students will know that the Holy Spirit directed Peter to go with Cornelius' men.
7. Students will know that Jewish men were forbidden to associate with foreigners such as Cornelius.
8. Students will know that Peter learned from the vision that it was okay to associate with foreigners since the Gospel is for all people.
9. Students will know that Peter shared the Good News with Cornelius, his family, and close friends.
10. Students will know that all the nonbelievers who were present at Cornelius' home followed Jesus and were baptized.
11. Students will know that they too can engage in evangelism through sharing the gospel and inviting others to church.

Micah the Prophet

BACKGROUND PASSAGES

Main Passage
Micah 1-7   Micah's prophecies

Related Passages
Jeremiah 26:16-19 Micah quoted by Jeremiah
Hosea   Preached similar message

Suggested Homiletic Passage
Micah 4:1-5

MEMORY VERSE

He has told you men what is good and what it is the Lord requires of you: Only to act justly, to love faithfulness, and to walk humbly with your God.
Micah 6:8

LESSON OBJECTIVE

God sent prophets to confront His people with their sin and to tell about future events. The Israelites would be disciplined for their sins, but God showed His enduring love by promising that one day a Savior would rule over the nations and provide for His people.

LESSON

This month our children will learn about Old Testament minor prophets, specifically the prophet Micah, and their messages from God. God loved His people but was grieved by their sinful ways. God would send judgment to turn their hearts back to Him. Since prophets were sent by God to confront His people with their sins and to foretell future events, Micah is a book of hope. God promised a savior and King (Jesus) to rule over all the nations and provide for His people.

Micah 1-7

The prophet Micah is one of the "minor prophets." The term "minor" is used only to compare the relative length of the prophetic books. Little is

known about Micah's personal life or background. Jeremiah wrote that Micah was from the town of Moresheth and prophesied during the time of King Hezekiah, who reigned from 715 to 686 B.C. (Jeremiah 26:16-19).

Like all of God's prophets, he came to God's people with a serious and life-changing message. God was displeased with how they were living, and as a result, there would be consequences.

God had made a covenant with the people of Israel. In this covenant, each party had responsibilities. The Israelites were to be faithful to God, and while God had always been faithful, the Israelites were not. Like all sinful people, they often followed their own way. There had been periods of time when they were close to God, but by the time of the prophets, the people's hearts were far from God.

The book of Micah can be viewed in three cycles. Each of which begins with a Hebrew word meaning "*hear*." (1:2, 3:1, 6:1). Each cycle is prophesied to begin with judgment and end with salvation. Much of the language in Micah resembles a court case where the evidence is presented and judgment pronounced. Micah was so distraught over the Lord's message that he went into mourning (1:8).

Because of the people's rebellion, Micah proclaimed, "Look, the Lord is leaving His place and coming down to trample the heights of the earth." (1:3). How had the people had rebelled? God held several things against them.

1. The leaders had created places of worship for false idols that drew the people away from God. (1:5-7).
2. People in high positions abused their power and stole land, homes, and property from others (2:1-2).
3. Women and children were displaced into abject poverty because of the greed of those in high positions (2:9).
4. The leaders had heard God's Word but shamelessly rejected it (2:2) .
5. The leaders hated good and loved evil (3:2).

Micah the Prophet

One of God's characteristics is His holiness. Another characteristic is His righteousness. God cannot tolerate sin in His presence; it demands His judgment. God disciplines those He loves, and Israel was no exception. The judgment of discipline was a common message delivered by prophets. God would discipline His people in a way that would turn their hearts and minds back toward Him.

This judgment would involve the invasion of two major powers: Assyria and Babylon. The judgment on Samaria (1:6) happened at the hands of the Assyrians during Micah's lifetime (723 B.C.) . Jerusalem would not fall to the Babylonians for another century (587 B.C.).

Micah's message was opposed by false prophets. In Micah 3:5 the Lord accused the false prophets of leading the people astray by saying that all was well and that judgment was not forthcoming. It seems that proclaiming this false truth was a lucrative enterprise as the prophets were rewarded financially for their "good news." (3:11).

Understandably, Micah's message of judgment was not popular, yet it was true. But despite the unfavorable aspect of the message, Micah also proclaimed a message of great hope and salvation.

God's perfect creation has been spoiled by sin. God's righteousness demands that sin be punished, but God's steadfast loyal love would not let His rebellious people go.[1] He had a plan to save His people from the penalty of sin.

In chapter five, Micah proclaimed that out of the soon-to-be besieged nation, a mighty ruler would come forth. "Bethlehem Ephrathah, you are small among the clans of Judah. One will come from you to be ruler over Israel for Me. His origin is from antiquity, from eternity." (5:2). The ruler foretold is Jesus.

700 years before His birth, Micah foretold the birthplace of Jesus. When Jesus returns, the armies of the nations of the earth will be in place, intent on destroying Israel once and for all. At that time Jesus will conquer them all and establish His earthly kingdom (5:4).

The Kingdom of God is also present today in the lives of believers who make up the church. While the arrival of an enemy army may not be impending, salvation can be found through a personal relationship with Jesus.

On that final day God will gather together all His people, and they will live with Him in exceeding joy. Micah concludes, "He will again have compassion on us; He will vanquish our iniquities. You will cast all our sins into the depths of the sea. You will show loyalty to Jacob and faithful love to Abraham, as You swore to our fathers from days ago." (7:19-20).

AGE GROUP CONSIDERATIONS

"Why did God get so angry at His people?" is a question some children may ask when studying the Old Testament prophets. Nonbelievers sometimes argue that wrath and judgment are incompatible with a loving God. They may use this as an excuse not to follow Him. How are we to understand God's acts of judgment?

It helps to view the question theologically as opposed to psychologically. Our society views all anger as a malevolent passion that must be suppressed. God's anger, however, is never irrational nor out of control, but rather, is righteously motivated by His concern for right and wrong.

God's love and concern are the sources of His anger. He cares about His people and is upset when they are indifferent toward sin. Acts of judgment are provoked by the actions of His people.

Thankfully, God is patient and long-suffering. His judgments have a twofold purpose: redemption and restoration. God will bring His people back to Himself. God does not hold onto His anger forever, because He delights in everlasting love.[2] "For His anger lasts only a moment, but His favor, a lifetime." (Psalm 30:5).

Love is not the opposite of anger. Indifference is the opposite of anger. God is personal. He actively and purposely works for the redemption of His people.[3]

Micah the Prophet

Supplemental Material

Elements of this lesson are abstract and may not easily lend themselves to narrative or rotational lessons. Since all the minor prophets proclaimed a similar message, teachers may wish to broaden the scope of this lesson by including the story of Hosea (as another prophet who obeyed God). Hosea's redemption of his unfaithful wife, Gomer, powerfully illustrates God's willingness to love us in spite of our sin.

Details of Gomer's unfaithfulness are not appropriate for young children. So, for them, simply state that Gomer did not take care of her spouse and children in the way that was pleasing to God.

SUGGESTED HYMNS/SONGS

1. *Living for Jesus*, 545, 2008 Baptist Hymnal.
2. *Wonderful Words of Life*, 338, 2008 Baptist Hymnal.
3. *God will Make a Way*, 85, 2008 Baptist Hymnal.
4. *Soon and Very Soon*, 599, 2008 Baptist Hymnal.

STUDENT APPLICATIONS

1. Students will know that the book of Micah is found in the Old Testament.
2. Students will know that Micah was a prophet who told his people the messages he received from God.
3. Students will know that Micah is considered a "minor" prophet only because his book is short, not because his message was any less important.
4. Students will know that God was displeased with how His people had rebelled against him.
5. Students will know that God was displeased with the leaders of Judah and Israel because they mistreated the people by misusing their authority.
6. Students will know that God sent an invading army to punish His people and to turn their hearts back toward Him.
7. Students will know that God also promised salvation. A Messiah would be born and care for His people.
8. Students will know that Micah prophesied the birth (and even location) of Jesus approximately 700 years before He was born in Bethlehem.
9. Students will know that they can be obedient to God by turning from their sins and trusting in His Son Jesus.
10. Students will know that holiness and righteousness are two of God's attributes.
11. Students will know that God only disciplines His children so that they will return to Him.

RESOURCES/CREDIT

1. Robert L. Cate. *Old Testament Roots for New Testament Faith* (Nashville: Broadman Press, 1982), 173.
2. *Ibid.*, 76-84.
3. Trent C. Butler, "*Praise our Incomparable God,*" *Explore the Bible Adult Commentary: Isaiah, Micah*, Lifeway (Spring 2006 Volume 10, Number 3): 138.

BACKGROUND PASSAGES

Main Passage
Luke 1:5-80   Mary & Elizabeth

Related Passages
Luke 2:1-22   The Nativity

Suggested Homiletic Passage
Luke 1:26-35

MEMORY VERSE

Younger version
    Now listen: You will conceive and give birth to a son, and you will call His name JESUS.

Luke 1:31

Older version
    Now listen: You will conceive and give birth to a son, and you will call His name JESUS. He will be great and will be called the Son of the Most High, and the Lord God will give Him the throne of His father David.

Luke 1:31-32

LESSON OBJECTIVE

    During the Christmas season believers celebrate the birth of Jesus. Elizabeth and Mary were ordinary women used by God as part of His plan for our redemption, showing that God can use anyone who submits to His will.

LESSON

    Thoughts about Christmas and the birth of Jesus usually bring to mind images of shepherds, animals, and a baby in a stable on a cold winter night. Obviously, there is more to the story. This Christmas rotation lesson will focus on the events that engulfed Mary and Elizabeth as the angel Gabriel announced their vital roles in God's plan through the births of

John the Baptist and the Messiah. God's use of these two ordinary women serves to remind that God can do anything, and He can use anyone in powerful and meaningful ways to accomplish His will.

Luke 1:5-80

    At the beginning of Luke's gospel we are introduced to Zechariah and Elizabeth. Both are descendants of Aaron. Zechariah was serving as a priest. They are described as, "... righteous in God's sight, living without blame according to all the commandments and requirements of the Lord." (v.6). As much as they delighted in serving God, there was one thing that brought them sadness. They were elderly and had no children.

    Zechariah was a priest in the division of Abijah. In King David's time, the priests were divided into twenty-four divisions (I Chronicles 24:3-19). Each division served in the temple for one week, twice a year. Twice daily, incense was burned in the Holy Place inside the temple. The priest who burned the incense was chosen by lot. The people would prostrate themselves (in prayer) outside the temple as the priest entered the Holy Place. After burning the incense, the priest would exit the temple and bless the waiting worshipers.[1] A priest was not allowed this privilege more than once in his lifetime, and many priests never had the privilege.[2] Once, while on temple duty, Zechariah was chosen for the honor of burning the incense.

    At the appointed hour, the assembly of worshipers watched as Zechariah entered the Holy Place. As Zechariah began his duties at the altar, the angel Gabriel appeared next to him. Zechariah was startled and overcome with fear. Gabriel told him he need not be fearful, for he brought good news. Elizabeth would bear him a son and they would name him John. John would be no ordinary baby. He would be filled with the Holy Spirit while still in his mother's womb. Perhaps most intriguing, Zechariah was told, "He will turn many of the sons of Israel to the Lord their God. And he will go before Him (the Messiah) in the spirit

Christmas - Mary & Elizabeth

and power of Elijah." (v.16-7). John would be the last of the Old Testament prophets and prepare the way for Jesus' ministry. Zechariah's reaction was to doubt and question. Because of his disbelief, Gabriel told Zechariah that he would be unable to speak until after John was born.

The encounter with the angel delayed Zechariah's exit from the sanctuary. When he finally came out, the worshippers, concerned about the extended absence, soon realized he had seen a vision because he had lost the ability to speak. After he returned home from his service, Elizabeth conceived, just as Gabriel had prophesied. She was thankful that God had removed the disgrace of barrenness, despite her advanced age.

In the sixth month of Elizabeth's pregnancy, Gabriel was sent by God to the town of Nazareth in Galilee. He appeared to Mary, who was engaged to a man named Joseph. Gabriel announced to Mary, "Rejoice, favored woman! The Lord is with you." (v.27). The greeting did little to calm Mary's fears. What the angel told her next was even more amazing than what Zechariah had been told:

"Now listen: You will conceive and give birth to a son, and you will call His name Jesus. He will be great and will be called the Son of the Most High, and the Lord God will give Him the throne of His father David. He will reign over the house of Jacob forever, and His kingdom will have no end." (v.31-3).

Mary 's first thought was that this could not happen since she had been intimate with any man.

She asked the angel how it would happen. Gabriel told her that the child would be conceived by the Holy Spirit. The Holy One born to her would be known as the Son of God. Gabriel assured her that nothing was impossible with God. Even her relative Elizabeth, who was considered barren, was expecting a child. Mary's response was one of acceptance, "I am the Lord's slave. May it be done to me according to your word." (v.38).

The virgin birth is critical to Christianity because it shows that Jesus is God, and not merely a great man.

Hobbs says it succinctly, "The virgin birth is morally necessary (Gen. 3:15), divinely possible (Luke 1:37), authentically recorded (Luke 1:1-3), and experientially affirmed (John 3:16).[3]

We do not know the exact relationship of Mary to Elizabeth, but after Gabriel's announcement, Mary set out quickly to Judah to visit Zechariah and Elizabeth. When she entered the house, she greeted Elizabeth. While they were greeting, Elizabeth's baby (John) "leaped in her womb," a sign that he was already filled with the Holy Spirit (as Gabriel had foretold) and recognized the presence of Mary and Jesus. The meeting was joyous.

Mary gave praise to God for the blessing of being privileged to be the mother of the Messiah, "... because He has looked with favor on the humble condition of His slave. Surely, from now on all generations will call me blessed." (v.48). Mary's praise honored Jesus' mercy and power. Jesus who was to be the hope for the nations.

Mary stayed with Zechariah and Elizabeth three months. Her departure would have been close to the time that Elizabeth gave birth. When Elizabeth did give birth to a son, her neighbors and relatives rejoiced because of the mercy God had shown to her. On the eighth day, her baby boy was to be circumcised, and, as was Jewish tradition, it was also the day on which the child was named. Those present at the circumcision expected that the child would be named Zechariah, after his father. Elizabeth interrupted and said, "No! He will be called John." (v.59). This caused confusion since no one in her family was named John. Zechariah (still unable to talk) motioned for a tablet. He wrote, "His name is John." Immediately, he regained the ability to speak and began to praise God. Fear came over all those who lived nearby, and word about John spread around the region. Many people wondered what would become of the child as it was obvious that God's anointing was on him.

Zechariah was filled with the Holy Spirit and prophesied. "Praise the Lord, the God of Israel, because He has visited and provided redemption for

His people. He has raised up a horn of salvation for us in the house of His servant David." (v.68-9). Jesus was to be a descendant of David, and the Messiah of whom the prophets had spoken hundreds of years previously. John would have an important role in preparing the people for the ministry of the Messiah, "And child, you will be called a prophet of the Most High, for you will go before the Lord to prepare His ways, to give His people knowledge of salvation through the forgiveness of sins." (v.76-7).

Little is known of Jesus' childhood, but less is known of John's. A single verse (v.80) states that he grew up in the wilderness and became spiritually strong. The next reference of John is as an adult ministering in the wilderness.

God works in ways that are often unexpected, as He did when He used Elizabeth and Mary in His plan of redemption. God can also use believers in a powerful and meaningful way when they submit to His will. At Christmas time, our children can take encouragement that God works through ordinary people as they celebrate the birth of the Messiah.

The Nativity: Luke 2:1-22

It would not seem to be Christmas without a look at the nativity. This lesson focuses on Mary & Elizabeth, but feel free to share the narrative about what actually happened at Jesus' birth. Two of the other lessons, *Christmas - The Messiah Prophesied* and *Christmas - the Shepherds* cover the events surrounding the nativity.

AGE GROUP CONSIDERATIONS

In-depth discussion about the virgin birth may lead to issues of sexuality that young children are not ready to learn. However, it is vital that children know that God was the Father of Jesus. Handle this topic with care, but do not compromise the truth.

SUGGESTED HYMNS/SONGS

1. *Mary Did You Know?*, 209, 2008 Baptist Hymnal.

2. *Gentle Mary Laid Her Child*, 219, 2008 Baptist Hymnal.
3. *Joy to the World*, 181, 2008 Baptist Hymnal.
4. *Emmanuel*, 201, 2008 Baptist Hymnal.
5. *O Come, O Come, Emmanuel*, 175, 2008 Baptist Hymnal.

STUDENT APPLICATIONS

1. Students will know that the story of Elizabeth and Mary is found in the New Testament book of Luke.
2. Students will know that a priest, Zechariah, was told by an angel, Gabriel, that his wife, Elizabeth, would give birth to a baby boy.
3. Students will know that Zechariah and Elizabeth's son was John the Baptist.
4. Students will know that the angel Gabriel announced to Mary that she would be the mother of Jesus the Messiah.
5. Students will know that the conception of Jesus was from the Holy Spirit.
6. Students will know that Mary visited Elizabeth while they were expecting their children.
7. Students will know that because of his disbelief, Zechariah was unable to speak until after John's birth.
8. Students will know that God can use them in a powerful and meaningful way if they submit to His will.

RESOURCES/CREDIT

1. Laurance E. Porter, *The International Bible Commentary*, Revised Edition, F.F. Bruce, ed. (Grand Rapids, Michigan: Zondervan Publishing House, 1979), 1187-8.
2. I.H. Marshall, *The New Bible Commentary : Revised, ed.* Donald Guthrie (New York: Wm. B. Eerdmans Co.), 890.
3. Herschel H. Hobbs, *Fundamentals of Our Faith* (Nashville: Broadman & Holman Publishers, 1960), 45-6.

Healing at Bethesda Pool

BACKGROUND PASSAGES

Main Passage

Verse	Summary
John 5:1-21	Healing of the lame man

Related Passages

Verse	Summary
Mark 2:1-12	Healing in Capernaum

Suggested Homiletic Passage
John 5:5-15

MEMORY VERSE

Younger version

I assure you: Anyone who hears My word and believes Him who sent Me has eternal life....

John 5:24a

Older version

I assure you: Anyone who hears My word and believes Him who sent Me has eternal life and will not come under judgment but has passed from death to life.

John 5:24

LESSON OBJECTIVE

Jesus has compassion on individuals who suffer from physical illness or affliction; however, a person's greatest need is not physical healing but the forgiveness of sins (leading to a life of pure living).

LESSON

While on earth Jesus performed many miracles, including many healings. These healings showed that He has great compassion for people in physical need. His healings also gave testimony to His divinity. Being fully God, yet fully man, Jesus could identify with and heal any sickness or disability. One day, while Jesus was in Jerusalem, he healed a man who had been sick for thirty-eight years. More important than physical healing, He taught the man the necessity of repentance leading to the forgiveness of his sins.

John 5:1-18

Jesus came to Jerusalem to observe one of the annual Jewish festivals (John does not tell us which festival). One of Jerusalem's gates was known as the "*Sheep Gate*." Near this gate was a water source known as the Bethesda pool.

The Bethesda pool can still be seen today in Jerusalem. In actuality, it is composed of two pools separated by a ridge of rock. Surrounding the pools were four covered colonnades with a fifth built on the ridge between the pools. The water was piped into the city from a reservoir known as Solomon's pools southwest of Bethlehem.[1]

The five colonnades gave shelter to a multitude of sick people: the blind, lame, and paralyzed. They gathered around the Bethesda pool because, from time to time, an angel would come and stir up the water. After the water had been stirred, the first (and only the first) person to enter the water was cured of his/her particular ailment.

There was a man at the pool who had been sick for thirty-eight years. Jesus noticed the man and asked him, "Do you want to get well?" (v.6). While it is easy to think the answer would be obvious, some people actually become so comfortable with reduced abilities that they do not have the will to face the challenge of a normal life, but would choose to remain in a condition of suffering. The man's answer revealed that he desired to be healed, but did not have the means to reach the pool. Due to his condition, the man could not move quickly, and when the water was stirred, another person always entered before him. It is unlikely that he had spent the last thirty-eight years by the pool, but it was also unlikely that he would ever be healed by entering the pool first.

Jesus commanded the man to "Get up, pick up your bedroll and walk!" (v.8). The man immediately stood up and began to walk — he was completely healed. The healing took place on the Sabbath, the day of the week for which the Jewish religious leaders had developed a detailed list of rules governing what could or could not be done. The laws had the original intent of preventing people from sinning, but instead of showing compassion or celebrating the miraculous healing, some of the religious leaders began to complain that the man was breaking one of their laws by carrying his bedroll (a mat or pallet of straw) on the Sabbath.

When they asked him, "Who told you to carry your bedroll?" the man said that he did not know. Jesus was no longer present, since He had slipped into the crowd immediately after the healing. Soon after this, while at the temple, the man saw Jesus once again. Jesus told the man, "See, you are well. Do not sin any more, so that something worse doesn't happen to you." (v.14). What could be worse than thirty-eight years of illness? Jesus was warning the man of the destructive power of sin. While illness can lead to physical death, sin leads to eternal, spiritual death. While the sick desire physical healing, they (along with the healthy) have a greater need for spiritual healing. Spiritual healing can only occur when an individual repents of his/her sins and follows Jesus.

The healed man's response to Jesus is not recorded. Did he repent? Did he ignore Jesus? We know he did report back to the religious leaders that it was Jesus who had healed him.

The religious leaders confronted Jesus and accused Him of breaking the Sabbath laws. God intended for the Sabbath to be a blessing to people, not a burden. Jesus said, "My Father is still working, and I am working also." (v.17). This only increased the anger of the leaders as they realized Jesus was now claiming to be equal with God (which He is).

In verses 19-23, Jesus talked about the special relationship He and God the Father have, as two of the three members of the Trinity. They are always in perfect unity. Jesus always does the will of the Father. All people will honor the Son just as they will honor the Father. The best news is found in verse 21. "And just as the Father raises the dead and gives them life, so the Son also gives life to anyone He wants to." What is required to gain the life of which Jesus spoke? Just as He had told the man whom He had healed: repent and turn from your sins. The eternal life that Jesus gives is greater than anything we Christians may experience, good or bad, in our time here on earth.

Jesus showed compassion on a man who could not help himself. Believers can pray in confidence, knowing that Jesus hears our prayers and cares when we go through times of sickness or physical affliction. Believers know that physical healing may or may not come in this life, but that the true miracle is that all who repent and follow Jesus will gain eternal life.

Artist's conception of the Bethesda Pool.

Healing at Bethesda Pool

AGE GROUP CONSIDERATIONS

Children may struggle with the concept of spiritual healing being more important than physical healing. It's natural to desire healing for ourselves and others when dealing with sickness or physical affliction. Remind the children that God works all things for the good of those who love Him. Suffering is a reality in this fallen world, though God may use illness or affliction to lead us and others to trust Him more. The Lord may even grant some physical healing. Ultimately, physical healing will only happen when believers receive their eternal, or resurrection, bodies.

SUGGESTED HYMNS/SONGS

1. *All Hail the Power of Jesus' Name*, 214, 2008 Baptist Hymnal.
2. *He is Lord*, 277, 2008 Baptist Hymnal.
3. *I Have Decided to Follow Jesus*, 434, 2008 Baptist Hymnal.
4. *In Christ Alone*, 506, 2008 Baptist Hymnal.

STUDENT APPLICATIONS

1. Students will know that the story of healing of the lame man at the Bethesda pool is found in the New Testament book of John.
2. Students will know that there was a water source in Jerusalem known as the Bethesda pool.
3. Students will know that an angel occasionally came and stirred the water in the Bethesda pool. When this happened, the first sick or injured person to enter the water was cured of his/her ailment.
4. Students will know that many sick and injured people gathered around the pool hoping for the chance to be cured of their illness or affliction.
5. Students will know that there was a lame man who waited by the pool, but had no hope of receiving healing because he had no one to help him into the pool.
6. Students will know that Jesus showed compassion to the lame man and healed him.
7. Students will know that Jesus later warned the man, whom He had healed, to avoid sinning.
8. Students will know that spiritual healing is more important than physical healing.
9. Students will know that Jesus did the will of Father God.
10. Students will know that some people, because of their hardened hearts, were upset that Jesus healed the man on the Sabbath.
11. Students will know that ultimate healing will happen when believers receive their resurrected bodies.

RESOURCES/CREDIT

1. Frederick Fyvie Bruce, *The Gospel & Epistles of John* (Grand Rapids: William B. Eerdmans Publishing Co., 1983), 122-3.

The Three Friends & the Fiery Furnace

Background Passages

Main Passage
Daniel 3:1-30 — Gold statue and the furnaces

Related Passages
Daniel 1 — Training of young Jewish men

Suggested Homiletic Passage
Daniel 3:24-29

Memory Verse

Younger
Do not make an idol for yourself...

Exodus 20:4a

Older
Do not make an idol for yourself, whether in the shape of anything in the heavens above or on earth below or in the waters under the earth. You must not bow down to them..."

Exodus 20:4-5a

Lesson Objective

Shadrach, Meshach and Abednego were faced with a tough decision. They chose to risk their lives by giving God the glory instead of worshipping a powerless idol.

Lesson

Shadrach, Meshach and Abednego (hereafter referred to as the three friends) were young men who had been taken from their homes and raised in a foreign land. Despite the circumstances they faced, they put their faith in God to lead and protect them during their time in Babylon. One day the three friends were forced to choose between their own lives and their faith in God. What happened that day proved that when God receives the glory He alone deserves, He will be faithful to bless.

Daniel 3:1-30

King Nebuchadnezzar decided to build a huge statue. No description of the statue is given, other than its height being ninety feet. It may have been a type of obelisk, but some translations, such as the ESV, use the word "*image*" instead of "*statue*" suggesting the monument resembled a person. In this lesson, we will refer to it as a "statue."

What was the purpose of the statue? Nebuchadnezzar might have built it as a monument to himself or to the greatness of the Babylonian empire. It might have been built to symbolically unify the many new peoples that had been conquered and assimilated into the empire. While his motivation is unknown, it is clearly seen that Nebuchadnezzar used the statue to test the loyalty of his officials.

After the statue had been erected, word was sent for all the officials who were responsible for the day-to-day operations of the kingdom to assemble in the court before Nebuchadnezzar and the statue. Among those assembled were rulers of the various provinces, Nebuchadnezzar's personal advisers, treasurers (who oversaw the kingdom finances), and judges. Comparing this gathering with the coming-together of American politicians for the annual *State of the Union* address may give a context to the importance of the event.

Once the officials had gathered, a herald called out, "People of every nation and language, you are commanded: When you hear the sound of the horn, flute, zither, lyre, harp, drum, and every kind of music, you are to fall down and worship the gold statue that King Nebuchadnezzar has set up." (v.4-5). There would be severe consequences for those who refused. Anyone who did not bow to the statue would be thrown into a furnace and killed by its blazing fire.

The Babylonian empire was made of many cultures, nations and peoples who worshipped many gods. Surely many of those present at the dedication found the command offensive? Would anyone dare

The Three Friends & the Fiery Furnace

to defy the command of the king? When the music played, all bowed ... all except three.

The three friends, along with Daniel, had been deported from their home to Babylon while they were still youth. By God's grace, Daniel and the three friends found favor in the eyes of successive Babylonian kings and were promoted to important positions in the government. The three friends were among the officials at the dedication. Because of their belief in the One True God, they refused to bow to the powerless, idolatrous statue.

While believers may not face the temptation to bow to a statue, anything that is given value or importance to that rightfully belongs to God is an idol. Idols for children may include video games, television, disrespect to parents, sports, or material possessions.

Their refusal to bow might have been overlooked, except that a group of Chaldeans took the opportunity to maliciously accuse the Jews (v.8). The Chaldeans were people who lived up and down the valley of the Tigris and Euphrates rivers.[1] In verses 9-12 the king is told of the three friends' actions. The Chaldeans apparently sought to stoke the king's wrath by saying, "These men have ignored you, the king; they do not serve your gods or worship the gold statue you have set up." (v.12).

During their Babylonian (and later Persian) captivity, several evil plots were devised against the Jews. Daniel was thrown into a lions' den because of the jealousy of three satraps (governors). Esther and Mordecai were the target of evil Haman's plot to wipe out all the Jews. In this case, the Chaldeans were the core people group from which the empire had its origin. They may have taken offense at the Jewish outsiders. Nonetheless, when God's people live faithfully for Him, they should expect opposition.

The three friends were brought before the furious king. Despite his anger, he gave the three one more opportunity to obey. If they would bow when the music was played, he would spare their lives. If they did not, they would be immediately thrown into the furnace. The king flaunted the authority of his position by asking, "... who is the god who can rescue you from my power?" (v15). The three friends replied, "Nebuchadnezzar, we don't need to give you an answer to this question. If the God we serve exists, then He can rescue us from the furnace of blazing fire, and He can rescue us from the power of you, the king. But even if He does not rescue us, we want you as king to know that we will not serve your gods or worship the gold statue you have set up." (v.16-18). The three friends, in good conscience, could not worship that which they knew to be false.

While the three friends intended no disrespect toward the king, their answer did nothing to soothe his anger. The HCSB version states, "the expression on his face changed toward Shadrach, Meshach, and Abednego." (v.19). He gave orders to heat the furnace seven times hotter than normal. He had some of his strongest soldiers bind and tie the three friends. The heat and flames were so intense that the men who threw the three friends into the furnace perished. The three friends fell into the furnace, fully clothed and bound, to their certain deaths.

While gazing into the furnace, Nebuchadnezzar suddenly jumped up in alarm! He asked his advisers, "Didn't we throw three men, bound, into the fire?" (v. 24). What the king saw was a fourth man walking around inside the furnace. Even more spectacular, the fourth man looked "like a son of the gods." The identity of the fourth man has been the subject of much debate. He may have been an angel, a member of the heavenly court, or a pre-incarnate appearance of Jesus. The only description we have is Nebuchadnezzar's observation.

Nebuchadnezzar realized he had misjudged the three friends and their God. He approached the furnace and called out to the three friends, asking them to come out. All the officials of Babylon present gathered around the three friends as they came out of the furnace. They saw that the fire had had no effect on the three friends. No effect at all! Their hair and clothing were unaffected; they did not even have the smell of smoke about them.

Then, instead of giving glory to the statue or his own authority, Nebuchadnezzar gave glory to God for saving the three friends. He admired how God had sent an angel or messenger to save the men. He also issued a decree that no one in the kingdom should speak anything offensive against the God of the three friends.

It should not be assumed that Nebuchadnezzar was converted. He most likely merely recognized that the God of the Jews was the most powerful of the many gods he believed existed.

Like the three friends, today's children are growing up in a pluralistic society with a myriad of beliefs competing for their affections. The Christian view of salvation coming only through Jesus is increasingly being met with hostility, but as the three friends found out, faithfulness to God, being possible only through Jesus, is always the right choice.

SUGGESTED HYMNS/SONGS

1. *Doxology*, 668, 2008 Baptist Hymnal.
2. *God Will Make a Way*, 85, 2008 Baptist Hymnal.
3. *Great is the Lord Almighty!*, 349, 2008 Baptist Hymnal.
4. *It is Well with My Soul*, 447, 2008 Baptist Hymnal.

STUDENT APPLICATIONS

1. Students will know that the story of Shadrach, Meshach, and Abednego is found in the Old Testament book of Daniel.
2. Students will know that Shadrach, Meshach, and Abednego were three young Jewish men taken from their families, their homeland, and raised in court of the king of Babylon.
3. Students will know that Nebuchadnezzar, king of Babylon, built a ninety-foot tall statue.
4. Students will know that Nebuchadnezzar commanded all his officials, including Shadrach, Meshach, and Abednego, to bow and to worship the statue.
6. Students will know that Shadrach, Meshach, and Abednego chose to worship only God no matter what.
7. Students will know that Shadrach, Meshach, and Abednego were thrown into a furnace for not bowing to the statue.
8. Students will know that God protected Shadrach, Meshach, and Abednego from harm while in the furnace.
9. Students will know that Nebuchadnezzar recognized the power of God because Shadrach, Meshach and Abednego chose to obey God and were miraculously protected by Him.
10. Students will know that God commands them not to worship idols.
11. Students will know that an idol is anything to which one gives value or importance to that rightfully belongs to God.

RESOURCES/CREDIT

1. *The Family Bible Dictionary*, 1958 ed. Avenir Books, s.v. "*Chaldeans.*"

Daniel & the Lion's Den

BACKGROUND PASSAGES

Main Passage
Daniel 6:1-28   Daniel and the Lions' Den

Related Passages
Daniel 5   Fall of the Babylonian empire

Suggested Homiletic Passage
Daniel 6:16-23

MEMORY VERSE

God is our refuge and strength, a helper who is always found in times of trouble.

Psalm 46:1

LESSON OBJECTIVE

Daniel's place in Babylon was envied by others in high positions, who recognized his faith and integrity, and sought to exploit these attributes for his downfall. Faithful believers can also expect opposition but should know that God will be faithful, as He was with Daniel, to help them deal with any situation they encounter.

LESSON

Many challenges arise as a believer seeks to grow in faith. Believers who consistently live a life pleasing to God can expect times of great joy and fellowship with the Lord. Believers can also encounter jealousy and opposition. Daniel is an example of a person who faced persecution for his faithfulness to God. God helped Daniel in his time of need and showed all that He is the one, True God.

Daniel 6:1-28

Daniel, a young Jewish man, was taken from his people in Judah and raised in the court of Babylon. His faith in God was so strong that it was written about him that "he had an extraordinary spirit" (v.3). God gifted Daniel to be a wise and able administrator. Daniel had served for many decades in two dif-ferent empires : first the Babylonian empire, and then the Persian empire, under several kings.

Daniel served under the Babylonian kings for many years. When the end of the Babylonian empire came, it came swiftly. One night the Persians swept in unexpectedly, killing the last Babylonian king, Belshazzar, and placing Darius the Mede (sometimes identified as Cyrus the Persian) on the throne. It is a testament to God's leading, and Daniel's administrative competence, that he not only survived the radical change of government but was elevated to a position of importance under the new king, Darius.

King Darius appointed 120 officials, or satraps, to help with the administration of the empire. Over these 120 were placed three men, one of whom was Daniel. Daniel so distinguished himself in this capacity that the king made plans to set him over the whole realm (v.3).

Whether out of jealousy or personal ambition, some of the other satraps and administrators sought to discredit Daniel and remove him from his position of responsibility. Despite their efforts, they could find no charge or corruption for which to accuse Daniel. Daniel was faithful and knowing this, all they could manipulate was something "... against him concerning the law of his God." (v.5).

The Persian kingdom was organized so that the king had priestly functions by virtue of his office.[1] While those duties most likely were delegated to others, the king was the final authority in any matter political or religious. The conspirators, aware that the king held Daniel in high esteem, crafted a cunning plan to deceive the king and trap Daniel. It was proposed to the king that a period of time, thirty days, be set aside in which no one in the kingdom would be allowed to make petition to man or god, except through (to) him. While this undoubtedly appealed to his ego, it would also serve as a demonstration of the king's authority. Those who broke the law would be tossed into the lions' den. The king was impressed enough to sign the edict, irrevocably, into law.

What did Daniel do when he found out about the law? He went into his house, got down on his knees and prayed, just as he had always done, three times every day. The conspirators, hoping to find Daniel praying, went to his house and caught him in the act.

The men then had the audacity to spring their trap in the presence of the king. They asked the king if he had ever signed a law forbidding prayer to anyone but himself for thirty days. The king acknowledged that he had signed such a law and that it was irrevocable. They then revealed that "Daniel, one of the Judean exiles, has ignored you, the king, and the edict you have signed, for he prays three times a day." (v.13). Immediately, the king knew he had been deceived. The law, instead of proving the king's sovereignty, had bound him.

The king sought to save Daniel from the consequences of the law. Despite the king's obvious displeasure towards them, the conspirators pressed home their point by reminding the king that the law could not be ignored. The king gave the order and Daniel was seized and thrown into the lion's den.

Have you ever wondered why a king would have a den of lions? There are several possible reasons: lions were a symbol of royal power and the captivity of the great beasts would have been a visual reminder of the king's authority, lions were a prized hunting animal and kings would sometimes keep a ready supply for personal hunts.[2] Darius may have had lions for either or both of these reasons. In this case, the threat of the lions was a savage deterrent toward anyone who would dare break the king's law.

As Daniel was placed in the den, the king called out, "May your God, whom you serve continually, rescue you!" (v.16). A stone was brought to close the den Then the king and his nobles sealed the stone with their signet rings. These unique rings, were used to confirm identity and prevent fraud in communications and transactions. The king returned to his palace. He was so upset that he could not eat, refused entertainment of any kind, and was unable to sleep.

But the king did not give up all hope. He had seen this foreign God work through Daniel, and thought it possible that He would save him after all. In the morning, as the den was opened, the king called out to Daniel. Daniel responded, "May the king live forever. My God sent His angel and shut the lions' mouths." (v.22). Daniel professed that he was innocent and had not committed a crime against the king. On the contrary, Daniel had shown wisdom in not following such a shortsighted and foolish law.

Overjoyed, the king had Daniel lifted out of the den. The king then ordered that the conspirators be gathered up and thrown in the den, along with their wives and children (please see Age Group Considerations below). In contrast to Daniel's uneventful night in the den, the conspirators were immediately overpowered and crushed by the lions. No one survived.

King Darius could not rescind the law he had signed, but in verses 26-27 he issued a new proclamation:

"I issue a decree that in all my royal dominion, people must tremble in fear before the God of Daniel: For He is the living God, and He endures forever; His kingdom will never be destroyed, and His dominion has no end. He rescues and delivers; He performs signs and wonders in the heavens and on the earth, for He has rescued Daniel from the power of the lions."

As with King Nebuchadnezzar, after the deliverance of Shadrach, Meshach and Abednego, it cannot be assumed that King Darius became a believer. It is known that, with God's continual leading, Daniel continued to prosper.

While there is great irony in facing persecution for doing what is right, we know that it is the way of the world. If a Christian seeks to live a life pleasing to God, there will come times when they will be tested because of that faith.

For a child, this may be a relatively minor happening. Perhaps, they will be teased for refusing to use inappropriate words, for giving up an activity, or forego participating in a sport in order to keep a church commitment. Graver consequences may come if a

Daniel & the Lion's Den

child must choose between being faithful to God or getting involved in rebellious activities such as drugs, or some such choices. Daniel could easily have decided to stop praying for thirty days rather than risk facing death. Our children need to know that making the right decision (to be faithful to God) is better than making the easy decision (not to obey).

AGE GROUP CONSIDERATIONS

It's difficult for us to understand the ancient practice of punishing an entire family for the sin of an individual. In the story of Daniel and the lion's den, we see that the children and wives of the conspirators were also sent to their death in the lion's den.

Ancient kings faced a plethora of perils, many of which often came from those closest to him. Family members of a man punished by the king might seek revenge. Persian and Israelite cultures (among others) also had a strong sense of communal guilt. What one member of a family did reflected on everyone within that family. This sense of responsibility towards beloved relatives would have been a strong deterrent to most.

Whatever Darius' motive might have been, it is best for younger children to simply know that the guilty men were thrown into the den. Do not dwell on the fate of the conspirators, instead emphasize how God protected Daniel because of his faithfulness.

SUGGESTED HYMNS/SONGS

1. *Be Strong in the Lord*, 504, 2008 Baptist Hymnal.
2. *In Christ Alone (My Hope is Found)*, 506, 2008 Baptist Hymnal.
3. *Living for Jesus*, 545, 2008 Baptist Hymnal.
4. *Oh, How He Loves You and Me*, 170, 2008 Baptist Hymnal.
5. *The Solid Rock*, 511, 2008 Baptist Hymnal.

STUDENT APPLICATIONS

1. Students will know that the story of Daniel and the lion's den is found in the Old Testament book of Daniel.
2. Students will know that Daniel was one of three administrators over the Persian empire who were answerable only to the king.
3. Students will know that Daniel was faithful to God, that he had an extraordinary spirit that distinguished him from his fellow administrators, and that he was a man of integrity .
4. Students will know that the other administrators were jealous of Daniel.
5. Students will know that some of the administrators deceived the king into signing a law which they knew could be used against Daniel.
6. Students will know that the law, which the king signed, allowed no one to pray to anyone but him for 30 days.
7. Students will know that Daniel continued to faithfully pray to God even after the law went into effect.
8. Students will know that Daniel was thrown into a lion's den after it was found out he had broken the law.
9. Students will know that the king was very worried about Daniel's safety.
10. Students will know that God sent an angel to shut the mouths of the lions and that Daniel was kept safe.
11. Students will know that the men who tricked the king into signing the law in order to catch Daniel were themselves thrown in the lion's den.
12. Students will know that when they were thrown in the den, the conspirators were quickly killed by the lions.
13. Students will know that the king issued a decree honoring the God of Daniel.

RESOURCES/CREDIT

1. A. R. Millard, *The International Bible Commentary, Revised Edition*, F.F. Bruce, ed. (Grand Rapids, Michigan: Zondervan Publishing House, 1979), 859.
2. *Ibid.*, 860.

BACKGROUND PASSAGES

Main Passages

Matthew 28	Resurrection & Great Commission
Acts 1:6-11	The Ascension

Related Passages

Luke 24:36-53	Upper Room/Ascension
John 14:25-28	Coming of Holy Spirit foretold

Suggested Homiletic Passage

Matthew 28:1-7

MEMORY VERSE

Younger

Go therefore, and make disciples of all nations, baptizing them in the name of the Father and of the Son and of the Holy Spirit.

Matthew 28:19

Older

Go therefore, and make disciples of all nations, baptizing them in the name of the Father and of the Son and of the Holy Spirit, teaching them to observe everything I have commanded you. And remember, I am with you always, to the end of the age.

Matthew 28:19-20

LESSON OBJECTIVE

Jesus' death on the cross (for our sins) was God's plan since before creation. After He arose, Jesus commanded His disciples, and all believers (empowered and filled with the Holy Spirit), to go to all nations and make disciples.

LESSON

After the crucifixion, Jesus' followers' hopes and feelings were crushed. They had been certain He was the promised Messiah. They had been convinced He would ascend to the throne of David and drive out the Roman oppressors. Now He had died an excruciating and painful death. Jesus had told His disciples several times (John 12:27-33, Matt. 20:17-19, Mark 10:32-34) that all this was just a part of a greater plan. He was going to die and then be resurrected. He would then rule at the Father's right hand and one day return victoriously. His believers still did not understand, nor remember what He had taught them.

Three days after the crucifixion, the believers received the greatest news imaginable — Jesus was alive! In the days following the resurrection, they would finally begin to understand why Jesus had to die on the cross. Jesus would give them a mission that still applies to all believers today. Jesus would command them to go in the power of the Holy Spirit and make disciples of all nations.

Matthew 28

It must have been a sorrowful Sabbath as Jesus' followers reflected on the crucifixion and grieved the loss of their Lord. Jewish Sabbath observance consisted of many restrictions, including a prohibition against touching dead bodies; thus Mary Magdalene and Mary (not the mother of Jesus) waited until the first day of the week to go to Jesus' tomb to anoint His body with spices. We know from Mark 16:3 that they were uncertain if they would be able to get past the stone blocking the tomb.

At Jesus' tomb there was a violent earthquake as an angel descended from Heaven and rolled back the stone. Guards had been posted at the tomb after the crucifixion to prevent tampering with its contents. At the sight of the angel, the guards "were so shaken from fear of him that they became like dead men." (v.4).

At the tomb, the women found an angel sitting on the stone. He told them to have no fear. Then he said, "He is not here! For He has been resurrected, just as He said." (v.6). He invited them to inspect the tomb and then told them to go share the good news with the disciples. The stone had not been rolled away so Jesus could get out, but rather, for the women to enter.

The women quickly departed "with fear and great joy" from the tomb. On their way to inform the disciples, the women met Jesus, who greeted them with "Good morning!" We can only imagine the emotions that washed over them as they fell at His feet and worshiped Him. He then commanded them to go and tell the disciples (HCSB uses the term "my brothers") to meet Him in Galilee.

Other events took place that day. The guards reported back to the chief priests everything that occurred at the tomb. The priests and elders assembled and came up with a plan. They gave the soldiers a large sum of money, and instructed them to lie, saying that Jesus' followers had come and stolen the body at night while they were asleep. The guards may have been Roman soldiers supplied by Pilate or Temple guards working for the religious leaders. The false story was circulated, and as a result many Jewish people were deceived (v.15).

The conclusion of the book of Matthew reads more like a beginning. Jesus spent forty days with His disciples after the resurrection (Acts 1:3), gave them a final command, and ascended into Heaven:

> "All authority has been given to Me in heaven and on earth. Go, therefore, and make disciples of all nations, baptizing them in the name of the Father and of the Son and of the Holy Spirit, teaching them to observe everything I have commanded you. And remember, I am with you always, to the end of the age." (Matt. 28:19-20).

The work Jesus had begun would continue after He ascended. These final instructions are often called *The Great Commission*.

Notice the command contains two main points. The first is to "go to all nations," and the second is to "make disciples of all nations." Jesus desired, then and now, for all people to hear about Him. Next, Jesus detailed the methods to be used in proclaiming the gospel. The disciples were to baptize in the name of the Father, the Son, and the Holy Spirit. Baptism

would be a natural progression for those who believe. They were to teach all new believers everything that Jesus had taught them.

Believers are not alone in this work, as Jesus gives the Holy Spirit to guide them. The task which God has given to His Church is both a responsibility and a privilege. Thus the Church has continued to grow through the centuries in the power of the Lord. While not every believer will go to another land, all believers have the responsibility of reaching out to the lost of this world.

Acts 1:6-11

Shortly before Jesus ascended, the disciples asked Him if this was when He was going to restore the kingdom to Israel. Jesus told them that they would soon receive the Holy Spirit (the Helper Jesus had promised in John 14:26) and would be His witnesses in Jerusalem, Judea, and to the ends of the earth (v.8). In doing so, the disciples and all believers were tasked with fulfilling The Great Commission. The Good News would be shared with all the nations.

After Jesus finished talking, He was taken up into a cloud and disappeared from their sight. Clouds, in the Bible, usually signify the presence of God. Two men (angels?) stood beside the disciples and asked, "Men of Galilee, why do you stand looking up into heaven?" They then continued, "This Jesus, who has been taken from you into Heaven, will come in the same way that you have seen Him going into heaven." (v.11). Jesus came to earth the first time as the humble Lamb of God. He left in a cloud and will reappear (at His second coming), in power, upon the clouds.

Has *The Great Commission* already been fulfilled? No, while it is likely the Gospel has been proclaimed within the geographic borders of every country at some point, *The Great Commission* still applies to believers today. Why? There are still many individuals, and even entire people groups who have never heard the name of Jesus, and many others who do not yet understand His message of salvation. Just as others shared and taught us about Jesus, we too are commanded to carry out *The Great Commission*. This work is never easy but helping people come to know and grow in their relationship with God is joyfully fulfilling.

AGE GROUP CONSIDERATIONS

The Great Commission applies not only to adults, but to children as well. Children can fulfill the commission in many ways. They can share how Jesus has changed their lives. They can invite friends to Sunday School, VBS and other church activities. They can pray. They can study the Bible in order to become more knowledgeable and effective disciples. They can study about, pray for, and support missionaries, both home and international. They can also participate in local mission efforts. All these, and more, when done out of love for God, can be powerful ways for children to do their part in fulfilling *The Great Commission*.

SUGGESTED HYMNS/SONGS

1. *Christ the Lord is Risen Today*, 270, 2008 Baptist Hymnal.
2. *Jesus, Keep Me Near the Cross*, 233, 2008 Baptist Hymnal.
3. *Jesus Paid it All*, 249, 2008 Baptist Hymnal.
4. *Nothing but the Blood*, 223, 2008 Baptist Hymnal.
5. *Because He Lives*, 449, 2008 Baptist Hymnal.
6. *We have heard the Joyful Sound*, 361, 2008 Baptist Hymnal.

STUDENT APPLICATIONS

1. Students will know that the account of The Great Commission is found in the New Testament book of Matthew.
2. Students will know that Jesus was crucified on a cross, so that they may have forgiveness of their sins.
3. Students will know that Jesus was resurrected three days after His crucifixion.
4. Students will know that Jesus is still alive today.
5. Students will know that a group of women were the first to learn (from an angel) that Jesus was alive.
6. Students will know that Jesus' disciples, along with many other believers, saw Him after His resurrection.
7. Students will know that the guards at the tomb were paid to spread the false story that Jesus' followers stole His body.
8. Students will know that Jesus commanded all believers to go and make disciples of all nations.
9. Students will know that they too can do their part to fulfill The Great Commission.
10. Students will know that Jesus ascended into the clouds and returned to Heaven and will return one day just as He left.

Pentecost & the Holy Spirit

BACKGROUND PASSAGES

Main Passage
Acts 2   Pentecost

Related Passages
Lev. 23:10-17   Background of Pentecost
John 16:8-10   Holy Spirit convicts of sin
John 16:13-15   Holy Spirit guides us to truth
Ephesians 1:13   Holy Spirit guarantees salvation

Suggested Homiletic Passage
Acts 2:37-42

MEMORY VERSE

But the Counselor, the Holy Spirit — the Father will send Him in My name — will teach you all things and remind you of everything I have told you.

John 14:26

LESSON OBJECTIVE

After Jesus ascended to Heaven, the Holy Spirit was sent to all believers at Pentecost. The Holy Spirit, as a member of the Trinity, indwells each believer whom He convicts of sin. He also comforts believers and teaches the truth about God.

LESSON

Christians often misunderstand and neglect teaching about the Holy Spirit. Yet it is only through His work as a member of the Trinity that one can ever understand anything about God. It is the Holy Spirit who convicts unbelievers of sin, their fallen condition, and their need for the Savior. He leads believers in spiritual growth, teaches, and assists in prayer. His presence in the life of a believer is continual and is the guarantee, or proof, that they are forgiven and belong to God.

To misunderstand the Holy Spirit is to misunderstand God. In the gospels, Jesus talked often about the Holy Spirit, but said that He, the Holy Spirit, could not come until Jesus' redemptive work was complete. After Jesus ascended, His followers waited patiently until the Holy Spirit came in power on the day of Pentecost.

Acts 2

After His resurrection, Jesus spent forty days with the believers before returning to Heaven (Acts 1:3). He commanded them to wait together in Jerusalem, stating, "But you will receive power when the Holy Spirit has come upon you, and you will be My witnesses in Jerusalem, in all Judea and Samaria, and to the ends of the earth." (Acts 1:8).

The believers gathered together and waited patiently. Ten days later, on the day of Pentecost, while the believers were gathered in a house, a sound like a rushing wind filled the place and flames of fire rested upon each person's head. Each believer was baptized by the Holy Spirit as promised by Jesus (Acts 1:5).

Each person began to speak in different languages. These languages were not some kind of spiritual utterance, but rather everyday languages in use at the time around the world. God used this miracle to prove that His Spirit was upon all believers and to bring many to belief in Christ, which greatly increased the number of believers.

Jews from throughout the ancient world gathered in Jerusalem for each of the feasts, including Pentecost. The sound of the arrival of the Spirit caught the attention of many in the city, who soon gathered in one place wondering what had happened. The location is not specified, but was likely the temple court as it was a focus of many followers during the feast and could easily accommodate a large crowd.

The gathered crowd was amazed to hear the believers speaking in their own languages. People from sixteen diverse regions, stretching from Rome (in the west) to Mesopotamia (in the east), are mentioned as being present that day. Each could understand what was being said by the believers. Astounded and perplexed, they began to wonder as to the cause of the phenomenon. Some accused the believers of being drunk (v.13). It was at this point that Peter stood up and began to preach.

Peter assured his listeners that the believers were not drunk. As evidence, Peter pointed out that it was only nine in the morning. It was unusual to eat or drink anything before the morning sacrifice was performed at the third hour (9 a.m.). On solemn festival days no food or drink was consumed before noon.[1] Peter then proceeded to preach the gospel to the crowd.

He first quoted from the book of Joel and talked about God's Spirit being poured out on people in the last days. He told of the "Day of the Lord" when Jesus will return and all who have called upon His name will receive their eternal reward. Peter then explained how Jesus is this Lord and that though He had been nailed to a cross and killed, He had arisen and was alive.

Peter quoted a Davidic psalm showing when God had promised David that one of his (David's) descendants would sit upon the throne. Peter then gives a personal testimony, "God has resurrected this Jesus. We are all witnesses of this." (v.32). Having testified, Peter concluded, "Therefore let all the house of Israel know with certainty that God has made this Jesus, whom you crucified, both Lord and Messiah!" (v.36).

Was Peter's sermon eloquent and powerful in presentation? Perhaps. What is known and certain is that the Holy Spirit was at work, convicting those present with the reality of their sinful condition and need for the Messiah. "When they heard this, they were pierced to the heart ..." (v.37). They asked Peter and the rest of the apostles what they must do. "Repent," Peter said to them, "and be baptized each of you, in the name of Jesus the Messiah for the forgiveness of your sins, and you will receive the gift of the Holy Spirit." (v.38).

Repentance is much more than saying one is sorry. It involves a change in behavior. To repent is to turn from an old way of living and to follow a new life or pattern. Baptism, while not a condition of salvation, is the natural first action of a new believer. Following Jesus' example of baptism gives testimony and evidence of the follower's repentance and new identity in Christ. It is also a commandment (Matt. 28:19).

The gift of the Holy Spirit is given to a new believer at the moment of conversion as a down payment, or guarantee, marking us as belonging to Christ Jesus. This is the baptism of the Holy Spirit, which should not be confused with the filling of the Holy Spirit (see *The Holy Spirit* later in this lesson). In this life, there will always be a struggle against the temptation to sin. As believers yield to God's leading, they will experience a deeper relationship with the Holy Spirit.

On the day of Pentecost, over 3,000 people repented and followed Jesus. Then, without delay, they were baptized. They actively devoted themselves to learning more about God from the teachings of the apostles, fellowship with other believers, and prayer.

This was a special time in the church as God worked many signs and wonders through the apostles. The believers loved one another, giving generously as each had need. They gathered together, not just on Sunday, but daily to study and worship. Each day more people were saved and joined the growing church.

The Spring Feasts

To understand the relevance of the Holy Spirit arriving at Pentecost (also called the Feast of Weeks), it is helpful to understand the background of the spring biblical feasts. God gave instructions in Leviticus 23 for annual observance of feasts. Passover, Firstfruits, and Pentecost are known as the spring feasts, since they take place in spring and early summer. Chronologically, Passover was the first Feast of the year, followed by Firstfruits. Pentecost (a Greek word for fiftieth) was observed on the 50th day after the Feast of Firstfruits.

The Passover observance brought to remembrance how God had delivered the Israelites from their Egyptian oppressors. It was only because they obeyed and "painted" their doorposts with the blood of spotless lambs that the Israelite firstborns avoided the fate of the Egyptian firstborns. Jesus was crucified during the week of Passover as the Lamb of God, and fulfilled the purpose of the feast for all humankind.

Passover week begins on the 14th of *Nisan*, the first month on the Jewish calendar, and ends on the 21st with the Feast of Firstfruits. During this feast, the Israelites offered thanks to God for His provision of food from the land. There was a national offering (Lev. 23:10-17) as well as individual offerings (Exod. 23:19, Deut. 26:1-11). The offerings went to support the priests. Jesus was resurrected on day of the Feast of Firstfruits. He fulfilled this feast by being the firstfruit of the resurrection (I Cor. 15:20). Believers will join Him in this resurrection at the end of time (I Cor. 15:23).

Pentecost (Leviticus 23:15-22) is only one day long, marking the end of the barley harvest and the beginning of the wheat harvest. It is considered to be the closing festival of the Passover season and the spring feasts. As Jesus had fulfilled the earlier feasts, the sending of the Holy Spirit fulfilled Pentecost. The Passover marked physical freedom from bondage for God's people. Pentecost, first through the giving of the law and later through the giving of the Holy Spirit, marked our spiritual freedom.

The Holy Spirit

All Christians, including children, need to understand the role and importance of the Holy Spirit. One common misperception is that the Holy Spirit is an impersonal force that can be manipulated by individuals, much like the force in Star Wars.

The Holy Spirit is personal and a member of the Trinity. The Holy Spirit convicts of sin and judgment (John 16:8-10). He makes nonbelievers aware of their fallen condition and their need for a Savior. He convicts believers whenever they fall into sin, calling them to repent and be restored to right relationship with God.

The indwelling of the Spirit guarantees salvation. He indwells a believer at the moment of conversion and remains thereafter. He is the deposit guarantee of a believer's salvation (Romans 8:9-11, Ephesians 1:13).

The Holy Spirit guides believers to know truth (John 16:13-15) and teaches believers all that they can know about God. The Holy Spirit communicates to believers what God wants us to know (I Cor. 2:10-12). The Holy Spirit helps believers to pray and intercedes for us (Romans 8:26).

It is important to note the difference between the "Baptism of the Spirit" and the "Filling of the Spirit." The Baptism happens once, at conversion and is part of our salvation. The Filling, also referred to as "the anointing of the Holy Spirit," happens continuously as believers daily yield to God's leading.

AGE GROUP CONSIDERATIONS

Avoid use of the term "Holy Ghost." While used in the King James Version, the term formerly meant "spirit." Today the term "ghost" is used almost exclusively to describe the wandering soul of a dead person.[2] Use of this term may confuse or even scare some children.

Refrain from referring to the Holy Spirit as "it." Referring to someone as an "it" renders them as a nonentity. The Holy Spirit is personal. We devalue God's glory by calling any member of the Trinity "it."

The indwelling of the Holy Spirit can potentially be a difficult and even scary concept for children. The thought of someone living inside of us might concern some children. Explain that the Holy Spirit is not a "man" living inside our bodies, but a presence that is always with us. He does not control us, but guides us in the way we should live.

The term "Filling of the Spirit" can cause confusion. If one can be "filled" it stands to reason that one can also be "empty." Remind the children that they can never, ever lose the Holy Spirit once they have been saved, adoption into the family of God is final. The "Filling of the Spirit" is important in that Christians need to daily seek God's leading or anointing.

SUGGESTED HYMNS/SONGS

1. *Spirit of the Living God*, 330, 2008 Baptist Hymnal.
2. *Sweet, Sweet Spirit*, 328, 2008 Baptist Hymnal.
3. *Pentecostal Power*, 496, 2008 Baptist Hymnal.
4. *Breathe on Me*, 332, 2008 Baptist Hymnal.
5. *Set My Soul Afire*, 533, 2008 Baptist Hymnal.

STUDENT APPLICATIONS

1. Students will know that the coming of the Holy Spirit at Pentecost is found in the New Testament book of Acts.
2. Students will know that Pentecost occurred fifty days after Jesus was resurrected.
3. Students will know that after Jesus ascended into Heaven, His followers waited together in a room in Jerusalem.
4. Students will know that on the day of Pentecost the sound of a violent rushing wind filled the house where the believers were gathered.
5. Students will know that the Holy Spirit appeared upon the believers as flames of fire and indwelt (baptized) each person in the house.
6. Students will know that the believers spoke different languages at Pentecost.
7. Students will know that many people were in Jerusalem to observe Pentecost.

8. Students will know that each nonbeliever at Pentecost heard the believers speaking in their own language.
9. Students will know that Peter preached a sermon, telling a large crowd the good news about Jesus.
10. Students will know that about 3000 people followed Jesus on the day of Pentecost.
11. Students will know that the "Baptism of the Holy Spirit" occurs as a one-time event, upon salvation, in which the Holy Spirit will indwell them once and forever.
12. Older students will know that the "Filling of the Holy Spirit occurs as we continually yield to the leading of the Holy Spirit.
13. Students will know that the Holy Spirit is a real being, just as Jesus is. The Holy Spirit is personal, and a member of the Trinity.
14. Students will know that the Holy Spirit convicts people of their sin, teaches believers the things of God, and makes intercession for us.
15. Students will know that the word "gospel," literally means "good news."

RESOURCES/CREDIT

1. James M. Freeman, *Manners & Customs of the Bible* (New Kensington: Whitaker House, 1996), 439-41.
2. Herschel H. Hobbs, *Fundamentals of Our Faith* (Nashville: Broadman & Holman Publishers, 1960), 52.

Creation

BACKGROUND PASSAGES

Main Passage

Genesis 1-2   Creation account

Related Passages

Psalm 8:3-9   Man and Creation
Romans 1:19-20   Creation points to God
Exodus 20:11   Confirmation of six-day creation
Isaiah 45:18-19   Earth created for inhabitation

Suggested Homiletic Passage

Genesis 1:26-31

MEMORY VERSE

Younger version

The earth and everything in it, the world and its inhabitants, belong to the Lord.

Psalm 24:1

Older version

The earth and everything in it, the world and its inhabitants, belong to the Lord, for He laid its foundation on the seas and established it on the rivers.

Psalm 24:1-2

LESSON OBJECTIVE

God created the heavens, the earth and all life, and called it good. He sustains all of creation. Human beings, created in His image, are His most-prized creation.

LESSON

How did the cosmos come about? How did life begin? Is there anything special about being human, or are humans just another kind of animal? These questions are asked and pondered by both children and adults. Thankfully, the Bible has definite answers about the origins of the universe, and humanity's special, God-given, place in creation.

What was the purpose of creation? The most forthright answer is that God did it for His Glory. Creation, through its order and majesty, points toward and glorifies God. Another reason is that God created it as an expression of His own nature. Some scholars have described creation as "God's provision of fellowship with His creatures, especially human beings."[1]

Genesis 1-2

Many people believe life on earth began in a primordial ooze of chemicals, or that life was somehow transported from elsewhere in the universe to our planet. The first verse of the Bible makes it clear that it was God alone who created all things, "In the beginning God created the heavens and the earth." (1:1). From this bold, nonnegotiable statement we learn that God is the Creator and that He was preexistent; furthermore, He is timeless. He exists outside of time as we know it.

The act of creation was accomplished over a period of six days. The creation account was not intended to be a scientific record. Since, however, the creation account is true, its teachings and science do not have to be at odds (See Why Teach a Six-Day Creation? at the end of this lesson). The work of creation made clear that God has power over every aspect of nature. Creation gives evidence of God's purpose and organization.

On the first day, God created light. He did not use any tools, construction vehicles or building materials. God spoke all of creation into existence, ex nihilo (out of nothing). The Word of God is powerful indeed!

On the second day He separated water from the sky. Some of the water was placed in the atmosphere (forming mists and clouds), while some was left on earth. Over the first two days, God gave form to the created order.

On the third day, God began to fill His creation. He gathered the water together into one place (oceans) and dry land appeared for the first time. He created vegetation which grew and bore fruit with seeds, according to their kind.

On the fourth day, God created sources of light in the heavens. He made two greater lights: the sun and the moon. Ancient cultures typically worshiped the sun and moon as gods. Here, God made it clear that He created all of the heavens and they were not to be worshiped. The sun and moon were created with the purpose of separating day from night, for tracking time, and for serving as "signs for festivals and for days and years." (1:14).

On the fifth day, God added sea animals and birds to the created order. Fish swarmed through the waters and birds flew across the expanse of the sky. He commanded them to be fruitful and multiply (1:22).

On the sixth day, He created land animals. He created livestock, creatures that crawled (an apparent reference to insects) and wild animals. Animals were not His only creation that day. God said, "Let Us make man in Our image, according to Our likeness." (1:26). "Us" is likely a reference to the Trinity.

Since he alone of all beings was created in God's image, man was given the place of highest importance in God's creation. God commanded man to "Be fruitful, multiply, fill the earth and subdue it." (1:28). Man would not be equal with other created beings, but was to rule over all. God also gave man seed-bearing plants, fruit-bearing trees, and every plant for food. God made sure His creation had everything it needed in order to thrive and endure.

At the end of each day, God saw that it was good. English usage of the term "good" typically expresses acceptance. To be judged "good" by God is to conform to His will; creation was exactly as He intended for it to be.[2] Nothing in creation was evil.

On the seventh day, God rested from the work of creation, called the day "holy" and set it apart from the other six days. This is not to mean He required rest from exertion, or that He did not stay around, or continue to sustain His creation. Rather, God set the example for us to follow: in how we work and in how we should rest. Jesus even reaffirmed this when He said, "The Sabbath was made for man and not man for the Sabbath." (Mark 2:27). We are to spend six days working and then observe a time of rest and worship on the seventh day. Work is a virtue, but proper rest is vital to a person's well being.

The second chapter of Genesis reveals details about the creation of man. Man was created from the dust of the ground and came to life only because God breathed life into him. Despite modern medicine and technical advances, humans cannot give life to anything. It is interesting to note that the man's name, Adam, is not revealed until Genesis 3:17.

God had prepared a garden, called Eden, for the man. All that the man needed to survive could be found in the garden. The garden was lush with food-bearing trees of all kinds. In addition, there were two trees in the garden, one was the tree of life, and the other the tree of knowledge of good and evil.

From the garden flowed a river that divided into four. Two of the rivers mentioned, the Tigris and Euphrates, have led to speculation that the location of Eden was in or near modern-day Iraq. The topography of the world probably changed drastically during the flood, so we cannot even be certain these are the same rivers, let alone say with certainty where Eden was located.

The man was given the responsibility to work and watch over the garden. There was only one prohibition: he was not to eat from the tree of knowledge of good and evil.

God said, "It is not good for the man to be alone. I will make a helper who is like him." (2:18). God was not caught off guard by the lack of a helper, He had a plan all along. First, God brought every kind of creature, each animal, each bird to Adam so that he could name them. This exercise raised Adam's awareness that there was no one else like him. After this, God caused Adam to go into a deep sleep. While Adam slept, God took one of his ribs and used it to form a woman (whom Adam named Eve, Genesis 3:20). Matthew Henry writes, "The woman was formed out of man — not out of his head to rule over him, but out of his side to be his equal, from beneath his arm to be protected, and from near his heart to be loved."[3]

Creation

When the woman was brought to Adam, he immediately recognized that, finally, there stood another created being like himself. "This one, at last, is bone of my bone, and flesh of my flesh; this one will be called woman, for she was taken from man." (2:23).

God gave marriage as a gift to Adam and Eve. In a marriage, the man leaves his parents and publicly promises to care for his wife. The two are united in their commitment to one another. In this safe and God-ordained environment husbands and wives can explore the mysteries of intimacy and becoming "one flesh." The man and woman were both naked, but since all of creation was pure and yet-untainted by sin, they were not ashamed.

All that existed, was present because God had created it. Because God is good and all-powerful, everything He created was good. Next month's lesson will reveal how sin was introduced into creation, separating people from God. It will be seen that even at that dark moment God was preparing a way for sinful humans to find peace with Him, through His Son, Jesus.

Why Teach a Six-Day Creation?

One would be hard-pressed to find a modern secular source that teaches anything other than that the earth and the universe are billions of years old. Many Christians accept without question the view of an "old" universe. Some go as far as to dismiss the Genesis account of creation as nothing more than allegory, if not outright fantasy.

This lesson is written from the perspective that within the context and normal definitions of language, God communicated in a straightforward manner that everything was created in six literal days. The Hebrew word used in Genesis 1 for "day," *yom*, occurs over 300 times in the Old Testament, each time in the context of meaning an ordinary day. Why should Genesis 1 be the exception?[4]

Compelling evidence confirming a young earth can be found in the giving of the Ten Commandments. In Exodus 20:11 God stated in a straightforward manner, "For the Lord made the heavens and the earth, the sea, and everything in them in six days; then He rested on the seventh day."

Several schools of thought, including the *Gap* and *Ruin-Reconstruction theories*, have sought to reconcile the Biblical account of creation with evolutionary thought. At the core of these theories, each creation day is viewed as an indeterminate period of time, during which fossil layers were laid down and the earth aged millions or even billions of years before the creation of Adam. What these theories fail to account for is that many, many animals would have died before Adam in order to build the fossil record. The Bible makes it clear that death, suffering and disease are a consequence of sin and did not occur until after the fall. Genesis 1:31 states, "God saw all that He had made, and it was very good." His creation was pure and uncontaminated. There was no death before Adam and Eve sinned.

Another argument brought against a six-day creation is that six days limits God's omnipotence. God could create instantly, so why six days? That argument limits what the proponent thinks God is capable of doing and why He would do it. Yes, He could have created everything in an instant; but, obviously He had other purposes in taking six days.

The purpose of this lesson is to learn about God as Creator and our place in His creation. The lesson does not serve as a historical or scientific treatise. While God can create in whichever way He chooses, to abandon the straightforward teaching of scripture on this topic is to challenge Biblical authority with tenuous and flawed theories. God finished the work of creation in six literal days.

AGE GROUP CONSIDERATIONS

The objective of this lesson is to teach children that God created and sustains everything, and that humans are his most-prized creation. Even when that is understood, it is to be expected that children will have questions about the specifics of creation. Did God create dinosaurs? What happened to them? How many years old is the earth? Why was there light before the moon and sun were created? Could Adam talk with the animals?

It is beyond the scope of this lesson to anticipate all the questions surrounding the "how" of Creation. If you do not have an answer to a question, do not give into the temptation to make up an answer. Simply say, "I don't know" or "Let me study that and see what I can find." We are blessed to have many good resources which explore the subject of Creation in detail.

Ken Ham, of Answers in Genesis, has written an excellent book, *The New Answers Book*" (Master Books, 2007), that addresses many questions on Creation, evolution, and the Bible. There are also several websites containing hundreds of well-researched articles, including:

Answers in Genesis	www.answersingenesis.org
Institute for Creation Research	www.icr.org
Christian Answers	www.christiananswers.net

While there may never be clear answers about some aspects of creation, believers can take hope and joy in knowing that God has revealed His love, and has provided the universe as both a testament to His greatness and to provide for our physical needs.

SUGGESTED HYMNS

1. *God, Who Stretched the Spangled Heavens*, 47, 1991 Baptist Hymnal.
2. *This is My Father's World*, 46, 2008 Baptist Hymnal.
3. *God, Who Made the Earth*, 50, 1991 Baptist Hymnal.
4. *For the Beauty of the Earth*, 638, 2008 Baptist Hymnal.
5. *All Creatures of Our God and King*, 11, 2008 Baptist Hymnal.

STUDENT APPLICATIONS

1. Students will know that the account of creation is found in the Old Testament book of Genesis.
2. Students will know that God spoke things into existence.
3. Students will know that God's creation was good, pure, and uncontaminated by sin.
4. Students will know that God continues to sustain His creation.
5. Students will know that God finished the work of creation in six days.
6. Students will know that God rested on the seventh day.
7. Students will know that reality, as we experience it, is not by chance nor by accident, but is by God's design.
8. Students will know that humans are God's most-prized creation.
9. Students will know that God created the first man, Adam, from the dust and breathed life into him.
10. Students will know that God created a garden, we call Eden, for the man to tend and to meet his physical needs.
11. Students will know that Adam, after viewing all the animals, realized there was no one else like himself.
12. Students will know that God caused Adam to fall into a sleep, during which, God removed a rib with which to create the first woman, Eve.
13. Students will know that Adam loved Eve and took her to be his wife.

RESOURCES/CREDIT

1. James Leo Garrett Jr., *Systematic Theology: Biblical, Historical, and Evangelical, Volume 1* (North Richland Hills: BIBLE Press, 2000) 351.
2. H. L Ellison, *The International Bible Commentary, Revised Edition*, F.F. Bruce, ed. (Grand Rapids, Michigan: Zondervan Publishing House, 1979), 114.
3. Sherwood Elliot Wirt & Kirsten Beckstrom, eds., *Topical Encyclopedia of Living Quotations*, (Minneapolis: Bethany House Publishers), 257.
4. Ken Ham, *The New Answers Book* (Green Forest, AR: Master Books, 2007), 93.

Adam & Eve Sin

BACKGROUND PASSAGES

Main Passage

Genesis 3	The Temptation and the Fall

Related Passages

Romans 3:23	All have sinned
I Cor. 15:22	In Adam all die
I Cor. 15:45	Last Adam a life-giving Spirit

Suggested Homiletic Passage

Genesis 3:17-24

MEMORY VERSE

For the wages of sin is death, but the gift of God is eternal life in Christ Jesus our Lord.

Romans 6:23

LESSON OBJECTIVE

Because Adam and Eve doubted God's goodness and gave in to temptation, sin has separated all people from God. God, however, had a plan in place, since before the beginning of time, to redeem all who repent and follow Jesus.

LESSON

Adam and Eve were the first human beings. They lived in the Garden of Eden, a wonderful place of perfection. They enjoyed perfect fellowship with one another and with God. Everything was good until Satan (the serpent) tempted Adam and Eve to doubt God's goodness. The couple gave in to the temptation, and sin was brought into creation. Death and suffering became part of the world. Everyone born since has been born in sin. Even though God must be consistent in His holy nature and not allow sin to go unchecked, He had a plan to bring people back into a right relationship with Him through His Son, Jesus.

Genesis 3

Genesis 3 introduces us to the serpent. While not named here, we know that it was Satan. Satan was an angel who rebelled against God and was removed from heaven and placed on the earth (Isaiah 14:12-5). He has always attempted to lead humans away from God. Perhaps he had tempted Adam and Eve previously. We only know of this one occasion when he came to Eve and inquired, "Did God really say, 'You can't eat from any tree in the garden'?" (v.1).

This "first" temptation set the pattern for all temptations that have followed. Temptation occurs in any situation in which one must choose between believing and obeying God, or doubting Him and doing things his/her own way and thus effectively attempting to usurp God's rightful place. Satan was subtle in how he tempted Eve. His statement to her implied that God is stingy or selfish, not wanting to share from the tree of knowledge of good and evil. Like Eve, whenever we sin, we put our desires and ourselves in the position of judging what is best for us, instead of trusting God.

Eve answered the serpent saying that they could eat of everything, except that they had been commanded to not eat from the tree of knowledge of good and evil lest they die. Eve actually modified what God said when she added a further restriction that they were not to touch the tree. The serpent also responded with a half-truth, "No, you will not die! In fact, God knows that when you eat it your eyes will be opened and you will be like God, knowing good and evil." (v.4-5).

The serpent told the truth in that by eating the fruit, Eve would become more like God, knowing good and evil, but he lied when he told her she would not die. Sin brought two deaths that day — spiritual and physical. One was immediate, the other lingering and wrought with suffering, and both permanently fatal without God's redemption through Jesus Christ.

While humankind's highest goal is to become more like God, we disobey when we attempt to take God's place rather than be more like Him.

There were severe consequences for disobeying God, with death as the ultimate penalty. As cunning and persuasive as Satan is, he could not force Eve to disobey. She had to make her own decision. Temptation usually manifests itself as welcoming and desirous. The fruit greatly appealed to Eve. She looked at the tree, saw that the fruit was "delightful to look at" (v.6), took the fruit, and ate it.

Eve also gave some of the fruit to Adam, who was with her at the time (v.6). Adam not only allowed Eve to eat the fruit, but also chose to disobey. While Eve has received the majority of blame, Adam is every bit as culpable as his wife. He too made a conscious decision to disobey God.

One of the realities of sin is that the sinner often gets exactly what he/she expected ... and more. Like the serpent had said, Adam and Eve's eyes were opened to know good and evil. However, their innocence was gone. They recognized they had done wrong and were ashamed because of it. They also became self-aware and ashamed of their nakedness. Comically, they attempted to cover themselves with loincloths made out of fig leaves. Sin cannot be hidden from God. Anything done to attempt to hide sin will be just as ineffective as Adam and Eve's fig leaves.

Late in the day, Adam and Eve heard God walking in the garden. They ran from God and attempted to hide among the trees. God called out, "Where are you?" (v.9). Adam answered that he was hiding because he was ashamed to be naked. God asked, "Who told you that you were naked? Did you eat from the tree that I had commanded you not to eat from?" (v.11). Their sins had broken their close relationship with God.

God already knew what Adam and Eve had done. He asked questions to see how Adam would respond.

When we sin, God usually gives us time to repent. We often try to blame others for our actions, and Adam was no exception. He told God that he ate the fruit because Eve had given it to him. God then confronted Eve. Eve blamed her actions on the serpent.

Sin always affects more than just the sinner. Adam and Eve's sin affected all of creation. Death and suffering is now a fact of life, as all creation now groans to be redeemed (Romans 8:22). Since the Fall, every person has been born with a sin nature that predisposes them to rebel against God.

God announced a curse upon the serpent. The serpent was cursed more than any livestock or wild animal. Today the serpent (or snake) is one of the most despised and feared of animals. The serpent would move on his belly (inferring that serpents likely had legs before the Fall), putting him at a disadvantage when confronted by man. The serpent would strike at man's heel, but man would crush his head. A strike at the heel is usually not serious, but a crushed head is fatal.

While this scene has played out countless times over the centuries in encounters between man and serpent, there is a much deeper theological meaning. Jesus would come from the seed of woman. Satan would strike at His heel, but Jesus would crush Satan's power through His death and resurrection. At the Fall of creation, God already had a plan to redeem it.

Sin always has unintended consequences. God told Eve three consequences that women would face: pain in childbirth, a longing for their husbands, and that their husbands would rule over them.[1]

Men would also face consequences for Adam's decision to listen to Eve and disobey God: The ground would be cursed and only yield food through hard labor, riddled with struggles against thorns, weather and the elements. There would always be an uncertainty to life as man would "...eat bread by the sweat of your brow until you return to the ground." (v.19). Man's chief glory is his ability to exercise dominion, so being at the mercy of droughts and pestilence is humiliating.[2]

Sin also brought consequences for creation including animal enmity and disease. Adam and Eve, and all their descendants would have to live with the consequences of their actions, but despite their rebellion, God still loved them. God made clothing for Adam and Eve out of animal skins. This was the first animal sacrifice and showed that God would still provide for His prized creation.

He also did something that might at first appear cruel, but was in keeping with His wisdom and grace. God drove the couple from the Garden of Eden. God knew if they stayed, they would be tempted to eat from the Tree of Life. If they did, they would have been forever stuck in their fallen condition.

The Bible is many things, but perhaps more than anything else it is a story of redemption, as God worked in the lives of sinful men and women. He set in motion a plan to draw them (and us) to Himself. Adam and Eve were the first to sin, and all have followed their example (Romans 3:23). But even at the time of the fall, God showed grace and patience towards sinners. Today we can rejoice that God sent Jesus as the perfect sacrifice to cover our sins so that we can stand blameless before Him.

AGE GROUP CONSIDERATIONS

This lesson has many deep, theological concepts. While it is important for teachers to know the nuances, some of the concepts may be too abstract for younger children. Explain words like "sin" and "redemption" in words they can understand. If nothing else, children should understand that Adam and Eve did wrong in God's sight, and everyone else (including themselves) has too. All have sinned and need a savior. God has provided a way to be fully forgiven through the Savior, Jesus Christ.

SUGGESTED HYMNS/SONGS

1. *Blessed Be the Lord God Almighty*, 37, 2008 Baptist Hymnal.
2. *Come Thou Long Expected Jesus*, 176, 2008 Baptist Hymnal.
3. *God Will Take Care of You*, 90, 2008 Baptist Hymnal.
4. *Holy, Holy, Holy*, 68, 2008 Baptist Hymnal.
5. *Rescue the Perishing*, 357, 2008 Baptist Hymnal.

STUDENT APPLICATIONS

1. Students will know that the story Adam and Eve and the Fall is found in the Old Testament book of Genesis.
2. Students will know that Adam and Eve lived in the Garden of Eden.
3. Students will know that the serpent (Satan) tempted Eve.
4. Students will know that Adam and Eve had been commanded by God not to eat from the tree of knowledge of good and evil.
5. Students will know that the serpent deceived Eve by convincing her to not trust God.
6. Students will know Eve ate fruit from the tree of knowledge of good and evil.
7. Students will know that Adam also ate fruit from the tree as well.
8. Students will know that after eating the fruit, Adam and Eve realized that they had sinned.
9. Students will know that Adam and Eve sewed together fig leaves to make coverings for themselves because after they had sinned and were ashamed to be naked.
10. Students will know that Adam and Eve attempted to hide from God.
11. Students will know that Adam and Eve made excuses for their sin.
12. Students will know that the serpent was cursed, and the future victory of Jesus foreshadowed.

13. Students will know that women were cursed with pain in childbirth, longing for their husbands, and to be under their rule.
14. Students will know that men were cursed with struggles to work and survive.
15. Students will know that God made clothing out of animal skins, the first blood sacrifice, for Adam and Eve.
16. Students will know that Adam and Eve were driven from the Garden of Eden by God for their own protection, lest they live forever separated from God.
17. Students will know that in spite of Adam and Eve's sin, God had a plan in place, since before the beginning of time, for our redemption through Jesus.

18. Students will know that sin is doing things our way by choosing not to trust and obey God.
19. Students will know that sin often looks rewarding and may feel good for a time.
20. Students will know that sin always has consequences.

Resources/Credit

1. H. L Ellison, *The International Bible Commentary, Revised Edition*, F.F. Bruce, ed. (Grand Rapids, Michigan: Zondervan Publishing House, 1979), 118.
2. *Ibid.*

Noah and the Flood

BACKGROUND PASSAGES

Main Passage

Genesis 6:5-9:17   Noah and the Flood

Related Passages

Isaiah 54:9   Never will be another flood
Ezekiel 14:20   Noah said to be righteous
Hebrews 11:7   Noah had faith
2 Peter 2:5   Righteous Noah protected

Suggested Homiletic Passage

Genesis 8:15-22

MEMORY VERSE

Younger

As long as the earth endures ... day and night will not cease.

Genesis 8:22

Older

As long as the earth endures, seedtime and harvest, cold and heat, summer and winter, and day and night will not cease.

Genesis 8:22

LESSON OBJECTIVE

God destroyed the surface of the earth in judgment of mankind's sinfulness. Through His grace He foreshadowed salvation through Jesus, by delivering Noah, a righteous man, and his family from the flood.

LESSON

It is ironic that the story of Noah, the flood, and the ark is typically one of the first stories taught in a church setting to children. Brightly-colored, cartoonish Noah's Ark art often adorns the walls of nurseries and children's classrooms. Rarely reflected is the horror and fear that swept over an evil generation that was consumed by the flood.

The reality is that the flood was the greatest, most catastrophic disaster in history, and a reminder that God is never pleased with sin. But, the flood also carried a message of hope: God always warns of judgment and has mercy on those who listen and follow Him. Noah and his family, were spared because Noah found favor in God's eyes and was a righteous man who walked with God. While only eight people were saved onboard the ark, centuries after the flood, God sent Jesus to make salvation available to everyone.

Genesis 6:5-9:17

God saw that wickedness was widespread on the earth. Wickedness was so pervasive that the Bible states about mankind, "...every scheme his mind thought of was nothing but evil all the time." (6:5). God made the decision to wipe every living thing off the face of the earth: humans, land animals and birds. While this may sound cruel, God, as Creator, has the moral authority to decide who lives and dies.

The faith of one man allowed mankind to avoid extinction: Noah had found favor with God. He was "a righteous man, blameless among his contemporaries; Noah walked with God." (6:9). Noah was the father of three sons, Shem, Ham and Japheth.

God warned of the coming judgment. Having seen how corrupted humanity had become, God informed Noah that He was going to destroy humanity and all other living things on the surface of the earth. God commanded Noah to construct an ark out of wood (the type of wood is uncertain). Building the ark would be no small task, it was a massive ship rivaling the size of modern day cargo ships.

While Noah was probably given more detailed instructions, we are given little more than the dimensions. The ark was 450 feet long, 75 feet wide, and 45 feet high. A low roof was built extending 18 inches above the sides. A door was built into the side, and three decks were built inside. A 1992 study found the dimensions of the ark to be optimal for a ship to survive the rough conditions likely encountered during a catastrophic flood.[1]

Noah and the Flood

Noah was to take his sons, his wife, and his sons' wives on board the ark. He was also to take two of every animal that God brought to him (New American Standard says "*two of every kind*"), male and female, on the ark. This included birds, livestock and "... every animal that crawls on the ground ..." (6:20). Noah also stored food and made all the necessary preparations for both his family and the animals.

What happened between the time Noah was told to build the ark and the flood? Building a boat the size of the ark almost certainly took years, if not decades. Much like with the nativity story, many extra-biblical traditions have been added to the story of Noah. While it is plausible and easy to imagine that hecklers laughed at Noah's supposed foolishness, that Noah and his sons worked alone on the ark's construction, and that people pounded on the ark doors as the flood waters rose, none of these events are recorded as fact in the Bible. Be careful to not teach these things as fact.

Another element often taught as fact about Noah is that he preached to his wicked brethren for years about the coming disaster. This is extrapolated from a reference in 2 Peter 2:5 that refers to Noah as, "a preacher of righteousness." While Noah almost certainly warned others of the coming catastrophe, albeit in futility, the Bible does not contain any specific accounts of him preaching.

Only one verse covers the time from when Noah received instructions from God until seven days before the rain commenced. Genesis 6:22 states, "And Noah did this. He did everything that God had commanded him." Noah was obedient.

Seven days before the rain began to fall, God gave Noah some final instructions. In addition to two of each kind of animal, Noah was commanded to take seven pairs of all clean animals on board the ark. Clean and unclean animals are described in detail in Leviticus 11, written well after the time of Noah. God somehow made sure Noah understood which animals were clean.

Noah was informed that it would rain for 40 days and nights. Again, Noah did all that God commanded him. The rain began to fall seven days later just as God had said. It was God who closed the door of the ark (7:16). Noah, his family, and the animals were safe.

Much speculation surrounds the source of the volume of water required to submerge all the land on earth. Genesis 6:11 describes two sources, "... all the sources of the watery depths burst open, the floodgates of the sky were opened ..."

One well-developed idea, the hydroplate theory[2] (but still just a theory) suggests that the earth's surface was much more even before the flood. The seas were smaller, as most water was trapped under the surface. When the water was released, it was jetted into the sky and then fell as rain, covering the earth. In a series of events caused by the release of the subterranean water, the continents shifted dramatically, crashing into one another, causing the land masses to fold accordion-like in places and creating today's taller mountains. The space vacated by the land masses are the vast ocean basins into which the flood waters were collected.[3]

What can be known from the Biblical narrative is that the flood was global, as the highest mountains were under water by more than 20 feet (7:20) and as God had said, it was catastrophic for any land or air creature not within the ark (7:21).

The rain ended after 40 days, but the waters surged for another 110 days. The well-designed ark endured the calamity and by the end of the 150 days, the waters had significantly subsided. The ark then rested on a mountain, named Ararat, which is commonly associated today with Mount Ararat in eastern Turkey. It was several more months before other nearby mountain peaks came into view.

After first releasing a raven, Noah sent out a dove as a test to see how far the waters had receded. The dove could not find a resting place and so, returned to the ark. Seven days later he again sent out the dove. The dove returned with an olive leaf. Noah waited another seven days before releasing the dove a third time. This time the dove did not return.

Approximately one year after boarding, Noah removed the covering on the ark. Soon, after the land was dry enough to exit the ark, God commanded Noah to bring his family and all the animals out of the ark. The total time they had spent within the ark was a little over a year.

The first thing Noah did was to build an altar. He sacrificed some of every kind of clean animal as a burnt offering to the Lord (remember that they had taken seven pairs of each clean animal on board the ark). God promised to not destroy the earth again until the final judgment (Rev. 21:1). Despite the sinfulness of men and women, God would continue to reconcile them to Himself.

What God said in Genesis 8:22 should give great comfort and remind believers of God's goodness, "As long as the earth endures, seedtime and harvest, cold and heat, summer and winter, and day and night will not cease." Each change of day and night, each change of season is a reminder of God's patient, faithful love for us. This verse speaks to one of the prominent issues of today: climate change. Children (and adults) are bombarded with the message that planet earth is in grave danger and can only be saved if each person does their part by taking drastic action. Saving an entire planet is a huge responsibility for one to shoulder, and the drastic actions suggested tend to be vague or conflicting, often causing great anxiety.

Christians recognize that they have a responsibility to practice good stewardship in caring for the earth. Genesis 8:22 serves to remind, however, that it is God who is sovereign over the earth. He planned and designed the planet to meet human physical needs until the final judgment. Christians can take comfort in knowing that humans cannot destroy the planet. Rather, God alone is to decide the time for the end of the earth.

God next commanded Noah (as he had Adam) to be fruitful, multiply and fill the earth. But this time some things would be different: animals would fear people because God gave the rule of them to man. God also gave every living moving thing to man for food. His only requirement was that it should be prepared without its blood still in it.

God told Noah that he would never again destroy the earth by flood. In 9:12-13 God said the rainbow would serve as a sign of the covenant. Rainbows do remind of God's promise, but Genesis 9:16 states that the rainbow is also a sign for God, "The bow will be in the clouds, and I will look at it and remember the everlasting covenant ..."

Noah trusted God even when His commands must have seemed strange or even impossible. Because of his faithfulness, Noah and his family survived the flood. From Shem, Ham, Japheth and their wives, all the nations of the world would spring forth. The ark serves as a picture of what Jesus did centuries later, providing salvation for those who could not save themselves. Unlike the ark, that provided salvation for only a few, salvation through Jesus is available to everyone who calls upon His name and repents.

AGE GROUP CONSIDERATIONS

Children will likely have dozens of questions about the details of the events surrounding Noah, the ark, and the flood. While most of these questions will probably have little relevance to the focus of the story, it is prudent to at least try to anticipate some of the questions. This is only a starting point. There are many good resources that discuss the flood and the ark in detail. There are also several websites containing hundreds of well-researched articles, including:

Answers in Genesis   *www.answersingenesis.org*
Institute for Creation Research   *www.icr.org*
Christian Answers   *www.christiananswers.net*

How long was Noah in the ark?

While the rain fell for 40 days and nights, Noah and his passengers actually spent a little over a year in the ark.

Due to how time is tracked on the Jewish calendar, there is some debate over the actual number of days. Most time lines put the length at between 370 and 378 days.[4,5]

Were there really two of each animal in the ark?

Today, scientists have cataloged tens of thousands of unique animals and insects, and it is believed that many more have not yet been discovered or identified. Could all these animals have fit in the ark? There are several things to consider that may help us better understand the feasibility of such an audacious undertaking.

Genesis 6:20 states that it was God Who brought the animals to Noah. Noah did not have to worry about missing any animals since it was not his responsibility. Aquatic animals were not on board the ark, reducing the number of animals.

The use of the term, *"kind"* in Genesis 6:19-20 opens the possibility that some, or all groups of animals may have had representatives on the ark. For example, all horses today may have descended from one pair of horses on board the ark. Variety within species occurs easily, as seen in the wide diversity of dog breeding. Remember, however, dogs come only from dogs; It is not possible to breed a dog with a cat (or any other type of animal) to make a new type of creature.

While this theory would greatly reduce the number of animals, it usually raises the next question...

How did all the animals fit on the ark?

The ark was a massive ship, larger than all but a few ships built before the twentieth century.[6] Visiting a museum battleship (not unlike in size to the ark) illustrates how easily a ship with multiple decks can house two thousand men in addition to all their food, gear, machinery and weapons . Noah's ark contained no weapons and no engines. It only needed to support eight people and the animals (many of which had space needs much smaller than that required by a human).

It is likely that the animals on board the ark were juveniles, rather than mature adults.[6] This would have reduced requirements of food and space. In addition, some of the animals may have entered a hibernation state that would have further reduced food requirements. We don't know, but this is a possibility with God in charge.

Did the flood really cover the entire world, and if so, where did all the water go?

The Bible is adamant that the flood was global and all-encompassing. The ark would not have been necessary if some parts of the world were not inundated.

If all the land on earth were perfectly smooth, water would cover the surface to a depth of nearly two miles! Even now water covers almost three-fourths of the earth's surface, and the mean depth of the sea is six times the mean height of land.[7] The flood almost certainly radically altered the topography of the earth. If the pre-flood mountains were shorter than today and a volume of water fell faster than it could drain, there is more than enough water to submerge the planet.

Did the dinosaurs become extinct because of the flood?

No. They may have died out before or after the flood. Death and extinction is a normal part our fallen world and still occurs today. If dinosaurs were not extinct by the time of Noah, they would have been on board the ark. Some Creationist scientists are convinced that dinosaurs did not die out until after the flood.[8] No one knows for sure, either way.

SUGGESTED HYMNS/SONGS

1. *Who Built the Ark?*, Track 16, Sharing God's Love: 25 Bible Songs for Children. Twin Sister Productions.
2. *Great is Thy Faithfulness*, 96, 2008 Baptist Hymnal.
3. *God Will Make a Way*, 85, 2008 Baptist Hymnal.
4. *Wherever He Leads I'll Go*, 437, 2008 Baptist Hymnal.
5. *Send a Great Revival*, 490, 2008 Baptist Hymnal.

Noah and the Flood

STUDENT APPLICATIONS

1. Students will know that the story of Noah is found in the Old Testament book of Genesis.
2. Students will know that God decided to destroy the earth in a flood because of the wickedness of its human inhabitants.
3. Students will know that one man, Noah, found favor in God's sight.
4. Students will know that God commanded Noah to construct an ark in which he, his wife, his sons and their wives would survive the flood.
5. Students will know that Noah was faithful to build the ark as instructed by God.
6. Students will know that God told Noah to take two of each kind of animal on board the ark.
7. Students will know that God told Noah to take seven pairs of each kind of clean animal on board the ark.
8. Students will know that God shut the door of the ark.
9. Students will know that forty days and nights of rain provided the water for the flood.
10. Students will know that the flood covered the entire earth.
11. Students will know that Noah sent out a dove three different times to measure how much the water level had dropped.
12. Students will know that it was over a year before Noah and his family and the animals were able to leave the ark.
13. Students will know that after exiting the ark, Noah made an offering to and worshiped God.
14. Students will know that God told Noah that the rainbow would serve as a reminder of His covenant to never again destroy the earth with water.
15. Students will know that day and night, and all the seasons will continue until it is God's timing to end the world.

RESOURCES/CREDIT

1. Ken Ham, *The New Answers Book* (Green Forest, AR: Master Books, 2007), 132-4.
2. Walt Brown, *In the Beginning: Compelling Evidence for Creation and the Flood, 7th Edition* (Phoenix, AZ: Center for Scientific Creation, 2001), 85-137.
3. Ham, 135.
4. *Flood Timeline* [article online]; available from http://www.answersingenesis.org/articles/am/v2/n2/ark-chronology
5. Michael Catellano, *Timeline of Noah and the Flood* [article online]; available from http://home.earthlink.net/~arktracker/ark/Timeline.html
6. Ham, 125.
7. A. R. Wallace, *Man's Place in the Universe* (McClure, Phillips & Co.: New York, 1903), 225-6.
8. Ham, 149-76.

Young Jesus in the Temple

BACKGROUND PASSAGES

Main Passage
Luke 2:41-52   Boy Jesus in Temple

Related Passages
John 10:22   Adult Jesus in Temple

Suggested Homiletic Passage
Luke 2:46-52

MEMORY VERSE

"Why were you searching for Me?" He asked them. "Didn't you know that I had to be in my Father's house?"

Luke 2:49

LESSON OBJECTIVE

While Jesus lived a normal childhood and adolescence, growing both physically and mentally, even at a young age there was evidence that He was the Son of God.

LESSON

What was Jesus like as a child? What would it have been like to be part of His family? The Gospels contain just one account about Jesus' life between the events surrounding His birth and the beginning of His public ministry at the age of thirty (Luke 3:23). The account occurs when he was twelve years old. Jesus went up to Jerusalem with His family to observe the Passover, as they did every year. Jesus demonstrated to his parents and many of the religious teachers that He was no ordinary child, but the long-awaited Messiah.

Luke 2:41-52

The Passover was one of three festivals that Jewish males were required to attend in Jerusalem each year (Deut. 16:16). Passover was considered the most important of the festivals. If it was possible to attend only one festival, Passover was the one they most likely attended. Joseph was faithful to bring his family every year (v.42).

When the days of observing the festival ended, the masses that converged on Jerusalem began to disperse. Since all men were required to attend, families typically traveled as a group with friends and relatives (out of concerns for security and safety). Along the way, the women would usually congregate, as would the men.

At the age of twelve, Jesus was leaving childhood and entering adulthood and was probably given a measure of freedom by his parents. Perhaps He was left behind in Jerusalem because Mary and Joseph each assumed He was with the other one as they began their journey home.

After a day's travel from Jerusalem, Mary and Joseph finally realized Jesus was missing. They first searched among their friends and relatives. When they still had not located him, they hurried back to Jerusalem. Typically, a day's journey was eighteen to thirty miles; however, there was an ancient custom to only travel three to eight miles on the first day. The reason was that if it was realized something was missing, it would only be a minor inconvenience to send someone back to fetch it. A popular stopping point, for groups traveling from Jerusalem, was the ancient town of Beer (*or* Beeroth), eight miles distant. If Mary and Joseph stopped there, they would have been only about three hours away from Jerusalem.[1]

Mary and Joseph certainly knew that God would protect His only Son. Still, they were likely filled with as much anxiety as any parents would be.

Once back in Jerusalem, it took another three days of searching to locate Jesus. When they found Him, He was in the temple complex. It is ironic that Jesus, Who would perfectly fulfill the duties of a priest, would not have been allowed into the temple proper since he was a young man and not a serving priest. An area outside the temple, aptly named the *Court of the Gentiles*, was open to everyone. Large colonnades surrounded the temple courtyard. In these colonnades teachers and rabbis would gather to teach and discuss many things, most of which were related to the Jew-

Young Jesus in the Temple

ish religion. During the annual feasts, the numbers of people gathered around the teachers were likely great.

When they finally found Jesus, Mary asked Him, "Son, why have You treated us like this? Your father and I have been anxiously searching for You." (v.48). While reading emotion into a text can sometimes lead to the wrong conclusion, Mary was probably both greatly relieved and somewhat upset. Jesus answered, "Why were you searching for Me? Didn't you know that I had to be in my Father's house?" (v.49). Jesus was aware of the divine mission that was ahead of Him. This would not be the last time for the teachers of the Law to be amazed. Jesus would later teach at the temple once He grew up and began His public ministry (John 10:22).

Joseph, Mary and Jesus returned to Nazareth. In a remarkable statement, the Bible tells that "He was obedient to them (his parents)." At an age when many young men are tempted to behave in a rebellious manner, God's Son willingly submitted to His earthly parents. If God's Son was willing to obey His earthly parents, how much more should we be willing to obey ours!

Like any loving mother, Mary carefully observed her child. She noticed what others did not, and she kept these things in her heart. Over time, other people began to notice there was something special about Jesus. He grew in wisdom and stature and gained favor with God and people.

While Jesus was no ordinary child, he lived a normal childhood and adolescence. He set the example for children to obey their parents. Children can also take comfort in knowing that God has a plan for their lives as they grow in wisdom and stature in their journey to adulthood.

Age Group Considerations

This is a wonderful lesson to reinforce the importance of obedience. Jesus willingly submitted to His earthly parents. Children may be reminded to always let their parents know where they are going, to be respectful, and to obey.

Suggested Hymns/Songs

1. *One Small Child*, 200, 2008 Baptist Hymnal.
2. *Tell Me the Story of Jesus*, 220, 2008 Baptist Hymnal.
3. *I Stand Amazed in the Presence*, 237, 2008 Baptist Hymnal.
4. *Let Jesus Come Into Your Heart*, 416, 2008 Baptist Hymnal.
5. *My Jesus I Love Thee*, 552, 2008 Baptist Hymnal.

Student Applications

1. Students will know that the childhood story of Jesus in the temple is found in the New Testament book of Luke.
2. Students will know that the story of Jesus in the temple is the only Biblical story recorded of Jesus as an adolescent.
3. Students will know that Jesus went with his family to Jerusalem to observe the Passover when he was twelve-years-old.
4. Students will know that Jesus remained in Jerusalem after his parents left to return to Nazareth.
5. Students will know that Jesus' parents realized that He was not in their group only after a full day's journey.
6. Students will know that it took three days for Jesus' parents to find Him.
7. Students will know that Mary and Joseph found Jesus in the Temple complex.
8. Students will know that Jesus was found sitting and talking with a number of teachers, who were amazed at His understanding and answers.
9. Students will know that Jesus was obedient to His parents.
10. Students will know that Jesus experienced a normal childhood in which He grew mentally, spiritually and physically (just as children do today).

Resources/Credit

1. James M. Freeman, *Manners & Customs of the Bible* (New Kensington: Whitaker House, 1996), 173-4.

Elisha

BACKGROUND PASSAGES

Main Passages
2 Kings 2:1-15	Elijah and the whirlwind
2 Kings 6:8-23	The Aramean war

Related Passages
2 Kings 2:16-6:7	Elisha's miracles
2 Kings 6:24-7:20	Aram defeated
2 Kings 13:14-21	Death of Elisha

Suggested Homiletic Passage
2 Kings 6:15-23

MEMORY VERSE

Younger version
This is the victory that has conquered the world: our faith.

I John 5:4b

Older version
For this is what love for God is: to keep His commands. Now His commands are not a burden, because whatever has been born of God conquers the world. This is the victory that has conquered the world: our faith.

I John 5:3-4

LESSON OBJECTIVE

Elisha, like Elijah before him, was a prophet whom God used to teach the kings and the people of Israel to trust in Him rather than their own power.

LESSON

God sent prophets at various times to remind Israel of their covenant with God and to call them to repentance. Elijah was one such prophet. He was one of only two men in the Bible to never experience a physical death. Enoch was the other (Gen. 5:24)]. Elisha followed Elijah, so he witnessed Elijah's depar-ture, and became God's vessel for many miraculous works. Through Elisha God taught many people that His power, though often unseen, is greater than anything they would ever encounter in this world.

2 Kings 2:1-15

Elijah ministered over fifty years in the northern kingdom of Israel. Elijah was Elisha's mentor, but that was about to change. "The time had come for the Lord to take Elijah up to heaven in a whirlwind." (v.1).

Elisha and Elijah were traveling from Gilgal, a hill town near Shiloh, to Bethel. Elijah told Elisha to stay where he was, for Elijah planned to go on to Bethel. But Elisha would not stay and insisted on going with Elijah. When they arrived in Bethel they were met by the sons of the prophets who knew that something was to happen to Elijah that day. Elisha did not wish to talk about it.

Elijah, led by the Lord, then prepared to leave for Jericho. This was the same Jericho destroyed by Joshua and rebuilt by Hiel (I Kings. 16:34). Once again, Elisha insisted on accompanying him.

Fifty men of the sons of the prophets watched from a distance as Elijah and Elisha approached the Jordan river. Elijah rolled up his mantle (an outer garment or overcoat) and struck the surface of the river. The water parted, allowing the two men to cross on dry ground.

As they walked, Elijah asked if there was anything he could do for Elisha before he was taken. Elisha boldly asked, "Please, let there be a double portion of your spirit on me." (v.9). In Israel the oldest son received a double portion of the inheritance. Elisha wanted to take Elijah's place in ministry. Elijah knew that what Elisha asked could only be granted by God. The sign confirming that Elisha was granted his request would be that he would witness the taking of Elijah.

As Elisha and Elijah continued walking, a chariot of fire pulled by horses of fire appeared and separated the two. Elijah cried out, "My father, my father, the chariots and horsemen of Israel!" (v.12). Elijah was then taken by a whirlwind, never to be seen again. Elisha tore his own clothes out of grief. The words cried out by Elisha were the same words that king Jehoash said years later concerning Elisha as the prophet was on his death bed (2 Kings. 13:14).

Elisha received the inheritance he had desired. Elisha took up Elijah's outer garment and repeated the crossing of the Jordan river. This bore witness to the sons of the prophets that Elisha was now Israel's leading figure among the prophets. God worked many miracles through Elisha, including the healing of Naaman (the subject of another rotation lesson), multiplying the widow's oil, and making an axe head float. These miracles showed the nation of Israel that God's hand was upon Elisha and challenged them to follow their Lord God.

2 Kings 6:8-23

Some time after Elijah was taken, Israel was at war with Aram. Aram was a nation to the northeast of Israel in the region of modern day Syria. Some translations, including the English Standard Version, use the term "Syria" instead of "Aram."

While traveling during his military campaign, the king of Aram realized he had a problem. His whereabouts and whatever he did were already known to Israel. Convinced that there was treachery in his midst, the angry king gathered his servants. One of the servants informed the king that, "Elisha, the prophet in Israel, tells the king of Israel even the words you speak in your bedroom." (v.12).

The king of Aram immediately began to make preparations to track down and capture Elisha. Once he learned Elisha was in the city of Dothan, he sent a large army with horses and chariots by night to surround the city.

The next morning one of Elisha's servants received a great shock as he got up and went out, only to discover that the city was surrounded. Despairing, the servant asked Elisha if there was anything that could be done.

Elisha knew this was an opportunity to teach his servant that God was in control of the situation. He said, "Don't be afraid, for those who are with us outnumber those who are with them." (v.18).

Elisha prayed, asking God to open the eyes of his servant. God opened his eyes, and as the servant looked at a nearby mountain, he saw it was covered with horses and chariots of fire. Though no one else could see, God was watching over Elisha.

As the Arameans closed in, Elisha prayed to God and asked Him to strike them with blindness. God struck the army with blindness. Elisha went out to the army and told them, "This is not the way, and this is not the city. Follow me and I will take you to the man you are looking for." (v.19).

Elisha led the army to the king of Israel in Samaria, about twelve miles from Dothan. Once there, Elisha prayed that their sight would be restored. Their sight returned and they realized where they had been led. The king of Israel asked Elisha what he should do with them. His first inclination was to kill all of them, but Elisha encouraged the king to treat the men with respect, give them food and drink, and send them back to their master.

The time and the name of the king in this incident cannot be definitively dated. It might have been during either the reign of Jehu or Jehoahaz.[1]

The king of Israel followed Elisha's advice and gave a feast for the Aramean army. He them sent them back to their homeland with an incredible story to tell. Realizing the futility of his efforts, the king of Aram left Israel alone and Israel experienced peace.

While it is easy to marvel at the faith and trust of Elisha, it should be remembered that while he was doubly-blessed, he was still only human, imperfect and fallible, just like all the other Old Testament prophets. In Jesus, however, believers have a perfect prophet, savior, and Lord who died on a cross to take away their sins. It is God alone that is deserving of trust and faith. While believers may not experience miracles of the type that God worked through Elijah and Elisha, they can know that God is at work, and trust Him to daily guide and protect.

AGE GROUP CONSIDERATIONS

Elisha performed many other miracles in the power of the Lord. These miracles are recorded in the first thirteen chapters of 2 Kings. Studying these passages will help you better understand the nature and grand scope of Elisha's five decades of ministry.

In your lesson preparation you may wish to include other events of Elisha's ministry in addition to the main lesson. One especially interesting story, which children would love to hear, actually happened after Elisha's death. Once a dead man was thrown into Elisha's tomb. The dead man revived after simply touching his bones (2 Kings. 13:21).

SUGGESTED HYMNS/SONGS

1. *Ancient of Days*, 62, 2008 Baptist Hymnal.
2. *Faith is the Victory*, 521, 2008 Baptist Hymnal.
3. *Great is the Lord*, 61, 2008 Baptist Hymnal.
4. *Jesus, Name Above All Names*, 320, 2008 Baptist Hymnal.
5. *O Magnify the Lord*, 134, 2008 Baptist Hymnal.
6. *Surely the Presence (of the Lord is in This Place)*, 158, 2008 Baptist Hymnal.
7. *Turn Your Eyes Upon Jesus*, 413, 2008 Baptist Hymnal.

STUDENT APPLICATIONS

1. Students will know that the life and events of Elisha is found in the book of 2 Kings in the Old Testament.
2. Students will know that Elijah and Elisha were prophets of God.
3. Students will know that Elisha asked for a double portion of the Spirit (of God) that was upon Elijah.
4. Students will know that Elijah did not experience death, but that a chariot and horses of fire appeared and carried him to Heaven in a whirlwind.
5. Students will know that Enoch and Elijah are the only two people in the Bible to not experience death.
6. Students will know that as a prophet of God, Elisha performed many amazing miracles,
7. Students will know that the king of Aram waged war against Israel.
8. Students will know that God spoke through Elisha, telling the king of Israel about what the king of Aram was planning and where his army was located.
9. Students will know that the king of Aram's army surrounded the city of Dothan, intending to capture Elisha.
10. Students will know Elisha's servant despaired at the siege of the king of Aram.
11. Students will know that Elisha informed his servant that God was protecting them with an army that could not be seen by normal human sight.
12. Students will know that God struck the Arameans with blindness and Elisha led them to the king of Israel in Samaria.
13. Students will know that instead of killing the Arameans, the king of Israel fed the army and sent them home, allowing Israel to be at peace.
14. Students will know that they can have faith in God, even when He works in mysterious, unseen ways.
15. Students will know that they can be confident that God is infinitely more powerful than any evil or trouble they may encounter.

RESOURCES/CREDIT

1. Charles G. Martin, *The International Bible Commentary, Revised Edition*, F.F. Bruce, ed. (Grand Rapids, Michigan: Zondervan Publishing House, 1979), 424.

David & Jonathan

BACKGROUND PASSAGES

Main Passage
I Samuel 20:1-42   Jonathan saves David's life

Related Passages
I Sam. 23:15-18   A final meeting
2 Samuel 9   David's kindness to Mephibosheth

Suggested Homiletic Passage
I Samuel 20:10-17

MEMORY VERSE

A friend loves at all times, and a brother is born for a difficult time.

Proverbs 17:17

LESSON OBJECTIVE

Loyalty, love, and self-sacrifice are qualities which Jonathan modeled in his friendship with David. These qualities exemplify true friendship.

LESSON

Over the course of a lifetime, an individual may interact with thousands of fellow human beings. Only a few of these interactions will go beyond the superficial and become relationships. Acquaintances are many, but friends are rare. True, intimate, God-centered friendships are the rarest of all. In the story of David and Jonathan, two men forged an unlikely friendship that proved stronger than their circumstances. Their love for one another shows that to have true friendship requires being a true friend. It is only when a person has personally experienced the love of Jesus that he/she can be the friend that God would have him/her to be.

I Samuel 20

David was on the run. King Saul had attempted several times to kill him. David fled from Naoith in Ramah, where Saul had tracked him down. He came to Gibeah, to talk with Jonathan, his friend, and Saul's son. Later, David would make Jerusalem the capital of Israel, but Saul lived and ruled form Gibeah. David approached Jonathan, wanting to know why Saul was so determined to kill him.

Saul believed that David was a threat to his throne. Led by God, Samuel had anointed David and prophesied that he would one day be king. Unlike many would-be rulers, David never desired to usurp Saul and had demonstrated multiple times that he refused to harm Saul. Instead, David waited on God's timing to become the next king. Jealousy was also a factor in Saul's anger toward David. God gave David much success in battle and favor with the people of Israel. When Saul heard the people singing praises about David, he became jealous from that day forward (I Sam. 18:6-8).

David and Jonathan, however, had already developed a deep friendship before this meeting. Jonathan had even made a covenant with David (I Sam. 18:1-4). At that time Jonathan gave David his royal robe and personal weapons. It was considered a special mark of respect to be presented with the personal garments of royalty. The giving of the military tunic ("*girdle*" in King James translation) showed the greatest confidence and affection.[1] The customs of power and succession made their friendship most peculiar. Jonathan, as Saul's heir, stood to lose the throne if David became king. David, understanding Jonathan's situation, showed great faith in trusting Jonathan.

Jonathan tried to calm David's fear, telling him that Saul did nothing great or small without first telling him. Jonathan had previously convinced his father to not harm David (I Sam. 19:1-6). David said that Saul knew of their friendship and was holding back information from Jonathan. "As surely as the LORD lives and as you yourself live, there is but a step between me and death." (v.3).

The two men put together a plan to determine if Saul truly desired to kill David. The next day was the festival of the new moon. The new moon festival marked the beginning of each month. While many ancient cultures observed celebrations based on the moon cycle, only the Israelites observed this feast at the new moon, when the moon is not seen. The absence of a visual representation in the sky helped insure that the Creator, and not the moon, was worshiped.

It was decided that David would hide in a field while Jonathan attended the feast. King Saul would expect all the members of his court to be present. If Saul asked of David's absence and became angry because of it, they would know that the he still intended to harm David. This allowed God to speak through circumstance and to guide them.

David asked Jonathan, that if he had truly done anything wrong, to kill him himself, rather than take him to the king. Jonathan emphatically refused and promised to tell David if ever the king had plans to harm him.

Once the feast ended, David would need a way to know how Saul had responded to his absence. It would be too dangerous for David to come out of hiding until he knew Jonathan was alone. They went to a field where Jonathan swore once again to tell David of any plans the king might have against him. He asked David to always treat him with brotherly love, along with all who were of his household. David agreed and plans were made.

The two men agreed on a meeting place. After the feast, Jonathan would come to the meeting place with a servant and shoot three arrows. Jonathan said, "Then I will send the young man [and say], 'Go and find the arrows!' Now, if I expressly say to the young man, 'Look, the arrows are on this side of you — get them,' then come, because as the LORD lives, it is safe for you and there is no problem. But if I say this to the youth: 'Look, the arrows are beyond you!' then go, for the LORD is sending you away." (vv.21-22). David agreed and then left and hid in the field, awaiting God's direction through his friend, Jonathan.

On the first day of the festival, Saul and his court gathered together for the meal. Saul noticed that David's place was empty but thought little of it. On the second day, when his place was still unoccupied, Saul inquired of Jonathan as to the whereabouts of David. Jonathan said he had gone to Bethlehem to observe a sacrifice with his family.

Saul was angered by Jonathan's response. He saw through the deception and accused Jonathan of protecting David. Saul suspected that Jonathan probably did know where David was and demanded that he call for him so that he could be killed. Jonathan stood up to his father and asked what it was that David had done to deserve death.

Saul lost control of his anger and hurled a spear at his son with intent to kill. This act was reminiscent of when Saul had previously thrown a spear at David (I Sam. 18:10-11). Jonathan, also greatly angered, got up and left, "grieved because of his father's shameful behavior toward David." (v.34).

The next morning, Jonathan went to the meeting place. He was accompanied by a servant referred to as a "young man." As Jonathan shot several arrows, he shot one beyond him. He said to the servant, "The arrow is beyond you, isn't it?" This was the sign to David that Saul truly did desire to kill him. After gathering the arrows, Jonathan handed his equipment to the young man, still clueless to the point of the exercise, and sent him back to the city.

Once Jonathan was alone, David came out of hiding. He bowed three times before Jonathan. They then kissed (a middle eastern tradition) and wept together, knowing that David must leave or face the wrath of Saul. Jonathan reaffirmed his intent to keep the agreement they had made earlier. David left and Jonathan returned to the city.

David and Jonathan would see each other at least one more time. Once while Saul was hunting David, Jonathan came to him in the Wilderness of Zin in Horesh, a desert area west of the Dead Sea and encouraged him that one day he would be king (I Sam. 23:15-18). David would not see him again as Jonathan met an untimely death, dying the same day as his father in battle against the Philistines (I Sam. 31:1-6).

David & Jonathan

David kept his promise to show love toward Jonathan's household. How is this known? It is seen after Jonathan's death when David took Jonathan's son Mephibosheth into his own household and provided for him all of his days (2 Sam. 9). This was no minor concession as Mephibosheth could have made a case that he was deserving of the throne.

God used Jonathan to protect David. It was through David's lineage that the Messiah was born. While Jonathan was a great and noble friend to David, he was not perfect. Jesus is the only friend who will always be perfect. Jesus will become the best friend of anyone who repents of his/her sins and chooses to follow Him. As the Holy Spirit works to sanctify a believer, he/she will become more like Him. This will enable him/her to be a better friend.

Age Group Considerations

Children may not be concerned with the attributes of true friendship. Their needs will be of a more practical nature. Remind them that they must be a friend if they want to have friends. They will find that not everyone will get along with them, but if they learn to listen, share, and put the needs of others ahead of theirs, then they will be a good friend and a witness to the love of God in their lives.

Suggested Hymns/Songs

1. *Serve the Lord with Gladness*, 382, 2008 Baptist Hymnal.
2. *The Bond of Love*, 387, 2008 Baptist Hymnal.
3. *What a Friend We Have in Jesus*, 154, 2008 Baptist Hymnal.
4. *Rescue the Perishing*, 357, 2008 Baptist Hymnal.
5. *Tell it to Jesus*, 425, 2008 Baptist Hymnal.

Student Applications

1. Students will know that the story of David and Jonathan is found in the Old Testament book of I Samuel.
2. Students will know that Jonathan was the son of Saul, king of Israel.
3. Students will know that God anointed David to be the next king of Israel.
4. Students will know that despite having made David a member of his court, Saul desired to kill him.
5. Students will know that Jonathan volunteered to find out if his father still wished to kill David.
6. Students will know that David promised not to harm any member of Jonathan's family when he became king.
7. Students will know that David hid while Jonathan attended a feast with the king, celebrating the new moon.
8. Students will know that King Saul was angry that David was not at the feast.
9. Students will know that King Saul was so angry with his son Jonathan for defending David, that he threw a spear at him with intent to kill. He missed.
10. Students will know that Jonathan used archery arrows to signal to David that his life was in danger.
11. Students will know that David and Jonathan departed sorrowfully, yet loving each other as friends.
12. Students will know that while earthly friendships are precious and worthwhile, only Jesus can be their perfect friend.
13. Students will know that Jesus was a descendant of David.

Resources/Credit

1. James M. Freeman, *Manners & Customs of the Bible* (New Kensington: Whitaker House, 1996), 138.

Christmas - Shepherds

BACKGROUND PASSAGES

Main Passage
Luke 2:8-20	Shepherds visit
Luke 2:39-40	Return to Nazareth

Related Passages
Micah 5:2	Messiah prophesied
Luke 2:1-7	Birth of Jesus
Luke 2:39-40	Return to Nazareth
Rev. 19:11-16	Second advent of Jesus

Suggested Homiletic Passage
Luke 2:9-13

MEMORY VERSE

Younger version
Today a Savior, who is Messiah the Lord, was born for you in the city of David.

Luke 2:11

Older version
Today a Savior, who is Messiah the Lord, was born for you in the city of David. This will be the sign for you: you will find a baby wrapped snugly in cloth and lying in a manger.

Luke 2:11-12

LESSON OBJECTIVE

The humble shepherds who were privileged to witness the birth of the Messiah are a reminder that Jesus came to earth as the Lamb of God to be the Savior and Lord of all who will accept Him.

LESSON

Each December Christians around the world celebrate the birth of the Messiah, Jesus Christ. Two of the four gospels, Matthew and Luke, describe Jesus' childhood, but only Luke talks specifically about the birth of Jesus.

His arrival came under the humblest of circumstances. Despite being the King of Kings, He was not born in a royal palace. His arrival was not announced by earthly heralds throughout a kingdom. Instead, He was born in a town that would not be His home, slept in a feeding trough (manger), and was visited by the fringe of society (the shepherds). This, however, was all part of God's plan as God became human in order to secure salvation for all who would believe on His name.

Luke 2:1-7

The Roman emperor Augustus Caesar declared that a census should take place throughout his empire. After the death of Julius Caesar, the term "Caesar" was adopted by his grandnephew Augustus and by subsequent emperors as a ruling title, much like "king" or "president" is used today. A census assisted the authorities in tax collection. A Roman census required all subjects to return to their hometown in order to be registered.

Joseph lived in Nazareth, in the region of Galilee, but had to return to Bethlehem because he was of the line of David (Mary was also a descendent of David). The journey was approximately 60 miles through rugged terrain. Joseph was engaged to Mary, who was expecting a child, the Messiah, who had been conceived by the Holy Spirit. Mary traveled with Joseph on the long journey.

In the Jewish culture of the time an engagement was as binding as marriage today, but precluded the consummation of the relationship until after the wedding. Engagements could only be terminated by divorce. During the engagement time the groom would build or otherwise secure a home, and the couple would make other necessary preparations for their future life together. Joseph considered quietly divorcing Mary after discovering she was pregnant, but he decided not to after a visit from an angel told him the baby was conceived by the Holy Spirit (Matt. 1:19-21).

Micah prophesied that the Messiah would be born in Bethlehem Ephrathah (Micah 5:2). There

Christmas - Shepherds

were multiple *Bethlehems*, but only one *Bethlehem Ephrathah*. God is sovereign over all history. He used the census undertaken by the Roman emperor Augustus to fulfill the prophecy of the location of Jesus' birth. Bethlehem was a tiny town near Jerusalem that had been the birthplace of King David approximately 1000 years before.

While the couple was in Bethlehem, the time came for Mary to give birth. Many extra-biblical traditions surround the circumstances of the nativity. All that the Bible describes is that the child was wrapped and placed in a feeding trough because there was no room for them at the inn.

It was common for a Jewish house to have an indoor area for smaller livestock that would likely include feeding apparatus, so it is possible that Jesus was born in a house (perhaps a relative?) and not a stable or cave as tradition holds. But that theory does not fully explain why Mary and Joseph tried to find lodging at an inn. Did Joseph no longer have relatives in Bethlehem? If they were in a stable, why are no animals mentioned? While speculation over the circumstances of Jesus' birth are intriguing, it is more profitable to study what is known.

The manger exemplifies the humble conditions under which Jesus came to earth. John Calvin wrote, "Such was his condition at his birth, because he had taken upon him our flesh for this purpose, that he might, 'empty himself' (Phil. 2:7) on our account."[1] It is difficult to fathom that the Lord, who will one day return as King of Kings in majesty and splendor riding on a white horse (Rev. 19:11-16) to judge the nations, once slept as a helpless babe in a feeding trough. It is comforting to know that Jesus understands what we go through in life because He has also experienced life as a human.

Luke 2:8-20

What kind of people would you expect to attend a celebration of the birth of a king? Royalty? Nobles? Powerful officials? None of these people were present to celebrate the birth of Jesus, with the possible exception of the wise men (they might not have seen Je-

sus until some time later). Jesus' birth was announced not by earthly heralds, but by angels. His birth was announced not to people of high position, but to shepherds tending their sheep in the countryside.

Shepherds were low in the social order of ancient cultures. They spent extended periods of time away from home and outside the normal social patterns of life. Shepherding was a full-time job. The work did not end as the sun went down, and in many ways took on more responsibility as the flock faced new threats in the darkness of the night. It was on one of these long nights that an angel appeared to shepherds tending their flock near the town of Bethlehem.

The shepherds were probably used to dealing with predators and other threats to their flocks, but were unprepared for and terrified by the sight of the angel and the brightness of the glory of God. The angel made an announcement, "Don't be afraid, for look, I proclaim to you good news of great joy that will be for all the people: today a Savior, who is Messiah the Lord, was born for you in the city of David. This will be the sign for you: you will find a baby wrapped snugly in cloth and lying in a manger." (vv.10-12). Not only had the promised Messiah arrived, the shepherds would be privileged to see Him!

God's gift of salvation through Jesus is not just for people of high position or honor, but it is for all people. Sadly, wealth, fame and power often prove to be a barrier to people accepting Jesus. Many people refuse God's gift because of their unbelief. This ingratitude for God is further evidence of the sinfulness of people.

The angel was suddenly joined by "a multitude of the heavenly host." They began to praise God saying, "Glory to God in the highest heaven, and peace on earth to people He favors!" (v.14). It was truly a wonderful moment as God showed His favor on the human race.

After the angels departed, the shepherds talked with one another and decided to go to Bethlehem to see the Messiah. They quickly headed for town. How they found Mary and Joseph is unknown (the star?), but find them they did. The baby was lying in a feeding trough just as the angel had said.

The shepherds could not contain their excitement about the arrival of the Messiah. They shared the good news, and all who heard it were amazed. The joy of the shepherds could not be contained as they glorified and praised God even as they returned to their work.

Since Bethlehem was so close to Jerusalem, it is likely that some of the sheep raised by the shepherds were used in sacrifice at the temple. In modern times it has been observed that shepherds still develop a special relationship with their flock. Shepherds develop an intimate knowledge about each sheep as they care for them when they are born, are sick, or wander from the flock.

It has been demonstrated that sheep recognize the voice of their shepherd, and ignore those who closely mimic their master. The shepherd even plays with his sheep, pretending to run away a short distance, only to have the sheep overtake and frolic about him.[2] These shepherds, of all people, would understand what a sacrifice truly meant as sheep were regularly taken to Jerusalem to be offered at the temple. It is only appropriate that those who cared for the sheep of Israel were the first to see the Lamb of God.

Luke 2:39-40

Joseph was warned in a dream to take Mary and Jesus to Egypt to avoid the wrath of King Herod (Matt. 2:13-15). After the time in Egypt, Joseph, Mary, and Jesus returned to Nazareth. There Jesus "... grew up and became strong, filled with wisdom, and God's grace was on Him." (v.40).

Jesus recruited disciples, taught extensively, and healed many people during His earthly ministry, but it was upon the cross that He did His greatest work. By dying on the cross and rising again, He conquered sin and the penalty of death.

It is sobering to think that God has every right to let people die in their sin, but, in His great love, He made a way of salvation. At Christmas, Christians celebrate the fact that God loved people so much that He sent His Son as a child who would grow up to the sacrificial Lamb of God who would save us from our sins.

AGE GROUP CONSIDERATIONS

Rather than explain the custom of Jewish engagement, it is probably best to tell younger children simply that Mary and Joseph were husband and wife. Older children will enjoy learning about the marriage customs of the day.

Each December lesson in this curriculum has focused on a different aspect of the advent of Jesus. However, all of them overlap one another. Feel free to add other elements of the story, including the wise men, Gabriel's announcement to Mary, etc. to your lesson presentation.

SUGGESTED HYMNS/SONGS

1. *While Shepherds Watched Their Flocks*, 203, 2008 Baptist Hymnal.
2. *Away in a Manger*, 205, 2008 Baptist Hymnal.
3. *Silent Night, Holy Night*, 206, 2008 Baptist Hymnal.
4. *What Can I Give Him*, 204, 2008 Baptist Hymnal.
5. *Hark the Herald Angels Sing*, 192, 2008 Baptist Hymnal.
6. *Angels We Have Heard on High*, 184, 2008 Baptist Hymnal.

STUDENT APPLICATIONS

1. Students will know that the story of the Shepherds is found in the New Testament book of Luke.
2. Students will know that Jesus was born in the village of Bethlehem Ephrathah, not far from Jerusalem.
3. Students will know that the job of a shepherd was tough, and often looked down upon by others.

Christmas - Shepherds

4. Students will know that an angel of the Lord appeared to shepherds near Bethlehem.
5. Students will know that the shepherds were scared of the angel until he told them to not be afraid.
6. Students will know that the angel told the shepherds the good news about the birth of the Messiah.
7. Students will know that the angel told the shepherds that they would find the baby wrapped in cloth and lying in a manger.
8. Students will know that a manger is a feeding trough for animals.
9. Students will know that the shepherds saw a multitude of the heavenly host praising God.
10. Students will know that the shepherds went to Bethlehem and found Jesus just as the angel had said.
11. Students will know that the shepherds told many other people, who were amazed at the story.
12. Students will know that Jesus is the Lamb of God who died for their sins.

RESOURCES/CREDIT

1. John Calvin. *Commentary on Matthew, Mark, Luke - Volume 1*, trans. and ed. by William Pringle (Grand Rapids: Christian Classics Ethereal Library, 1999), 83.
2. Fred H. Wright, *Manners & Customs of Bible Lands* (Billy Graham Evangelistic Association published by Moody Press.: Chicago, 1994), 158-62.

Abraham Receives a Promise

BACKGROUND PASSAGES

Main Passages

Genesis 12:1-7	Call of Abram
Genesis 15:1-6	God reassures Abram
Genesis 17:1-8	Name changed to Abraham
Genesis 21:1-7	Isaac born to Abraham
Genesis 22:1-18	Abraham tested

Related Passages

Genesis 12-25:11	Full account of Abraham
Genesis 22:1-18	Abraham tested
Romans 4	Abraham justified by faith
James 2:20-23	Abraham's faith perfected
Galatians 3:6-9	All blessed from Abraham
Hebrews 11:8-12	Faith of Abraham and Sarah

Suggested Homiletic Passage

Genesis 12:1-7

MEMORY VERSE

Abram believed the Lord, and He credited it to him as righteousness.

Genesis 15:6

LESSON OBJECTIVE

By faith, Abraham obeyed God when he left his home and moved to a foreign land. From Abraham's descendants came the nation of Israel, and Jesus Christ, the Messiah.

LESSON

The importance of Abraham's spiritual journey is attested to by the 12 chapters of Genesis devoted to his life. In the years following Noah, humanity returned to their sinful ways. God chose Abram for a new beginning. It was through Abram (later known as Abraham) that God would build His chosen people into the nation of Israel. Abraham believed God even though he did not see all of the promises fulfilled. Today, through the redemptive work of Je-sus on the cross, all who believe in Him are part of God's people.

Genesis 12:1-7

At the advanced age of 75, Abram's adventure began. Abram was living in Haran, near the border of modern day Turkey and Syria, when God spoke to Him. He told Abram to leave his relatives and all that he knew and go to a land that God would lead him. There were four parts to the promise.

1. Abram's descendants would be given a land. (v.1)
2. Abram's descendants would be a great nation. (v.2)
3. Abram's name would be greatly revered. (v.2)
4. All the peoples on earth would be blessed because of Abram. (v.3)

Abram would become the father of the nation of Israel. Through the nation of Israel would come the Messiah. Jesus Christ would be (and still is) a blessing to all the world, both to Jews and Gentiles.

Often what is not said in a Bible passage raises more questions than what is actually written. Was Abram overwhelmed by this announcement? Did he deliberate over whether to be obedient? How did his family and friends react? The Bible does not give any of these details. All that is revealed is that Abram was obedient and did exactly as God commanded. Abram packed up his possessions, along with his wife Sarai, nephew Lot, and their servants, and set out for the land of Canaan.

God led Abram to Canaan, where he stopped at Shechem, at the oak of Moreh. Shechem was a cross-roads in northern Palestine and the oak of Moreh may have been a Canaanite worship site.[1] But there was a problem: there were already people living in Canaan. The Lord appeared to Abram and told him that his descendants would be given the land. Abram believed God, built an altar and worshiped Him.

Genesis 15:1-6

Several events passed between the time since Abram had arrived in the land of Canaan and the events of chapter 15. Abram spent time in Egypt and had also engaged in a quarrel that led to the departure of Lot. Later, when Lot was in trouble, Abraham led his men into battle to free Lot and his family. Finally, Abraham had had an audience with a mysterious priest named Melchizedek.

After all these events Abram and Sarai were still childless. While it is impossible to know with certainty Abram's frame of mind, he apparently began to fear that he might never have an heir. God appeared in a vision and told him to not be afraid. God would protect and reward him.

Abram lamented to God that he still did not have any children and therefore, under the custom of the time, his household would pass to one of his servants. God told him that his heir would come from his own body. God led Abram outside and told him to try and count the stars. "So shall your offspring be." (v.5) God said to him. In a time without electricity and pollution to cloud his view, Abraham likely gazed upon thousands of stars. It was a proverbial illustration of the uncountable.

Any fear or doubt Abram might have had was gone. "Abram believed the Lord, and he credited it to him as righteousness." (v.6). Abram still did not have specific answers, but was convinced that God would fulfill His promises in a time and way of His choosing. The word "credited" is probably best understood as meaning "to judge favorably." The word "righteous" simply means "right living." Abram did not earn favor from God for his good works, but as Paul wrote in Romans 4:5, "But to the one who does not work, but believes on Him who declares righteous the ungodly, his faith is credited for righteousness."

Genesis 17:1-8, 15-21

At the age of 99, God appeared again to Abram. God reaffirmed His earlier promises. He said, "I am God Almighty. Live in My presence and be devout. I will establish My covenant between Me and you, and I will multiply you greatly." (v.2). 24 years had passed since Abram first heard this promise, yet from a human perspective it appeared to be no closer to fulfillment. God at that time changed Abram's name to Abraham, meaning "father of a multitude."

Sarai's name also changed. She was thereafter known as Sarah, meaning "princess." From her would come kings of peoples. Not only would elderly Abraham have a child with elderly Sarah, but entire nations and kings would be among their descendants.

Abraham's reaction to this was rather undignified: he fell to the ground in laughter. Perhaps Abraham had given up on the idea that God would fulfill the promise through conventional means with Sarah. Perhaps it was a of joyful anticipation. We do not know Abraham's motivation for laughing.

By this time Abraham had already fathered a child, Ishmael, with Sarah's servant Hagar. Abraham said to God, "If only Ishmael could live in Your presence!" (v.18). Ishmael would not be the child of the covenant. God confirmed to Abraham that the child of promise would be born of Sarah. Abraham was surely encouraged at what God revealed next, the child, to be named Isaac, would be born by that time the next year.

Ishmael, however, would play a major part in God's promise. He would be the father of another great nation as promised by God.

Genesis 18:1-15

Abraham was sitting in the entrance of his tent one day, at the oaks of Mamre, sheltered from the hot part of the day. He saw three men near the tent. He ran(!) before them and bowed. He convinced them to stay, and offered them food, water and rest.

Hospitality was a virtue and a characteristic of the faithful in ancient times. Hospitality towards strangers provided opportunities to minister, and also allowed the host to assess if a stranger might be a threat. Abraham spared no effort in caring for his visitors. He ordered seven quarts of flour be baked and took a calf from the herd to be prepared for the guests. Abraham served the men as they sat under a tree.

The men asked where Sarah was. Abraham said she was in the tent. One of the men then reaffirmed what God had previously told Abraham, "I will certainly come back to you in about a year's time, and your wife Sarah will have a son!" (v.10). One of the men was the

Lord Himself, a pre-incarnate appearance of Jesus.

Sarah heard what the Lord said, but knowing that she was past the age of childbearing, laughed to herself. The Lord asked why Sarah laughed. Out of fear, she denied laughing. The Lord reminded Abraham and Sarah that nothing was impossible for God. In a year's time they would have a child. We know from Hebrews 11:11-12 that Sarah's faith was strengthened until she too joined Abraham on his journey of faith.

Genesis 21:1-7

God's promise to Abraham was fulfilled, "at the appointed time God had told him." (v.2). Sarah conceived and gave birth to a son. Abraham named the child Isaac, meaning "laughter." Sarah remembered what the three visitors had said about the Isaac. She said, "God has made me laugh, and everyone who hears will laugh with me." (v.6). Sarah certainly took delight in how God had blessed her and Abraham in their old age. Abraham was 100 years-old when Isaac was born; Sarah was 90 years-old.

God had kept His promise, and fulfilled it in such a way, that only He could receive the glory for it. He did all these things, not to please Abraham and Sarah, but to further His historic plan of redemption. Christians can know that, like Abraham and Sarah, their greatest joys and blessings will be found when they are in the center of God's will.

Abraham would live 75 more years to the age of 175. After Sarah died at age 127, Abraham took another wife, Keturah, and had other sons. He did not live to see all of God's promises fulfilled, but did live to see his grandsons Esau and Jacob born. He lived out his days as a nomadic stranger in the land of Canaan. It would not be until approximately 600 years later that Joshua would lead a great multitude of Abraham's descendants in to conquer the promised land. It was not until 42 (or more) generations and almost 2000 years later that the greatest fulfillment of God's promise occurred: it was through the line of Abraham that Jesus was born (Matt. 1). Jesus was and is the greatest blessing the nations of the earth could ever desire. In Him is the sure hope of salvation.

Despite his faults, Abraham fully believed that God would do what he had promised. Abraham's faith was cited as a model to be followed by several New Testament authors, including Paul and Peter. The unknown author of Hebrews names both Abraham and Sarah as heroes of faith (Heb. 11). Abraham serves as an example of how God can do the impossible in the life of one who trusts and obeys.

Age Group Considerations

The events surrounding Abraham's journey of faith could easily expand to several lessons. You may wish to add some of the other events of Abraham's life to fill out the lesson. Some of the events contain material that is too strong for young children, including circumcision, the sin of Sodom and Gomorrah, and the testing of Abraham in offering Isaac as a sacrifice. As always, be sensitive to your children's needs as you prepare your lesson.

Suggested Hymns/Songs

1. *There Shall Be Showers of Blessing*, 495, 2008 Baptist Hymnal.
2. *Be Strong in the Lord*, 504, 2008 Baptist Hymnal.
3. *Amazing Grace! How Sweet the Sound*, 104, 2008 Baptist Hymnal.
4. *Trust and Obey*, 500, 2008 Baptist Hymnal.

Student Applications

1. Students will know that the story of Abram/Abraham is found in the Old testament book of Genesis.
2. Students will know that God made a covenant with Abram when he was 75 years-old.
3. Students will know that despite the fact that Abram had no children, God promised that his heirs would outnumber the stars.
4. Students will know that Abram believed and obeyed God.
5. Students will know that Abram obediently took his family and moved to the land of Canaan.

Abraham Receives a Promise

6. Students will know that God changed Abram's name to Abraham, meaning "father of a multitude."

7. Students will know that three Heavenly visitors, including the Lord, visited Abraham to announce that he and Sarah would have a child in one year's time.

8. Students will know that Abraham was 100 years-old, and his wife Sarah was 90 years-old when their son Isaac was born.

11. Students will know that Abraham became the father of the nation of Israel.

12. Students will know that Jesus was a descendent of Abraham, fulfilling the promise that Abraham would be a blessing to all the nations.

RESOURCES/CREDIT

1. E. LeBron Matthews, "*Genesis,*" *Explore the Bible Adult Commentary,* Lifeway (Winter 2007-08 Volume 11, Number 2): 73.

Jonah and the Fish

BACKGROUND PASSAGES

Main Passage
Jonah 1-4   Story of Jonah

Related Passages
Isaiah 10:5-12   Nineveh's ultimate judgment
Matthew 12:38-42   Jesus and the sign of Jonah

Suggested Homiletic Passage
Jonah 4:5-11

MEMORY VERSE

Do not remember the sins of my youth or my acts of rebellion; in keeping with your faithful love, remember me because of Your goodness, Lord.

Psalm 25:7

LESSON OBJECTIVE

God's will was accomplished even though Jonah was disobedient (and faced severe consequences). God accomplishes all that He plans.

LESSON

The story about Jonah and the "big fish" is a children's Sunday School favorite; however, the lessons to be learned from Jonah have powerful and eternal implications for both children and adults. In studying the story of Jonah it is learned that God's will cannot be thwarted. It is both a responsibility and a privilege for believers to allow God to work through them. His Will, will be accomplished, while it is also clear that our life decisions have consequences. Disobedience to God will have consequences not only for the disobedient, but the consequences of sin will impact others.

Jonah 1-4

The author of Jonah does not ease into the story. In just the first two verses, it is revealed that Jonah received a call from God to go to the city of Nineveh, a leading city of the powerful Assyrian empire, and an enemy of Israel. Jonah rejected God's command and, instead, boarded a ship in Joppa, and sailed in the opposite direction from Nineveh. Joppa was a port city on the Mediterranean Sea, not far from Jerusalem. The location of Tarshish is a little mysterious. It may have been a city in Spain or a trading group known for its journeys to faraway lands.[1] Tarshish is mentioned in several Old Testament passages in the context of being the location of the "*ends-of-the-earth.*" While uncertain of which reference applies, what is known is that Jonah desired to flee as far as physically possible from Nineveh.

Jonah's voyage was no pleasure cruise. God raised up a storm that threatened to break the ship apart. The sailors tossed the cargo overboard and fought to keep the ship afloat. Jonah, meanwhile, had managed to fall into a deep sleep. He was awakened by the captain, who pleaded with him to "Call to your god. Maybe this god will consider us, and we won't perish." (1:6).

The superstitions of the crew were confirmed. They were certain the storm was not natural, but had been sent as punishment against one of the people onboard. They decided to draw lots to determine who was the guilty party. The lot fell to Jonah. Jonah confessed that he was attempting to flee God's presence. The sailor's fears grew at this revelation. The condition of the sea continued to deteriorate as they asked Jonah what they should do. He told them that if they tossed him into the sea the storm would cease.

The sailors made one final, futile, attempt to row back to land. The sailors, not wanting to further incite God, called out, "Please Yahweh, don't let us perish because of this man's life, and don't charge us with his blood." (1:14). The sailors then tossed Jonah into the sea and the storm immediately ceased. While the sailors offered a sacrifice of thanksgiving to God, Jonah was swallowed by a great fish.

What kind of sea animal swallowed Jonah? The Hebrew word *dag* includes an array of sea life: shellfish, crustaceans and sea mammals such as seals. While

Jonah and the Fish

dag might also apply to a whale, the most common translation is "*fish*." Zoologically speaking, the only place under the surface to find replenishable oxygen is in the pharynx of an air-breathing mammal; thus a man swallowed by a fish would drown as quickly as in the water.[2]

The supernatural aspect of the storm, the timing of the fish swallowing Jonah, and the providence of surviving three days in the deep all point to a miraculous work of God Almighty. While the nature of the word for "fish" is highly intriguing, we should not be so obsessed by what was going on inside the whale to the point we miss focusing upon what was going on inside Jonah.[3]

While inside the fish, Jonah prayed to God. It would be natural to assume the prayer was a desperate prayer for deliverance, but this was not the case. Counter intuitively, his prayer was one of thanksgiving. Jonah 2:2 states, "I called to the Lord in my distress, and He answered me. I cried out for help in the belly of Sheol; You heard my voice." While it's inconceivable that this time inside the fish was pleasant for Jonah, he clearly recognized God's providence in his position. He had expected to drown, but God had another plan. In 2:9 Jonah prayed, "but as for me, I will sacrifice to You with a voice of thanksgiving. I will fulfill what I have vowed. Salvation is from the Lord."

After three days and three nights, God commanded the fish to spit Jonah out onto dry land. After this (the length of time is not specified), God again told Jonah to go to Nineveh. This time Jonah obeyed. The journey to Nineveh was nearly 500 miles. What went through Jonah's mind as he traveled to the great city? Did he have second thoughts?

Nineveh, near modern day Mosul in Iraq, was located in the ancient fertile crescent and would have been an ideal location for growing the food to support such a large population. Jonah was probably used to towns and villages in Israel that tended to be small and compact. Traversing Nineveh, however, required a three day walk. One theory suggests that the city of Nineveh was so large due to its being part of a larger district comprised of outlying towns and settlements.[4]

As Jonah walked through the city, he proclaimed, "In 40 days Nineveh will be overthrown." (3:4). Was it possible that the citizens of this great city would believe Jonah, a foreigner? But the citizens of Nineveh did believe what Jonah told them. God had prepared their hearts to receive Jonah's message. They dressed in sackcloth and proclaimed a fast. Even the king exchanged his royal clothes for sackcloth and sat on ashes as a sign of repentance. He issued a decree and ordered all his subjects to turn from their evil ways in the hope that God would forgive them and turn from His anger.

One of God's many wonderful attributes is His mercy. God never changes in His essential nature, but when people repent, He shows mercy. When He saw that the Ninevites had repented, He relented and spared the city. Today, God still shows mercy to sinners who are willing to repent.

How did Jonah react to these events? He had feared what might happen to him by going to Nineveh, but now, not only was he safe physically, but he had succeeded. The Ninevites had taken God's message to heart. Jonah's reaction to all this was most unexpected: he became furious (4:1).

The motive behind Jonah's anger is unclear. He professed the knowledge that God is merciful and compassionate. Perhaps he was upset and embarrassed that the prophecy did not come to pass. Perhaps he looked down upon the Ninevites as undeserving foreigners outside of God's covenant grace with Israel. Regardless, despite all that Jonah had learned of God's mercy, he had more to learn.

God asked Jonah a simple question, "Do you have the right to be angry?" (4:4). Only God, as creator and sustainer, has the right to begin and end life. To be upset that the Ninevites were not destroyed, showed that Jonah, perhaps, presumed he knew better than God.

Jonah and the Fish

Jonah left the city, but stopped where he could still observe it. He built a shelter and sat inside to wait and see what would become of Nineveh. In just a day, God caused a plant to grow near the shelter. The plant provided a comforting shade to Jonah and pleased him.

The next morning, God sent a worm to attack the plant. It died and soon withered. As the sun rose, a "scorching wind out of the east" (4:8) blew upon Jonah. As the sun rose higher in the sky, the heat became so intense that Jonah fainted. He complained, "It's better for me to die than to live." (4:8).

"Is it right for you to be angry about the plant?" (4:9) God asked Jonah, paralleling the question He had asked in verse four. Jonah replied, "It is right. I'm angry enough to die." (4:9). God then pointed out to Jonah that he had done nothing to make the plant grow and that it had only lived for little more than a day. People, too, are created, live, grow and die by the will of the Lord, and they are worth far more than a plant, yet Jonah was emotionally anguished as a result of the death of the plant.

God contrasted the value of the plant with the value of the 120,000 people living in Nineveh. They were people created and loved by God. They were of infinite worth in comparison to a lowly plant. God had shown mercy on them, especially as they could not "... distinguish between their right and their left." (4:11). This is proof of God's love as He always takes the initiative in making people aware of their fallen condition.

The book of Jonah ends abruptly at this point. What happened in Jonah's life after this time is unknown. Hopefully, he learned from his experiences. Regardless, perhaps we too can learn from the lesson of Jonah. Nineveh did eventually face judgment (in 612 B.C.) as the Babylonians sacked and conquered the Assyrian city. But that did not happen until after God had used them as a tool of judgment on Israel (Isaiah 10:5-12). What is certain is that humans are not to judge whether someone is beyond God's grace. As long as a person lives, Christians are to obediently and lovingly minister to those to whom God leads.

AGE GROUP CONSIDERATIONS

Some children may develop the idea that if they are not obedient, God will drastically discipline them (like what happened to Jonah). During the lesson, remind them that while there are consequences to all our actions (or in some cases, inaction), God loves them and will never do anything that is not for their own good. God will lovingly teach and correct all believers to be more like Him.

SUGGESTED HYMNS/SONGS

1. *I Surrender All*, 433, 2008 Baptist Hymnal.
2. *Speak, O Lord*, 432, 2008 Baptist Hymnal.
3. *Open the Eyes of My Heart*, 66, 2008 Baptist Hymnal.
4. *Have Thine Own Way, Lord*, 544, 2008 Baptist Hymnal.

STUDENT APPLICATIONS

1. Students will know that the story of Jonah is found in the Old Testament book of Jonah.
2. Students will know that Jonah was a prophet of God.
3. Students will know that God commanded Jonah to go and preach to Nineveh, a powerful and wicked city in the Assyrian empire.
4. Students will know that Jonah disobeyed God. He did not go to Nineveh, but, instead, boarded a ship and fled in the opposite direction.
5. Students will know that Jonah's ship encountered a storm sent by God.
6. Students will know that Jonah told the sailors to toss him overboard in order to end the storm.
7. Students will know that a large fish swallowed Jonah.

Jonah and the Fish

8. Students will know that Jonah survived inside the fish for three days, until it spit him up onto dry land.
9. Students will know that Jonah went to Nineveh and delivered God's message to its inhabitants.
10. Students will know that the people of Nineveh repented and God did not destroy the city.
11. Students will know that Jonah was upset that the city was not destroyed.
12. Students will know that God used a plant as an object lesson to teach Jonah just how much He cares for all people.

RESOURCES/CREDIT

1. *The Family Bible Dictionary*, 1958 ed. Avenir Books, s.v. "*Tarshish*."
2. Michael C. Griffiths, *The International Bible Commentary, Revised Edition*, F.F. Bruce, ed. (Grand Rapids, Michigan: Zondervan Publishing House, 1979), 923.
3. *Ibid.*
4. Alec Motyer. *Eerdmans' Handbook to the Bible* (Grand Rapids: William B. Eerdmans Publishing Company, 1973), 448.

Return of Jesus

BACKGROUND PASSAGES

Main Passage
Revelation 19:11-16   Rider on white horse
Revelation 20:7-10   Satan defeated
Revelation 21:1-8   New heaven and earth
Revelation 22:1-13   Description of heaven

Related Passages
II Peter 3:1-13   The Day of the Lord
Revelation 1-18   Final days
Revelation 22:8-21   The time is near

Suggested Homiletic Passage
Revelation 22:1-7

MEMORY VERSE

Younger version
"Look! I am coming quickly ..."
Revelation 22:12a

Older version
"Look! I am coming quickly, and My reward is with Me to repay each person according to what he has done. I am the Alpha and Omega, the First and the Last, the Beginning and the End."
Revelation 22:12-13

LESSON OBJECTIVE

One day Jesus will literally and bodily return to Earth, in power, as the King of kings, vanquishing evil and rewarding all believers with eternal life. Christians are to anticipate and prepare for His return.

LESSON

People are fascinated with the future. What will happen to the world? What will happen to them personally? Does the future hold prosperity or doom? Even Christians, with the help of the Bible, wonder how the end times will be. Though many books and articles have been written presenting different views and interpretations, one thing is absolutely, positively certain: Jesus will return to Earth. He will reward His followers with eternity in Heaven and pronounce judgment on His enemies and those who choose to reject Him.

Revelation 19:11-16

Many fantastic events will take place in the final days of earth. It is beyond the scope of this lesson to explore all the various theories about how events will unfold. This lesson takes the perspective that Jesus' return marks the beginning of the millennial reign. However, the most important truth of this lesson is that it is absolutely certain that Jesus will return to earth. In many places throughout the Old and New Testaments this day is referred to as "*The Day of the Lord.*"

There is a great contrast between Jesus' first and second coming. In His first coming, Jesus came in obscurity and poverty as a humble baby; at His second coming everyone will see and recognize Him. When Jesus arrived at Jerusalem before the Passover week, he rode humbly on a donkey; at His second coming He will ride an animal more appropriate for royalty: a white horse.

The return of Jesus will be unmistakable, "Look! He is coming with the clouds, and every eye will see Him..." (Rev 1:7). John wrote that when Jesus returns, He will be on a white horse. "Its rider is called Faithful and True, and in righteousness He judges and makes war." (v.11). Wars waged by men are tragic and misguided. Jesus, however, judges perfectly and is the only one who can wage a righteous war.

In a vision, John described Jesus as having eyes of fiery flames that can see all. He wore many crowns, signifying His position as King of kings. He wore a robe stained with blood and was followed by the armies of Heaven. He had a sword with which to judge and an iron scepter with which to rule. On His thigh and robe were written, "KING OF KINGS AND LORD OF LORDS." (v.16). Ancient kings often had an identifying name or mark on their thigh to verify their identity.

Return of Jesus

The return of Jesus will be a day of joy for all believers, but for Satan and those who have rejected Jesus, only judgment will remain.

Revelation 20:7-10

When the Lord returns, Satan will be crushed. At the end of the millennial reign, Satan will be released for a time. He will deceive many into following him. He will lead a great army to surround Jerusalem. Unlike a Hollywood movie, where good and evil struggle to tip the balance of power in their favor, this battle will not be a fair fight as the one and only omnipotent God will send a fire to consume Satan's army.

Satan will meet his judgment as he is cast into Hell, here described as a lake of fire, where he and all who have rebelled against God will be tormented forever.

Revelation 21:1-8

Revelation 21 reveals the ultimate fate of the earth and the universe. I Peter 3:10 states, "... the heavens will pass away with a loud noise, the elements will burn and be dissolved." The universe as we know it will cease to exist, destroyed by fire, and will be replaced by a new universe and earth (v.1).

While this may sound unsettling, Christians can know that they will be with the Lord on that day. They can also take comfort that the earth does not face imminent destruction because of climate change, menacing aliens, a rogue asteroid, or any other number of frightening disaster scenarios.

The focus of this passage, however, does not dwell on the old, but the new. The focus of the passage is on Heaven, described here as the New Jerusalem. John, in his vision, saw it descending to the new earth. Just as God came to humankind in Jesus, He brings Heaven to be among His people

A voice from God's throne announced the great news, "Look! God's dwelling is with men, and He will live with them. They will be His people, and God Himself will be with them and be their God." (v.3). Just as Genesis opened with God creating the universe, Revelation concludes with Him making all things new.

The finality of judgment is once again made clear. The victors are those who are faithful in following God. To reject God is to be separated from Him, and to share in the lake of fire with Satan and his followers.

Revelation 22:1-13

Popular culture has done much to diminish the truth about Heaven. Heaven is typically portrayed as a tranquil, but boring place, where there is nothing better to do than spend all day floating around on clouds while playing a harp. Sometimes Hell is portrayed as the preferable destination! Nothing could be further from the truth. Heaven will be a place of joy and excitement, without a single dull moment.

While the Bible gives many clues about the nature of Heaven, we must remember that much is beyond our comprehension. Revelation 22 gives additional details, after chapter 21, about Heaven.

John described a river of living water flowing from the throne of God. The tree of life grows alongside the river. Unlike the curse brought on by the fruit from the tree of knowledge of good and evil found in the garden of Eden, fruit from this tree will produce health and strength as everyone eats freely from it (v.2). Eating from the tree will not merely be a privilege, but a right, "Blessed are those who wash their robes, so that they may have the right to the tree of life..." (v14).

Believers will have work to do in heaven. They will serve God. Work is gratifying and can give a sense of purpose when things go well. Unfortunately, because of the curse of Adam, work in this world is full of problems and inefficiencies, often leading to frustration. Whatever work believers attempt in Heaven will be satisfying and meaningful.

In the Bible, whenever someone entered the presence of God, they typically immediately found themselves face down in fear. In Heaven believers will see God's face (v.4). There will be no more darkness, no place to hide anything, no fear, as God's light will shine for all eternity. Since there will be no more death or separation, God's people will reign with Him "forever and ever" (v.5).

Jonathan Edwards, in his book *Charity and Its Fruits* wrote this beautiful passage about relationships in Heaven:

"In heaven there shall be no remaining enmity, or distaste, or coldness, or deadness of heart towards God and Christ. ... Those that have a lower station in glory than others, suffer no diminution of their own happiness by seeing others above them in glory. On the contrary, all members of that blessed society rejoice in each other's happiness, for the love of benevolence is perfect in them all."[1]

John was told by an angel that the Lord God wanted his followers to know what must take place so they could be prepared (v.6). Those who heed the words of Revelation will be blessed. Believers are reminded by the words of Jesus, "Look! I am coming quickly, and My reward is with Me to repay each person according to what He has done. I am the Alpha and Omega, the First and Last, the Beginning and End." (vv.12-3).

No one can know what will happen in his/her life tomorrow, let alone in the coming years. No one knows the day or time of Christ's return, but believers can take comfort in knowing, "...the message of Revelation is the final and complete victory of Christ over all his enemies and his resultant reign over all the universe."[2]

Likewise, while our understanding of Heaven is incomplete, all believers can look forward in anticipation knowing, "What no eye has seen, and no ear has heard, and what has never come into a man's heart, is what God has prepared for those who love Him." (I Cor. 2:9). Heaven is a wonderful and awesome place. Christians need to joyfully anticipate and prepare for the Lord's return.

AGE GROUP CONSIDERATIONS

Talking about end-time events may be unsettling to some children. To say that it challenges their everyday routines and expectations of the future is an understatement! Be sensitive to children who may express anxiety over the thought of being separated from family, pets, toys or home to "move" to Heaven. Remind them that God is loving though true, and always knows what is best for us.

It may help to explain to children that waiting for Jesus to return is much like waiting by the front window in anticipation of the special arrival of a beloved relative who has not been seen in a long time. How exciting it is when they pull into the driveway and can be seen! For a believer, the excitement of Jesus' return and their subsequent time in Heaven will be greater that any joy previously experienced.

While the focus of this lesson is on the physical return of Jesus and the Christian's reward of Heaven, please do not ignore the aspect of judgment that is an integral part of Christ's purpose in returning. Christ's return will not be a pleasant experience for those who have rejected Him. Judgment and Hell are real. Hell is a place of complete separation from God, devoid of hope and love. Children need to know the truth. Teach that one's final destination is based upon one's choice, not God's forcing. Do not try to scare or press for a decision, but gently teach the students the biblical truth and allow the Holy Spirit take it from there.

SUGGESTED HYMNS/SONGS

1. *Soon and Very Soon*, 599, 2008 Baptist Hymnal.
2. *When the Roll is Called Up Yonder*, 600, 2008 Baptist Hymnal.
3. *I'll Fly Away*, 601, 2008 Baptist Hymnal.
4. *When We All Get to Heaven*, 603, 2008 Baptist Hymnal.
5. *The King is Coming*, 291, 2008 Baptist Hymnal.
6. *Worthy of Worship*, 3, 2008 Baptist Hymnal.

STUDENT APPLICATIONS

1. Students will know that the return of Jesus is found in the New Testament book of Revelation.
2. Students will know that Jesus will return to earth in bodily form one day as King of kings and Lord of lords.

Return of Jesus

3. Students will know that no one knows when Jesus will return.
4. Students will know that Jesus' return will be sudden and dramatic. Everyone on earth will see Him.
5. Students will know that God will judge all people.
6. Students will know that at the judgment Satan, all the demons, and those who choose to reject Jesus will be eternally separated from God in Hell.
7. Students will know that those who follow and love God will receive their reward in Heaven at the judgment.
8. Students will know that God will create a new heaven and a new earth to replace the old.
9. Students will know that Heaven will be an amazingly beautiful place.
10. Students will know that believers will spend eternity in the presence of God.
11. Students will know that there will be no pain, suffering, loss, fear or lack of anything in Heaven.
12. Students will know that there will be no ugliness between people in Heaven; everyone will rejoice in each other's happiness.
13. Students will know that God wants all believers to anticipate and prepare for His return.

RESOURCES/CREDIT

1. Jonathan Edwards, *Charity and its Fruits* (Edinburgh: The Banner of Truth Trust, reprinted 2000), 335.
2. Herschel H. Hobbs, *Fundamentals of Our Faith* (Nashville: Broadman & Holman Publishers, 1960), 160.

Easter - Passover & Lord's Supper

BACKGROUND PASSAGES

Main Passage
Luke 22:7-20	Lord's Supper
I Cor 11:23 -31	Instructions for Lord's Supper

Related Passages
Exodus 12:1-28	Background of the Passover
Matt 26:17-30	Lord's Supper
Mark 14: 12 - 26	Lord's Supper
Rev 19:7-9	Lord's Supper in Heaven

Suggested Homiletic Passage
Luke 22:14-20

MEMORY VERSE

For as often as you eat this bread and drink the cup, you proclaim the Lord's death until He comes.

I Cor 11:26

LESSON OBJECTIVE

In observing the Lord's Supper, believers remember Jesus' love and the need to be in right standing with God and man. The Lord's Supper also reminds us that one day all believers will participate in the marriage feast of the Lamb in Heaven.

LESSON

During the Easter season, Christians remember the crucifixion, burial, and glorious resurrection of Jesus. Many events took place during that world-changing week. This lesson will focus on how all Christians today should remember the Lord's resurrection through observance of the *Lord's Supper* (Communion). The Lord gave His life on the cross for all. As followers of Christ, we must examine our lives and be worthy of Him. In observing the Lord's Supper, we remember Jesus' love for us and our need to be in right standing with God and man. We are also to be encouraged, knowing that one day all believers will participate in the marriage feast of the Lamb in Heaven.

The sacrificial nature of the Passover, in the Old Testament, foreshadowed the work of redemption that Jesus did as the spotless, perfect, sacrificial Lamb of God. The Lord's Supper is the New Testament picture of the Lord giving mankind redemption from death.

During the Passover, it was not the blood of the lamb which had power to redeem, but rather the mighty and merciful God. So, too, it is not in the elements of the Lord's Supper, baptism, or acts of personal sacrifice that one finds forgiveness of sin. It is only by accepting the sacrifice of the spotless lamb (*i.e.,* Christ) can one be spared the judgment of God (eternal death) through forgiveness of sin.

During the original Passover, all those who chose to place the blood of the lamb on their doorpost, in a simple act of obedience, were provided protection from the very judgment of God. By following God's plan, death passed over them; hence the term *Passover*.

Today the same is true. Anyone who will obey the Lord and give his/her life to Jesus, will be freed from the judgment of God and have the penalty of sin (eternal death) removed forever.

Once saved, we are to be baptized and, in our church life, observe of the Lord's Supper. Both of these ordinances remind us of His victory over death and our need to walk daily with Him.

Luke 22:7-20

In the New Testament one can see how plans were made for the observance of the Passover. The disciples asked where Jesus wanted to eat the Passover supper, and He replied by telling them (specifically Peter and John), "Listen, when you've entered the city, a man carrying a water jug will meet you. Follow him into the house he enters." (v.10-11).

The disciples went and found the man. After they had entered the house they asked the man where a guest room could be found in which to observe the Passover. The man led them to a large, furnished upper room. Peter and John set about making preparations. The Passover had been observed for over a millennium. Little did they realize that this time, it would be much different.

During the Passover meal, Jesus and the disciples were likely to be reclining at the table, as this was the custom of the day. The famous painting by Leonardo da Vinci is almost certainly not an accurate representation of the event. The disciples were probably not all clustered to one side of the table but would have been around three of its sides. This arrangement, common in Roman times, was called a *triclinium*. The U-shaped table allowed one side to remain open for servant access.

As Jesus participated in the normal Passover ritual, He broke the bread (known as matzah or unleavened bread) and took the cup. He then did something unusual; He said the bread was His "body" and that the cup was His "blood." Jesus was initiating a new covenant. "This cup is the new covenant established by My blood; it is shed for you." (v.20). It is worth noting that this cup, within the Passover ceremony, is called "the cup of blessing." Jesus used this cup to show that the new covenant that would be established through the shedding of His blood on Golgotha (the Place of the Skull) which would provide for the forgiveness of sins and be a blessing of mercy to all who would believe.

Jesus had changed (and fulfilled through His sacrificial death) an ancient feast, which praised God for His mercy and provision, into an ordinance of remembrance for all He was about to do. Each time we observe the Lord's Supper, we remember what he did. We remember the past and look forward to the great feast in heaven (Rev19:7-9) and many other blessings as promised of God through Jesus (John 14:1-4).

Other events transpired that night that are covered in other Easter rotation lessons, including the revelation of a traitor, Judas, and the prediction of Peter's denial. As the dinner drew to a close, those gathered sang a hymn and departed for the Mount of Olives (Matt.26:30). The hymn was a regular part the Passover observance and

was probably from the book of Psalms. Jesus and the disciples sang praises to and of the Lord, just as believers do today. Children can learn to sing to God and to praise Him. This blesses Him, the worshiper, and others. It also reminds of all the many things He has done out of His love (including sending Jesus).

In Corinthians 11:23-31, Paul reminds us of all that Jesus said during His final Passover and, like the Corinthians, believers are reminded (cautioned) that partaking of the Lord's Supper in an unworthy manner is a sin. The Lord's Supper is to be observed in a serious and solemn manner but also as a time of encouragement and hope. As individual believers, we are to remember how Jesus gave His life. We are to examine our lives and walk worthy of His death, resurrection, and calling.

Although an important ordinance, the Lord's Supper is still only a picture of Jesus' victory over sin and death. The supper, in and of itself, does not make one right with God; but, rather, is a special reminder of His gift of eternal life as obtained through the cross. When we celebrate the Lord's Supper, we celebrate His sacrifice, resurrection, and victory.

AGE GROUP CONSIDERATIONS

Remind the children that the bread and wine (grape juice) of the Lord's Supper are symbolic. Children from some church backgrounds have been taught that the communion elements actually turn into the flesh of Jesus. This is not Biblical. Jesus died once (Rom 6:10) and is not being continually sacrificed for our sins. Do not embarrass the children, simply explain why we believe the elements to be symbolic.

Older children can be introduced to the concept of ordinances and authoritative commands from Christ Himself. You may wish to refer to your church or denomination Statement of Faith. *The Baptist Faith & Message (2000)* states "The Lord's Supper is a symbolic act of obedience whereby members of the church, through partaking of the bread and the fruit of the vine, memorialize the death of the Redeemer and anticipate His second coming."[1]

ROTATION SUNDAY SCHOOL AND EASTER

Easter encompasses much more than is presented in this lesson. Each of the six Easter rotations in this book focus on a different aspect of the Easter story. For a fuller context in preparing your lesson, gospel accounts of the "Easter story" are found in the following places:

Matt 26:47 through Matt 28:10
Mark 14:43 through Mark 16:13
Luke 22:39 through Luke 24:12
John 18 :1 through John 20:18

Many believe Mark's version is the most concise.

Depending on the age of your group, you might want to relate your own short version of Jesus' arrest, crucifixion, burial, and resurrection in addition to the account of the Lord's Supper.

SUGGESTED HYMNS/SONGS

1. *Because He Lives*, 449, 2008 Baptist Hymnal.
2. *The Lord's Prayer*, 431, 2008 Baptist Hymnal.
3. *The Communion Hymn,* 404, 2008 Baptist Hymnal.
4. *He Is Lord*, 277, 2008 Baptist Hymnal.

STUDENT APPLICATIONS

1. Students will know that the first Lord's Supper is found in the New Testament book of Luke.
2. Students will know that the Lord's Supper reminds of Christ's love and sacrifice on the cross (providing eternal life).
3. Students will know that The Lord's Supper is sometimes referred to as communion.
4. Students will know the elements of the Lord's Supper are symbolic.
5. Students will know the bread represents Christ's body and the cup represents Christ's blood.
6. Students will know that the Lord's Supper is observed only after receiving Christ as our Savior and after having examined our lives.
7. Students will know that one day in Heaven, there will be another supper, the marriage feast of the Lamb, and many other wonderful things with Jesus.
8. Students will know that the Lord's Supper finds its roots in the Old Testament observance of the Passover.
9. Students will know that Jesus was the perfect, spotless Lamb of God and fulfilled the Passover through His death and resurrection.

RESOURCES/CREDIT

1. *The Baptist Faith and Message*, 2000. The Southern Baptist Convention.

Jesus Calls Disciples

BACKGROUND PASSAGES

Main Passage
Matthew 4:18-22   The calling of the disciples

Related Passages
Luke 5:1-11	Luke's version of the calling
Mark 2:13-14	The call of Matthew
John 1:35-51	Andrew, Peter, Phillip & Nathanael
Mark 3:13-19	The list of 12 Disciples
I Cor. 1: 26-31	Consider your calling
Ps. 119:11	Know His word
I Pet. 3:14-17	A cost to discipleship
Rev. 3: 20	Jesus still calls, "Follow me."
Matt. 28:19-20	The Great Commission

Suggested Homiletic Passage
Matthew 4:18-22

MEMORY VERSE

And He said unto them, Follow Me, and I will make you fishers of men.

Matthew 4:19 (KJV)

LESSON OBJECTIVE

Jesus asked people to follow Him. The disciples followed, leaving much behind. Jesus taught them the word and how to love. The disciples obeyed and many people heard the gospel and were saved.

LESSON

The call of the disciples can be mirrored in every believer's life. Jesus still asks people to follow Him. In this lesson our children will study the call of the disciples and learn how they can be prepared to follow Jesus.

Some scholars speculate that several of the disciples knew Jesus (and each other) as they grew up in Galilee, in northern Israel. In fact, we know that Simon Peter and Andrew had met Jesus previously (John 1:35-41) and that Andrew had already professed Jesus as the Messiah.[1] The disciples were living very normal and mundane lives before Jesus called them. But God knew what was to come and was preparing the disciples. We must understand that what happens in our lives may also be what is needed to make future decisions.

Matthew 4:18-22

In Matt 4:18-22, Peter and Andrew were hard at work, casting their nets into the water. It was an ordinary day of fishing, until Jesus arrived. That day, Jesus called and asked them to "Follow Me, and I will make you fishers of men." (v.19, KJV). They heard and understood that "following" meant leaving everything to follow Jesus. It meant listening to and learning of His teachings. It meant to work, walk, talk, and live (or die) as He did. Jesus' call would change their lives... but only if they listened, heard (understood), and chose to follow.

Peter and Andrew had a choice to make ... and it was a big one. Following Jesus they would not only change their lives, but the lives of all believers who would come after them. Jesus would use these men to start the New Testament church. What they would do would impact all those who teach, help, pray for, and love in Jesus' name.

Their choice would mean giving up the 'right' to live the way they wanted to choose. They would now need to live a life that pleased Jesus, instead of their own desires. Their choice would have to be sacrificial, kind and loving. Their choice also had to be immediate. In Matthew 4:20, we see immediate obedience when we see Peter and Andrew drop what they were doing to follow Christ. They were ready to follow Him without delay.

We must be prepared to trust Jesus no matter what is happening in the world around us. We must be ready to pray even when we are tired. We must be ready to forgive, even when we are still hurting. We must abide by rules (respect all our authorities) even when we don't feel like obeying. We must be willing to trust Jesus and follow His teachings, even while we are still learning and may not have a complete understanding. Obedience will save us much pain and sorrow. We must remember God loves us and will make a way for us (I Cor 10:13).

The choice to follow Jesus was also given to others. In verses 21-22, James and John, brothers, were in a boat mending fishing nets with their father, Zebedee. When Jesus called, they too, left all and immediately followed Him. James, according to tradition, was beheaded by Herod in 44 A.D. John would live to an old age and write five New Testament books: John, I John, II John, II John, and Revelation.

Jesus called twelve to be his special followers. The disciples were men who would learn His word and be willing to give their lives teaching others. Even more, they were men who would live as Christ, that others may hear His call and also follow (Matt 28:19-20). Jesus still calls today. He expects believers to follow Him immediately and to learn His word, so that they can wisely choose what to say, how to act, and how to love as Jesus. All of this, and more, may be learned from the Bible in Sunday School and church, in prayer, and through the guidance of the Holy Spirit as believers commit to follow Jesus and be His disciples.

Children should be given an opportunity to commit to Jesus so that they may also be His disciples.

AGE GROUP CONSIDERATIONS

In teaching younger children, remember to tell them that a disciple is a person who is a learner, helper, and follower of Jesus.

In teaching older children, you may wish to study the related passages and emphasize how we each must be prepared for life circumstances (I Cor 7:20-24) and trials (I Pet 3:14-17). Emphasize that being a disciple is a lifelong walk with Christ (Ps 119:11). They can be assured that His never-ending presence will provide direction not only for eternal hope, but for life and for daily strength.

You may also wish to include the Great Commission (Matt 28:19-20) in your lesson planning. Christ was preparing the disciples to carry on the ministry and expects all believers today to do the same as He has gifted them.

Children need to understand that they too can be followers of Christ. Therefore, they need to answer Him (receive Christ and choose to obey daily), follow Him (that is, live/love as Christ), and be ready (that is, know /follow the Word). This lesson provides a wonderful opportunity for children to be given an opportunity to express that Christ is calling them to be His follower. Do not press for a decision as the Holy Spirit does His work. Do pray for discernment as children may express a desire to make a decision solely to please an adult or seek the approval of the group.

SUGGESTED HYMNS/SONGS

1. *Come, Now Is the Time to Worship*, 30, 2008 Baptist Hymnal.
2. *Since Jesus Came into My Heart,* 624, 2008 Baptist Hymnal.
3. *Jesus Loves the Little Children*, 651, 2008 Baptist Hymnal.
4. *We've a Story to Tell*, 356, 2008 Baptist Hymnal.

STUDENT APPLICATIONS

1. Students will know that accounts about the calling of the disciples are found in all four of the New Testament gospels.
2. Students will know that the disciples were willing to give up everything in order to follow Jesus.
3. Students will know that four of the disciples were fishermen: Andrew, Peter, James and John.
4. Students will know that Jesus wants them to be His disciples and still calls people today.
5. Students will know that disciples need training.
6. Students will know that Sunday school and other church times are important times of learning and training for all believers.

Jesus Calls Disciples

7. Students will know that they need to learn, and grow in God's Word, to be ready for all that may happen in their lives.
8. Students will know that they need to learn how to choose what they say, how they say it, how they behave, what they do, as well as, what they choose not to do in a way that pleases God.
9. Students will know that there are costs in being a disciple, but God will be faithful to His promises, and offers many blessings and rewards to His followers in this life and beyond.

10. Students will know that being obedient to authorities (parents, guardians, teachers, etc.) is also obedience to Christ.
11. Students will know that following God is a lifelong commitment.

RESOURCES/CREDIT

1. Steven Short, *The International Bible Commentary, Revised Edition*, F.F. Bruce, ed. (Grand Rapids, Michigan: Zondervan Publishing House, 1979), 1158.

Joseph Part 1 - Joseph's Colorful Coat

BACKGROUND PASSAGES

Main Passage
Genesis 37   Coat of Many Colors

Related Passages
Luke 12:15-34	Life is not in possessions
Rom. 8:28	God has a plan for your life
Psalms 37:7-8	Wait on the Lord, don't fret
Jeremiah 19:11	God plans are not for harm

Suggested Homiletic Passage
Genesis 37:3-8

MEMORY VERSE

Younger Verse
We know that all things work together for the good of those who love God.

Romans 8:28a

Older Verse
We know that all things work together for the good of those who love God: those who are called according to his purpose.

Romans 8:28

LESSON OBJECTIVE

The lives of Joseph and his brothers show that God loves all of His children and makes sure they have what they need, when they need it. Believers should not be jealous of what God gives to others and be thankful for what they have received.

LESSON

The origin of the twelve tribes of Israel is found in Genesis 35:23-26. Chapter 37 begins the story of Joseph, one of the sons of Israel (Jacob). This lesson is the first of a three-part study on the life of Joseph. The first part warns against envy, the second will show how God works providentially through Joseph and saved many (including Israel), and the third will show forgiveness and fulfillment of God's promises in Joseph's reunion with his family.

Genesis 37

The story of Joseph's colorful coat is often taught as a story of a father's love. Another approach explores the darker story of envy, hate, and God's provision in the midst of seemingly unwarranted betrayal. Joseph's story begins, in Genesis 37:2, which shows him as a young man tending the flocks with his older brothers: Dan, Naphtali, Gad, and Asher. They were, by birth, the children of slaves. After tending the flocks, Joseph brought an evil report, about his brothers, to Israel. Did Joseph often report back to his father? Did other brothers report on other days? Why was this report an evil one? No one knows. Some believe that this verse shows either that these four brothers were already of a "bad sort" or that in this very act of reporting, Joseph was marked a "betrayer."

Joseph was one of two sons born through Israel's wife Rachel. Israel loved Rachel more than his other wife Leah, and that favoritism extended to Rachel's children. Verse 3 clearly states that Joseph was Israel's favorite child and that Israel made him a brightly colored coat as a special gift. In Joseph's day, a coat was an everyday garment, covering undergarments, keeping one warm, carrying one's things during a trip, and such; yet, this coat was different. Joseph's coat had many colors, which was something that was usually reserved for royalty. 2 Samuel 13:18 describes a richly ornamented coat as having royal character. This symbol of special privilege became a constant reminder of Israel's favoritism towards Joseph. Whether love, favoritism or both, it was obvious to Joseph's brothers that he held a special place in the family and they "hated him and could not bring themselves to speak peaceably to him." (v.4).

Was Joseph sad, lonely, angry, or hurt by the actions of his brothers? Why did his brothers not kid him about "getting too big for his britches?" Did they hate him, because they knew that he was special in some way? Have you ever been hated, mistreated, or ignored? Has someone ever given you special treatment?

Joseph Part 1 - Joseph's Colorful Coat

In the midst of all this, Joseph had a dream. In his dream, he and his brothers were in a field binding sheaves of grain. The brother's sheaves gathered around Joseph's and bowed to it. Joseph told his brothers all about his dream, only to find that it led them to hate him all the more. Why? It seems that the brothers believed the dream meant Joseph thought he would one day rule over them. Since Joseph was Israel's eleventh son and lived in a culture that glorified elder children (usually at the expense of younger), this was truly a presumptive "claim."

Joseph had another dream. In this dream the sun, moon and eleven stars were bowing down to him. This time, he described the dream to both his brothers and his father. Joseph's family interpreted (correctly!) the dream to mean that Joseph would rule over, not only his brothers, but his parents as well. Israel rebuked Joseph. Notice, however, that Israel's rebuke was not for Joseph to mind his position nor to apologize, but was simply: "What kind of dream is this you had?" (v.10). Also notice, that Israel "kept the matter in mind." Perhaps Israel pondered the working of God much as Mary did many, many years later (Luke 2:19). Most likely it simply means that Israel took note that the Lord might be working through Joseph.

In verse 12 Israel sent Joseph to check on his brothers, who were tending the flocks near Shechem. Knowing of the family squabbles, why did Israel send Joseph? Notice that Joseph simply said, "I'm ready" (*i.e.,* "Here am I" or "I will go").

Joseph traveled to Shechem in the valley of Hebron only to discover that his brothers had moved on (perhaps to Dothan). Being so directed by a kind man, Joseph goes to Dothan, and as the brothers see him still in the distance, they plotted to kill him. The Bible doesn't record which brothers instigated or led the plotting, it simply states "they" in verse 19. However, in verse 21 it is revealed that Reuben wanted no part of their plot and attempted to save Joseph. He suggested to the other brothers that they place him in dry cistern. Reuben's intention was to come back later and save Joseph. Was Reuben really trying to be the good guy? His motive is unclear. We know that Reuben was not always wise, nor righteous (Gen. 35:22), but here he did prevent Joseph from being killed.

After stripping Joseph of his robe and placing him in the cistern, the brothers sat down to eat (v.25); however, note that Reuben had gone away a second time and was not present when a caravan of Ishmaelites from Gilead, bound for Egypt, arrived on the scene. Seeing the caravan gave Judah an idea. He suggested selling Joseph rather than killing him, saying: "... he is our brother, our own flesh." (v.27) The brothers agreed. Joseph was sold, for twenty pieces of silver, and taken, as a slave, to Egypt.

What did Joseph think, feel, or pray about while he was in the cistern? Did he hear his brothers discussing his fate? Did he hope in the Lord? Was he afraid? Did he yell or beg? Did he wait on the Lord? Was he quiet or did he sing? Hated and envied by his brothers, betrayed, and sold into slavery, Joseph joined the caravan, not knowing what would happen next. His nomadic life, with a large family clan and a loving father, was over. What did God have in mind for him?

The brothers, believing to have succeeded and profited by their heinous sin, now schemed to cover their actions and deceive their father. They did not tell Israel about Joseph, they simply dipped Joseph's coat in a young goat's blood, returned it to Israel (v.32), and said, "We found this. Examine it. Is it your son's robe or not?" It is interesting how they did not even use Joseph's name. Why the phrase "your son's robe?" Israel bought the deception and concluded that a wild animal had killed Joseph. He tore his clothes, put on sackcloth, and mourned for many days.

As a result of the brother's hatred and envy, Israel sank into a deep mourning that found no consolation. The brothers had to live with the knowledge of what they had done. The broken spirit of their father served as a daily reminder.

Though the brothers had intended evil, God was already at work to providentially provide for His chosen people. God had a plan for all of Israel's family. God had a plan for Joseph to rise in power. Verse

Joseph Part 1 - Joseph's Colorful Coat

36 is the first indication of where God was leading. Joseph was purchased, taken into the household of Potiphar (Pharaoh's captain of the guard), and from this point on, Joseph's future is intertwined with that of the Pharaoh. God, through Joseph, was preparing to save His people.

When God's path for our children leads them into seemingly strange places, they can trust that He is still at work and that He is still in control? They can truly believe that God makes no mistakes and that He has His best for all in mind.

Are you willing to serve, sacrifice, and wait while God is at work? Do you realize that, sometimes, God plans to bless thousands upon thousands through a work in YOUR life? Think about it.

The next rotation will pick up where this lesson leaves off. The children will learn how God worked providentially through Joseph to save many (including Israel) and will cover the events of Joseph's life in Egypt.

AGE GROUP CONSIDERATIONS

1. Focus on the coat portion of the story for younger children. Joseph's father loved him, showed his affection, and provided for him.
2. Discuss how God loves us, shows us His affection, and daily provides for all our needs.
3. Discuss that God knows everything, isn't ever scared, and does what is best - according to His plan.
4. Discuss that God's timing is not the same as ours and that, since God is forever, He may take many, many, MANY (!!!) years to finish His plan (Habakkuk 2:3, Lamentations 3:25, Isaiah 55:8-9, others). We must trust He loves us while we wait.

SUGGESTED HYMNS AND SONGS

1. *Stand Up, Stand Up for Jesus*, 665, 2008 Baptist Hymnal.
2. *The Solid Rock*, 511, 2008 Baptist Hymnal.
3. *He Leadeth Me! O Blessed Thought*, 81, 2008 Baptist Hymnal.
4. *Near to the Heart of God*, 458, 2008 Baptist Hymnal.

STUDENT APPLICATIONS

1. Students will know that the story of Joseph's colorful coat is found in the Old Testament book of Genesis.
2. Students will know that God changed Jacob's name to Israel and that his 12 sons would become the tribes of Israel.
3. Students will know that Joseph was one of twelve sons.
4. Students will know that Israel favored Joseph over his other sons.
5. Students will know that Israel gave a precious, colorful coat to his son Joseph.
6. Students will know that Joseph had two dreams that foretold that all of his family would bow to him.
7. Students will know that Joseph's brothers were jealous of the preferential treatment he received from their father and angered by his dreams.
8. Students will know that the brothers imprisoned Joseph in a dry well.
9. Students will know that Joseph's brothers sold him to slave traders who took him to Egypt.
10. Students will learn to not be jealous of someone who has better talents, abilities, or possessions than themselves.
11. Students will know that they should be thankful with what God has blessed and trust that they have what they need, work fairly, ask God, and seek His will diligently.
12. Students will know that God has a plan for them to bless and not to harm them, regardless of how circumstances may appear.
13. Students will know that hatred and envy are sins and have serious consequences.

Joseph Part 2 - Joseph in Egypt

BACKGROUND PASSAGES

Main Passages
Gen. 39:1-19	Joseph accused
Gen. 39:20 - Gen. 40	Joseph in prison
Gen. 41	Joseph exalted

Related Passages
Romans 8:28	All things work for good
1 Cor. 15:58	Our labor is not in vain

Suggeste Homiletic Passage
Gen. 41:28-36

MEMORY VERSE:

Younger version
"...the Lord was with (Joseph) and made everything he did successful."

Genesis 39:23b

Older version
The warden did not bother with anything under Joseph's authority, because the Lord was with him, and the Lord made everything that he did successful.

Genesis 39:23

LESSON OBJECTIVE

Joseph was faithful to God even when all appeared horribly wrong. God honored and blessed Joseph for his faithfulness. God will also honor and bless believers who are faithful to Him.

LESSON

This is the second part of a three-part study on the life of Joseph. Despite many hardships, Joseph was faithful to trust God. As a result, God used Joseph in an amazing and unusual way. This lesson picks up at the point after Joseph's brothers sold him into slavery.

Gen. 39:1-19

After his arrival in Egypt as a slave, Joseph was sold to a high ranking Egyptian official named Po-tiphar. The Bible states, "The Lord was with Joseph and he became a successful man, serving in the household of his Egyptian master." (v.2). Even as a lowly slave Joseph prospered. Potiphar, captain of Pharaoh's guard, saw that the Lord was with Joseph. Joseph was put in charge of Potiphar's household, as well as, everything Potiphar owned. Amazingly, from that moment, God blessed all that Potiphar had (in his home and in his fields). God so blessed, through Joseph, that Potiphar's only concerns were about what he ate (v.6).

When you are in a seemingly bad circumstance, do you strive to do your best as unto the Lord? Do you let others see God taking care of you? Do you really believe that nothing will come your way, except that it is allowed by God?

Sadly, Potiphar's wife was not content with her abundance, but lusted after Joseph. Joseph was resolute and told her that her husband had "withheld nothing from me except you, because you are his wife. So how could I do such a great evil and sin against God?" (v.9). Notice that Joseph did not merely say "no," but informed her that she was tempting him to sin against God. Even from the position of slavery, Joseph recognized who was his true Lord.

In the midst of trying times, when someone has wronged you or lied about you, do you see how God can still be at work? Can you be honest, when no one else is? Is it your fault when others choose to do wrong? Who is responsible for how others respond, when you are doing what you know God requires?

Potiphar's wife was persistent and would not listen to Joseph. She tempted him day after day. He continued to refuse and would have nothing to do with her (v.10).

Temptation is difficult to resist because it appeals to human nature. The best way to deal with temptation is to avoid situations or things that one knows will be tempting. When faced with temptation the best thing to do is ... run (I Cor. 10:13, I Cor. 6:18, II Tim. 2:22). God has promised that He will always make a way out for a believer. Sometimes, like it appeared in Joseph's situation, believers may feel as if they are trapped. All things happen for a reason within the hands of God. Even in Joseph's circumstances God was at work.

One day Joseph went into the house to attend to his duties. No other servants were present, but Potiphar's wife was at home. Finding herself alone with Joseph, she grabbed him by his cloak and said, "Sleep with me!" (v.12). Joseph responded with the appropriate action, by refusing and fleeing the house. In his haste, he left his cloak behind in her grasp. Potiphar's wife then called out to her servants. After they arrived, she lied to them saying that Joseph had made advances, and presented his cloak as evidence.

She kept Joseph's cloak until Potiphar came home and then lied to him also, saying: "These are the things your slave did to me." (v.19). Furious, Potiphar threw Joseph in the prison of the king.

Gen. 39:20 - Gen. 40

What had Joseph thought, felt, or prayed while he was being accused? Betrayed once more, and cast away, Joseph joined the prisoners, not knowing what would happen next. His relatively comfortable life in Potiphar's household was over. What did God have next in store for him?

Once again God prospered Joseph. Gen 39:21-23 shows that Joseph was granted favor by the warden and put in a place of authority within the prison. God blessed all that he did.

At this point please note that:

- Joseph was born the eleventh child, in a world where that meant he was not going to be noticed.
- Joseph tended to the flocks, in a world where that meant he wasn't going to be important.
- Joseph was a slave, in a world where that meant he wasn't anything more than a piece of property.
- Joseph was now a prisoner, in a world where that meant that you were forgotten, even if you survived.

God had other plans, for over and over, Joseph was placed in a position of trust and responsibility. He was blessed and made a leader. God gave him suc-

cess, and the prison warden came to completely trust Joseph. God blessed and Joseph served where he was and whomever God brought his way.

Sometime later, two of Pharaoh's servants were thrown into prison and placed under Joseph's care. The servants were the Pharaoh's chief butler (called a cup bearer) and the chief baker. Both were positions of high standing and trust. The cup bearer's job was to taste Pharaoh's food and make sure it was safe to be eaten. The baker's job was to prepare Pharaoh's food. Both servants had somehow offended the Pharaoh and were now, like Joseph, in prison. They had been imprisoned for quite awhile, when they each dreamed a dream - the very same night. The dreams disturbed them enough that it affected their demeanor and caused Joseph to question them.

The men informed Joseph that they had had dreams and lamented that there was no interpreter. Joseph then asked, "Don't interpretations belong to God?" (Gen 40:8) rightly ascribing the ability of interpretation to God. Joseph then asked them to tell him their dreams. God blessed and revealed the meanings to Joseph. This glorified God.

The cup bearer was told that he would be restored to his former place in three days, while the baker was told that he would be executed, also in three days. As morbid as it may sound to have knowledge that one's demise is imminent, the baker did have three days warning. Believer's may never have that foreknowledge and should never presume to have even one more heartbeat.

What did each of the men think? How did each man do during the three days? How did Joseph feel having to tell the baker that he was going to die soon, and in a bad way? Believers must, in love, always share God's truths with others. Believers must not compromise, simply because the truth is not comfortable.

Joseph asked the cup bearer to show him kindness and remember him when all went as God had promised. Joseph asked that when the cup bearer was before the Pharaoh, would he please tell Pharaoh about him and ask Pharaoh to get him "... out of this

Joseph Part 2 - Joseph in Egypt

prison. For I was kidnapped from the land of the Hebrews, and even here I have done nothing that they should put me in a dungeon" (40:14-15). Joseph had told his story to someone whom God had revealed would be at Pharaoh's side and could intercede for him. Are you prepared to talk, move, or act as God makes a way for you? If you had been Joseph, would you have thought to ask the cup bearer to approach the Pharaoh on your behalf?

The interpretations came true just as God had revealed to Joseph (40: 21-22). After resuming his position in the court of Pharaoh, the cup bearer forgot about Joseph. Two years passed. Joseph had been in Egypt for 13 years; 13 long years away from his family. Did Joseph find a peace in the midst of all this, while in prison? Would you have? When overlooked, do you wait on God? Joseph did.

Genesis 41

At the beginning of chapter 41, Pharaoh had a dream. Seven sleek and fat cows came out of the river Nile and were devoured by seven ugly and gaunt ones. Pharaoh awoke but went back to sleep only to have a second dream. This time seven healthy heads of grain were growing on a single stalk and seven thin heads of grain, scorched by the east wind, sprouted up and swallowed the healthy ones. Pharaoh woke up once again.

The dreams troubled Pharaoh, so he called together all the magicians and wise men of Egypt. None of them could interpret his dreams. It was, at this point, that the chief cup bearer remembered his promise to Joseph and told Pharaoh everything.

Pharaoh sent for Joseph. He was quickly brought from the prison. Joseph was cleaned and clothed for his audience with Pharaoh. Upon entering Pharaoh's presence, Pharaoh said that he had heard Joseph could interpret dreams. Joseph, once again gave God the glory, and admitted that he could not, but that God would.

After hearing the Pharaoh's dreams, Joseph confirmed what Pharaoh probably already suspected. God revealed that the dreams meant one and the same thing. Egypt would see seven years of great abundance, followed by seven years of great famine. God had given Pharaoh his dream in two forms, because it would happen quickly (v.32).

Since it was to occur soon, plans were needed and immediate action was of the utmost importance. Joseph proposed a bold idea to Pharaoh: "So now, let Pharaoh look for a discerning and wise man and set him over the land of Egypt. Let Pharaoh do this: Let him appoint overseers over the land and take one-fifth of the harvest of the land of Egypt during the seven years of abundance." (Genesis 41:33-34)

However Pharaoh, like the Potiphar, recognized the presence of God upon Joseph and said, "Since God has made all this known to you, there is no one as intelligent and wise as you." (v.39)

So Joseph was elevated to "placing you over all the land of Egypt." (v.41) and was second only to Pharaoh himself. He was given a signet ring, fine clothing, gold chains, and the company car of the day, a chariot. Assuming they were still living, one can easily wonder how Potiphar and his wife reacted when they had learned of Joseph's promotion. All Egypt knew for the Pharaoh had said, "I am Pharaoh, but without your permission no one will be able to raise his hand or foot in all the land of Egypt."

Joseph had suffered much, but clearly God had providentially prepared Joseph for this time. His obedience to God would save the lives of an untold number of people. The next rotation study will examine how God used Joseph to save his own family, who would bow before him, just as God had foretold in Joseph's own dreams. Joseph's family would ultimately become the twelve tribes of Israel.

AGE GROUP CONSIDERATIONS

The portion of the lesson where Potiphar's wife makes advances towards Joseph are sexual in nature. For the younger children it would be best to say simply that she tried to convince Joseph to do something which he knew was wrong. When he refused, she told a lie that got him into trouble.

Joseph Part 2 - Joseph in Egypt

Suggested Hymns and Songs

1. *Only Trust Him*, 465, 2008 Baptist Hymnal.
2. *His Eye Is on the Sparrow*, 93, 2008 Baptist Hymnal.
3. *Have Faith in God*, 508, 2008 Baptist Hymnal.
4. *Just When I Need Him Most*, 160, 2008 Baptist Hymnal.

Student Applications

1. Students will know that the story of Joseph in Egypt is found in the Old Testament book of Genesis.
2. Students will know that God changed Jacob's name to Israel and that his 12 sons would become the tribes of Israel.
3. Students will know that Joseph was one of 12 sons.
4. Students will know that Joseph had been sold into slavery by his jealous brothers.
5. Students will know that Joseph was sold to Potiphar, a high ranking Egyptian official.
6. Students will know that Joseph proved so capable and trustworthy in his servant duties that Potiphar entrusted him with the care of his entire household.
7. Students will know that Potiphar's wife tempted Joseph to sin, but that Joseph refused.
8. Students will know that Potiphar's wife accused Joseph of wrongdoing, and he was unjustly thrown in prison.
9. Students will know that Joseph proved so capable and trustworthy in prison that the prison warden entrusted him with all the prisoners.
10. Students will know that God allowed Joseph to interpret the dreams of two of the prisoners.
11. Students will know that Joseph asked the cupbearer to seek Pharaoh's favor for him.
12. Students will know that the cupbearer forgot about Joseph until reminded when Pharaoh had a dream he did not understand.
13. Students will know that Pharaoh summoned Joseph, whom God allowed to interpret the dream.
14. Students will know that in the dream God told Pharaoh that there would be seven years of plenty followed by seven years of famine.
15. Students will know that Pharaoh lifted Joseph to second-in-command in order to prepare in advance for the seven years of famine.
16. Students will know that God is sovereign over all, evil and good, and that everyone will one day answer to Him.
17. Students will know that they may be wrongly accused but that God can use even unpleasant things to carry out His will within(or through) their lives.
18. Students will know that God has a plan for them that is to bless and not to harm them, regardless of how circumstance may appear.
19. Students will know that we don't know what tomorrow will bring and need to live a righteous life today and always.

Joseph Part 3 - Joseph Reunites with His Family

BACKGROUND PASSAGES

Main Passage

Genesis 42-44	Back to Egypt
Genesis 45	Joseph makes himself known
Genesis 46-47:11	Moving to Egypt

Related Passages

Genesis 37:6-9	God given dreams fulfilled
Genesis 48-50	Life and death in Egypt

Suggested Homiletic Passage

Genesis 45:2-10

MEMORY VERSE

Younger version

But Joseph said to them, "Don't be afraid. ... God planned it for good..."

Genesis 50:19

Older version

But Joseph said to them, "Don't be afraid. Am I in the place of God? You planned evil against me; God planned it for good to bring about the present result — the survival of many people."

Genesis 50:19-20

LESSON OBJECTIVE

God in His providence, had a plan for Joseph's life. What others intended for harm, God used to save His people. Joseph recognized this and forgave those who tried to harm him.

LESSON

This is the final part of a three-part study on the life of Joseph. In last month's lesson Joseph was elevated to a position of authority, in which he was second in the land of Egypt only to Pharaoh. He oversaw the collection of grain during seven years of plenty. The years of plenty were followed by the famine God had warned about. "The whole world came to Joseph in Egypt to buy grain, for the famine was severe all over the earth." (Gen. 41:57).

Genesis 42-44

In chapter 42, the narrative switches back to Jacob's family, who were also affected by the famine and heard that grain was available in Egypt. Ten of the eleven brothers went to Egypt, leaving only Benjamin to behind. This was likely Jacob's (*also known as* Israel) idea, as Benjamin was Joseph's only full-blood brother and the child of Rebecca, Jacob's true love.

Once in Egypt, the brothers appeared before Joseph and bowed, fulfilling the dreams God had given Joseph long ago (Gen. 37). The brothers did not recognize Joseph. It had been at least twenty years; Joseph's appearance had likely changed. Also, even if they thought Joseph was still alive, the very idea of him being a high official in the Egyptian government would have been incomprehensible.

Joseph, however, did recognize his brothers but chose not to reveal his identity. Joseph chose rather to speak harshly to them. He accused them of being spies and demanded that one brother remain behind in Egypt until the others returned with the youngest brother. It seems that, upon being accused, they stressed that they were not spies but were all the sons of one man and that their family was of twelve children: them, one dead, and the youngest left at home. Why Joseph asked for them to fetch the youngest child (Benjamin) is the subject of much speculation. Most likely it was simply Joseph testing his brothers to see if they had changed over the years.

The brothers had no choice, so Simeon stayed in Egypt while the others returned to get Benjamin. Jacob was very distressed by the news. Also troubling was that each brother found, hidden within the bags of grain, their money had been returned (Gen 42:27-28). Jacob initially refused to allow the brothers to return. Eventually, however, their grain ran out and they were forced to return.

Jacob had already lost one son, Joseph, so he was protective of Benjamin. Before their second trip Judah promised his father that nothing would happen

Joseph Part 3 - Joseph Reunites with His Family

to Benjamin. Jacob grudgingly agreed and sent an array of gifts, hoping to find favor with the Egyptian official (Joseph).

When the brothers arrived, Joseph was pleased to see Benjamin with them. He ordered that the brothers be brought to his home and a meal prepared for them. They were to be the guests of Joseph, but this did not assure them, as they assumed they were being made accountable for the returned money (which they had found in their bags of grain). They were frightened and approached the steward. He quickly assured them all was fine, and then Simeon was freed to rejoin the brothers.

What was this reunion like? What did Simeon say? We don't know, but we do know that they all prepared for the meal (they washed) and that they got ready to meet Joseph. When Joseph arrived at the house, the brothers presented the gifts. Joseph asked many questions about their family. He asked God to be gracious to Benjamin and, deeply moved at the sight of his brother, he retreated to his room and wept.

After composing himself, they dined. Notice that Joseph ate alone and that the Egyptians and Hebrews did not mix. Sometimes cultural rules dictate how something is done. Something that astonished the brothers was that they had been seated "in the order of their ages." (43:33). Also notice that Benjamin was given more food than his brothers. They all ate and drank freely. What did they talk about? Was Joseph able to hear all they said? What did Joseph feel as he watched his brothers?

The brothers had come for more grain and, little did they know that Joseph had prepared for all their silver to once again be put in their grain sacks. He also asked his steward to place his silver cup in Benjamin's sack. The cup was an important symbol of Joseph's authority. To steal it would be a serious offense.[1]

As the next morning dawned, the brothers left for home. They had not gone far, when Joseph sent his steward to chase after them and accuse them of stealing his silver cup. The brothers resolutely denied any

such actions and promised that if the cup be found in any of their sacks, then that person could be killed and the rest made slaves. The steward replied that, instead of death, the guilty party would become a slave and the rest could go free.

Joseph's cup was found in Benjamin's sack. Stricken with grief, the brothers tore their clothes (a common way to express sorrow) and then they all returned to Joseph. Joseph tested the brothers' resolve to look out for Benjamin. Had they learned anything over the past twenty years? Would they stand up for Benjamin or "sacrifice" him like they had Joseph? They had not stolen the cup, and Judah stated that they were innocent, and then he acknowledged that they were guilty before their God and willing to stay and be slaves along with and beside Benjamin (44:16).

"The man in whose possession the cup was found will be my slave" (44:17) said Joseph. A second time they had been told they could go free. Would they save themselves and abandon Benjamin? They did not. Judah came forward to defend Benjamin and humbly pled with Joseph. Judah explained how important Benjamin is to Jacob and offered to become a slave in Benjamin's place (44:33).

Genesis 45

Joseph saw the change he had hoped for in his brothers. He told his servants to leave him alone with the brothers. Joseph proclaims to his brothers "I am Joseph! Is my father still living?" (v. 3). The brothers did not answer right away because they were terrified by the unexpected revelation. Joseph reassured them that by selling him, lives had been saved, even theirs, and that it was God who had sent him ahead of them to "establish you as a remnant in the land." (v. 7). Indeed, it was God who had orchestrated the fantastic chain of events.

Joseph then told them that there was to be five more years of famine and that they must all move to Egypt where he could care for and provide for them. He told them to bring the whole family and even their livestock. But most importantly that they

Joseph Part 3 - Joseph Reunites with His Family

should bring their father quickly! They all talked, hugged, kissed, and cried.

When news of the reunion reached Pharaoh's palace, Pharaoh encouraged Joseph to bring his family to Egypt and offered them some of his best land. He told them not to mind about their belongings, because the best of all Egypt would be theirs.

In verse 26 the brothers returned and told Jacob the good news. Stunned, Jacob did not believe the news at first; but, all the carts Joseph had sent to carry the family back to Egypt convinced him and he proclaimed, "Enough! My son Joseph is alive. I will go to see him before I die." (v. 28). Did the brothers confess to their father what they had done to Joseph two decades previously? It is never mentioned, but Genesis 44:16 reveals that the brothers knew they had been wrong. Imagine carrying that guilt for over twenty years!

Genesis 46-47:11

In Genesis 46 Jacob and all his family moved to Egypt. God had provided for His future nation in their time of need. God had big plans for the future of His children. Egypt would not be their permanent home, but it would be many years and many adventures would occur before they would leave. Meanwhile, God worked providentially through Joseph to save many. In the midst of famine there was plenty, and Joseph was the honored leader, the shepherd boy who was bowed to by many, and the prisoner who was free and honored.

Remind students that God has a plan for them also, and that it is to bless and not to harm them, regardless of how things sometimes seem. It took a long time for Joseph to see where all his life would lead. Many years later, God saved many and provided food for them all.

AGE GROUP CONSIDERATIONS

Younger and Older

Help explain cultural differences in Joseph's day. Perhaps explain that in America, men might open a door and let the lady enter first, while in Germany men open and enter first but hold the door for the lady (supposedly they were taught that the men were to make sure the way was safe). Use this to explain why:

1. It was a great work of God for Joseph to be so high in power (a Hebrew in Egypt) and to be so trusted and honored of Pharaoh.
2. Joseph would look so different wearing the fine Royal Egyptian clothes and makeup that his own brothers did not know him.
3. The brothers were afraid while in Egypt.
4. It was a great work of God to have all the honors they received from Pharaoh

Older only

If you wish to continue the story, explain how Jacob (Israel) and Joseph did not want to be buried in Egypt and how they were honored by the Egyptians, even in death. Explain how, when Israel died, the brothers were afraid of what Joseph might do but that Joseph made sure they understood that he had forgiven them and that it was God who had worked within it all, stating: "You intended to harm me, but God intended it for good." Also point out how Joseph encouraged his brothers to know that God would surely come to their aid and take them out of Egypt (Gen. 50:24).

SUGGESTED HYMNS AND SONGS

1. *I Need Thee Every Hour*, 423, 2008 Baptist Hymnal.
2. *A Child of the King*, 632, 2008 Baptist Hymnal.
3. *God of Our Fathers*, 642, 2008 Baptist Hymnal.
4. *How Deep the Father's Love for Us*, 101, 2008 Baptist Hymnal.

STUDENT APPLICATIONS

1. Students will know that the story of Joseph's family in Egypt is found in the Old Testament book of Genesis.
2. Students will know that God changed Jacob's name to Israel and that his 12 sons would become the tribes of Israel.

Joseph Part 3 - Joseph Reunites with His Family

3. Students will know that Joseph was one of twelve sons.
4. Students will know God allowed Joseph to interpret Pharoah's dream that foretold of a great famine to soon come.
5. Students will know that Pharoah placed Joseph as second-in-command in Egypt to prepare for the famine.
6. Students will know that Joseph worked during the seven years of plenty to store grain and make other preparations for the famine.
7. Students will know that seven years of famine did indeed follow the seven years of plenty.
8. Students will know that the famine affected Joseph's family in Canaan.
9. Students will know that Israel sent 10 of his sons to Egypt to buy grain, leaving only Benjamin at home.
10. Students will know that Joseph recognized the brothers, but they did not recognize him.
11. Students will know that Jospeh asked his brothers to bring the other brother (Benjamin).
12. Students will know that Joseph returned the brothers' money without their knowledge.
13. Students will know that Joseph's family ran out of food again and made another trip to Egypt.
14. Students will know that all 11 brothers, including Benjamin, went on the second trip.
15. Students will know that Joseph planted a silver cup in Benjamin's sack to see how the brothers would respond when he was "caught."
16. Students will know that Joseph knew his brothers had changed when he saw them pleading for Benjamin.
17. Students will know that Joseph revealed his identity to his brothers and told them God had used their treachery for His own good.
18. Students will know that Israel and all his family, at the request of Pharoah, moved to Egypt.
19. Students will know that God always makes provision for His people.
20. Students will know that Joseph recognized God's providence and did not retaliate against his brothers.
21. Students will know that God used Joseph to make certain the future nation of Israel survived the famine.
22. Older students will know that Egypt was a temporary home for the sons of Israel. One day they would return to God's promised land.

RESOURCES/CREDIT

1. *Life Application Bible.* (Zondervan Publishing House, Grand Rapids, Michigan. 1991), 88.

Elijah vs. the Priests of Baal

Background Passages

Main Passage

I Kings 17	Drought and faith
I Kings 18	The Mount Carmel challenge

Related Passages

Psalm 37:3-9	Trust in God and He will...
Proverbs 29:25	Trust God do not fear man
Matthew 10:28-31	Fear those who kill eternally
Matthew 28:19-20	God is with you always
Luke 1: 37	Nothing is impossible for God
Hebrews 11:1 & 6	Faith, required

Suggested Homiletic Passage

I Kings 18:30-39

Memory Verse

Younger version

Trust in the Lord ... and He will guide you.

Proverbs 3:5-6a

Older version

Trust in the Lord with all your heart, and do not rely on your own understanding; think about Him in all your ways, and He will guide you on the right paths.

Proverbs 3:5-6

Lesson Objective

The God of the Bible is the one and only true God and He is in control of everything. Believers must be faithful and trust that God knows their needs and will provide even when it appears that everyone else does not, for the lives of many may depend upon their life of faith.

Lesson

Elijah was believed to have been born somewhere in Gilead. There is no record of his family or background. Elijah's name means "*Yahweh*

is my God." God called Elijah to prophesy during the reign of King Ahab. Ahab led the nation of Israel astray by worshipping pagan idols, and even marrying a pagan priestess, Jezebel. Because of the poor example of Ahab and his wife, Israel turned from God, killed God's prophets, and worshipped the false gods Baal and Asherah (prophets of the groves). Ahab provoked God to anger more than any of the kings of Israel who had reigned before his time.

I Kings 17

God told Elijah to announce to Ahab that there would be a drought in Israel and then to go into hiding as the king would surely seek to have him killed. Elijah hid by the Cherith Brook where each morning and evening he was fed by ravens, as sent by God with bread and meat. Elijah drank from the brook and remained there until, as a consequence of the drought, it ran dry. Surely Elijah wondered what God had planned for his future.

Once the brook was dry, the Lord sent him to Zarephath, a town in Phœnecia on the Mediterranean coast, where a widow and her son allowed him to stay. Even though food and water were scarce, they were faithful to meet the man of God's needs, sacrificially, and God honored them. They fed Elijah and God made sure to meet all of their needs.

Meanwhile not a drop of rain had fallen in the land. The lack of water had caused a famine in Samaria. Ahab and Israel were suffering the consequences of their rebellion against God.

I Kings 18

Three years had passed since God had spoken through Elijah and announced the drought in Israel. God spoke to Elijah and told him to go and show himself to Ahab for He would again send rain upon the land.

In Ahab's palace was a man named Obadiah. He was the palace governor and a devout believer in the Lord. Even though Ahab was allowing Jezebel to kill off the Lord's prophets, Obadiah was faithful to the Lord. He had risked much by hiding many of the

Elijah vs. the Priests of Baal

Lord's prophets, as well as making sure they had bread and water. It was to Obadiah that Elijah first showed himself, and it was Obadiah who brought word to Ahab that Elijah had come (v.16).

In verse 17, Ahab is seen greeting Elijah as the "troubler of Israel." How ironic and wrong was Ahab's accusation! It was Ahab who had caused trouble, and it was Ahab who had rebelled against God and brought suffering to all of Israel.

Elijah told Ahab to summon all of Israel along with 850 pagan priests to a meeting at Mount Carmel. After the people had gathered Elijah asks the people, "How long will you hesitate between two opinions? If Yahweh is God, follow Him. But if Baal, follow him." (v.21). Their failure to answer shows how far the people had wandered from God. Realizing Elijah was correct, they said nothing in their own defense.

In verses 22-24, Elijah announced a challenge even though he was vastly outnumbered. In this contest both sides would build an altar and prepare a sacrifice. Each side would then pray and "the god who answers with fire-he is God." The people agreed to abide with the results of the contest saying to Elijah, "That sounds good."

Full of faith and absolutely confident in God, Elijah allowed the priests of Baal go first. After building the altar, the priests of Baal spent the entire morning leaping and dancing around the altar entreating Baal to answer their plea. At noon Elijah began to mock them, saying, "Shout loudly, for he's a god! Maybe he's thinking it over; maybe he has wandered away; or maybe he's on the road. Perhaps he's sleeping and will wake up!" (v.27). In verse 28 we see a practice that seems incomprehensible to us today — the priests began to intentionally cut and injure themselves in an attempt to garner the attention and favor of their god. All afternoon they frantically called, but no one answered, responded, nor paid attention.

Then Elijah said to everyone, "Come near me" and they came. With twelve stones, symbolic of the twelve tribes of Israel, Elijah rebuilt the Lord's abandoned, ruined altar. Around the altar he dug a large

trench and arranged the sacrificial offering upon the wood. Elijah called for water to be poured upon the altar. This was done three times, so that the water actually ran down around the altar, wet everything, and filled the trench (an amazing thing to witness after three years of drought, though Mount Carmel is close enough to the sea that undrinkable salt water might have been used).

It was the time of the evening sacrifice, Elijah stepped forward and prayed. He asked God to answer him so that everyone would know that "... You, Yahweh, are God and that You have turned their hearts back." (v.37). Elijah's faith and God's faithfulness were about to change a nation.

In answer to Elijah's simple prayer, God's fire fell and not only burned up the offering and wood, but the stones, soil, and trench water too! Imagine such a fast, powerful, and mighty answer for an act of faith to redeem a lost and deceived people.

The people understood, fell on their faces and cried "Yahweh, He is God! Yahweh, He is God!" While certainly convinced, hopefully many of the people were also converted. Matthew Henry's commentary states, "Blessed are they that have not seen what these saw, yet have believed, and have been wrought upon by it, more than they they that saw it."[1]

Just as a wound must be cleansed of dirt in order to not become infected, so those who follow the Lord must remove anything that will hinder a faithful life with God and lead to sin and death. Here God called for the removal of those who had led his people away from Him and had killed in the name of false deities. Elijah ordered the people to seize the priests and not let anyone get away (v.40). The priests were taken to the Kishon Valley, also called a *wadi* (a desert stream bed lower than the surrounding ground that only seasonally contains water), and there they were killed. Some scholars believe that everyone would have understood the consequence of losing the contest; the pagan prophets fate was not unexpected.[2] This part of the lesson is not appropriate for younger children.

Elijah vs. the Priests of Baal

Finally, Elijah remembered God's promise to bring rain back to the land, and he would not be still until God did exactly that. In verse 41, Elijah turned to Ahab and said, "Go up, eat and drink, for there is the sound of a rainstorm." Elijah did not immediately leave the mountain. There on top of Mount Carmel he bent to the ground and put his face between his knees. He told his servant to go and look toward the sea. Six times he did this, and six times his servant said, "There's nothing." The seventh time, however, the servant answered that he saw a "cloud as small as a man's hand coming from the sea." Elijah arose, knowing God was about to send rain, as He had promised, in answer to the faithful servant's prayers.

Though he was greatly outnumbered, Elijah had kept his faith in God. Often times today our faith is under attack. It seems like the forces of darkness have the upper hand. Believers can learn from Elijah and know that God is in absolute control. No matter how things look, who is on our side, or who is against us, we must remember that God will always keep His promises, and God will honor faith in Him, (even when it seems what we are asked to do, or give, is impossible) for nothing is impossible with God.

Age Group Considerations

Self-cutting, modern definitions of idols (a rather abstract concept), and the slaughter of the priests is not appropriate material for younger children.

Older children can better understand how important holiness is to God. Anytime false teachers or leaders were found in the Bible, God dealt with them harshly. God's Word repeatedly shows that sin leads to death, both physical and spiritual. In this lesson the results of sin can be seen quite literally. Remind the children that only God, as Creator of all life, is uniquely qualified to decide when a life should end.

Also note, that while we would never consider cutting ourselves in worship to God, many people often gravely hurt themselves worshipping the idols of this world. God has our best interest at heart when we follow Him. We must trust Him and be faithful to all He asks of us (remind the children that this means they need to know what God wants by faithfully studying and memorizing His Word).

Suggested Hymns/Songs

1. *Shout to the Lord*, 133, 2008 Baptist Hymnal.
2. *The Potter's Hand*, 441, 2008 Baptist Hymnal.
3. *I Know Whom I Have Believed*, 353, 2008 Baptist Hymnal.
4. *Tell Me the Story of Jesus*, 220, 2008 Baptist Hymnal.
5. *All Hail the Power of Jesus' Name*, 314, 2008 Baptist Hymnal.

Student Applications

1. Students will know that the story of Elijah versus the priests of Baal is found in the Old Testament book of I Kings.
2. Students will know that there is one true and living God: the Creator, Redeemer, Sustainer, and Ruler of all creation.
3. Students will know that Elijah was a prophet of God.
4. Students will know that Ahab was a king of Israel.
5. Students will know that Elijah, under God's direction, challenged 400 prophets of Baal and 450 prophets of Asherah to a contest.
6. Students will know that the prayers of the priests of Baal and Asherah were not answered because their gods do not exist.
7. Students will know that Elijah prepared an altar, set an offering on it and had water poured on it three times.
8. Students will know that when Elijah prayed, God sent fire to consume the offering, the altar and even the water.
9. Students will know that the people of Israel worshiped God as a result of the contest.
10. Students will know that God can protect them even when it all seems impossible.
11. Students will know that God answers prayers.

12. Students will know that God wants us to follow Him, not idols.
13. Students will know that an idol does not have to be a statue, but is anything in which we place more importance than God.
14. Students will know that even when only a very few believe, and those who do are persecuted, they must continue to trust in God and be faithful to all He has asked.

Resources/Credit

1. *Matthew Henry Commentary on the Whole Bible: Condensed Version*. The Ages Digital Library on CD, 455.
2. *The International Bible Commentary*. Charles G. Martin. F.F. Bruce, general editor. Zondervan Publishing House, 1979, 415.

Giving Back to God (Stewardship)

BACKGROUND PASSAGES

Main Passage
Mark 12:41-44   Mark's version of
                     Widow's Offering

Related Passages
Luke 21:1-4   Luke's version of
                    Widow's Offering
James 1:19-27   Faith exhibited through actions
Luke 16:13   Can't serve God and money
Matthew 6:19-21   Treasure is where your heart is
Proverbs 3:9-10   Honor God with the first fruit
Philippians 2:4   Look out for needs of others

Suggested Homiletic Passage
Mark 12:41-44

MEMORY VERSE

Younger version
For where your treasure is, there your heart will be also.

Matthew 6:21

Older version
But collect for yourselves treasures in heaven, where neither moth nor rust destroys, and where thieves don't break in and steal. For where your treasure is, there your heart will be also.

Matthew 6:20-21

LESSON OBJECTIVE

God in His sovereignty gives all things and has commanded all believers to also give of their money, time, and talents.

LESSON

Giving should be as natural as breathing for a believer. Giving helps those in need. When needs are met, the gospel is more readily shared, believed, and received. Giving shows obedience to God, shares His love, meets the needs of others, and demonstrates a life of faith.

This lesson focuses on a story about giving traditionally known as "*The Widow's Mite*." On the surface, the story appears to deal solely with financial stewardship of all that the Lord has given to believers. Stewardship means much more than handling finances. It involves total submission to God in all areas of life (money, time, attitude, speech, friendships, possessions, etc.).

Mark 12:41-44

"*The Widow's Mite*" is only three verses long in the book of Mark and four in Luke. While often called '*mites*', the two small copper coins are translated literally as "*two lepta*." A *lepton* (sing.) was the smallest and least valuable Greek coin. Two *lepta* were equal to a *quadrans*, the smallest of the Roman coins and estimated to be approximately 1/63 of a day's wages.[1]

In the verses preceding the widow's story, Jesus had berated the scribes for making a public show of their false piety. The widow provided a perfect contrast to the scribes. The widow that Jesus observed brought her offering to an area of the temple complex known as the Court of Women, where boxes were available for freewill offerings. Separate boxes were available for Jewish males to pay the temple tax.

Giving in this setting was not a private experience. In verse 41, Jesus observed that many rich people had brought large sums to be deposited in the treasury. Unlike contemporary velvet lined offering plates, it was likely that the act of placing money in the boxes created a fair bit of noise. This naturally would draw attention to the giver. Was the widow self-conscious about not having as much to offer? We do not know as nothing is written about this in the Bible. Surely, it took courage for the widow to make her offering in such a public setting.

After witnessing her unselfish giving, Jesus calls the disciples together to teach them an object lesson. He stated, "I assure you: This poor widow has put in more than all those giving to the temple treasury.

Giving Back to God (Stewardship)

For they gave out of their surplus, but she out of her poverty has put in everything she possessed — all she had to live on." (v. 43-44).

Offerings are not valued monetarily by God. Indeed, God needs nothing from His children, as He already has all the world for His very own (Psalms 50:7-15). Instead, offerings are valued by gratitude, humility, and the understanding that all things come from the loving hands of our Heavenly Father, without whom nothing would be enough or of consequence (James 1: 16-18). Christians are to be like Christ, tender hearted, kind, and compassionate towards those in need (Matt 5:43-48; Mark 12: 28-33; James 2:15-16; Matt 10:42).

Children may have very little in the way of financial means to give to God. The value of their offering, like the widow's, is magnified when given with a spirit of thanksgiving. God values praise and thanksgiving far above earthly offerings (Psalms 69: 30-32). Giving is an act of worship. Children should be reminded that God considers the heart and is pleased with those who, in Jesus, seek to serve others. Those who give in order to get a reward or to be noticed will not be rewarded by God as they have already been rewarded (Matt 6:1-4).

Giving the tithe to God is just the beginning of obedience. One must also be ready to willingly give an offering (which could be money, but may be a time of prayer and praise to God, food or clothes to those in need, or time with someone who is lonely). Service encourages hope, faith, and more service (Heb 10: 23-24)!

As stated earlier, stewardship encompasses much more than financial giving. The book of James integrates faith with everyday practical living. James emphasizes that works are the evidence and natural result of faith. There is nothing a person can do to earn God's favor. All believers are saved, through faith in Christ, for works.

Believers are called to be stewards, not only financially, but practically. We meet needs in order to share the gospel. "Pure and undefiled religion before our God the Father is this: to look after orphans and widows in their distress and to keep oneself unstained by the world." (James 1:27) In the most practical of terms, we are commanded to look after those who have no one to look after them. Who fits this description in the lives of your children today? Is there a need in our church (Acts 4:32-35)? Is there a need in your community? Is there a ministry opportunity at a local shelter or children's home? Is there a bigger need which can be met by many sharing the burden (such as in Southern Baptist churches through offerings for the World Hunger Fund, Annie Armstrong, Lottie Moon, state children's home, etc.)?

There are many ways children practice good stewardship by the "giving" of their lives. Children can "give" the respect due to their parents and other authority figures. Children can "give" back to God through praise and worship (at home or at church by praying, singing, and learning the Bible). Eph. 6:15 reminds believers that they are to be in a state of "readiness" that comes from the gospel of peace. Children can "give" back to God through learning what God says and by doing it daily (Deut.6:6-7; Heb 3:13). Children can "give" to God by helping with various mission projects such as assembling a shoe box for *Operation Christmas Child* or going with a parent to deliver canned goods to a food bank.

As a believer learns to trust God and give back freely, he/she will discover the truth that it is impossible to out give God. One's effort will be rewarded many times over as he/she sees God's kingdom grow.

AGE GROUP CONSIDERATIONS

It is quite likely a child will ask: *Does God want all of my money?* God will rarely ask anyone to give up everything he/she physically owns. He simply wants believers to trust Him with all He has given. God has His eye on each sparrow. He feeds and cares for each lowly bird (Matt. 6:26; Matt.10:29-31). God says each person means more to Him than a sparrow, and He will be faithful to care for us too.

Giving Back to God (Stewardship)

With younger children, emphasize the different ways they can give to God through obedience, prayer, and praise. Financial giving should be taught but not be overly emphasized.

Suggested Hymns and Songs

1. *I Surrender All*, 433, 2008 Baptist Hymnal.
2. *How Great is Our God*, 5, 2008 Baptist Hymnal.
3. *To God Be the Glory*, 28, 2008 Baptist Hymnal.
4. *Jehovah Jireh*, 124, 2008 Baptist Hymnal.

Student Applications

1. Students will know that the story of the Widow's mite is found in the New Testament books of Mark and Luke.
2. Students will know that while the monetary value of the widow's offering was insignificant, her offering was valued by God because she gave sacrificially.
3. Students will know that God is the sole provider of all that they have and has blessed them greatly.
4. Students will know that God commands them to give back just a portion of what they have received from Him.
5. Students will know that things of this world are temporal, but things of heaven are eternal.
6. Students will know that they can bless God and others through financial giving.
7. Students will know that they can bless God and others by giving of their time.
8. Students will know that they can bless God and others by obeying parents and authority figures
9. Students will know that they can bless God and others through their praise and worship.
10. Students will know that when someone's earthly needs have been met, he/she will likely be more willing to hear the gospel.

Resources/Credit

1. *Holman Christian Standard Bible Red-Letter Text Edition.* (Holman Bible Publishers: Nashville, Tennessee, 2004), 859

Resurrection of Lazarus

Background Passages

Main Passage

John 11:1-44   Resurrection of Lazarus

Related Passages

Passage	Summary
John 14:6	Jesus is the Way
Luke 10:38-42	Jesus visits Mary and Martha

Suggested Homiletic Passages

John 11:21-27

Memory Verse:

Younger version

"I am the resurrection and the life. The one who believes in Me ... will live."

John 11:25b

Older version

"I am the resurrection and the life. The one who believes in Me, even if he dies, will live. Everyone who lives and believes in Me will never die — ever."

John 11:25-26

Lesson Objective

Jesus showed that he has power over physical death by resurrecting his friend Lazarus. Jesus showed that he had power over spiritual death by dying on the cross for our sins and rising again.

Lesson

The death and resurrection of Lazarus is a moving account told only in the book of John. It was Jesus' final major act before His last Passover. It was also the event that galvanized the Sanhedrin into forming a plan that would succeed (though only by the will of God) in killing Jesus. But Jesus would conquer both physical and spiritual death. The story of Lazarus teaches that Christ has power over death and life, both physical and spiritual.

John 11:1-44

Mary, Martha and Lazarus were close friends with Jesus. At the beginning of John 11 Lazarus is sick enough that his worried sisters sent word to Jesus to come quickly. In verse four, Jesus made it clear that events surrounding Lazarus would play out for God's glory.

In verse six Jesus did something that would seem odd to most of us. After affirming his love for Lazarus and his family, Jesus stayed where he was for two more days. God's mercy should not be judged based on the conditions before our eyes. Whatever the delay, God does not forget His people. As Jesus had stated in verse four, this was to be for God's glory.

Lazarus died, possibly even before Jesus received news of his illness, and was buried in his home town of Bethany in Judea.

When Jesus announced that he was returning to Judea, his disciples tried to dissuade him. They knew that while many were following Jesus, many of the religious leaders in Judea desired to see Jesus killed. The disciples resisted further when Jesus said "Our friend Lazarus has fallen asleep; but I'm on My way to wake him up." (v.11). The disciples thought Jesus was talking about normal sleep, not death. This is despite the use of the term 'sleep' as a metaphor throughout the New Testament and the Jewish world of their day. Pointing again to a lack of understanding, Thomas stated in verse 16 "Let's go so that we may die with him."

Upon arriving in Bethany, it is learned that Lazarus had already died and been buried four days previously. Martha came to meet Jesus and lamented that he had not arrived sooner. Jesus told her that her brother would (will) rise again. Martha thought that Jesus was referring to the resurrection at the last day. It is true that Lazarus will rise again at last day (the *Day of the Lord*), but Jesus had something more immediate in mind.

Resurrection of Lazarus

What Jesus said next in verses 25-26 is one of the more profound and powerful statements made in the Bible:

"I am the resurrection and the life. The one who believes in Me, even though He dies, will live. Everyone who lives and believes in Me will never die — ever. Do you believe this?"

Here Jesus stated that He has power and authority over life and death in the spiritual realm. This was probably said to Martha as a reminder that Christ promises an unimaginably more excellent life beyond the many God-given blessings on earth. In addition, Christ planned to soon prove he had power over physical death by His death on the cross and resurrection.

In verses 28-30, Mary was alerted to the arrival of Jesus. Note that the Jews mourning with Mary followed her as she went to meet Jesus. Upon approaching him, she fell at his feet and lamented that he had not arrived sooner. This expression of sorrow deeply moved Jesus, to the point that Jesus himself wept (v.35). Some of those watching Jesus recognize his genuine compassion. Others criticized him for not having come in time to heal Lazarus and doubted His power. They would soon learn that God's timing is perfect.

Jesus arrived at the tomb along with Mary, Martha, and others. Tombs of the day were often caves carved into a limestone hillside. A tomb might hold several or many bodies while allowing for walking room inside. The tomb would be closed with a large stone. Jesus commanded the stone in front of Lazarus' tomb to be rolled away.

Martha protested, thinking it pointless since Lazarus had already been dead four days. Jesus reminded her of the importance of belief. Why was it important enough to be mentioned that Lazarus had been dead four days? Four days proved to everyone that Lazarus was truly dead, and had not merely swooned or been sick. Another reason for the four days may have been that some Jews believed that the spirit of the dead hovered over the body for up to three days. Four days countered that argument.

The stone was rolled away and Jesus prayed aloud. Jesus said, "...I know that You always hear Me, but because of the crowd standing here I said this, so that they may believe You sent Me." (v.41-42). The purpose of this miracle would prove to those present that Jesus was sent by God. After praying, Jesus called in a loud voice "Lazarus, come out!" (v.43). The dead cannot hear. Jesus wanted those present to realize that He was sent of God and was God in the flesh. Only God can give life or raise the dead. Lazarus, bound in burial linens, walked out of the tomb. Jesus commanded Lazarus be unwrapped and let go.

All the miracles of Jesus' ministry had led up to this final, dramatic miracle. Upon hearing of this miracle, the chief priests and the Pharisees met to discuss the event. Instead of expressing joy over the miracle, they were incensed. While they had attempted to kill Jesus before, it was now God's timing for Christ to die. This would be the plan that would succeed. Passover week was at hand. It was to be the Passover when Jesus would become the perfect, once-for-all, sacrificial lamb for our sins.

Age Group Considerations

Older students may confuse this Lazarus with the one who ate from the rich man's table. This Lazarus was the brother of Mary and Martha.

Students may ask why Jesus' resurrection was so special when Lazarus and others in the Bible were also resurrected. Colossians 1:18 states, "He is the beginning, the firstborn from the dead, so that He might come to have first place in everything." The difference is that Jesus was the first to be resurrected and stay that way. Lazarus eventually died once more and awaits his resurrection body. As "firstborn" Jesus holds a position of preeminence in regards to resurrection.

Resurrection of Lazarus

Suggested Hymns and Songs

1. *I Have Decided to Follow Jesus*, 434, 2008 Baptist Hymnal.
2. *Jesus is Lord of All*, 294, 2008 Baptist Hymnal.
3. *He Lives*, 269, 2008 Baptist Hymnal.
4. *I Stand Amazed in the Presence*, 237, 2008 Baptist Hymnal.

Student Applications

1. Students will know that story of Lazarus' resurrection appears in the New Testament gospel of John.
2. Students will know that Lazarus, Mary and Martha were friends of Jesus whom lived in Bethany.
3. Students will know that Jesus received word that Lazarus was gravely ill.
4. Students will know that Lazarus died four days before Jesus arrived in Bethany.
5. Students will know that Jesus commanded Lazarus to come out of the grave, and he did.
6. Students will know that Jesus, as God, has power over life and death.
7. Students will know that Jesus showed love for His friends by meeting a physical need.
8. Students will know that Jesus can meet all their needs, the most important of which is their spiritual need for salvation.
9. Students will know this miracle was the last miracle performed by Jesus before His final Passover.
10. Students will know that Jesus has compassion for those in mourning.
11. Students will know that Jesus showed human emotions, including weeping.

Christmas - The Messiah Prophesied

Background Passages

Main Passages
Isaiah 7:13-14   His name *Immanuel*
Isaiah 9:6-7   Unto us a child is born
Luke 2:1-22   Nativity/Shepherds

Related Passages
Matt. 1:18-2:12   Nativity/Wise Men
Isaiah 11:1-2   Christ from line of David
Micah 5:2   Christ born in Bethlehem
Rev. 22:16   Christ is offspring of David

Suggested Homiletic Passages
Isaiah 7:13-14, 9:6-7

Memory Verse

Younger version
For a child will be born for us, a son will be given to us ...

Isaiah 9:6a

Older version
For a child will be born for us, a son will be given to us, and the government will be on His shoulders. He will be named Wonderful Counselor, Mighty God, Eternal Father, Prince of Peace.

Isaiah 9:6

Lesson Objective

God, through Isaiah, foretold of His coming to earth as the Messiah. Christians recognize the fulfillment of this prophecy each Christmas, as we celebrate the birth of Christ.

Lesson

The rotation curriculum is designed to take place over a number of years. In each December rotation there will be an emphasis on a specific part of the Christmas story. For this rotation, the focus will be on the prophecy of Isaiah concerning the future birth of the Messiah.

Approximately one-third of the Bible consists of prophetic literature. The majority of prophetic literature is found in the latter part of the Old Testament. Isaiah, a prophet, ministered for a period of more than forty years, from 740 B.C. until after 701 B.C.[1] He was one of several prophets God used to speak to the nation of Israel during its decline. While Isaiah and the other prophets spoke directly to the nation of Israel, most prophecy can potentially have three applications.[2]

1. The prophecy will contain meaning for the original audience. Isaiah prophesied God's judgment to the nation of Israel at the hands of the Babylonians and reconciliation with God.

2. Prophecy can have an application to the future, perhaps even beyond the present day. Some future prophecies speak in the past tense. This is 'prophetic perfect' tense, speaking of a future event as if it has already happened because it is so certain.[3] This is the application focused on in this study. The prophecy of the birth of the Messiah was not fulfilled until many generations after Isaiah spoke to the Israelites.

3. Finally, prophecy may teach eternal principles of right and wrong that apply to all generations. In Isaiah there are the principles of judgment and reconciliation.

Remembering these principles can help believers to better understand prophecy.

Isaiah 7:13-14

Isaiah chapter 7 contains what is often referred to as "The Immanuel Prophecy." One scholar states, "Scarcely any verse in the Bible has been more debated and discussed than Isaiah 7:14"[4] Despite the various debates that have arisen over the interpretation of this verse, one thing is certain "No Christian who takes Matthew 1:20-23 seriously can deny an ultimate fulfillment in Christ."[5]

Immanuel, meaning "*God with us,*" was to be a unique sign. Some scholars think this sign had a special meaning for the original audience in that it was meant specifically for the reigning king of Israel, Ahaz. If this is true, the woman in the verse may have referred to Isaiah's betrothed and the child his son, Maher-shalal-hash-baz. Another possibility is that it

Christmas - The Messiah Prophesied

was a mark of faith on the part of the mothers of Israel. Shortly after the prophecy, perhaps many mothers named their newborn children Immanuel. This would have been out of gratitude for God driving away the two kings who were terrorizing Israel (7:1 and 7:16).

So what is the relevance of the "Immanuel" of Isaiah's day to the Christmas story? God in the flesh, coming to earth would be the final and permanent salvation of His people and the one true Immanuel. The Messiah would come out of David's lineage. The fulfillment of this prophecy is noted in Matthew 1:22-23.

Isaiah 9:6-7

In chapter nine more details about the Messiah were revealed. Israel would one day have a perfect king. He would stand in stark contrast to the contemporary, relatively impotent Israeli kings. The Messiah was given four names, which the Life Application Bible defines as:

Wonderful Counselor — He is exceptional, distinguished, and without peer, the one who gives right advice.

Mighty God — He is God himself.

Everlasting Father — He is timeless; he is God our Father.

Prince of Peace — His government is one of justice and peace.[6]

Verse seven tells that his reign will be characterized with justice and righteousness as his priestly rule increases and never ends.

Luke 2:1-22

Moving ahead almost 700 years to the actual birth of Jesus, only one gospel, Luke, detailed the actual nativity scene. While Matthew detailed the visit of the magi, only in Luke do we read about the actual birth scene. Even in Luke, the details are scant. Much of what many Christians believe today about the birth has come down through tradition or assumptions. What is evident is that Christ's arrival came under humble and quiet circumstances. It is in stark contrast to His future second coming when He will come in majesty for all to see (Revelation 19:11-16).

At the beginning of Luke chapter 2 an imperial decree had been issued throughout the Roman empire declaring a census. Everyone was commanded to return to their home town to be counted. Joseph and his betrothed, Mary, returned to Joseph's home town of Bethlehem. Bethlehem had also been the home town of David. Luke calls attention to this fact since Jesus was of the lineage of David (Matthew 1).

In the Jewish culture of the day, betrothal was not marriage, but unlike engagements of our day it was a binding commitment. Tradition claims that Mary rode a donkey on the journey. The Bible makes no mention of the mode of transportation. At this time Mary's pregnancy was nearing the time of birth. Details about the birth are limited to two verses:

While they were there, the time came for her to give birth. Then she gave birth to her firstborn Son, and she wrapped him in cloths and placed him in a manger, because there was no room for them in the inn.[6]

Today, tourists can visit Bethlehem and see a cave where Jesus was alleged to have been born. A large metal star marks the "exact spot." Whether this is truly the location is possible, but cannot be proven. Inns as we know them today did not exist at that time, though towns on trade routes often had a *caravanserai*; open air courtyards in which animals would stay while the humans slept under enclosures around the courtyard edge.

A manger was a feeding trough for animals. As the only prop mentioned in the narrative, it has led to the tradition of Jesus being born amongst the animals in a stable or cave. Perhaps Jesus was born in the house of Joseph's relatives. Families often had one-room homes with a lower and upper area. The upper area was living space while the animals lived in the lower one. Perhaps because of the census, the house was crowded and the only place to lay Jesus was in the animal's trough. The point of mentioning the manger is to show the lowly state of Christ's birth. Paul stated Jesus "became poor." This is a literal example.

In verse 8 the scene shifted to the fields outside Bethlehem. Shepherds were spending the night

Christmas - The Messiah Prophesied

watching over their flocks. Shepherds ranked low on the social scale. That God would choose to announce the birth to shepherds is curious to us, but in keeping with the humble nature of the event.

An angel appeared to the shepherds. Verse nine says that this appearance terrified them. The angel made his announcement and told the shepherds that they would find the child wrapped in cloths lying in a manger. There is no mention of the star that the wise men later followed.

In verse 13 "a great company of the heavenly host" appeared and said (the text does not say that they sang) "glory to God in the highest heaven, and peace on earth to people He favors!" Inspired by this heavenly display, the shepherds made haste and found Mary, Joseph, and the baby lying in the manger just as they were told.

In verse 17 the shepherds spread the word about what they had seen. Those who heard "wondered at the things which were told them by the shepherds." (Luke 2:18. NASB). In verse 20 the shepherds return to the fields glorifying and praising God.

The Messiah had been born, in accordance with what God had spoken through Isaiah 700 years previously. In His first coming Jesus arrived as a helpless infant. In his second coming He will arrive as the King of all creation.

Age Group Considerations

Younger children may view the Bible as just one book written all at one time. Emphasize that there was a great period of time between the writing of Isaiah and Christ's birth. The accuracy of the fulfillment of the prophecy is proof that God's Word is trustworthy and relevant to their lives.

Suggested Hymns

1. *Emmanuel*, 201, 2008 Baptist Hymnal.
2. *Come, Thou Long-Expected Jesus*, 176, 2008 Baptist Hymnal.
3. *Away in a Manger*, 205, 1991 Baptist Hymnal.
4. *What Child is This*, 198, 2008 Baptist Hymnal.
5. *Majesty*, 297, 2008 Baptist Hymnal.

Student Applications

1. Students will know that the book of Isaiah is found in the Old Testament.
2. Students will know that Biblical prophecies had meaning for the original audience .
3. Students will know that many Biblical prophecies hold meaning for the future.
4. Students will know that the account of the birth of Jesus is found in the New Testament.
5. Students will know that Jesus is the Messiah promised in Isaiah's prophecies.
6. Students will know that Jesus was God born in the flesh (as a human).
7. Students will know that Immanuel means "God with us."
8. Students will know that Jesus was born under the humblest of circumstances.
9. Students will know that angels proclaimed the birth of Jesus to shepherds.
10. Students will know that the shepherds found baby Jesus lying in a manger.

Resources/Credit

1. R.C. Sproul, ed. *The Reformation Study Bible*. (Orlando, Florida: Ligonier Ministries, 2005), 948.
2. Debbie Fisher, *Rotation.org* writing team.
3. Vaughan Roberts, *God's Big Picture: Tracing the Storyline of the Bible* (Downer's Grove, Illinois: IVP Books), 96.
4. F.F. Bruce, ed., *The International Bible Commentary, Revised Edition*. (Grand Rapids, Michigan: Zondervan Publishing House, 1979), 726.
5. *Ibid.*
6. *Life Application Bible*. (Grand Rapids, Michigan: Zondervan Publishing House, 1991), 1185.

Sample Calendar

Year 1

January	Jesus Teaches Forgiveness
February	Joshua and the Conquest of Canaan
March	Philip and the Ethiopian
April	Easter - Peter's Story
May	Solomon asks for Wisdom
June	The Centurions's Faith
July	Queen Esther
August	Jesus Helps on the Sabbath
September	Samuel Listens to God
October	Ark of the Covenant
November	The Ten Lepers
December	Christmas - Anna & Simeon

Year 2

January	Gideon
February	Healing of Namaan
March	Jesus is Tempted
April	Easter - Emmaus Road
May	Conversion of Saul
June	Jeremiah - Fall of Judah
July	Daniel Stays Pure
August	Nehemiah/Ezra
September	Jesus Teaches about Prayer
October	Zacchaeus
November	David Becomes King/Psalms
December	Christmas -Wise Men

Year 3

January	Armor of God
February	Nicodemus
March	Easter - Crucifixion
April	Early Church - Peter Rescued
May	Josiah the Boy King
June	Moses Part 1 - Birth to Midian
July	Moses Part 2 - Plagues & Exodus
August	Moses Part 3 -Ten Commandments
September	Martha & Mary
October	The Lost Son
November	Elijah and the Widow
December	Christmas - Joseph

Year 4

January	David & Goliath
February	Jesus is Baptized
March	Ruth
April	Easter - Trial/Judas
May	Jesus' Miracles
June	Paul & Silas
July	Paul's Missionary Journeys
August	Paul's Letters
September	Faith of Job
October	Peter & Cornelius
November	Micah the prophet
December	Christmas - Mary & Elizabeth

Year 5

January	Healing at Bethesda Pool
February	The Three Friends and the Fiery Furnace
March	Daniel & the Lion's Den
April	Easter - Upper Room/Great Commission
May	Pentecost & the Holy Spirit
June	Creation
July	Adam and Eve Sin
August	Noah and the Flood
September	Young Jesus in temple
October	Elisha
November	David & Jonathan
December	Christmas - Shepherds

Year 6

January	Abraham receives a Promise
February	Jonah and the Fish
March	Return of Jesus
April	Easter - Passover & Lord's Supper
May	Jesus Calls Disciples
June	Joseph Part 1 - Joseph's Colorful Coat
July	Joseph Part 2 - Joseph in Egypt
August	Joseph Part 3 - Joseph Reunites with His Family
September	Elijah vs. the Priests of Baal
October	Giving Back to God (Stewardship)
November	Resurrection of Lazarus
December	Christmas - The Messiah Prophesied

Easter Dates

While the date of Christmas is predictable and fits easily in the rotation schedule, preparing for Easter requires a critical look at the calendar every year. In years that Easter is in March, you may switch the March and April lessons. If the date of Easter is in early April, you must decide whether to teach it in March and build up to the actual date, or to teach it in April, including the Sundays that come after Easter Sunday. The wonderful thing is that for believers every Sunday is Resurrection Sunday, and therefore, it is always appropriate to make any Sunday "Easter."

Here are the dates of Easter until 2030

April 4, 2010	April 16, 2017	March 31, 2024
April 24, 2011	April 1, 2018	April 20, 2025
April 8, 2012	April 21, 2019	April 5, 2026
March 31, 2013	April 12, 2020	March 28, 2027
April 20, 2014	April 4, 2021	April 16, 2028
April 5, 2015	April 17, 2022	April 1, 2029
March 27, 2016	April 9, 2023	April 21, 2030

*Many people contributed to creating **The Village** at Oak Crest Baptist Church. This mural for the media room was painted by JoAnn Lancaster.*

Bibliography/Sources

Randall L. Adkisson, "*A Man named Nicodemus*," **Biblical Illustrator**, Lifeway (Winter 2006-07 Volume 33, Number 2).

The Baptist Faith and Message, 2000. The Southern Baptist Convention.

Flood Timeline [article online]; available from http://www.answersingenesis.org/articles/am/v2/n2/ark-chronology

David Alexander & Pat Alexander, eds. *Eerdmans' Handbook to the Bible* (Grand Rapids: William B. Eerdmans Publishing Company, 1973).
Donald Guthrie. *Eerdmans' Handbook to the Bible* (Grand Rapids: William B. Eerdmans Publishing Company, 1973).
Derrick Kiddner. *Eerdmans' Handbook to the Bible* (Grand Rapids: William B. Eerdmans Publishing Company, 1973).
Alec Motyer. *Eerdmans' Handbook to the Bible* (Grand Rapids: William B. Eerdmans Publishing Company, 1973).

William Barclay, *The Daily Bible Series: The Letters to the Galatians and Ephesians* (Philadelphia: The Westminster Press, 1976).

Robert Bergen, "*Moab*," **Biblical Illustrator**, Lifeway (Spring 2006 Volume 32, Number3).

Henry T. Blackaby and Claude V. King. *Experiencing God: Youth Edition* (Nashville: Lifeway Press).

Walt Brown, *In the Beginning: Compelling Evidence for Creation and the Flood, 7th Edition* (Phoenix, AZ: Center for Scientific Creation, 2001).

Trent C. Butler, "*Praise our Incomparable God*," **Explore the Bible Adult Commentary: Isaiah, Micah**, Lifeway (Spring 2006 Volume 10, Number 3).

Frederick Fyvie Bruce, *The Gospel & Epistles of John* (Grand Rapids: William B. Eerdmans Publishing Co., 1983).

Frederick Fyvie Bruce, *Paul: Apostle of the Heart Set Free* (Grand Rapids: William B. Eerdmans Publishing Co., 1995).

David J. A. Clines, *The International Bible Commentary, Revised Edition*, F.F. Bruce, ed. (Grand Rapids, Michigan: Zondervan Publishing House, 1979).
H. L Ellison, *The International Bible Commentary, Revised Edition*, F.F. Bruce, ed. (Grand Rapids, Michigan: Zondervan Publishing House, 1979).
Robert P. Gordon, *The International Bible Commentary, Revised Edition*, F.F. Bruce, ed. (Grand Rapids, Michigan: Zondervan Publishing House, 1979).
Michael C. Griffiths,The International Bible Commentary, Revised Edition, F.F. Bruce, ed. (Grand Rapids, Michigan: Zondervan Publishing House, 1979).
Charles G. Martin, *The International Bible Commentary, Revised Edition*, F.F. Bruce, ed. (Grand Rapids, Michigan: Zondervan Publishing House, 1979).
A. R. Millard, *The International Bible Commentary, Revised Edition*, F.F. Bruce, ed. (Grand Rapids, Michigan: Zondervan Publishing House, 1979).
Charles A. Oxley, *The International Bible Commentary, Revised Edition*, F.F. Bruce, ed. (Grand Rapids, Michigan: Zondervan Publishing House, 1979).
Laurance E. Porter, *The International Bible Commentary, Revised Edition*, F.F. Bruce, ed. (Grand Rapids, Michigan: Zondervan Publishing House, 1979).
Steven Short, *The International Bible Commentary, Revised Edition*, F.F. Bruce, ed. (Grand Rapids, Michigan: Zondervan Publishing House, 1979).

John Calvin. *Commentary on Matthew, Mark, Luke - Volume 2*, trans. and ed. by William Pringle (Grand Rapids: Christian Classics Ethereal Library, 1999).

Robert L. Cate. *Old Testament Roots for New Testament Faith* (Nashville: Broadman Press, 1982)

Michael Catellano, *Timeline of Noah and the Flood* [article online]; available from http://home.earthlink.net/~arktracker/ark/Timeline.html

Bob Dunston, "*Ezra, Nehemiah, Esther*" **Explore the Bible Adult Commentary, Lifeway** (Winter 2006-07 Volume 11, Number 2).

Bibliography/Sources

Jonathan Edwards, *Charity and its Fruits* (Edinburgh: The Banner of Truth Trust, 2000 (reprint)).

The Family Bible Dictionary, 1958 ed. Avenir Books,

James M. Freeman, *Manners & Customs of the Bible* (New Kensington: Whitaker House, 1996).

Everett Ferguson, *Backgrounds of Early Christianity* (Grand Rapids: William B. Eerdmans Publishing Co., 1993).

James Leo Garrett Jr., *Systematic Theology: Biblical, Historical, and Evangelical, Volume 1* (North Richland Hills: BIBAL Press, 2000).

Joel B. Green, *The Gospel of Luke: The New International Commentary on the New Testament*, ed. Gordon D. Fee (Grand Rapids: William B. Eerdmans Publishing Co., 1997).

Gary Hardin, "*Jewish Sabbath Laws*," **Biblical Illustrator, Lifeway** (Spring 2006 Volume 32, Number 3).

Ken Ham, *The New Answers Book* (Green Forest, AR: Master Books, 2007).

Matthew Henry Commentary on the Whole Bible: Condensed Version. The Ages Digital Library on CD.

Herschel H. Hobbs, *Fundamentals of Our Faith* (Nashville: Broadman & Holman Publishers, 1960).

Holman Christian Standard Bible Red-Letter Text Edition. Holman Bible Publishers: Nashville, Tennessee, 2004.

F.F. Bruce, *The New Bible Commentary : Revised, ed.* Donald Guthrie (New York: Wm. B Eerdmans Co.).
A.E. Cundall, *The New Bible Commentary : Revised, ed.* Donald Guthrie (New York: Wm. B Eerdmans Co.).
Hywel R. Jones, *The New Bible Commentary : Revised, ed.* Donald Guthrie (New York: Wm. B Eerdmans Co.).

I.H. Marshall, *The New Bible Commentary : Revised, ed.* Donald Guthrie (New York: Wm. B Eerdmans Co.).
William Sanford LaSor, *The New Bible Commentary : Revised, ed.* Donald Guthrie (New York: Wm. B Eerdmans Co.).
Hywell R. Jones, *The New Bible Commentary : Revised, ed.* Donald Guthrie (New York: Wm. B Eerdmans Co.).

Life Application Bible. (Grand Rapids, Michigan: Zondervan Publishing House, 1991).

E. LeBron Matthews, "*Genesis*," **Explore the Bible Adult Commentary**, Lifeway (Winter 2007-08 Volume 11, Number 2).

Steven R. Miller, "*The Egypt Joseph Knew*," **Biblical Illustrator**, Lifeway (Spring 2008 Volume 34, Number 3).

Burk Parsons, ed., "*True Israel*," **Tabletalk**, Ligonier Ministries (January 2008 Volume 32, Number 1).

Bibliography/Sources

Burk Parsons, ed., *"One with His People,"* **Tabletalk**, Ligonier Ministries (January 2008 Volume 32, Number 1).

Gregory T. Pouncey, *"First-Century Armor,"* **Biblical Illustrator**, Lifeway (Summer 2005 Volume 31, Number 4).

Vaughan Roberts, *God's Big Picture: Tracing the Storyline of the Bible* (Downer's Grove, Illinois: IVP Books).

Franklin M. Segler (Revised by Randall Bradley), *Understanding, Preparing for, and Practicing Christian Worship* (Nashville, TN: Broadman & Holman).

"Session 85: Saul's Conversion Bible Background," **Fuel: Igniting New Life with God's Story**, Lifeway (2006, 2.4).

Charles H. Spurgeon, *All of Grace* (Chicago: Moody Press).

R.C. Sproul, ed. *The Reformation Study Bible*. (Orlando, Florida: Ligonier Ministries, 2005).

J. Mark Terry, *"Threshing Floors,"* **Biblical Illustrator**, Lifeway (Spring 2008 Volume 34, Number 3).

A. R. Wallace, *Man's Place in the Universe* (McClure, Phillips & Co.: New York, 1903).

William Whitaker, *Disputations on Holy Scriptures*, trans. and ed. by William Fitzgerald(Orlando: Soli Deo Gloria Publications).

Sherwood Elliot Wirt & Kirsten Beckstrom, eds., *Topical Encyclopedia of Living Quotations*, (Minneapolis: Bethany House Publishers).

V. Gilbert Veers, *Family Bible Library* (Nashville: The Southwestern Company, 1971).

Fred H. Wright, *Manners & Customs of Bible Lands* (Billy Graham Evangelistic Association published by Moody Press.: Chicago, 1994).

USEFUL WEBSITES

www.rotation.org
www.answersingenesis.org

Bible Verse Index

About the Author

Clark Highsmith lives in Midlothian, Texas with his wife and son. He has a Bachelor of Science in Commercial Art from Southwest Baptist University and a Master of Arts in Christian Education from Southwestern Baptist Theological Seminary. He teaches a youth Sunday School and believes that Vacation Bible School is the best week of the year. This is his first book.

Visit the Alacrity Press website at
www.alacritypress.com
for supporting materials for this book
and quality classical books and educational resources

Made in the USA
Middletown, DE
03 July 2022